Adventure Guide

The Alps

Krista Dana

HUNTER

HUNTER PUBLISHING, INC,
130 Campus Drive, Edison, NJ 08818
☎ *732-225-1900; 800-255-0343; fax 732-417-1744*
www.hunterpublishing.com

Ulysses Travel Publications
4176 Saint-Denis, Montréal, Québec
Canada H2W 2M5
☎ *514-843-9882, ext. 2232; fax 514-843-9448*

Windsor Books
The Boundary, Wheatley Road, Garsington
Oxford, OX44 9EJ England
☎ *01865-361122; fax 01865-361133*

ISBN 1-58843-391-9
© 2004 Hunter Publishing, Inc.

This and other Hunter travel guides are also available as e-books through Amazon.com, NetLibrary.com and other digital partners. For more information, e-mail us at comments@hunterpublishing.com.

Maps by Kim André and Lissa Dailey, © 2004 Hunter Publishing, Inc.
Index by Elite Indexing

Acknowledgements

Although there is only one author's name listed on the front cover, this book is the result of a great many contributions. First thanks go to my outlandishly supportive family and friends, who allowed me to neglect real-world responsibilities during the year I spent researching this project. I am blessed to call you mine. Particular thanks go to Jacq and Lee Collins, Wags and Deanne Wagner, and the Sooners of Cohort 3; to Carol Barker, for hours spent proofreading; and to my husband, for his expertise in European history. May mounds of gratitude be heaped as well upon editor and publisher Michael Hunter and the many publishing, editing, and tourism professionals who made this project click. Recognition goes also to those countless strangers on mountain trails, ferry crossings, and ski slopes that offered their opinions and advice – some of it solicited, some of it not. Much of their insight is represented here. Finally, and most forcefully, I thank Jethro. Life with him turns out to be the best adventure of all.

Photographs throughout the book are used courtesy of picswiss.ch, swiss-image.ch, Tourismus Salzburg, Tourismusverband Neustift im Stubaital, Nationalpark Hohe Tauern, Tourismusverband Sölden-Ötztal, Lech Tourismus, Silvretta Galtür, Tourismusverband Ischgl, Val Thorens Office de Tourisme, Tourismusverband St. Johan in Tirol, Office du Tourisme de Méribel, Tourist Board Mayrhofen, Office du Tourisme Val d'Isère, Füssen Tourismus, A.P.T. del Comasco, Oberammergau Tourismus, Verbier/Bagnes Tourism, Swiss Travel System, Luzern Tourismus, Interlaken Tourismus and the author.

Contents

About the Author

A native of Southern California, Krista Dana has chased the sun to live in Europe, Asia, and Salt Lake City, Utah. Along the way she's wrestled cocktails from thieving primates in Kenya, drifted on a broken-down boat through the Indonesian islands, and raced Chinese school children to the top of The Great Wall. An avid skier and hiker, she has explored terrain ranging from Switzerland's Matterhorn to South Korea's Muju Mountain. Today, when not basking in the glow of her computer monitor, Krista plays in the dirt and snow near her current home in southern Germany. Krista has written over 800 travel features, hotel reviews, and destination guides. She holds a master's degree in Cross-Cultural Human Relations.

Dedication

To my mom and dad,
who roused in me this wanderlust;
And to my husband and dog,
who now put up with it.

Going Metric

To make your travel a bit easier, we have provided
this chart that shows metric equivalents for the measurements
you are familiar with.

GENERAL MEASUREMENTS

1 kilometer = .6124 miles

1 mile = 1.6093 kilometers

1 foot = .304 meters

1 inch = 2.54 centimeters

1 square mile = 2.59 square kilometers

1 pound = .4536 kilograms

1 ounce = 28.35 grams

1 imperial gallon = 4.5459 liters

1 US gallon = 3.7854 liters

1 quart = .94635 liters

TEMPERATURES

For Fahrenheit: Multiply Centigrade figure by 1.8 and add 32.

For Centigrade: Subtract 32 from Fahrenheit figure and divide
by 1.8.

Centigrade	Fahrenheit
40°	104°
35°	95°
30°	86°
25°	77°
20°	64°
15°	59°
10°	50°

Introduction

Alpine History

 Man has long wandered the Alps, and evidence suggests that the earliest Paleolithic hunter-gatherers had already moved into local caves some 100,000 years ago. Following the last ice age, Neolithic settlers entered the lower valleys, where subsequent generations established farms, mines, and transalpine trade routes.

The earliest of these settlers were the Celts – a name derived from the Greek word *Keltoi*, or barbarian. They migrated from the east, gradually settling into the lowlands of central Europe around 1200BC; eventually they would settle as far west as Ireland. The oldest of the Celtic cultures settled in Hallstatt, a lakeside Austrian village that now gives the anthropological era its name. Here and in other Alpine regions, the Celts lived as farmers, herders, and miners – mostly for iron and valuable salt. The Celtic word for salt is *hall*, a root word still observed in the names of the ancient Celtic salt-mining and trade towns.

Around 400BC, the Celts' migration approached the fertile Po Valley in northern Italy, where they fought and defeated the local Etruscan inhabitants. However, the Etruscans appealed to their Roman allies and, after a mild rattling of swords, the Celts signed onto a peace agreement with their neighbors to the south. However, the Romans promptly reneged on the deal, inciting the Celts – renowned through history for ferociousness and bravery – to lay siege to Rome, sacking the city in 390BC.

However, Celtic dominance began to crumble when, in 49BC, a young Roman Caesar named Julius set his sights on Gaul, where the Celtic up-and-comer Vercingetorix was organizing a threatening unification of tribes. Julius Caesar prevailed in the ensuing conflict, Vercingetorix was imprisoned in Rome, and the Roman Empire was off and running in the Alps. They built roads, established trade centers, and laid the foundational stones of the cities we visit today. Eventually, as Roman power weakened in the Alps, other empires followed, including those under Charlemagne and the Hapsburgs of Austria – subsequent eras addressed in later chapters of this book.

The Land

■ Prehistory

 Hundreds of millions of years ago, the Alps began their formation with the upward surge of the earth's crust. Over the course of millions of years more, limestone forced up along the Alpine axis, granite thrust into the western Alps, and – some 20 million years ago — the African continent collided with the Eurasian landmass, pushing, folding, and rippling the Alps to their current height. Nonetheless, the shape of the Alps has forever been in flux, as ever-present glaciers grow and recede, whittling valleys and ravines as they go. Additionally, these glaciers serve as the headwaters for many Alpine streams and rivers – forces of water that shift and erode the land, changing the layout of the mountains as they go. Together, the prehistoric subterranean collisions and glacial processes have sculpted one of the world's great mountain ranges.

Today, the Alps span some 1,000 km from east to west. Starting in France, the range forms a crescent that arches through Switzerland, Liechtenstein, Austria, Germany, and Italy, and then drops down into Slovenia and the former Yugoslavia. The range includes several hundred peaks over 4,000 m, with the tallest peak, Mont Blanc, reaching 4,810 m.

■ Climate

 The Alps harbor a variety of localized micro-climates, with climatic zones stacking up the long, narrow wall of mountains at steep gradients; in the south, for example, travelers go from just above sea level at the foot of the Alps to over 2,500 m above sea level with just a short drive. Further complicating the matter, the range runs east to west, dividing northern and southern Europe, and sides of the mountain range see very different amounts of precipitation and sunlight through the course of the seasons. Below, I offer weather statistics from a representative sample of Alpine destinations. For comparison purposes, I've included a couple of more familiar cities, too.

DENVER CO, USA												
	Jan	Feb	Mar	Apr	May	Jun	Jul	Aug	Sep	Oct	Nov	Dec
Max. °F	43	46	54	61	70	82	88	86	77	66	52	45
Min. °F	16	19	25	34	45	54	60	57	46	36	25	16
Precip. inches	.5	.5	1.3	2	2.4	1.6	2.2	1.8	1.1	1	1	.6

GENEVA, SWITZERLAND											
Max. °F	37	43	47	56	64	72	75	75	70	57	46	39
Min. °F	28	30	34	38	45	52	54	52	48	43	36	30
Precip. inches	3	3	3	2.4	2.8	3.4	2.6	3.2	3.2	3	3.6	3.2
INNSBRUCK, AUSTRIA											
Max. °F	34	40	52	62	70	75	79	75	70	57	46	36
Min. °F	19	25	30	40	46	52	56	54	48	40	32	25
Precip. inches	2.1	1.6	1.7	2.3	3	4.2	4.8	4.6	3	2.4	2.3	2.1
MUNICH, GERMANY											
Max. °F	34	37	45	56	64	70	74	74	66	56	43	36
Min. °F	23	25	32	38	45	50	54	54	46	40	32	25
Precip. inches	1.8	1.7	1.9	2.2	3.6	4.4	4	4	2.8	1.9	2.2	2.2
VENICE, ITALY											
Max. °F	43	45	54	62	70	75	81	81	74	64	52	44
Min. °F	30	34	38	47	54	61	64	63	58	48	40	32
Precip. inches	2.3	2.1	2.3	2.6	2.8	3	2.6	3.4	2.6	2.8	3.4	2.1

■ Flora

 Nowhere on the globe has such an ecologically rich region been developed so thoughtfully. It's an admirable accomplishment. Tens of thousands of visitors venture to the Alpine wilderness each weekend but, even after centuries of use, much of this pristine wilderness remains intact. Preservation efforts continue, particularly in the national parks, and travelers are apt to witness a memorable display of plant and animal life.

Botanists categorize habitats into several vegetation belts, each delineating the types of flora that thrive there. The span of each categorical belt, however, can vary considerably among regions and even from one side to the other of a single mountain peak. (Some glaciers, in fact, sit at lower altitudes than do neighboring mountains' tree lines.) Thus, the altitude approximations offered below can be no more than mere estimations. In any case, Alpine travelers will witness a vast array of vegetation clinging to rock crevices, peeking through springtime snowbanks, and padding high-altitude pasturelands in a mat of lush grasses and flowers.

Vegetation Belts

The first and lowest of the Alpine vegetation zones are the lowland **Planar** and **Collin belts**. These include much of the Alpine region surrounding Italy's lakes. The region produces olives, oaks, evergreens, and lemons. In addition, vines crawl up the sunny hillsides of the interior Alps' deep valleys. The Planar and Collin belts extend up to approximately 700 m. Above, the **Mountain Belt** shows a mix of deciduous trees — primarily larch, oak, beech, and sycamore – a region similar in climate to that of lower Canada or the American northeast.

Above 1,500 m or so, the terrain gives way to the **Subalpine Belt**, home of the lush high pasturelands that have for centuries drawn farmers and their herds during the summer months. A fertile blend of grasses enriches the herd's diet, infusing the dairy products with a delicious, herby tang. Trees here include spruce, fir, and larches, gradually changing to low-lying berries and dwarf shrubbery at higher altitudes.

The **Alpine Belt** lies above approximately 2,300 m, encompassing the terrain between the tree line and the lowest permanent snowcaps. Despite its high altitude and lack of trees, there is a tremendous variety of plant life in this region, as shrubs and juniper give way to Alpine grasslands. Beyond, above approximately 2,800 m, the **Nival Belt** embraces the upper glacial regions, nurturing a still varied mix of plant life, including mosses, lichen, and algae.

Alpine Flowers

Although Alpine slopes offer a rich variety of flora year-round, the most vivid display of wildflower color comes between May and August, as the prime blooming season works its way up from the valley floors to the glaciers above. Fall colors are at their most spectacular in late September through early November. Still-green valleys grow gradually to bright gold larch fields, dark coniferous forests, red algae-covered slopes, and white snowcaps high above – and all, if you're lucky, set against a deep blue sky swept clear by an autumn breeze.

 Much of the Alpine flora here is protected by law, and the look-but-don't-pick policies are well-respected by European adventurers. I hope you'll do the same.

Most common among the Alpine blooms are a variety of buttercup, bellflower, and gentian families. The spring **pasque flower**, or *Pulsatilla vernalis*, is a buttercup derivative with tough leaves and petals purple on the outside and white within. The small flower blooms from April through July in dry grasslands and stony soils at altitudes up to 3,500 m. Look for the hairy, light-blue petals of the

Bearded bellflower

down-turned bearded bellflower, or *Campanula barbata*, throughout the summer in high-altitude pastures up to 3,000 m.

Several species of **gentian** thrive throughout the Alps, running the gamut from the yellow gentian, or *Gentiana lutea*, which grows up to one-meter high, to the more typical trumpet gentian, or *Gentiana acaulis*, which grows just a few centimeters from the earth. Several gentian species are appreciated, too, for their medicinal properties – and monks have for centuries used the plant to make a potent schnapps.

Gentian

Fire lily

Among the showiest of the early Alpine blooms is the **white crocus**, or *Crocus vernus*, its sturdy lavender petals pushing up through the melting snow. The bright orange **fire lily**, or *Lilium bulbiferum*, draws attention, too. Look for its eye-catching blooms from June through July in woodland pastures and grasslands between 300 and 2,000 m. Less extravagant and ever so dainty, the **lady's slipper**, or *Cypripedium calceolus*, is a lucky find; legend dictates that whoever finds one of these little orchids will enjoy true love – but adds that whoever purposely looks for the flower will never find one.

Edelweiss

Finally, the **edelweiss**, or *Leontopodium alpinum*, remains the most venerated of the Alpine flowers – a fame due in no small part to the popularity of the movie *The Sound of Music*. Look for the little woolly gray stars in sunny beds of limestone rock and grasslands, normally between 1,700 and 3,500 m and blooming from July through September.

■ Fauna

Although several majestic species such as brown bears and wolves have long disappeared from the European Alps, the mountains still play home to an extensive array of animals. Many are difficult to spot, however. To up your odds, visit in autumn, when animals move into the valleys to escape the coming snows. Keep watch, too, in the evenings and early mornings, when animals are active and foraging. (Feeding wild animals is, of course, always a bad idea – both for their health and your safety.) To further increase your chances of spotting wildlife, head for one of the national parks, where a wide range of birds and mammals are protected. Below, I list some favorites:

- ■ **Berchtesgaden National Park**, Germany
  www.nationalpark-berchtesgaden.de

- **Gran Paradiso National Park**, Italy
  www.granparadiso.net
- **Höhe Tauern National Park**, Austria
  www.nationalpark.at
- **La Vanoise National Park**, France
  www.vanoise.com
- **Swiss National Park**, Switzerland
  www.nationalpark.ch

 If all else fails, head for the **Alpine Zoo** in Innsbruck. All the animals listed here are represented in the zoo – along with a few species now extinct in their natural habitats. The zoo actively participates in preservation, research, and rehabilitation projects, so your entrance fee is actually doing alpine wildlife some good.

The **Alpine ibex**, or *Capra ibex*, is recognizable first for its enormous horns. It's almost twice the size of the chamois, and both males and female have horns – although the male's are much more grand. The highly maneuverable bovid prefers a habitat of rocky outcroppings at high altitude. Look for the ibex in La Vanoise National Park, which was created for its protection.

Alpine ibex

The **chamois**, or *Rupicapra rupicapra*, delights onlookers with Alpine acrobatics, leaping nimbly among rocks and along cliffs using its non-slip hooves. Male chamois mark tree branches with a musky scent secreted out of glands from just behind their horns. Look for these mountain goats in high Alpine terrain, particularly the Gran Paradiso and Vanoise national parks.

Alpine marmots

The **Alpine marmot**, or *Marmota marmota*, proves the favorite animal of many visitors. These big, beaver-like fur-balls live in large family groups, occupying extensive interconnecting burrows that provide both summer and winter homes – upper rooms for playful summer days and lower rooms to be sealed off during the winter hibernation. Marmots live throughout the Alps, and sightings from cableways and mountain trails are frequent. Look for them on sunny slopes; listen, too – marmots whistle to warn others of danger.

The **red fox**, or *Vulpes vulpes*, disperses widely throughout the region. As it is usually the largest mammalian predator in its habitat, it rarely goes wanting for food. The omnivorous fox prefers to feed on mice, marmots, and carcasses and inhabits a wide range of climatic zones. Look throughout the Alps for its rusty coat, black tail, and slinky, cat-like movements.

The **snow hare**, or *Lepus timidus*, ranks low on the food chain and is the favored prey of the golden eagle. Nonetheless, it's a clever little thing, camouflaging its coat with white in winter and brown in summer. Look for the mountain hare all across the Alps.

The white-headed **bearded vulture**, or *Gypaetus barbatus*, is enormous – with a wingspan of almost three meters, it is, in fact, Europe's largest bird of prey. Although extinct in parts of the Alps, the birds have made a feeble comeback in the high mountain terrain. Look for the paired mates nesting on cliffs and feeding on rabbits and marmots around the Höhe Tauern National Park in Austria.

The **golden eagle**, or *Aquila chrysaetos*, remains king of the peaks, and their numbers have increased dramatically since near-extinction in the late 19th century. The grand bird prefers to feed on hares and marmots in summer and carcasses in winter – much of the meat salvaged from avalanche kill. Eagles create huge nests at altitude, but hover in forested areas to hunt for food. Look for the bird around the high-pine pastures that serve as their hunting grounds.

Golden eagle

Finally, we draw attention to the much less glamorous **Alpine chough**, or *Pyrrhocorax graculus*. This little black bird ranks among the heartiest of the Alps' feathered fauna, nesting at extreme elevations and toting food up from far below. A member of the Corvid family, the crow-like chough is glossy black with a yellow beak and red legs. It's a sociable breed. You will see them soaring on the updrafts around high-mountain lift stations.

Travel Basics

■ When To Go

Setting a date to visit the Alps does, of course, involve all of the normal travel concerns – planning around temperature, weather, holidays, festivals, and such. In other parts of the world, I'm a big fan of off-season travel. I like to go when few others do, enjoying lower rates and less crowded destinations. However, it doesn't work out that way in the Alps.

Many of the destinations in this guidebook shut down almost entirely between seasons. Local residents go on their own vacations or spend closure days completing maintenance and renovation tasks – and in some villages you'll be hard-pressed to find an open hotel, bak-

	JAN			FEB			MAR			APR			MAY			JUN			JUL			AUG			SEP			OCT			NOV			DEC		
Arosa	❄	❄	❄	❄	❄	❄	❄	❄	❄	❄							☼	☼	☼	☼	☼	☼	☼	☼	☼	☼	☼	☼							❄	❄
Berchtesg.	❄	❄	❄	❄	❄	❄	❄	❄	❄	♦	♦	♦	♦	♦	☼	☼	☼	☼	☼	☼	☼	☼	☼	☼	☼	☼	☼	☼	♦	♦	♦	♦	♦	♦	♦	❄
Bregenz	♦	♦	♦	♦	♦	♦	♦	♦	♦	♦	♦	♦	♦	♦	♦	♦	♦	♦	♦	♦	♦	♦	♦	♦	♦	♦	♦	♦	♦	♦	♦	♦	♦	♦	♦	♦
Chamonix	❄	❄	❄	❄	❄	❄	❄	❄	❄	❄	❄	♦	♦	♦	♦	♦	☼	☼	☼	☼	☼	☼	☼	☼	☼	☼	☼	☼	♦	♦	♦	♦	♦	♦	❄	❄
Cortina	❄	❄	❄	❄	❄	❄	❄	❄	❄	❄	❄	♦	♦	♦	♦	♦	☼	☼	☼	☼	☼	☼	☼	☼	☼	☼	☼	☼	♦	♦	♦	♦	♦	♦	❄	❄
Courmayeur	❄	❄	❄	❄	❄	❄	❄	❄	❄	❄							☼	☼	☼	☼	☼	☼	☼	☼	☼	☼	☼								❄	❄
Davos	❄	❄	❄	❄	❄	❄	❄	❄	❄	❄								☼	☼	☼	☼	☼	☼	☼	☼	☼									❄	❄
Engelberg	❄	❄	❄	❄	❄	❄	❄	❄	❄	❄	❄	❄						☼	☼	☼	☼	☼	☼	☼	☼	☼	☼								❄	❄
Garm.-Part.	❄	❄	❄	❄	❄	❄	❄	❄	❄	❄	♦	♦	♦	♦	♦	☼	☼	☼	☼	☼	☼	☼	☼	☼	☼	☼	☼	☼	♦	♦	♦	♦	♦	♦	❄	❄
Geneva	♦	♦	♦	♦	♦	♦	♦	♦	♦	♦	♦	♦	♦	♦	♦	♦	♦	♦	♦	♦	♦	♦	♦	♦	♦	♦	♦	♦	♦	♦	♦	♦	♦	♦	♦	♦
Innsbruck	♦	♦	♦	♦	♦	♦	♦	♦	♦	♦	♦	♦	♦	♦	♦	♦	♦	♦	♦	♦	♦	♦	♦	♦	♦	♦	♦	♦	♦	♦	♦	♦	♦	♦	♦	♦
Interlaken	❄	❄	❄	❄	❄	❄	❄	❄	❄	❄	♦	♦	♦	♦	♦	☼	☼	☼	☼	☼	☼	☼	☼	☼	☼	☼	☼	☼	♦	♦	♦	♦	♦	♦	♦	❄
Ischgl	❄	❄	❄	❄	❄	❄	❄	❄	❄	❄	❄	❄							☼	☼	☼	☼	☼	☼	☼	☼								❄	❄	❄
Kitzbuhel	❄	❄	❄	❄	❄	❄	❄	❄	❄	♦	♦	♦	♦	♦	♦	♦	☼	☼	☼	☼	☼	☼	☼	☼	☼	☼	☼	♦	♦	♦	♦	♦	♦	♦	♦	❄
Lucerne	♦	♦	♦	♦	♦	♦	♦	♦	♦	♦	♦	♦	♦	♦	♦	♦	♦	♦	♦	♦	♦	♦	♦	♦	♦	♦	♦	♦	♦	♦	♦	♦	♦	♦	♦	♦
Méribel	❄	❄	❄	❄	❄	❄	❄	❄	❄	❄	❄								☼	☼	☼	☼	☼	☼											❄	❄
Milan	♦	♦	♦	♦	♦	♦	♦	♦	♦	♦	♦	♦	♦	♦	♦	♦	♦	♦	♦	♦	♦	♦	♦	♦	♦	♦	♦	♦	♦	♦	♦	♦	♦	♦	♦	♦
Munich	♦	♦	♦	♦	♦	♦	♦	♦	♦	♦	♦	♦	♦	♦	♦	♦	♦	♦	♦	♦	♦	♦	♦	♦	♦	♦	♦	♦	♦	♦	♦	♦	♦	♦	♦	♦
Salzburg	♦	♦	♦	♦	♦	♦	♦	♦	♦	♦	♦	♦	♦	♦	♦	♦	♦	♦	♦	♦	♦	♦	♦	♦	♦	♦	♦	♦	♦	♦	♦	♦	♦	♦	♦	♦
St. Anton	❄	❄	❄	❄	❄	❄	❄	❄	❄	❄							☼	☼	☼	☼	☼	☼	☼	☼	☼	☼	☼								❄	❄
St. Moritz	❄	❄	❄	❄	❄	❄	❄	❄	❄	❄								☼	☼	☼	☼	☼	☼	☼	☼	☼									❄	❄
Turin	♦	♦	♦	♦	♦	♦	♦	♦	♦	♦	♦	♦	♦	♦	♦	♦	♦	♦	♦	♦	♦	♦	♦	♦	♦	♦	♦	♦	♦	♦	♦	♦	♦	♦	♦	♦
Vaduz	♦	♦	♦	♦	♦	♦	♦	♦	♦	♦	♦	♦	♦	♦	♦	♦	♦	♦	♦	♦	♦	♦	♦	♦	♦	♦	♦	♦	♦	♦	♦	♦	♦	♦	♦	♦
Val d'Isère	❄	❄	❄	❄	❄	❄	❄	❄	❄	❄	❄	❄						☼	☼	☼	☼	☼	☼	☼										❄	❄	❄
Venice	♦	♦	♦	♦	♦	♦	♦	♦	♦	♦	♦	♦	♦	♦	♦	♦	♦	♦	♦	♦	♦	♦	♦	♦	♦	♦	♦	♦	♦	♦	♦	♦	♦	♦	♦	♦
Verbier	❄	❄	❄	❄	❄	❄	❄	❄	❄										☼	☼	☼	☼	☼	☼											❄	❄
Zermatt	❄	❄	❄	❄	❄	❄	❄	❄	❄	❄	❄	❄	♦	♦	♦	♦	♦	☼	☼	☼	☼	☼	☼	☼	☼	☼	☼	☼	☼	♦	♦	♦	♦	❄	❄	❄
Zürich	♦	♦	♦	♦	♦	♦	♦	♦	♦	♦	♦	♦	♦	♦	♦	♦	♦	♦	♦	♦	♦	♦	♦	♦	♦	♦	♦	♦	♦	♦	♦	♦	♦	♦	♦	♦

☼ = summer season ❄ = winter season ♦ = normal town activity blank = closing period ery, or café. So, when planning, first consider opening and closing periods in the destinations you hope to visit.

The chart below illustrates the *approximate* opening and closing dates for the major destinations we cover. However, opening and closing dates are rarely definite and, although most resorts throw big opening and closing bashes, many hotels, restaurants, and cable networks gradually spin up to full operations. So, if you plan to travel along the edges of the opening season, do check in with the tourist office first.

SCHEDULING TIPS

- In **August**, many European countries take vacations *en masse*, crowding tourist destinations, jamming roads, and pumping up hotel rates. That said, August is the balmiest month of the calendar, its festivals are frequent, and its villages are fully open.

- The same effect comes around in **February**, when the ski season hits its high point for the midwinter school breaks.

- **January** is the least crowded month of the European ski season, as tourists head home after the holidays. It's cold on the slopes – but if you can take it, bargains abound.

■ Transportation

Getting Here

Visitors who come to Europe specifically to visit the Alps can book convenient flights into the gateway cities below. From the US, non-stop flights are in general most frequent to and from Zürich, Milan, and Munich. (Direct and connecting flights make convenient connections into the other gateway cities as well.) A mind-boggling array of airlines offer flights to and from Europe; we suggest consulting both the airlines' direct reservation lines and the bargain-hunting search engines online. For gateway airport information, see the guide below:

PASSPORTS

International travelers to Europe must carry a passport – and getting one can take several months. Aside from the strict passport controls at airports, however, visitors will find that, due to the European Union merger, most countries here no longer check passports at borders. However, any nation can at will reinstate passport control, so do keep yours handy. You may also be asked for your passport upon arrival at your hotel, where it's still common practice for the front desk to keep your passport overnight in order to record registration information.

GATEWAY AIRPORTS			
Gateway	**More Info**	**Location**	**City Transfers**
Geneva, Switzerland	www.gva.ch	4 km west of Geneva	Bus, train
Innsbruck, Austria	www.innsbruck-airport.com	3 km west of center	Bus
Milan, Italy Malpensa Airport	www.sea-aeropimilano.it	45 km northwest of the center	Bus, train
Milan, Italy Linate Airport	www.sea-aeropimilano.it	7 km east of the center	Bus
Munich, Germany	www.munich-airport.de	28 km northeast of the center	Train, bus
Zürich, Switzerland	www.uniqueairport.com	In Kloten, 10 km north of the center	Train, bus

Getting Around

By Car

Private autos remain the most convenient way to get around the Alps. Adventurers traveling in pairs or groups will find that renting a car is not prohibitively expensive; and most nations accept US drivers' licenses in lieu of an international permit – check with your rental agency upon reservation. Major US and European car rental agencies serve the Alps gateway cities – try Alamo, Avis, Budget, Europcar, Hertz, and Sixt. Several online search engines offer discounted rates as well.

For good deals on car rentals, check AutoEurope's search engine at www.autoeurope.com.

DRIVING TIPS

All cars are required by law to carry a first-aid kit, a warning triangle, and registration information. These should be provided by your rental agency. In addition, those planning to travel in Alpine areas between October and early spring should carry tire chains. Car rental agencies rent out these too, but most require prior arrangements – confirm your request when you reserve a car.

European roads – even the superhighways – frequently come to a standstill during holiday travel periods. Transalpine routes prove particularly painful during the winter season on Saturdays, when the ski resorts' weekly guests swap out. It's extremely frustrating (and I try to schedule around it), but Europeans have come to expect and accept the traffic as part of the ski holiday tradition.

Expect gas prices to run approximately three times more than in the United States. Some cars run on unleaded fuel, while others use diesel – something to know before you drive out of the rental agency's lot.

GASOLINE LINGO

English	German	French	Italian
Diesel	Diesel	Diesel	Diesel
Gasoline/petrol	Benzin	Essence	Benzina
Unleaded	Bleifrei	Essence sans plomb	Senza piombo

■ Parking

Europeans rely heavily on public transportation, and central parking facilities are in short supply. Parking spaces are often either time-limited short-term spots or in public garages. For short-term spaces showing time limits, you'll need a parking disk placard. Most cars will come with one in the dash compartment. Spin the time wheel on the placard so it indicates the time you arrived and place it on the dash. Most public garages operate on an automated payment system. Grab a ticket on your way in, park your car, and carry the ticket with you. On departure, pay your fee either at the window or at the automated machine before returning to your car. A second variation on lot parking requires you to log your parking spot number at a central machine, pay for the needed time in advance, and then place the receipt on the dashboard.

International Road Signs

Stop

Speed Limit
Kilometers per hour
or miles per hour in U.K.

No Passing

Trucks Forbidden
to Pass

Yield to
Oncoming Vehicles

Closed to
Vehicles

Closed to Trucks
Heavier than
2.8 metric tons

Closed to
Automobiles

Closed to
Motor Vehicles

No Entry

No Parking

No Stopping

Customs Station:
Stop

Automobiles Only
Zone Ends

Dead End

Recommended
Maximum Speed

Minimum Speed

One Way

Keep Left
(Keep Right on
Right Arrow)

Turn Left
(Turn Right on
Right Arrow)

No Passing
Zone Ends

Speed Limit
Zone Ends

Derestriction Sign
(Multiple Diagonal Lines)

National
Speed Limit Applies
(Single Diagonal Line)

Danger

Yield

Curve

S-Curve

Uneven Road

Crossroads or Junction
Yield to Traffic from
the Right

Two-Way
Traffic

Railroad Crossing
with Barriers

Steep Upgrade

Steep Downgrade

Hazardous
Crosswinds

Right of Way
on Priority Road

Bicycles Only

Cyclists and
Pedestrians Only

Expressway
Begins

Expressway
Ends

Alternate Route
for Express Traffic

300 Meters to Exit

Access to
Expressway

International
Route

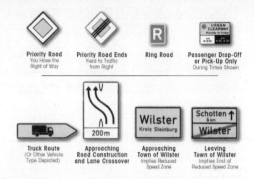

Priority Road
You Have the
Right of Way

Priority Road Ends
Yield to Traffic
from Right

Ring Road

Passenger Drop-Off
or Pick-Up Only
During Times Shown

Truck Route
(Or Other Vehicle
Type Depicted)

Approaching
Road Construction
and Lane Crossover

Approaching
Town of Wilster
Implies Reduced
Speed Zone

Leaving
Town of Wilster
Implies End of
Reduced Speed Zone

SPEED LIMITS & ROAD TOLLS

	Austria	Italy	France	Germany	Switzerland & Liechtenstein
In town	50 km/hr	50 km/hr	50 km/hr	50 km/hr	50/km/hr
Open roads	110 km/hr	110 km/hr	110 km/hr	110 km/hr	80 km/hr
Highways	130 km/hr	130 km/hr	130 km/hr	130 km/hr	120 km/hr
Road tolls	*Vignette* sticker	Pay-as-you-go	Pay-as-you-go	None	*Vignette* sticker

Police officers stop cars using a lollipop-like stick. If pulled over, you may be assessed a fine on the spot. Hidden cameras track speeding violations as well, in which case tickets show up months later in the mail.

Vignette stickers are required for travel on superhighways where indicated above. Rental cars come with one attached, or buy one at gas stations near the border.

By Train & Bus

Train travel remains one of the joys of European tourism. Systems are modern, fast, and timely, though not always inexpensive. Most Alpine destinations – right down to the smallest villages – are well served by rail or, at a minimum, by a convenient bus connection from the nearest rail station. A wide range of services is available, most available through the websites listed below; look for information on trip planning, baggage services, bike rentals, theme trips, and combination itineraries via rail, bus, boat, and cableway. If you go by rail, I recommend traveling with little baggage and, for longer rides during high season, paying the small fee to reserve a seat. (You don't have to sit there, but it's nice to know you can.) Ticketing procedures vary by country and rail line; for more information check the websites below.

EUROPEAN TRAIN TRAVEL

Austria . . . . www.oebb.at

France . . . . . www.voyages-sncf.com

Germany . . . . www.bahn.de

Italy . . . . www.fs-on-line.com

Switzerland . . . . www.rail.ch

Rail Europe offers one-stop shopping and a host of information regarding European rail passes. Check in at www.raileurope.com. For international bus transportation, inquire with Eurolines at www.eurolines.com.

By Cableway & Mountain Train

We hope that every European visitor experiences the thrill of ascending the Alps via one of the region's extensive uplift networks. Lifts serve pedestrians, paragliders, and snow-sport fans through the winter, and most resorts operate lifts in summer, too. Hikers and mountain-bikers (and their dogs) head for the hills via cable car, gondola, chairlift, funiculars, and mountain trains. The variety of engineering is astounding in itself – let alone the views once you reach the top. For more information on mountain transportation, see the *Getting Around* detail listed for each destination.

Car-Carrying Trains

One of the Alps' most interesting forms of transportation is the car-carrying train. Drivers load their cars onto a flatbed train, which then tugs the line of occupied autos through a mountain tunnel, saving motorists what in some cases would be a several-hour roundabout drive. Leaving a light on inside your car will make the bouncy ride a bit less bizarre, but beware the rookie mistake – when it comes time to disembark, a dead battery will make you the least popular traveler aboard. In the Swiss Alps, try the **Loetschberg Tunnel** between Kandersteg (near Interlaken) and the Valais region; the **Vereina Tunnel** between Klosters and Susch; or the **Furka Tunnel** between Realp and Oberwald.

■ Currency

With the exception of Switzerland & Liechtenstein, the currency of the countries in this guide is the euro (€). There are 100 cents to €1 and coins are in denominations of 1, 2, 5, 10, 20 and 50 cents, as well as €1 and €2. Notes are in denominations of €5, 10, 20, 50, 100, 200 and 500.

Whereas the value of the US dollar was approximately €1.20 when work began on this guide, the dollar has slipped since that time and in early 2004 stood at about €0.79. So, if you see an item priced at €1, the dollar equivalent would be $1.26, €10 would be $12.60, €100, $126.

Switzerland and Liechtenstein use the Swiss franc, abbreviated as CHF. The current value of 1 CHF is $0.79 or €0.64. It is divided into 100 cents. Coins come in denominations of 5, 10, 20 and 50 cents, as well as 1, 2 and 5 CHF. Banknotes come in values of 10, 20, 50, 100, 200 and 1,000 CHF.

■ Where to Sleep

 This guide attempts to round up hotels for each destination that have both a prime location and reasonable standards of comfort. Our hotel picks are categorized by price range – but you should be aware that seasonal fluctuations can be great, particularly in the resort areas. While luxury houses across Europe maintain similarly exquisite standards, ho-

HOTEL PRICE CHART	
Double room without tax; $$$-$$$$ always with bath.	
$	Under €80
$$	€81-150
$$$	€151-250
$$$$	Over €250

tels at lower ends of the scale tend to vary by region in comfort and cleanliness. In general, budget hotels in Italy and France offer less bang for your lodging buck than, say, Germany and Switzerland, where comfortable rooms and good service are common. The undisputed queen of Alpine hospitality is Austria. Here, cozy accommodations, duvet-topped beds, and family-style hospitality are the rule rather than the exception. Particularly in small towns and villages, Austria offers Europe's warmest welcome.

Lodging Tips

- If you enter town without a room, head for the tourist office or simply browse the streets for a vacancy sign – in German, *zimmer frei*; in French, *chambre libre*; in Italian, *camera / stanza libera*.

- Shared baths are common in budget hotels, hostels, B&B guesthouses, and mountain huts, so I recommend you pack a pair of shower flip-flops. In addition, traditional European towels are flimsy cotton affairs. While

I've seen a lot more terrycloth in recent years, I still usually pack along a washcloth.

■ Breakfasts are normally included in room rates. However, the meal is not an American-style feast, but a modest buffet spread of bread, meat, cheese, and jam, normally served with a choice of juices and coffee or tea.

■ Bidets are a common European feature, a great little gadget intended for washing your nether regions. I've heard of some creative uses, too, ranging from a sock-soak to a baby bath. High-tech versions prove a real hoot, with water jets that have controls for pressure, temperature, and pattern; built-in blow dryers; and (requiring some imagination) portable remote controls.

■ A wide range of accommodations are available, including youth hostels, private rooms, mountain huts, guesthouses, hotels, and spa resorts. I've included mostly hotels here. When booking lodging at the lower end of the price range, expect to share a bath; at the upper end, expect to pay extra for breakfast.

■ Dining

Alpine Europe offers a wide array of dining, and for each destination I've attempted to give a sample, ranging from pricey gourmet to picnic groceries. Although our guide covers six countries, the region is home to three main culinary traditions: Italian, Germanic, and French.

DINING PRICE CHART	
Average entrée, with tax.	
$	Under €10
$$	€10-25
$$$	Over €25

Italian cuisine permeates the Alps, just as it has the entire world: Diners enjoy fresh pastas and traditional *pizze* made with thin, cracker-like crusts, baked in a wood-fired oven, and served with a wonderful array of toppings – each pie hanging over the edges of a large plate. Even better, it's all yours. Traditional pizzas are intended as servings for one, even though most could easily provide a snack for three. Other culinary treats include fresh, homemade pastas – some varieties in northern Italy are stuffed with delicious meat, cheese, or squash concoctions and topped with rich sauces of butter, tomato, or walnuts. Grilled meats are popular in the Alpine regions, as are risotto (rice) dishes. Those unaccustomed to the art of Italian dining will be surprised to find that the main meal is served at midday and that it's often accompanied by copious quantities of red wine. Also notable: pasta dishes are served as a first (rather than main) course, and salads usually wrap up (rather than kick off) a full meal.

Austria and Germany are the strongholds of hearty Germanic fare. Germany offers the world its variety of sausages, or wurst, which come grilled and with bread, making a great afternoon snack, particularly when served with a liter-size mug of *bier*. Farther south, in Austria, delicious hearty meals run to a wide array of meat-and-potatoes fare – always a huge hit with both the men and the kids in our groups. Traditional *Wiener schnitzel* is a solid choice, but I hope you'll branch out to try *gröstl*, a meat and potato pan fry, and *käsepatzle*, a Vorarlberg specialty of noodles and grated cheese, baked together and topped with fried onions. Kids love *kaiserschmarren*, a sweet mound of shredded pancake served with preserves, and adults love the *schnapps*, warm *gluhwein*, and potent *jagertee* – all three, drinks with a kick.

While Switzerland shares cuisines with each of its neighbors, its most intimate culinary relationship is with France. Along with the northwestern corner of Italy, Switzerland and France dish out an astounding array of cheese dishes. The *fondue Savoyarde* is the most famed of the cheese mixes here, a bubbling pot of *fromage* made tangy with white wine and a shot or two of *kirsche* liqueur. Raclette, too, proves another oozy favorite: The traditional service involves a large block of cheese melted tableside over an open flame – and served with a mix of steamed potatoes and pickled vegetables. Other open-flame affairs include chunks of meat with fondues bourguignonne, a pot of hot oil; chinoise, a pot of boiling bouillon; and Bacchus, a pot of spiced local wine. Grilled specialties, mixed salads, and a variety of sweet and savory crêpes all prove popular, too.

Dining Tips

- Unless there's a host posted at the door, European restaurants intend for you to come in and seat yourself. (Leave your coat and umbrella at the door.) In casual and traditional settings, it's not uncommon for strangers to share your table. Although it seems an oddly intimidating question to pose, you shouldn't be afraid to join a stranger's table, either. You're not necessarily expected to chat – although it is a pleasant way to meet strangers.

- Many cafés and mountain huts offer both self- and table-service. If you find a table without a cloth, menu, and such, it's a fairly good indicator that it's a cafeteria-style self-service arrangement. If there are menus on the table, stay put and you'll be served eventually. Also, if some tables are set with fine silver and others have just paper napkins, sit at the dressed table for a meal, at the undressed table for just a drink or snack.

■ Many cafés also offer stand-up service. Pay for your drink and snack at the cashier, take your receipt to the barman, and he'll dispense the goods, which you then consume standing up at the bar.

■ We hear many complaints about "poor" restaurant service, but I think the issue has less to do with quality than culture. In general, service is slow. Europeans dine out to relax and to enjoy – to rush you would be rude. Service is unobtrusive rather than obsequious, and so, to North Americans, the service may seem inattentive, too.

■ Multi-course meals line up in varying orders depending on where you sit in the Alps. (Italians, for instance, often eat salad at the end of the meal.) In any case, don't be surprised to be asked in which order you'd like your meal. Also worth mentioning is the small glitch of timing. Lest food grow cold or stale, kitchens tend to serve individuals as their plates become ready rather than serving the table as a group.

■ In most cases, you'll need to flag down your server in order to ask for the meal check. (Some cafés ask you to settle your bill immediately upon service.) A tip is still a gratuity in Europe, and no set amount is expected. However, it is customary to round up a euro or two when paying your bill. Hand the extra to your server; leaving change on the table is considered an impersonal slight.

■ Connections

Language

 Three major languages and a host of minor dialects babble through the Alps. Visitors will find the "high" versions of German, French, and Italian most useful, although a fast-growing number of Europeans speak English. And, although even the feeblest linguistic attempts are appreciated, more often than not the reply will come back in English. I do suggest, of course, that every visitor learn some basic phrases. Give our *Lan-*

guage Primer a quick study – it's in *Appendix B* at the back of this book.

Telephone

Telephone numbers are changing rapidly in European countries – as the old system has become inadequate. Area codes are changing, as are phone-number formats. In general, foreign phone numbers are dialed using *00* + *country code* (see below) + the *phone number* without the 0 prefix. Domestic numbers are dialed using the phone number with the 0 prefix. Tobacco shops, newsstands, post offices, and tourist offices sell two types of phone cards: one with a scratch-to-see bar code; the other with a program chip or strip to be inserted into public phones. (We like the scratch-off variety, as it can be used from hotel rooms, too.)

INTERNATIONAL COUNTRY CODES	
Austria	+43
France	+33
Germany	+49
Italy	+39
Liechtenstein	+423
Switzerland	+41

Internet

Internet service is widely available, both in hotels and in a growing number of bars and cafés. Whenever possible, I've indicated surf stations for each destination; find them in each chapter under *Getting Connected*.

Time Zone

The Alpine nations lie in the Central European Time Zone, GMT + 1 hour, or, from the last weekend in March till the last weekend in October, GMT + 2 hours. If it's easier, think Eastern Standard Time + 6 hours year-round.

Electricity

Electrical outlets in Europe supply 220-volt alternating current for a variety of plug shapes. Unless specifically designed for dual-voltage use, 110-volt electrical appliances will work only when connected to large, heavy, voltage transformers. (Common plug adapters – those lightweight kits found in travel shops – adapt only shape, not voltage.) That said, appliances designed for dual-voltage use work when fitted with these lightweight plug adapters. European plug shapes vary somewhat even within national borders. Your best bet is to pack along an adapter set; hotels have loaners if yours don't work.

 Consider leaving the blow-dryer at home; most hotels either loan hairdryers or stock them in rooms.

∎ Health & Safety

 Europe has a modern medical infrastructure and, although some corners of the Alps lie far from urban centers, the emergency and airlift operations are well organized. The high Alpine terrain inspires many adventurers to stretch the limits of their physical and mental bounds. Done with reason, such challenges can land you triumphant amid some of the world's most spectacular scenery; done with haste, they can land you in a foreign hospital bed (or worse). Some tips for Alpine travelers.

EMERGENCY!

Dial 112, Europe-wide.

Safety Tips

- **Health insurance** policies vary in their international coverage, and I advise that you check your own before you go. A plethora of companies specialize in additional travel and sports insurance; you may even be asked upon purchasing your lift pass if you'd like rescue insurance tacked on.

- **Sunburn** threatens both skin and eyes, particularly at high altitudes and on snow. Spread on some sunscreen, take a hat and sleeves, and wear UV-protected sunglasses.

- **Frostbite**, or hypothermia, endangers Alpine adventurers as well. Dress warmly in layers whenever venturing out; wear a hat to prevent heat loss through your head; and don moisture-wicking under-layers and waterproof outerwear. Mild hypothermia causes fatigue, numbness, cramps, shivering, and slurred speech. Warm victims slowly without rubbing,

■ All but the fittest will feel a bit winded when exercising at altitudes over 2,500 m. The effect can be severe, however, and oxygen depletion can lead to **acute mountain sickness**. Headaches, dizziness, and breathlessness can lead to more extreme symptoms such as confusion, vomiting, and even death. Infants and children are particularly susceptible, and some experts recommend not taking youngsters to altitude at all.

■ If you're heading out on a mountain trail, let someone know where you're heading and when you expect to return. (Your hotel's staff is a likely candidate; leave your key behind so they'll know when you return.) And, by the way, if you do end up needing helicopter assistance, get your signals right: Both arms up in a V means help is needed; one arm up waves them off.

■ **Avalanches** can be a serious threat in many parts of the Alps, particularly to those who venture into the backcountry (which they should never do, of course, without a guide). Pay attention to avalanche warnings. The system rates danger on a scale from one to five, one being the lowest risk. Posted flags go from yellow to black, growing darker with graver avalanche danger. Local tourist offices and mountain guiding operators post notices, too.

■ Getting More Information

Throughout this guide, I have given web addresses for the various outfitters, hotels, tourist offices and other information sources. In some cases, these websites are in the local language only. If you do not speak the language, one solution is to go to www.google.com and insert the web address in the search box at the top. Then click on "Translate this page." Google will display the website in English.

For general information, check in with the national tourism offices:

Austria. . . . . www.austria-tourism.at

France . . . . . www.franceguide.com

Germany. . www.germany-tourism.de

Italy . . . . . www.italiantourism.com
Liechtenstein . . . . www.tourismus.li
Switzerland. www.myswitzerland.com

Pick-A-List Planning

■ Pick-A-Theme

Top Old-Towns

Historical town centers welcome with shops, cafés, and quaint hotels:

- Aosta *(page 242)*
- Feldkirch *(page 42)*
- Kitzbühel *(page 95)*
- Oberammergau *(page 202)*
- Salzburg *(page 107)*
- Zürich *(page 343)*

Peak Experiences

The Alps' most spectacular mountains, each easily accessed by year-round cableway or train:

- Jungfrau (Interlaken and region)
- Matterhorn (Zermatt)
- Mont Blanc (Chamonix or Courmayeur)
- Titlis (Engelberg)
- Valluga (St. Anton)
- Zügspitze (Garmisch-Partenkirchen)

The Sightseer

Must-see sights – check out *Peak Experiences*, too:

- Eagle's Nest (Berchtesgaden)
- Grand Canal (Venice)
- Hofbräuhaus Munich
- Linderhof Castle (Oberammergau)
- Milan's Cathedral
- Neuschwanstein Castle (Füssen)
- Salzburg's Old Town
- St. Mark's Square (Venice)

Historical Hotels

Elegant, creaky old dames from centuries gone by:

- Badrutt's Palace (St. Moritz)
- Belvedere (Davos)
- Gritti Palace (Venice)
- Hospiz Alm (St. Christoph)
- Kulm (St. Moritz)
- Miramonti Majestic (Cortina d'Ampezzo)
- Villa d'Este (Como Cernobbio)
- Villa Serbelloni (Como Bellagio)

Olympic Legacies

Veterans of the world stage, these Olympic hosts still put on a good show:

- Albertville, Méribel, & Val d'Isère (1992)
- Chamonix (1924)
- Cortina d'Ampezzo (1956)
- Garmisch-Partenkirchen (1936)
- Innsbruck & surroundings (1964, 1976)
- Lausanne (International Olympic Committee Headquarters)
- Munich (1972)
- St. Moritz (1928)

Museum Towns

An art-and-history hound's dream – towns with multiple museums:

- Innsbruck
- Lucerne
- Munich
- Salzburg
- Venice
- Winterthür
- Zürich

National Parks

The Alps' most pristine wilderness:

- Berchtesgaden National Park
- Gran Paradiso National Park

- Höhe Taurern National Park
- Swiss National Park
- Vanoise National Park

Dramatic Drives

These roads venture into the high Alps, skirting glaciers and traversing barren terrain – in spring, fall, and winter, check road conditions before you go:

- Gerlos Pass (Zillertal - Krimml)
- Great St. Bernard Pass (Val d'Aosta - Valais)
- Grossglockner Hochalpenstrasse (Höhe Tauern National Park)
- Petit St. Bernard Pass (Val d'Aosta - Tarantaise)
- Silvretta Hochalpenstrasse (Arlberg)
- Timmeljoch Hochalpenstrasse (Ötztal - Italy)

■ Pick-A-Vibe

Alpine Charmers

Traditional mountain hamlets oozing with allure:

- Lech
- Mürren
- Oberammergau
- Saas-Fee
- Seefeld
- Wengen

Scenic Splendor

Mother Nature's best work:

- Cortina d'Ampezzo
- Jungfrau region (Interlaken)
- Königsee
- Bellagio (Como)
- Venice

Family-Friendly Playgrounds

Fun destinations for parents and kids:

- Arosa
- Interlaken

- Lech
- Malbun/Steg
- Méribel
- St. Johann
- Zermatt

Party-Hearty Winter Resorts

Where the revelry starts early and lasts long:

- Chamonix
- Ischgl
- Kitzbühel
- Ötztal (Sölden)
- St. Anton
- Verbier
- Zermatt

Genteel Hideaways

No *paparazzi* here. Try these discreet retreats for a refined holiday:

- Courchevel
- Lech
- Mürren
- Seefeld
- St. Christoph

Glamour Girls

Expensive, fur-lined resorts where socialites show up just to show off:

- Cortina
- Courmayeur
- Kitzbühel
- St. Moritz
- Zermatt

City-Shopper

Havens of hedonism for shopping, dining, and entertainment:

- Milan
- Munich
- Salzburg

- Venice
- Zürich

City-Sportster

The best of both worlds – big-town conveniences with big mountains nearby:

- Geneva
- Innsbruck
- Lucerne
- Salzburg
- Vaduz

■ Pick-A-Sport

Mountaineering Classics

The historical towns where alpinism got its start:

- Chamonix
- Cortina
- Courmayeur
- St. Anton
- Zermatt
- Jungfrau region

Walking & Hiking

Long, short, shallow, and steep – these resorts please with a variety of trails:

- Cortina
- Jungfrau region
- Méribel
- Seefeld
- St. Moritz
- Val Gardena
- Zermatt

Mountain Biking

Put wheel to trail at these varied resorts:

- Chamonix
- Garmisch-Partenkirchen
- Innsbruck
- Interlaken

Introduction

- Ischgl
- Méribel
- Zell am See

Airborne Sports

Parasailing, sightseeing flights, helicopter rides, and ballooning – take a flying leap at these destinations:

- Chamonix
- Interlaken
- Silvaplana
- St. Moritz
- Verbier
- Zermatt

Lake Sports

Sailors, swimmers, water-skiers, and kite-surfers head for these Alpine waters:

- Chiemsee
- Davos
- Geneva
- Interlaken
- Silvaplana
- Zell am See

Whitewater

Wild rides on Alpine rapids – get set to get wet:

- Interlaken
- Lucerne
- Ötztal
- Zell am See
- Zillertal

Oddball Extremes

Europe's adventure sport outfitters bring on the adrenaline rush:

- Cortina
- Engelberg
- Interlaken
- Verbier
- Zillertal

Summertime Glacier Play

With skiing, tubing, dog-sledding, and ice caves, these glacier resorts stay cool in summer, too:

- Hintertux (Zillertal)
- Jungfrau
- Kaprun
- Saas-Fee
- Stubaital
- Val d'Isère
- Zermatt

■ Snow-Sliding for Distance

With extensive lift networks and moderate slopes, these resorts please intermediate-level skiers:

- Cortina
- Courchevel
- Davos
- Méribel
- Selva (Val Gardena)
- Val d'Isère
- Val Thorens

Snow-Sliding for Speed

Experts go steep and deep with high-gradient slopes, heli-skiing drops, and extreme off-piste opportunities:

- Argentière
- Chamonix
- St. Anton
- Val d'Isère
- Verbier
- Zermatt

Snow-Sliding for Families

Homey resorts with mild slopes and good ski-school programs:

- Arosa
- Courchevel
- Lech

- Obergurgl
- Saas-Fee
- Wengen

Snow for Those Who Don't Ski

Ice-skating, tobogganing, sleigh rides, and more. There's a lot to do here off skis, too:

- Cortina
- Davos
- Jungfrau region
- Saas-Fee
- Seefeld
- St. Moritz
- Zermatt

Austria

(Österreich)
Languages: German
Population: 8,169,929
Phone Country Code: +43
Currency: Euro

History

The ebb and flow of Austrian history began with its settlement by wandering tribes who valued its position at the gateway between southern Europe and the plains of northern and western Europe. In 803, Charlemagne declared the Dan-

ube Valley "Ostmark," and Austria was born. In 1278, the Hapsburgs gained control of Austria and maintained their rule up to World War I. By leveraging real estate purchases and arranging marriages, the Hapsburgs expanded Austria's holdings east into much of southeastern Europe and west into Spain. The Hapsburgs eventually gained control of the Spanish throne, and thus the Hapsburg house divided into two distinct lines, the Spanish and the Austrian.

Despite the Thirty Years War and several sieges of Vienna by the Turks, Austria Hapsburgs sustained their empire for over six centuries. The Napoleonic Wars and the subsequent Austro-Prussian War at last began to whittle away at the dynasty, and, in 1870, Austria lost its influence in Bavaria. The empire eventually became the dual monarchy of Austria-Hungary. However, the nation continued its expansionist policy, eventually invading Bosnia-Herzegovina and kicking off World War I, the aftermath of which saw the independence of several Austria-Hungarian lands – what today comprises much of Eastern Europe.

Under Hilter's rule, Germany annexed Austria in 1938, ushering World War II onto the country's doorstep. At the end of World War II, Austria saw the most recent restructuring of her borders and was divided into separate occupation zones that remained under Allied control. Although Austria was formally recognized by the Western powers in 1946, it wasn't until 1955 that the country saw her full sovereignty restored.

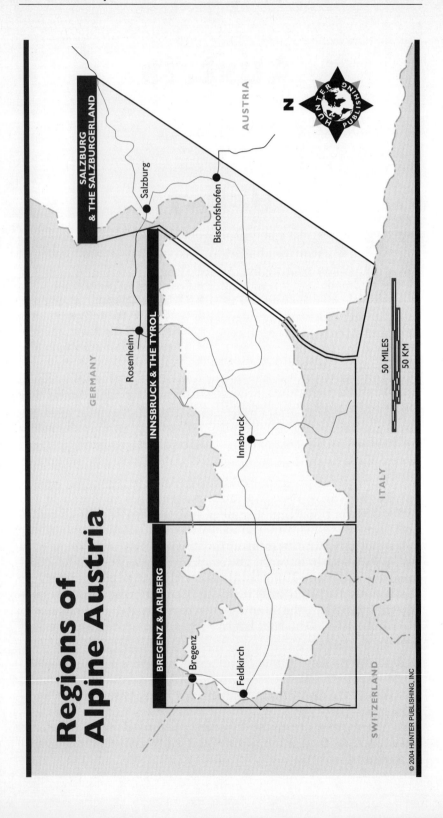

Regions of
Alpine Austria

BREGENZ & ARLBERG

INNSBRUCK & THE TYROL

SALZBURG
& THE SALZBURGERLAND

SWITZERLAND

ITALY

GERMANY

AUSTRIA

Bregenz

Feldkirch

Rosenheim

Innsbruck

Bischofshofen

Salzburg

N

50 MILES

50 KM

© 2004 HUNTER PUBLISHING, INC

Maria Theresa

The only female ruler in the 650-year history of the Hapsburg Dynasty, Maria Theresa ascended the Austrian throne in 1740 as the daughter of Emperor Charles VI. She is often considered the "Savior of the Hapsburg State." It was under her reign that Austria developed into a modern state: government control was centralized, civil services were greatly expanded, public education was introduced, and reforms of the military were instituted. Almost immediately upon Maria Theresa's assumption of the throne, Prussia challenged her authority. Seeing that Austria had been weakened during the last years of Charles VI's rule, they invaded and occupied Silesia. Bavaria and France soon joined in and invaded Austria from the west. Maria Theresa did not falter. She strengthened the army, reorganized the tax structure, and centralized control efforts to build a force capable of reclaiming these lands. However, in 1756, with preparations nearly complete for a retaliatory campaign, Austria suffered a surprise attack from the Prussians – the onset of the Seven Years War. Despite these setbacks, Maria Theresa is credited with laying the groundwork for a resumption of Austria's eastward expansion. Maria Theresa reigned until her death in 1780.

Overview & Government

The Republic of Austria spans some 83,853 square km in south-central Europe. The entire western third of the nation lies in the Alps, and much of its central and southern territories are Alpine as well – some 75% of the country is mountainous. The nation boasts a greater percentage of forested land than any other European nation – about 39% of its terrain is covered with trees. Austria shares its borders with eight other nations: Switzerland and Liechtenstein to the west, Germany and the Czech Republic to the north, Slovakia to the northeast, Hungary to the east, and Italy and Slovenia to the south.

Austria's government is partitioned into nine states; its capital is Vienna. It maintains a parliamentary democracy, with a strong central government. The president presides as the chief of state, and the head of government is the chancellor. From 1955, Austrian politics have vacillated between conservative and socialist policies. Recent issues include the influx of Yugoslav refugees and subsequent right-wing anti-immigration movements. Also controversial over the past decade have been growing unemployment levels, tax increases, and cuts in social services. Austria's unemployment rate hovers around 4.3%.

People & Culture

Austria's population is approximately 98% ethnic Austrian, with the remaining 2% split among several eastern European ethnicities, including Croat, Hungarian, Slovene, and Czech – minorities that cluster along Austria's eastern border. Approximately 80% of the population claims a Roman Catholic religion, with 5% claiming some faction of the Protestant faith. Some 65% of all Austrians reside in urban settings, with 25% of the population living in the country's five largest cities: Vienna, Graz, Linz, Salzburg, and Innsbruck. The population density is approximately 97 people per square kilometer.

National Holidays

1 January	New Year's Day
6 January	Epiphany
March/April	Easter; Easter Monday
1 May	Labor Day
10 days before Whit Sunday	Ascension Day
7th Sunday after Easter	Whit Sunday
Day after Whit Sunday	Whit Monday
Thursday after 8th Sunday after Easter	Corpus Christi
15 August	Assumption Day
26 October	National Day
1 November	All Saints Day
8 December	Immaculate Conception
25 December	Christmas Day
26 December	Boxing Day

For additional tourist information, contact the Austrian National Tourist Office at www.austria-tourism.

Bregenz

Bregenz & the Arlberg

This chapter spans the westernmost region of Austria, that pointy piece of territory that juts along the borders of Germany, Switzerland, and Liechtenstein. The region covered here includes pieces of two Austrian provinces, the Vorarlberg to the west and, to the east, the westernmost fringes of the Tyrol. Bregenz is western Austria's cultural capital, an up-and-coming artsy town on the shore of Lake Constance. Medieval **Feldkirch** sits just south, the **Bregenzerwald forest** lies east, and the **Montafon Valley** stretches toward Silvaplana to the southeast. The terrain climbs its way east toward the high-altitude passes along the border of the Tyrol. Here, in the area region known as the Arlberg, the **Lechtaler Alps** are home to **St. Anton**, **Lech**, and **St. Christoph**, while the **Paznaun Valley** to the south harbors **Ischgl** and neighboring **Galtür**. The region ranks among our favorite places in the Alps, home to both Austria's friendliest people and its most extreme mountain terrain.

■ Bregenz

Population: 28,000

Base elevation: 398 m

Tourist city

Other than its old town, Bregenz boasts no extraordinary historical sites; other than its lake, Bregenz boasts no extraordinary recreational

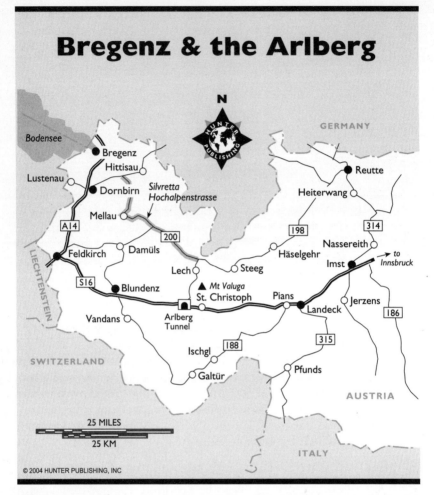

Bregenz & the Arlberg

sites. Nonetheless, culture-hounding tourists adore the city – for its artsy aspirations, its gutsy experimental architecture, and its fabulous lakeside festival.

History & Orientation

First a Celtic and then a Roman settlement site, Bregenz originally hit the map as "Brigantium." Regional wars wiped out the town by the mid fifth century, and it was not to be significantly settled again until the 10th century, when a castle that still remains was raised near the site of the old walled town. Today, however, Bregenz makes less of its history than it does of its contemporary architecture and modern art exhibits. It serves as the capital of the Vorarlberg region, and is the most culturally active city in the province.

Bregenz lies amid hilly terrain on the easternmost shore of the Bodensee or, in English, Lake Constance. It's the third-largest lake in central Europe, spanning 540 square km, plunging to a depth of 252 m, and with a shoreline circumference of 273 km. To the south and west of Bregenz stretch the Bregenzerwald forest and the Vorarlberg Alps. The city lies 120 km east of Zürich, 190 km south-west of Munich, and 200 km west of Innsbruck. Its position at the junction of Austria, Switzerland, Liechtenstein, and Germany makes it an easily accessible day-tripping base for those wishing to explore the lake region.

The Town

When writer Alexandre Dumas first entered Bregenz, he portrayed Lake Constance as "a piece of heaven framed in earth to serve God as a mirror." Although you might utter a somewhat less poetic phrase, it is undeniably a lovely lake. Your personal assessment of central Bregenz, however, will rely entirely on your taste for contemporary architecture, small-city bustle, and modern art.

The town stretches along the eastern edge of the lake, separated from the shore and its **Seepromenade Park** by train tracks and a busy road. The lakefront attractions here are anchored to the west by the **Strandbad beach** facilities and the festival's floating stage and, to the east, by the jetty and the **Mili swimming pool**. The city center lies in-between, stretching back toward the hills and up toward **Oberstadt**, the walled old town. **Mt. Pfander** rises a modest 1,064 m to the east of the town center, its cable car departing from a valley station on the northeastern edge of town.

Getting Here & Around

The nearest international airports to Bregenz are in Zürich, Munich, and Innsbruck. Trains pull into the main station city center; it's at the lakefront between the casino and the tourist office. Although the town's sights are all within easy walking distance, **Stadtbus Bregenz** provides bus service to outlying areas. For taxi service, head for the train station or contact ☎ 05574 422 45.

*Those planning on staying three days or more should consider the **Lake Constance Adventure Card**. The card offers free travel on all lake ferries and numerous cable cars. Entry to 195 museums, castles, pools, and spas is included as well, covering attractions across one huge lake and four countries. The three-day card runs €49; contact the tourist office for more information and prices for longer stays.*

Getting Connected

 The tourist office is in the Tourismushaus at Bahnhofstrasse 14 at the corner of Montfortsrasse, in the western corner of the pedestrian area. Its helpful staff offers room reservation assistance, sightseeing advice, and the informative *Discover Bregenz* pamphlets. For more information, contact ☎ 05574 495 90, www.bregenz.at.

 The main post office lies along Seestrasse just north of the Kunsthaus cube.

 For Internet access, try the tourist office, or head up Kirchestrasse to house number 47, the **S'Logo Café**.

The Sights

 Any town tour should start with a lakeside stroll, wandering from the festival stage and out to the jetty along the Seepromenade. In the center along the lakeshore lie three of the main attractions. Farthest west, the Festspiel und Kongresshaus complex anchors the festival's **Seebuhne**, or lake stage, the largest of its kind in the world. Farther east, across the main road from the jetty, are the Landesmuseum and Kunsthaus. The **Bregenz Landesmuseum** at Kornmarktplatz 1 documents the Vorarlberg's history; Tuesday through Sunday from 9 am-12 pm and 2 pm-5 pm, ☎ 05574 460 50, €2. Nearby, the **Kunsthaus Bregenz**, or KUB, occupies a celebrated architectural landmark designed by Peter Zumthor and draws 60,000 visitors each year. The museum runs rotating exhibitions of contemporary artists. It's open Tuesday through Sunday from 10 am-6 pm, Thursday till 9 pm, ☎ 05574 48 59 40, €5. Behind the lakefront and east of Montfortstrasse road lies the modern **pedestrian center**. It's lined with shops, cafés, and restaurants with pragmatic rather than tourist appeal and is a good place to taste "real life" in Bregenz.

Vorarlberg Architecture

The region's traditional architecture uses grayed untreated wood, scale-like shingle siding, and light balconies, which can still be seen outside the city. But the cities of the Vorarlberg – particularly those at the eastern edge of Lake Constance – now use traditional Vorarlberg methods, but focus on simplicity and economic functionality, using glass, steel, concrete, and raw local wood. Both Bregenz and Dornbirn have good examples – check out the Festival and Conference Center and the Bregenz Art Gallery cube.

AUTHOR'S PICK

Bregenz's **old town** lies up hill from the center and is here known as the *Oberstadt*. Although it can be reached by car via Kirchstrasse, the most scenic route up is by foot along the Maurachgasse and the old-world Stadtsteig road, which leads up to the fortified old town. When you reach the walls at Martintor, don't miss the petrified sea creature dangling above the gate – a delightfully scary sight during a midnight thunderstorm. The Oberstadt remains largely residential, but at the northern corner of the walled complex rises the **Martinsturm**, Bregenz's signature landmark. Built in 1601, the tower boasts central Europe's largest onion-dome; the Martinskappelle chapel next door is home to some interesting 14th-century frescoes.

The Adventures

Of Bregenz's adventure opportunities, **ferryboat rides** on Lake Constance prove the most popular. The *Weisse Flotte* ferry fleet cruises between several Bodensee ports in Austria, Germany, and Switzerland – including the island of Lindau, the town of Friedrichshafen and its Zepplin Museum, the wine-producing town of Meersburg, and the flower-happy island of Mainau. In addition to regular ferry service, several theme cruises and package tours are available. Contact ☎ 05574 428 68. The *Höhentwiel*, an elegant old-world paddle steamer, has been plying these waters since 1913; www.hohentwiel.com. Boats depart from the harbor just east of the jetty.

In the summer, waterlovers can rent **rowing, pedal, and electric boats** from along the Seepromenade just east of the festival stage. **Fishing** is possible along the Rhine Delta and in Lake Constance. Contact the tourist office for permits and information. **Swimmers** head for the 27-km stretch of lakeshore with several beaches and an old U-shaped dockside pool on the northern edge of town. The pool is nicknamed "Mili," as it was originally a military swimming pool. Three more pools dot the Strandbad area west of the festival stage, and a year-round indoor pool, the Seehallenbad, lies just behind.

Those looking for adrenaline-inspiring watersports can contact **Canyoning Team Vorarlberg** at ☎ 05574 52024, www.canyoning-team. com. They coordinate a variety of **canyoning**, **rafting**, **paragliding**, and **on-snow adventures**.

Adventurers climb from the edge of town up to Mt. Pfander for excellent lake views and visits to the **game park, cable car museum, and falconry exhibit**. **Hikers** can climb up or take the Pfanderbahn **cable car**, which tugs up the hill in just six minutes. It's open daily from 9 am-7 pm; €9.80 round-trip. One favorite hiking excursion from the top follows the Käsewanderweg, or "cheese route," between several hospitable dairies, farmhouses, and guest-houses. The tourist office offers a map.

The city's shoreline trails are well suited to **cycling, skating,** and **running**. Cyclists head out on the Bodensee Radweg, a 268-km loop around the lakeshore. It's do-able either as an eight-day tour or in single-day, round-trip chunks by utilizing the ferryboats. For more info, check www.bodensee-radweg.com. **Mountain bikers** head for the hills on the Pfanderbahn cable car, which carries bikes at no extra charge. The cable car station also sells a handy little pamphlet laying out 10 popular mountain routes.

*Bird-loving bicyclists can explore the largest of the region's nature reserves, the **Rhine River Delta**, a 5,000-acre meadowland with over 330 bird species, sandy beaches, and several welcoming snack stops. The 27-mile "Living on the Water" cycle route loops from Bregenz.*

Where to Stay

Many of Bregenz's hotels cater to the business-oriented folks who come to this provincial capital with work in mind. Rather characterless establishments are the norm, but a few hostelries stand out. Rates soar at all hotels during the July-August Bregenzer Festival.

HOTEL PRICE CHART	
Double room without tax; $$$-$$$$ always with bath.	
$	Under €80
$$	€81-150
$$$	€151-250
$$$$	Over €250

First among the hotels here is the enchanting **Hotel Deuring Schlössle** ($$$$). The only hotel within the Oberstadt's walls, the Deuring Schlössle boasts lake views, one of the region's best restaurants, and a homey castle atmosphere. Reserve at ☎ 05574, www.tiscover.at/at/guide/5,de/objectId,ACC126693at/home.html. In the center, try the **Hotel Weisses Kreuz** ($$-$$$). It's next to the pedestrian shopping area and has rooms with pretty painted furniture; ☎ 05574 498 80, www.bestwestern-ce.com/weisseskreuz.

With considerably less charm, but with a lake- and park-side locale, the **Hotel Mercure Bregenz City** ($$) is a reasonable businesslike choice; ☎ 05574 461 00, www.mercure.com. Budgeting visitors should consider the central, but very simple **Pension Sonne** ($) in the pedestrian shopping area; ☎ 05574 425 72, www.bbn.at/sonne.

Austria's Zillertal in summer

Above: Innsbruck cable car

Below: The Spullersee near Lech am Arlberg, Austria

Getreidegasse, the shopping street, Salzburg

Above: Galtür, Austria

Below: Ischgl, Austria

Or, for more character, try the old **Hotel Zum Grauen Bären** ($) in the center behind the Kunsthaus; ☎ 05574 428 23. Several private rooms are available in the vicinity of the Pfander cable car station; stop by the tourist office to make arrangements.

Where to Eat

Bregenz's 120 restaurants, cafés, and bars offer a solid choice of fare, including traditional Alpine cooking and local fish specialties.

DINING PRICE CHART	
Average entrée, with tax.	
$	Under €10
$$	€10-25
$$$	Over €25

AUTHOR'S PICK

The **Hotel Deuring Schlössle** ($$$) harbors one of western Austria's best gourmet dining rooms. The restaurant occupies one corner of the old town's wall, a splendid setting with views of the lake below. In dining rooms decked out with elegant residential décor, guests dine on light, creative cuisine and fine wines. Have a brandy by the massive fireplace to top off a wonderful meal. Reserve a table and room at ☎ 05574 478 00, www.deuring-schloessle.com.

The two restaurants at the Hotel Weisses Kreuz also have good fare. The **Stadtgästhaus** ($$$) gourmet room does elegant menus, while the less formal **Kreuzstuben** ($$) offers hearty Austrian specialties; ☎ 05574 498 80. In the center, at Anton Schneider Strasse 5, the **Restaurant Neubeck** ($$) serves up excellent cuisine with a French-Mediterranean flair; ☎ 05574 436 09, www.neubeck.at.

For enormous meals of wholesome traditional cuisine, head for the half-timbered **Wirsthaus am See** ($$) on the lakeside promenade, or cozy up in the old **Goldener Hirschen** ($$) at Kirchstrasse 8. South of the city but worth the trek is the **Burgrestaurant Bebhardsberg** ($$), an old mountainside refuge with big views and a menu featuring local beef, fish from the lake, and Austrian wines; ☎ 05574 425 15, www.greber.cc. Budgeting diners can try the **Gunz** ($), in the center at Anton-Schneider Strasse 38, or head for the **Coop** ($) grocery and deli in the basement of the pedestrian area's indoor shopping mall.

Where to Party

Bregenz's nightlife tends toward low-key café lounging. At Kornmarktstrasse, the **Erste Akt** maintains a casual atmosphere and pub amenities. For dancing, head for the **Kanzlei** near the museums at Kornmarktplatz 5 or the

Tanzbar Nachtigall at Rheinstrasse 64. There's dancing, too, at the panoramic **Calypso Club** at Bahnhofstrasse 14 and, nearby, **Cuba Bar** DJs pump a Latin beat. On the lakeshore across from the train station, the **Casino Bregenz** offers blackjack, roulette, poker, slot machines, and European seven-eleven. The gaming house claims to stand on lucky ground, as more Austrian lottery jackpots have been won here than at any other locale. Try your luck daily, 3 pm-3 am, Friday and Saturday till 4 am, ☎ 05574 45 12 70.

Where to Play

Although Bregenz sets its cultural sights toward more mature pursuits, kids enjoy its lakeside setting for the beaches, pools, rental boats, swans, and ferryboat rides. Cable car rides up to the Pfander mini-zoo prove popular as well. **Playgrounds** are near the lake across the tracks from the main train station, tucked away along St. Anna Strasse off of Römerstrasse, and up behind the old town Oberstadt. On the mountain, kids play behind the cable car arrival station.

Festivals & Events

From March through May, the **Spring Festival** kicks off the festival season, featuring a wide array of dance performances. The **International Fleet Rally** opens the summer ferry season in mid-April. Four ferry companies participate to determine who has the fastest, most maneuverable ships.

From mid-July through mid-August, the famed **Bregenz Festival** brings internationally renowned musical theater performances to the largest floating stage in the world. (If you want a hotel room during this period, book far, far in advance.)

Every other year at the end of August, the **Kubelregatta**, or tub regatta, floats out onto Lake Constance. Participants run the race in whatever oddball floating vehicle they choose. The **Three Countries Marathon** in early October ranks as the area's largest sporting event, with over 4,000 competitors.

Feldkirch

A small, charming city on the western border of Austria, halfway between Bregenz and Vaduz, Feldkirch is a seldom-visited place loaded with medieval ambiance. The city got its start as a market and university town, developing its central network of alleys and squares along the Ill River by late in the 13th century. Today, much of the town's action continues to revolve around the old center's pedestrian marketplace.

Day tourists will enjoy a simple wander through the **old town** along its cobblestone alleys, which link two long, parallel squares, the **Neustadtplatz** to the east and the **Marktplatz** to the west. The Neustadt is now a bustling ring street with cramped parking; the Marktplatz remains a narrow market area encircled by elegant arcades. The **St. Johanneskirche** anchors the southern edge of the old town, and the 15th-century cathedral **St. Nikolaus** and the nearby **Katzenturm** bell tower rise to the north. At the northwestern corner of town, the 14th-century **Churertor** still guards the city gates. Outside of the center, on a hill south of town, is **Schattenberg Castle**. First built in the 12th century, the **Montfort castle** has four-meter-thick walls that alone make the steep hike or drive worthwhile. To get there, drive up Burgasse or follow the footpath up the Schlosssteig steps. Inside are a restaurant and museum, the latter open Tuesday through Sunday from 9 am-noon and 1-5 pm; December through January, only 11 am-4 pm; closed November.

AUTHOR'S PICK Several medieval festivals highlight the Feldkirch calendar, and if you can catch one, it's likely to be one of your trip's most memorable events. The **Montfort Markt**, the city's famous old-world festival, comes each May to the foot of the Schattenburg Castle. The **Feldkircher Weinfest** fills the Marktplatz in early July and, later in the month, the **Gauklerfestival**, or Jugglers' Festival, brings 100 street artists to the Feldkirch, delightfully crowding the old medieval center with clowns, mimes, comedians, and, of course, jugglers. Finally, the Christmas season enlivens the old town with the **Blosengelmarkt**, **Advent singing**, and the **Feldkirch Christmas Market**.

Want to stay? The coziest place in town – and it has the best restaurant, too – is the lovely **Hotel Alpenrose** ($$), with a gracious staff, antique-heavy décor, and a 450-year-old history. The hotel is in the old center at Rosengasse 4. Reserve at ☎ 05522 721 75, www.alpenrose.net.

 The Feldkirch tourist office is at Herrengasse 12, near the Katzturm. For more information, contact ☎ 05522 734 67, www.feldkirch.at.

■ St. Anton am Arlberg

Population: 2,580

Base elevation: 1,300 m

Mountain resort village

There's a lot to love about St. Anton. I adore it above all for its people, both its friendly residents and its spirited, hard-driving visitors. Although famed throughout the world as a winter resort, the village also claims a respectable following among summertime hikers, bikers, and climbers. But St. Anton comes into its own as a superb playground for expert skiers; it's Austria's premier ski-bum resort – the rip-roaring bad boy of the Arlberg.

History & Overview

 The Arlberg region occupies the western panhandle of Austria, the nation's most mountainous terrain. Once farmland, the region was opened to visitors in the 19th century by the arrival of the railway and the construction of the Flexen Pass road – basically a tunnel with an open gallery on one side. The now-famous Arlberg Ski Club was formed in St. Christoph in 1901. Member Hannes Schneider offered ski instruction here for the first time in 1907, assisted the Austrian military in the development of on-ski Alpine troops, and eventually developed the distinctive feet-together Arlberg style. Schneider also played host to British skier Sir Alfred Lunn, with whom he together coordinated the 1927 inaugural running of the Kandahar Race. Several local racers have gone on to great success and worldwide sporting fame in this and other World Cup competitions. World champions Karl Schranz and Marina Kiehl are just two of those. Today, the village enjoys a historical significance that spans an entire century – as home to Hannes Schneider, the father of modern skiing, and as host of the World Alpine Skiing Championships in 2001.

The Town

St. Anton sprawls along the Rosanna River, 30 km west of **Landeck**. The elongated town connects at its eastern edge with the neighboring villages of **Nasserein** and, farther down-valley, **St. Jakob**. The main valley road, the **Arlbergstrasse**, runs up from Innsbruck and into the center on its southern side. (Through traffic ducks into the Arlberg Tunnel, which empties out 14 km west of here.) The main train station sits on the hillside opposite town, across the main road and the river. St. Anton's action centers on its pedestrian zone and a long street called Dorfstrasse, which runs from the traffic circle at its western end downhill toward Nasserein. Paralleling Dorfstrasse just up the hill, Hannes Schneider Weg runs from the lifts to the wellness center along a lovely park, site of what was until just a few years ago an unsightly train yard. The main cable cars depart from just above the center, with other stations up the valley, above the wellness center, and at Nasserein.

Getting Here & Around

 Visitors arriving by air will fly into Innsbruck, 100 km to the east; Zürich, 200 km to the west; or Munich, 250 km to the north. Airport transfers from Zürich are provided by **Arlberg Express**, ☎ 05582 226. The new, ultra-modern train station lies at the southern edge of the center, and train connections are frequent to both Innsbruck and Zürich.

Drivers will likely arrive via Landeck in the east or Feldkirch and the Arlberg Tunnel in the west. (Tunnel toll at last count was €8.50). As the center of the village is a car-free zone, parking areas line the main road into town. Local and regional buses serve the area well. In winter, free shuttle buses operate between the villages of St. Anton and St Jakob; between the bases of the Galzig and Rendl areas; and between Alpe Rauz and the nearby village of Zurs. Tickets must be purchased for travel between St. Anton and St. Christoph, Alpe Rauz, Zurs, and Lech. For taxi service, contact **Taxi Harry** at ☎ 0554 23 68 or **Taxi Griesser** at ☎ 0554 37 30.

Mountain transportation includes 41 local lifts, six of which run in summer for lift-served hiking and mountain biking. A variety of passes are available.

LIFT PASS PRICE SAMPLES

Winter

1-day adult Arlberg Pass €38.50

6-day adult Arlberg Pass €179

Summer

7-day all-mountain Wanderpass €30

Pedestrian round-trip to the Valluga Summit €18

Getting Connected

i The **tourist office** is in the center near the traffic circle, at the top of Dorfstrasse. New arrivals appreciate the electronic hotel map in the corridor outside; and skiers appreciate the resort Info Team, a group of eight multi-lingual ladies that disperse across the mountain with the sole purpose of providing up-to-date information. Contact the tourist office at ☎ 05446 226 90, www.stantonamarlberg.com.

 The **post office** is along the main road into town, next door to the St. Antonerhof Hotel.

 The **Mail Box Café** in the pedestrian zone offers Internet access. It's open 9 am-10 pm in season. **Jennewein Sport** also offers Internet access from its rental and sport shops.

The Sights

 St. Anton is a sporting resort, and few sights stand out. Chief among them is the **St. Anton Ski Museum**, which documents the development of St. Anton, local cultural traditions, and the history of the local ski club. The museum is located in the Arlberg Kandahar Haus chalet – and its lovely interior is alone worth the price of admission. It's open Sunday through Friday, 3 pm to 10 pm in winter, less frequently in summer; ☎ 05446 24 75, €3. Also of interest to history buffs is the **Thöni Haus**, dating from the Middle Ages and thereby among the region's oldest homes. The old wooden house is tucked inconspicuously away at Im Greis, and today remains in private hands.

 The tourist office offers guided village tours every Monday at 4 pm; the tours are free of charge.

AUTHOR'S PICK The 360° view from 2,650-meter-high **Valluga Summit** offers one of the most spectacular panoramas of the Alps. The trip up entails a three-stage cable car ride – the Galzigbahn from the village center; the Valluga I cable car to the Valluga Grat area; and finally, the Valluga II cable car (actually, something more akin to a telephone booth) to the 2,811-meter Valluga peak. From the small viewing platform at the top, views extend to the Lechtal Alps in the north, to the Zügspitze of Germany in the northwest, to the Silvretta and Switzerland's Bernina in the south, and to the Stubaital glaciers and Italy's Dolomites in the southeast.

The Adventures

On Foot

 Hikers enjoy 110 km of well-posted paths. Six summertime lifts access the local mountains, and 33 mountain huts offer refreshment. The tourist office runs a program of guided walking tours Tuesday through Friday in summer. Walks include an outing to an Alpine dairy farm, a walk through mountain flowers, a photo tour, and a two-day trek, with an overnight in a mountain hut. Contact the tourist office for information and to make reservations, ☎ 05446 226 90, www.stantonamarlberg.com.

The Arlberg Climbers' Track

Experienced climbers consider the Arlberg Climbing Track one of the Alps' most demanding and scenic fixed routes. The track stretches 2.8 km along the Lechtal Alps and takes around five hours to complete. To access the starting point, walk approximately 20 minutes east from the Valluga Grat cable car station toward the Einstieg or, from the Kapall chairlift, approximately 15 minutes west. Proper equipment, weather conditions, and expertise are required.

In Water

 Swimmers head year-round for the **ARLBERG-Well.com** and its pool facilities, which include an indoor pool, waterfalls, an outdoor river current, and excellent sauna area; contact ☎ 05446 2269 54, www.Arlberg-well.com, for current open hours. The **Sporthotel St. Anton** and the **Hotel Grieshof** also open their indoor pools to the public. In the summer, the **Waldschwimmbad** provides an outdoor pool in a forested locale. Watersport fans looking for more extreme action pair up with **H2O Adventures** (see *Sports Services, Outfitters & Guides* below, page 69) for canyoning, rafting, and such. Fishing is an option, too, both in the Rosanna River and at Lake Verwall. Make inquiries at the tourist office for permits and regulations.

On Wheels

 Summertime **mountain bikers** take advantage of 60 km of timber access road and designated trails. Routes run along the Rendlalpe, Tritschalpe, and Putzenalpe; one favorite 1.5-hour run climbs past the Verwallsee up to the Konstanzerhütte and, if you're game, another two hours up to the Heilbronnerhutte at 2,308 m. The tourist office sells maps and guidebooks specifically for mountain bikers.

In the Air

Paragliding flights include training, trial course, and tandem jumps. For more information, contact Simon Penz at **Flight Connection Arlberg**, ☎ 0664 141 51 66, www.fca.at.

*The **Arlberg Adventure Pass** includes free cable car rides and entry to the swimming complex, the minigolf park, and the local museum. It's good for seven days, and can be purchased at the tourist office; cost is €45 for adults, €24 for children.*

On Snow & Ice

St. Anton is Austria's signature resort, a name well known throughout the **skiing** world; a mecca for on-ski experts, and a magnet for après-ski addicts. The ski region surrounding St. Anton includes 260 km of groomed runs served by 83 lifts in six resorts: St. Anton, St. Christoph, Stuben, Lech, Zurs, and Sonnenkopf. The 41 local lifts access the region's largest section of slopes, a 40-km network of steep, groomed pistes.

During the summer of 2003, €13 million was invested in efforts to open up additional runs for beginning- and intermediate-level skiers. Improvements target the Rendl and Fang areas. Mid-level skiers can enjoy most of the mountain, including the area's longest run, a 10.2-km descent from the Vallugagrat down to the village. Experts head for the steep slopes at Schindlerkar or plunge off the Valluga peak for an exhilarating ride. (Certified guides must accompany you on the Valluga route; if you don't have a guide, the bouncer manning the Vallugapitze cable car won't allow your skis on board.) Due to ecological concerns, helicopter skiing is no longer allowed.

Ski Safety

St. Anton is one of the world's great resorts for expert skiers. If your skills do not fall into this category, take some care when on the local slopes. Piste difficulty is notoriously under-graded here, and I've encountered chopped up sections of "blue" piste that would easily qualify as black in a lesser resort. Avalanches are a very real threat – note the protective gates high above the village and heed all posted warnings. That said, there's no reason to fret, and there's always a way down – I just hope it's not with the services of St. Anton's sixteen rescuers, here unnamed, and four avalanche dogs: Tasso, Dando, Arco, and Rambo.

St. Anton is predominately a skiing, rather than snowboarding, resort – up-and-comer Ischgl, just over the hill, has cornered that youthful niche market. Nonetheless, **free-style skiers** of all persuasions find funpark action, including a halfpipe and various jumps, on the Rendl. The lodge there, known as "Rendl Beach," proves popular on sunny afternoons. A total of 18 **mountain huts** stud the slopes, offering food, drink, and high-altitude hospitality.

Cross-country skiers enjoy 35 km of loipe (trails), including the lovely Verwall Trail, which tucks back into the Verwall Valley, looping around the lake and back to town. For **horse-drawn sleigh rides** along the same route, contact the tourist office or Martin Tschol, ☎ 05446 23 80. **Tobogganers** enjoy the four-km run at Gampen – rent sleds at the Rodelhütte below – and **ice-skating** and **curling** takes place on the small natural rink fronting the wellness center. Finally, some 15 km of cleared **winter walking paths** wind around the village, including a nice hike up to the Rodelhütte restaurant.

Sports Services, Outfitters & Guides

- **H20 Adventures** organizes a number of high-energy outings, including canyoning, tubing, rafting, ropes courses, and mountain biking tours. If what you've got in mind isn't on the list, they'll custom-tailor activities to your request. Contact ☎ 05446 39 37, www.events-more.at.

- **Alber Sport** is my favorite among the 15 sports equipment and rental shops in town. They have four outlets scattered around town. Contact ☎ 05446 34 00.

- The **Arlberg Arena Mountain Hiking School** centralizes the expertise of several mountain guides. For treks throughout the Ferwall and Lechtal Alps, contact Ferdl Nöbl, ☎ 05446 28 66, www.Arlberg-arena.at.

- The **Ski School Arlberg** and the **Ski and Snowboard School St. Anton**, the village's two ski schools, employ a total of 320 instructors and over 150 group courses at all ability levels. The Arlberg school is the older, traditional school, in operation since 1921, ☎ 05546 34 11, www.skischool-arlberg.com. The St. Anton school is under the direction of Franz Klimmer, ☎ 05446 35 63, www.skistanton.com. Both are good.

Austria

Where to Sleep

St. Anton boasts a wide range of accommodations, some scattered into far-flung neighborhoods in Nasserein and St. Jakob – both of which are friendly, quiet villages but not what most visitors come here to experience. Most outlying accommodation remains closed through the summer, and rates soar at the height of winter.

HOTEL PRICE CHART	
Double room without tax; $$$-$$$$ always with bath.	
$	Under €80
$$	€81-150
$$$	€151-250
$$$$	Over €250

Although the luxurious **St. Antoner Hof** ($$$$) is the only house to pull five stars here, its location along the busy main road makes it less than ideal; ☎ 05446 29 10, www.antonerhof.at. I like instead the elegant **Schwarzer Adler** ($$$), a rambling old hotel with what must be St. Anton's most genteel staff. The rooms in the new wing are bright, the lounge has an open fire, and there's a pool and wellness center on the ground floor; ☎ 05446 224 40, www.schwarzeradler.com. Try the large, chalet-style **Hotel Post** ($$$) for cozy rooms and two popular in-house bars; ☎ 05446 221 30, www.st-anton.co.at. Or, for on-mountain lodging near the Mooserwirt (and with an in-house après-ski scene to boot), book the Kössler Family's cozy **Kaminstube**; ☎ 05446 26 81, www.kaminstube.com.

In the center, I liked the convenient location of the **Angelike** ($$), ☎ 05446 22 54; the country-style **Hotel Garni Montana** ($$) in the pedestrian area, ☎ 05446 32 53; and, tucked away on a back street, the **Hotel Manfred** ($$), with a hodgepodge of homey décor and an enormous St. Bernard, ☎ 5446 27 20. It's open most of the year, and the restaurant serves excellent fondue as well. A short walk uphill from the center, near the lifts in the vicinity of the racing stadium, try the **Haus am Fang** ($$), ☎ 05546 35 43, for cozy residential accommodations at the slopes. Up Arlbergstrasse, hidden away on Rudi Matt Weg, the **Haus Lisun** ($), ☎ 05446 33 59, and the **Haus Olympia** ($), ☎ 05446 25 20, both offer simple accommodations in a convenient, quiet locale.

Where to Eat

One of the village's most elegant dining venues is, oddly, the **Museum Restaurant and Café** ($$). The restaurant occupies the ground floor of a forest-ensconced fairytale chalet, its cozy rooms surrounding a massive fireplace and each decked out in old-world chalet décor. Reserve a table at ☎ 0556 24 75. On the mountain at St. Christoph, don't miss the **Hospiz Alm** (see *St. Christoph* below**). For traditional cuisine, the **Fuhrmannstube** ($$) draws locals to Dorfstrasse 74; across from the tourist office, try the **Hax'n Stub'n** ($$) – it's cozier inside than it might first appear, and there's upstairs seating, too. The simple **'S Wirtshaus am Alten Bahnhof** restaurant ($$) in the old train station offers good traditional food as well.

DINING PRICE CHART	
Average entrée, with tax.	
$	Under €10
$$	€10-25
$$$	Over €25

The **Rodelstall** ($-$$), at the foot of the tobogganing run, boasts an open fireplace, regional cuisine and, on advance request, delicious spareribs; ☎ 0699 178 588 55. For less expensive fare, **Pomodoro Pizzeria** ($) at Dorfstrasse 5 is popular for its good selection of pizzas and convivial ambiance. **Bobo's** ($) specializes in American and Mexican food, and the **Dorfstuben** ($) next door serves food till late. Near the tourist office, the **Café Haferl** ($) serves up a good selection of light snacks, and **Café Schneider** ($) down the street does the same throughout the year. For inexpensive picnic fare, head for the **Spar grocery store** and its **Murr Deli**.

Where to Party

St. Anton's reputation as a party town is well deserved, at least in winter, when adult crowds descend upon the village with revelry in mind. In summer, the village is a great deal quieter.

AUTHOR'S PICK

If you love après-ski parties, don't miss the afternoon action at the **Mooserwirt** mountain lodge in the hamlet of Moos, just above town. A deck full of picnic tables fills up early, as skis pile up outside. Inside, a DJ plays music to a house packed from dance floor, to stairway, to balcony – where a cross-cultural mix of international visitors drinks beer and dances on tables, ski boots and all. Beware, however, as the party slows down around dinnertime, at which point you must navigate the icy slope down to the village on skis. The cries of tumbling drunks oft echo through the village center.

The **Krazy Kangaroo** just across the slope shares an equally renowned reputation and a lively – if younger and poorer – après-ski crowd. Down the hill at village center, après-ski action congregates at several scattered locales, although most places quiet down during the dinner hour before picking up again late (after everyone's had a shower and a nap). At the base of the slopes, near the ski school, the

Austria

Base Camp gazebo bar offers a heated deck and a long list of warm drinks. Favorite afternoon-and-evening attractions include the **Underground,** a two-story bar with a dark basement and an upstairs pub; **Jacksy's** next door, for low-key conversation; the **Bar Cuba** for self-service beer; and the **Funky Chicken** for big, cheap beers and young, rollicking fun. For late-night dancing, try the **Piccadilly Pub** or the **Post Keller**, both in the Hotel Post. My favorite late-night bar, however, remains the **Platzl**, a dark, smoky dive with a fireplace and occasional live music.

Where to Play

 Although St. Anton wholeheartedly welcomes children in all seasons, the difficulty of the local ski slopes and the raucousness of the clientele here makes it less than ideal for families in winter. (However, the standard ski school operations are available.) But in the summer, St. Anton's lively festival calendar and village ambiance makes for a great family atmosphere. The **kindergarten** accepts potty-trained children, the tourist office can help arrange **childcare**, and two great **playgrounds** entertain. The first, near the wellness center, on the site of the old train yard, offers water play, a fountain, and several toys. The second, up Rudi Matt Weg, at the foot of the town museum, delights with a good collection of wooden toys and – the kicker – a small fishing pond. A third playground is a 10-minute walk outside of the center, next to the lake at Verwall.

Festivals & Events

 St. Anton opens its winter season in early December with the **Radio 7 Ski Opening** party and pop concert for which fans bus in from Germany, Italy, and Switzerland. **Holiday season festivities** follow, including a torch-lit race and musical fireworks, a mountain celebration at St. Jakob's church, and the **Arlberg New Year Concert**. In mid-February, **World Cup** slalom and downhill competitions bring the world's fastest skiers to town, and various races run throughout the spring. July brings traditional folklore and the **St. Anton Festival**, while August features the **Tent Feast**, during which local and visiting folklore bands parade through town in traditional costumes. Mountain bikers flock to town for the **Arlberg Mountain Bike Trophy** in August, when some 200 bikers race on the 20-km extreme downhill run. The **St. Anton Film Festival** takes center stage in mid September, showing international and regional takes on mostly mountain-related themes; and, later in September, the **Almabtrieb Harvest Festival** celebrates the return of the cattle from their summer Alpine pastures.

LANDECK CASTLE

Landeck sits 30 km east of St. Anton, on the way to Innsbruck. On a hill above the town perches Schloss Landeck, a 13th-century fortress that today houses the local museum. Inside the castle is a good collection of costumes and art and a cultural center that mounts a variety of events and exhibitions. Stop by between mid-May and the end of September, Tuesday through Sunday, 10 am-5 pm, €3.70. For more information, contact ☎ 05442 632 02, www.schlosslandeck.at.

St. Christoph

Some 17 buildings comprise the hamlet of St. Christoph, a secluded, exclusive satellite resort of St. Anton that boasts a history all its own. (See *The Brotherhood of St. Christoph* below.) The settlement lies at the top of the barren Arlberg Pass, a six-km climb above St. Anton along a dramatic tunnel road that's avalanche-protected with an opening on one side, and is home to a ski school, six expensive hotels, and a national ski team training center. If you're not staying here – and given local room rates, the odds are good you're not – St. Christoph provides little more than a lunch stop on a day-tripping ski route; but, if you head for the Hospiz Alm, St. Christoph is a stop well worth making.

AUTHOR'S PICK

The **Hospiz Alm** ($$) restaurant is owned and operated by the same family that runs the swanky Arlberg Hospiz Hotel down the road. The atmosphere in this old farmhouse, however, is much more fun. Rough-hewn wood, lots of stone, and a roaring fire create a cozy ambiance – and don't miss the stairway slide down to the bathrooms. (One of the region's best wine cellars lurks downstairs as well.) Excellent traditional cuisine makes this a favorite on-slope lunch stop for skiers, and the gourmet creations of Stefan Hofer make this *the* place in the Arlberg for a romantically rustic dinner; ☎ 05446 36 25, www.hospiz.com, open winter only.

The Brotherhood of St. Christoph

As was the custom in medieval times, the Christian men's order *Johanniter* maintained a network of high-altitude chapels en route to the holy land, offering shelter, food, and drink to travelers in need. So, although a chapel may have existed along the path prior his time, Heinrich Findelkind, a St. Anton pig herdsman, is attributed with founding the first hostel on this site in 1387. Findelkind was known to serve far beyond the duties expected of a hostel host, actively seeking out stranded travelers and bringing them to safety, even in the harshest winter weather. The Pope took note in 1386, and the Brotherhood of St. Christoph was officially established. After extensive recruiting throughout Italy, Bohemia, Poland, Germany, the Netherlands, and Switzerland, Heinrich Findelkind and the Brotherhood of St. Christoph had the financial and prayerful support of some 2,000 members by the time of the man's death around 1415.

Emperor Joseph II disbanded the brotherhood in 1780, and the hostel passed through several private ownerships before falling into ruin by the 19th century, when the new Arlberg railway line largely eliminated traffic over the pass. Government preservation efforts kicked in during 1898, and the hostel and its chapel found new life as a ski lodge for early sportsmen. On January 3rd of 1901, the legendary Arlberg Ski Club was founded here, a moment documented on a Hospiz tablecloth. Sadly, in Jaunary 1957, a fire destroyed all but the exterior walls of the structures – an event that, tragic as it was, resulted in the reestablishment of the ancient brotherhood, which was enacted in efforts to rebuild the historical site. Today, the Arlberg Hospiz Hotel stands on the site of the original hostel, and the Brotherhood of St. Christoph numbers over 13,000 members worldwide. Funds raised through membership fees pay for the upkeep of the chapel and donations to varied charities, including the sponsorship of children orphaned in mountain accidents.

 Want to stay? Well, unfortunately, a night at St. Christoph's famed hostel is these days far from free. If you've got the change to spare, however, by all means book accommodations at the **Arlberg Hospiz Hotel** ($$$$), shown on the previous page. Its rooms, suites, and apartments vary in décor, but all are luxurious; its private ski instructors rank among the region's best; and the sofa fronting its enormous lobby fireplace is the mountain's most perfect place for a nightcap. Reserve at ☎ 05546 26 11, www.hospiz.com; hotel open winter only. If you'd prefer a less extravagant stay, the least expensive of the hotels here is the **Gästhof Valluga** ($$$), a cozy but still pricey place; ☎ 05446 28 23, www.arlberg.com/gasthof-valluga; gasthof-valluga@arlberg.com. The hotel is open in winter only.

 St. Christoph shares the St. Anton tourist information office. Contact ☎ 05446 226 90, www.stantonamarlberg.com.

Lech am Arlberg

Lech

Although it technically lies within the borders of the Vorarlberg province, Lech is the Arlberg region's favorite family resort. The traditional village lies up the Flexen Pass, on the northern side of the Valluga mountain, approximately 20 km north of St. Anton. Lech, for me, is the quintessential Alpine holiday village; chalets dot forested hillsides, a crystal-clear river runs through the center, and horse-drawn carriages await fares next to a covered bridge. Although it is one of the Alps' more expensive resorts, the village is less pretentiously exclusive than St. Christoph, and a country-style gentility prevails. First and foremost, Lech is loved by families, many of whom have been coming here for years.

Some 300 m up the hill from the village center perches the hamlet of **Oberlech**, a car-free village served by a lift that runs late into the night. Also near Lech are the satellite hamlets of **Stuben** and **Zug**, quiet hideaways perfect for walking, cross-country skiing, and horse-drawn sleigh and carriage rides. Between Lech and St. Christoph is **Zurs**, a treeless ski resort that largely closes up in summer.

Lech for Kids

Lech's children's programs are some of the best in the Alps. Its Mini and Junior Club adventure day programs entertain kids from three to 12 years old with a wide range of age-appropriate activities, including river rafting, pool swimming, fishing, picnicking, skating at the local fun park. For kids staying in Lech, the program (except for lunch) is absolutely free. In winter, the Mini Club and the Oberlech kindergarten take kids three years and up; for guests staying in Oberlech, kindergarten childcare is free. The tourist office can help arrange babysitting year-round.

From late November through April, Lech is a snowy wonderland. For skiers, the village partners up with nearby resorts to offer the **Arlberg Ski Pass**, which includes 83 lifts and 260 km of groomed runs and 185 km of ungroomed routes at resorts including St. Anton, St. Christoph, and Zurs, among others. The 110 km of groomed skiing above Lech is less extreme than that above St. Anton – another feature attractive to families. Other winter attractions include many sporting activities for non-skiers, such as a lighted tobogganing run, 19 km of cross-country runs, 25 km of cleared walking trails, and sleigh rides day and night.

In summer, the valley's low-key relaxation brings loyal guests from all over Europe. From late June through late September, visitors hike on 250 km of trails, head into the hills on four lifts, enjoy a large forest pool, fish in mountain lakes, and mountain bike on a variety of trails. The local mountaineering school organizes classes and outings for a variety of sports across a full range of ability levels. In addition, free hikers' buses serve outlying trails, including the fascinating Sea of Stone Trail. Beginning near the crater-like Formarinsee, this four-hour, geology-themed loop encircles the Formaletsch peak, passing through a limestone treasure trove of fossils – some up to 200 million years old. Stone markers indicate fossil sites..

Want to stay? It's neither the quietest nor the quaintest place in town, but the **Hotel Tannbergerhof** offers a good array of services directly in the village center – and at relatively reasonable rates. It's at house number 111, just across from the river, and it welcomes guests for both the summer and winter seasons. In winter, the hotel's sidewalk café is a popular après-ski hangout. For reservations, dial ☎ 05583 220 20, www.tannbergerhof.com.

The local tourist office is along the main road in the center of town. For more information, contact ☎ 054483 31 55, www.lech-zuers.at.

■ Ischgl

Population: 1,500

Base elevation: 1,377 m

Mountain resort village

Once a mildly prosperous mining town, Ischgl is a place where both "hard rock" and "gold" have taken on entirely different meanings. I love wintertime Ischgl for its young, party-hearty spirit, its famed on-mountain concerts, and its trendy, pricey façade. The town lies largely dormant during its summer recuperation, although expanded summer lift service and a growing following among hard-core mountain bikers promise to change all that.

History & Overview

The old settlement of "Yscla" first hit the maps as Rhaeto-Romans ventured over the Fimberpass in search of summer pasturelands. In 1319, German-speaking Walsers migrated from the upper Valais to settle near Galtür and were later joined by an influx of Bavarians. From the 15th through 19th centuries, the now-settled Fimba and Paznaun valleys served as a trade route and mining center. Finally, in the mid-20th century, the village began developing its tourist infrastructure and cable uplift network in earnest.

Ischgl sits 100 km west of Innsbruck, a long way up the long Paznaun Valley. The resort village occupies a 1.5-km stretch of the southern bank of the Trisanna River and boasts a lovely setting smack dab among the Silvretta, the Samnaun, and the Verwall mountains. Today, with 10,000 guest beds and growing occupancy rates, Ischgl sets the standard for modern resorts and was recently deemed the European Alpine Show's "Best International Ski Resort."

The Town

Although the village has a lengthy history, little of Ischgl's historical core remains today. Restaurants line the narrow streets, sporting goods shops flaunt the latest in high-tech equipment, and glossy hotels stretch out along the southern foothills, each vying for a coveted "ski-in" lot. All that said, Ischgl does not feign the pretension of such highbrow resorts as Kitzbühel and St. Moritz, but instead adopts a

Austria

Biking above Ischgl

welcoming friends-and-fun atmosphere suitable for its young clientele.

Ischgl centers on its little hilltop church and crowds its way downhill, toward the Prenner area and the Pardatschgratbahn cable car to the northeast and toward the Pasnatsch area and the Silvrettabahn gondola to the southwest. These two sides of town sandwich a maze of tiny streets, a relatively large pedestrian area, and a very convenient foot tunnel between the pedestrian center and the Fimbabahn lift. The village streets remain unnamed and, as buildings are randomly numbered, locations are best described by landmark rather than address. (Pick up a map and take a familiarization stroll as soon as you hit town.)

Ischgl's quiet summer season runs from late June through mid-October, although what summer action there is here seems to peter out by mid-September. Winter season rolls around in mid-December and rocks on through April.

Getting Here & Around

Ischgl sits mid-way up the Paznaun Valley, approximately 100 km west of Innsbruck. Those arriving by air will find Innsbruck, Munich, and Zürich reasonably accessible, while those arriving by train will have to bus in to Ischgl from the train station at Landeck, 30 minutes down-valley. Buses ply the length of the Paznaun Valley, and taxi service is on call at **Ischgler Taxi**, ☎ 05444 5999, www.taxi-ischgl.com.

The village itself is a maze of tiny streets and pedestrian-only alleys and is therefore best maneuvered on foot. (Lots along the main road make parking easy.) The village's knoll-side setting makes for some long winding walks, although the 190-m Village Tunnel mitigates this difficulty a bit with conveyor belts connecting the center of Ischgl with the Fimba cableway valley station.

Mountain transportation is offered year-round – at least to some extent. Check with the tourist office to confirm lift operations, particularly during the spring and fall shoulder seasons, when maintenance, weekend-only service, and extended lift lunch breaks may interfere with your plans.

LIFT PASS PRICE SAMPLES

Winter

1-day adult €37.50

6-day adult €163.50

Pedestrian round-trip to Idalp €14.50

Summer

Pedestrian round-trip to Idalp €12.30

Getting Connected

 The **Ischgl tourist office** is tucked away in the center under the Spar grocery store, an inconvenient locale for new arrivals. You'll have to park below or in the garage and walk up the hill. Brochures, a hotel reservation board, and recreational arrangements are available during the office's changeable opening hours. Dial ☎ 0544 5366 or check www.ischgl.com for more info. For further information regarding the opening status of Silvretta area cableways, check with www.silvretta.at.

 Next to the tourist office, the post office is open weekdays from 8 am-5 pm (with a break for lunch) and on Saturdays from 9 am-noon.

WWW Most hotels here now offer Internet access in their lobbies. An Internet café operates out of the Silveretta Sall Community Center.

The Sights

 Ischgl is a recreational resort through-and-through, and few cultural sights are to be found. The Kurz Family maintains the **Bauernmuseum** in nearby Mathon, four km up-valley toward Galtür. The museum offers a look at the historical lives of local peasant farmers and is open daily except Saturdays in winter and daily except Tuesdays in summer. The **Mathias Schmid Museum** presents a collection of the local artist's work and keepsakes as well as items of cultural and historical interest. Opening hours vary, so check in at ☎ 0664 35 79 174 or look for info posters around the village. The village's **St. Nikolaus Church** is worth a peek for its ornate interior and flower-strewn cemetery – just wander uphill toward the bell tower.

Austria

The Adventures

*The **Silvretta Card** offers free and discounted use of summer recreational facilities in Ischgl and surrounding area for three, seven, 10, or 14 days. Included is free use of cable networks, swimming pools, and museums. Discounts on equipment rental, guided hikes and bike tours, paragliding, and children's programs also apply. The seven-day card costs €39.50 for adults – a bargain if you put the card to adequate use. Reductions for seniors and children apply. Buy your card at the tourist office.*

On Foot

The village offers 300 km of **hiking** trails and 18 Alpine huts in its immediate vicinity. The cable uplift network runs throughout the summer season, and numerous themed and guided walks are available. In addition to many hotel-based programs, Ischgl Reservations, ☎ 05444 5266 44, runs daily guided hikes, including nature walks, high peak excursions, Alpine pasture walks, and low-intensity family excursions. Our favorite outing, however, is a lift-assisted trek to Samnaun, Switzerland – see the *Smugglers' Run* info box below.

*For hikers straying farther from home base than daylight or endurance will allow, try one of the village's hiker transportation options. Daily shuttle service runs to nearby trailheads from **Hotel Piz Tasna**, ☎ 05444 52 77, and the **AlpenTaxi** service will make private pick-ups, ☎ 05444 5757. Do make arrangements before you go.*

Climbing enthusiasts head for the Greitspitz, a 2,850-m peak accessible by a short hike from the Silvrettabahn and Idjochbahn lifts. The equipped route rises 120 m in elevation – contact the tourist office, Ischgl Reservations, or Galtür's mountain climbing school for instruction and guiding information. Additional climbs within reach include the Piz Buin and the Filmspitze and, for practice, Fun Sport City maintains a climbing wall.

In Water

Kayaking, rafting, canyoning, and hydrospeed (river-running by boogie-board) are options on the Trisanna River and along the nearby Alpine valleys. Fishing for trout and char are popular pastimes as well. Contact Ischgl Reservation for more information, gear, and licensing. Swimmers head for the Silvretta Center and its indoor adventure pools, sauna, solarium, and sundeck, although in summer the outdoor Waldbad Silvretta, or forest pool, draws a bigger crowd.

On Wheels

Mountain biking is Ischgl's reason-for-being from mid-June through early October. The region's Mountain Bike Arena maintains 35 marked tours between 5 and 45 km in length and with a vertical drop of over 2,000 m. In-the-know riders will appreciate the local influence of superstar biker Hans Rey, who oversees the trail network here. Rey is currently supervising the development of additional single-trail networks – a move that could raise Ischgl from *a* great Alpine biking destination to *the* great Alpine biking destination.

The Silvretta Card (see page 60 above) brings riders unlimited access to the uplift network, hotels offer all-inclusive biking packages, and the Bike Guiding Center runs at least five guided tours a week. Instruction is offered throughout the summer. Request the excellent Silvretta Mountain Bike Arena guidebook from the tourist office, and book Bike Guiding Center activities through Ischgl Reservations. For rentals, check **Intersport Mathoy** (see *Sports Services, Outfitters & Guides*, page 62 below) or **The Mountain Bike Shop** in the center of the pedestrian zone, ☎ 05444 5262.

In the Air

Fun Sport City boasts a high-wire climbing garden and **ropes course** suspended 14 m above the ground. Cables, nets, bridges, and poles make up this challenging course. Equipment rental and instruction are available on-site. **Bungee-jumping** fans will enjoy the leap from the 94-m-high Pitzenklamm bridge. Arrangements can be made through the tourist office and Ischgl Reservations, ☎ 05444 5266 44, reservation@Ischgl.com. **Paragliding** instruction and tandem flights are offered through both **Ischgl Reservation** and the **Flugschule Silvretta** in Galtür, ☎ 05443 8256 or www.silbertaler.at.

On Snow & Ice

 Ischgl's continually improving **ski** facilities now include 205 km of groomed trails and an uplift system with two cable cars, three gondolas, 20 chairlifts, and 17 tows. The downhill runs here suit intermediates best, but advanced skiers hire guides and head off-piste, while beginners take to the Idalp's sunny runs. Europe's **snowboarding** set loves Ischgl as much for its partying as for its on-slope attractions, which include a funpark with four areas and 30 obstacles, a half-pipe, and a competition schedule that includes FIS World Cup events. Skipass options are plentiful, the most popular being the VIP Ischgl/Samnaun pass, valid on 42 lifts serving 205 km of local trails, and the Regional Silvretta pass, valid on 67 lifts across Ischgl, Samnaun, Galtür, Kappl, and See.

THE SMUGGLERS' RUN

The Smugglers' Run is a cross-border route from Ischgl to Samnaun, Switzerland. The attractions? Duty-free shopping and the enduring thrill of crossing an international border on skis, foot, or bike. Although the most direct route between the two villages is via ski and lift, pedestrians can make this run year-round with the purchase of the Schmugglerticket lift pass (€23.50 for adults). The pass is good for a round-trip journey on the four lifts en route to Samnaun, and bikes can tag along, too, for no additional charge. A planning tip: Many duty-free shops close Sundays.

Cross-country skiers enjoy 48 km of valley trails looping from Ischgl up to Galtür, and **winter walking trails** line the river bank and loop at altitude near Trida Sattel and Idalp. **Ice-skating** is on a small outdoor rink near the village center, and night-time **tobogganing** hits the slopes twice each week on the seven-km trail from Idalp down to the village. **Horse-drawn sleighs** ply through the village day and night – call Fronzls Hoamat for reservations, ☎ 05444 5365.

Sports Services, Outfitters & Guides

- **Ischgl Reservations** serves as a central clearinghouse for all manner of warm-weather, adrenaline-inspiring adventures – if in doubt, call them. To make arrangements for biking, mountain-climbing, themed walks, glacier safaris, paragliding, kayaking, canyoning, rafting, river surfing, river trekking, river boogie-boarding (and the list goes on), contact ☎ 05444 5266 44, reservation@ischgl.com, or the local tourist office.

- **Ski and Snowboard School Ischgl Silvretta** offers group and private instruction for carving, snowboarding, cross-country, and a wide range of variant ski techniques. Kids can join a group or stay and play at the kindergarten. Contact ☎ 05444 5257 for more information.

- **Fun Sport City** offers a wide range of activities from June to September. It's really a converted parking lot, but kids enjoy the street soccer field, a skate park, beach volleyball, a playground, and – the highlight here – a climbing and rope garden. Equipment rental and instruction are available nearby. Contact Ischgl Reservations (see above) for more info.

- For a wide range of sporting goods, try **Intersport Mathoy** across from the Hotel Post and, toward the eastern end of the village, at its second shop near the Pardatschgratbahn cable car base. The outfitter rents all manner of sporting equipment during both the summer and winter seasons – inquire or reserve at ☎ 05444 5759.

Where to Sleep

Hotels abound in this small town, although most close during the shoulder seasons and many close during the summer. Look for accommodations away from the busy road.

The **Hotel Trofana Royal** ($$$$) is Ischgl's premier house, a chalet-style complex located between the base of a ski run and near the Silvretta gondola. A luxurious health center, stellar service, and a celebrated in-house chef round out the amenities here. ☎ 05444 600, www.trofana.at. Its sibling up the hill, the **Trofana** ($$$), ☎ 05444 601, is less luxurious but cuts rates by half.

The **Hotel Tirol** ($$$) offers a wide range of four-star attractions, including an at-the-gondola location, a wide range of package plans,

HOTEL PRICE CHART	
Double room without tax; $$$-$$$$ always with bath.	
$	Under €80
$$	€81-150
$$$	€151-250
$$$$	Over €250

Austria

and a small children's playroom. Reserve at ☎ 05444 5216, www.tirol-ischgl.at. Just up the hill, neighbors **Hotel Post** ($$$), the **Goldener Adler** ($$$), and the **Hotel Yscla** ($$) boast central locations and year-round biking, skiing, hiking, and dining packages. Reserve the Post at ☎ 05444 5232, www.post-ischgl.at; the Goldener Adler at ☎ 05444 5217, www.goldener-adler.at; and the Hotel Yscla at ☎ 05444 5275, www.yscla.at. The winter-only **Astoria** ($$), ☎ 05444 5520, sits in après-ski central just across from the Silvrettabahn gondola station church. For central, budget accommodations within reach of the Fimbabahn, try the **Almfried** ($), ☎ 05444 5234, or the homey **Fimba** ($), ☎ 05444 5240.

Ischgl is a party town in winter, and bars and discos hop well into the wee hours. Prospective guests – at least those who plan to sleep – are wise to inquire about the location of their lodging relative to the nearest noisy nightclub.

Where to Eat

Although most visitors to Ischgl stay on half-board plans where meals are provided, a good selection of mostly hotel-based restaurants offer meals to non-guests as well. For traditional fare in cozy surrounds, try the **Trofana Alm** behind the Hotel Trofana Royal ($$) or the **Goldener Adler** ($$).

DINING PRICE CHART	
Average entrée, with tax.	
$	Under €10
$$	€10-25
$$$	Over €25

CULINARY ROYALTY

Ischgl's luxurious Hotel Trofana Royal is home to the Tyrol's only 3-Toque chef, **Martin Sieberer**. Repeatedly honored by Gault Millau with prestigious titles such as Newcomer of the Year and Chef of the Year, the young Tyrolean heads up the **Paznaunerstube Restaurant** ($$$), with creative and healthy takes on the region's hearty traditional cuisine. It's pricey — as well it should be — but if you're going gourmet, go all out and try the chef's six-course tasting menu. Here, you're in good hands. Reservations required; dial ☎ 05444 5216.

Several outlets have good pizzas; I liked the **Dorf Café** ($$) – look for the skiing marmots across from the pedestrian tunnel. **La Bamba** ($) offers a handful of Tex-Mex options. On the mountain, I liked the **Bodenalpe** ($$), a cozy, rustic house accessible in winter by both walkers (from the Silvrettabahn Mittelstation) and skiers. For picnic fare, stock up at the **Spar Grocery** or splurge on gourmet goodies at the **Ladali Deli** in the Gästhof Goldener Adler.

Where to Party

 Although Ischgl hosts very mellow guests in the summer, its winter visitors keep schedules something like this: eat, ski; drink, eat, drink; drink, eat, drink... sleep. So, as you might imagine, Ischgl boasts plenty of drinking establishments – so many that it seems futile to recommend just a few.

In winter, après-ski parties heat up at the foot of the Pardatschgratbahn with sing-a-longs at **Niki's Stadl** and table-dancing at the **Shatzi Bar**. Party places ring the base station of the Silvrettabahn as well – try the **Kuhstahl**, **Feuer & Eis**, or the **Niko's Hexenkuche**. Behind the Trofana Royal Hotel, the **Trofana Alm** offers both après-ski action and a late-night disco. Other popular disco options include the **Hölle Bar**, the **Livingroom** at Hotel Grillalm, and **Feuer & Eis** at the Silvrettabahn station. For a more elegant setting, cigars, and scotch, try the **Guxa** cocktail bar.

Evening entertainment runs to **Tyrolean folklore shows** each Thursday at the Silvretta Center and, in July and August, Wednesday evening **church concerts**. Three hotels run small **casinos** – place your bets at Hotel Madlein, Hotel Post, or Hotel Seespitz.

Where to Play

 Childcare is scanty in Ischgl, but the tourist office can provide contacts for **babysitters**. In winter, children three years and older can join the ski or non-ski kindergartens and organized youth programs. Make arrangements at the **guest kindergarten** at the Silvretta cable car valley station, 10 am-4 pm, ☎ 05444 5257. A small **playground** is in the park across from the tourist office. Older kids enjoy the tourist office's **youth programs** and, in summer, the beach volleyball, skate park, climbing garden, street soccer field, and playground at **Fun Sport City**.

Festivals & Events

 First and foremost, Ischgl knows how to throw a party. The resort is renowned for its **mountain concerts,** held at the open and close of each season and during the Christmas and Easter holidays. But these are not run-of-the-mill *oompah* affairs: this little village brings in the crowds with big-name pop artists, performers that in the past few years have included Jon Bon Jovi, Bob Dylan, Tina Turner, Rod Stewart, and Sting. Other festivals include the mid-January **Shapes in White snow-sculpting competition** and its summer-time cousin, the late-June **European fire-sculpting competition**, during which flame artists build elaborate frames before setting them afire over a small lake. Mountain-biking events, including the brutal **Ischgl Ironbike** in mid-August, highlight the warmer months and, in late-August, a new **Jazz Festival** closes out the summer season. Dial ☎ 0544 5366 or check www.ischgl.com for more info.

Galtür

Tucked up at the end of the Paznaun Valley at the foot of the Ballunspitze, 10 km southwest of Ischgl, quiet Galtür draws visitors for its isolated rural location and its convenient skiing, biking, and hiking trails. It's both much more peaceful and considerably less expensive than Ischgl, its raucous neighbor. Galtürers are proud of their headstrong, resilient reputation – a willfulness directed at the preservation of their village traditions and the natural environment.

The village is known, too, for it avalanches. In February of 1999, 31 people died when a devastating icefall rolled into the center of town, and less damaging avalanches occur every year. Lest I scare you away, however, much has been done to protect the town and its visitors from harm. Under a midwinter blanket of snow, houses along the foothills appear to be built into the mountain, and the summertime

Hiking, Galtür

thaw reveals the village's enormous, boulder-built protective walls. Whatever the season, visitors should leave Galtür with a profound respect for the power of nature.

The new **Alpinarium** complex cleverly combines an avalanche protection wall with a climbing route, an underground garage, a museum and exhibition room, and a nearby network of themed walking paths. Adventurers come to hike, bike, climb, and ski. In winter, 11 lifts serve mostly easy and intermediate runs, groomed cross-country trails lead off to the Silvrettasee and down toward Ischgl, and a ski school staffed entirely with locals provides instruction. The mountaineering school is well known, too, offering instruction at all levels and operating special courses for children.

 For accommodations in the center, try the lovely **Gästhof Zum Rössle** ($$), ☎ 05443 82 320, www.roessle.com. In a quiet location near the ski lifts in Whirl, try the family-friendly **Whirlerhof** ($$$), ☎ 05443 8231, www.huber-hotels.at.

 For more information, contact the tourist office on the central square, ☎ 05443 8521, www.galtuer.com.

The Silvretta Hochalpenstrasse

Built in 1953 to connect the Paznaun and Montafon valleys, the Silvretta Hochalpenstrasse offers an awe-inspiring look at western Austria's high Alpine landscape. The 22-km road winds its way through rugged terrain above Galtür to Bielerhöhe and the Silvretta Reservoir, interesting for its blue glacial waters, boat tours, and hiking opportunities. The reservoir is dammed at both ends, and the Ill River sheds its waters toward both the Rhein and Danube rivers. Past the lake, the road labors down into the forested Montafon Valley toward Bregenz. Be prepared for a hefty toll (€10.90 at last count) and boulder-colored cows along (and in) the road. The pass closes for snow from November through May. Simple accommodations are available at the roadside-yet-remote **Berggästhof Piz Buin** ($), ☎ 5558 4231, www.pizbuin-silvretta.at.

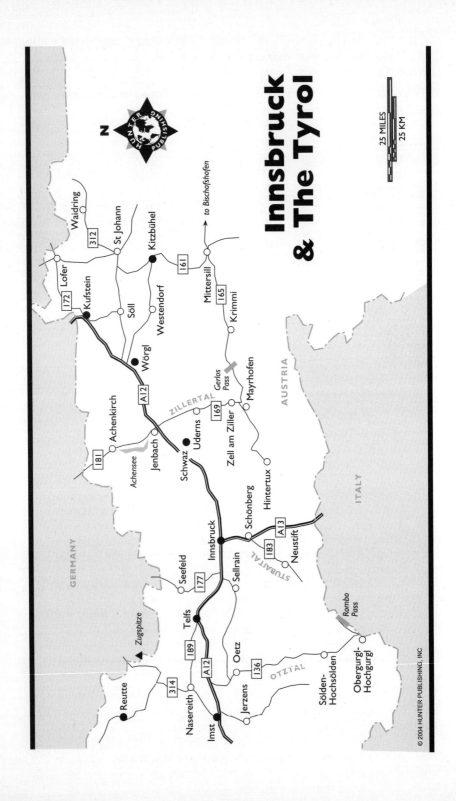

Innsbruck & The Tyrol

Innsbruck & the Tyrol

Austria's Tyrol draws travelers year-round for its picturesque villages and its warm hospitality. The region squeezes between Germany and Italy, stretching the length of the Inn Valley along a wide river; at the region's center, the lively university city of Innsbruck. All around **Innsbruck**, within an hour's drive, valleys jut off into high-Alpine glacial terrain. It's into these valleys – the **Ötztal**, the **Stubaital**, and the **Zillertal** – that adventurers escape the city each weekend. The charming resort of **Seefeld** rests just south of the Zügspitze and the German border, and chic **Kitzbühel** puts on a good show to the east. Unlike the more extreme steeps of the Arlberg to the west, the rolling pastures here prove a family-friendly place to play. Catering to sightseers and adventurers of all ages and abilities, the Tyrol greets visitors with an ambiance of rustic coziness here called *gemutlichkeit*.

■ Innsbruck

Population: 128,000

Base elevation: 575 m

Gateway tourist city

Innsbruck is both the political capital and the cultural core of the Tyrol – a dynamic university town at once stirred by student energy and entrenched in traditional conservatism. With 15 Alpine resorts on its doorstep and two Olympic Winter Games under its belt, it's also the most athletically active city in the Alps. More than any other city I know, Innsbruck offers an ideal combination of city sightseeing and Alpine adventures.

History & Overview

 Innsbruck sits on a site inhabited by Stone Age settlers as early as 4000 BC. The area's position at the intersection of the Inn and Wipp valleys made it a coveted stop along the early trade routes through the Alps, a convenient locale that continues to enrich the city today. The region saw stints under both Roman and Bavarian rule during the first millennium, and mention is first made of "Insprucke," or "a bridge over the Inn River," in the 12th century. The new town flourished from the 14th through the 19th centuries, enjoying booming growth as a cultural, administrative, and mining center. The ruling Hapsburg Family adored Innsbruck, making it their official residence and thereby attracting to the city the greatest artists, musicians, and writers of the time. The two world wars in the early 20th century brought the city's rise to an abrupt halt; but, even though extensive damage befell the city during World War II, it rebounded quickly, taking the world stage once more as host of the Olympic Winter Games both in 1964 and again in 1976.

Innsbruck lies in western Austria, along the Inn River at the crossroads of the Inntal and Wipptal valleys. The Nordkette mountain range rises dramatically to the north, and the Ötztal, Stubaital, and Zillertal Alps stretch out to the south. Two autobahns, the A12 and the A13, converge just south of town – the A12 running east toward Salzburg and west toward Landeck, and the A13 running south over the Brenner Pass into Italy.

The Town

Central Innsbruck fills a triangular chunk of land bordered by a kink in the wide Inn River and the autobahns to the south. The old town, or **altstadt**, lies at the western edge of the center and remains the focus of the city's tourism. The nucleus of the *altstadt* district is a pedestrian area along Herzog Friedrich Strasse, a cobblestone road lined with shops, arcades, and cafés. The university and most of the churches and museums of note sit on the old town's northeastern edge. **Markt Graben** and **Burg Graben** loop around the southern edge of the *altstadt*, perpendicular to Maria Theresienstrasse, the inner city's wide boulevard and its shopping district. The main station – now under dramatic reconstruction – sits at the southern side of town, a 10-minute walk southeast of the *altstadt*.

Getting Here & Around

 Visitors arriving by air will land at the Innsbruck Airport just west of town or transfer from Munich, 146 km north, or from Salzburg, 190 km northeast. Zürich is 250 km west. For local transportation, Innsbruck operates a complicated network of buses and trams, most of which hub at the main train station on the southeastern edge of old town. (In addition to its modern trams, the city operates nostalgic streetcars with original wood-paneled interiors from June through September – look for them along the tramline to Igls.) For taxi service, ☎ 0512 53 11.

*The free **Club Innsbruck Card** is issued to hotel guests upon check-in. Guests receive discounts on sightseeing, activities, and transportation and an invitation to participate in free guided hiking tours. Your hotel can issue and validate a card upon your arrival. **The Innsbruck Card** is not free, but includes cable car rides, museum admissions, and use of The Sightseer tourist bus. Cards come in 24- , 36- , and 72-hour increments and are sold at the tourist office, attraction ticket counters, and many hotels. 24-hour cards run €21, which you'll make back after one round-trip ascent to the Seegrube; www.innsbruck-ticket-service.at.*

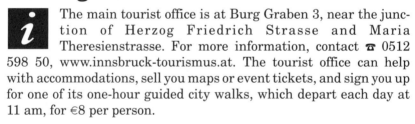

Getting Connected

The main tourist office is at Burg Graben 3, near the junction of Herzog Friedrich Strasse and Maria Theresienstrasse. For more information, contact ☎ 0512 598 50, www.innsbruck-tourismus.at. The tourist office can help with accommodations, sell you maps or event tickets, and sign you up for one of its one-hour guided city walks, which depart each day at 11 am, for €8 per person.

✉ The main post office is at Maximilianstrasse 2; a second post office is at Bruneckerstrasse, just north of the train station.

The Sights

Innsbruck's small but charming **old town** is the center of the city's tourist action. Here, visitors wander back alleys, shop in the boutiques, and dine in outdoor cafés. Additionally, Innsbruck boasts 18 museums on topics ranging from alpinism to bells, running second only to Vienna among Austria's museum cities. At Herzog Friedrich Strasse 15, beneath the landmark **Goldenes Dachl**, or Golden Roof, is the **Maximilianeum Museum**. The museum memorializes the life of Emperor Maximilian I, great patron of Austrian art, music, and architecture. Visit May through September daily from 10 am-6 pm, and October through April, Tuesday through Sunday from 10 am-5 pm; ☎ 0512 58 11 11; €4. The **Tiroler Volkskunst Museum**, or Tyrolean Regional Heritage Museum, documents the Tyrol's history with fascinating displays of interior design and artistic craftsmanship. It's at Universitatsstrasse 2, near the Hofkirche, and is open Monday through Saturday from 9 am-5 pm; ☎ 0512 58 43 02. The nearby

Hofkirche houses the tomb of Emperor Maximilian I and is open to visitors daily from 9 am-5 pm when services are not in session.

A visit to the **Innsbruck Alpenzoo** is a hit with kids, and involves a ride up the Hungerburgbahn funicular at the base of the Seegrube and a pleasant stroll through the woods. The zoo is home to more than 2,000 Alpine animals – 150 species are represented. The park can also be reached by car. It's open daily from 9 am; ☎ 0512 29 23 23, www.alpenzoo.at.

Just south of town, the new **Bergisel Ski Jump** offers tours of its 47-m tower. The sports stadium below was the site of the Olympic Winter Games ski jumping events and today hosts training and competitions throughout the year. Visit daily, 6 am-5 pm, €6. Also south of town, near a stop along the Igls tram route, **Schloss Ambras** offers a nice collection of historical art, armor, and artifacts, all housed within the splendid surroundings of the 16th-century palace grounds. It's open daily, December through October, from 10 am-5 pm; ☎ 05252 47 45, www.khm.at/ambras.

Swarovski Crystal World

Discerning shoppers will recognize the Austrian trademark Swarovski as one of the great manufacturers of precision-cut crystal. It all started here, just east of Innsbruck, when in 1895 Daniel Swarovski founded the company's first mill. Today, savvy shoppers visit Swarovski Crystal World, a complex gleaming with water, glass, and crystal – a display that's more avant-garde exposition than museum. The newly expanded complex is in Wattens, approximately 20 km east of Innsbruck along the A12 Autobahn. It's open daily except Christmas and Easter from 9 am-6 pm; entry is €5.45. For more information, contact ☎ 05224 510 80, www.swarovski-crystalworlds.com.

The Adventures

On Wheels

Innsbruck remains one of Europe's most outdoorsy cities, and its adventures span all seasonal sports. In summer, **mountain bikers** take to over 100 km of designated trails along the Nordkette range, and the new **Nordparktrail** free-ride run drops 1,040 m between the Seegrube and Hungerburg mountains – a huge hit with technical riders.

On Foot

Innsbruck's popular panoramic **climbing route** surmounts seven summits from Hafelekar to the Frau-Hitt-Sattel along a 3,000-m secured climbing route. It's not a particularly difficult climb, but newcomers should ask the advice and services of the **Alpinschule Innsbruck** in Natters at ☎ 0512 546 000, www.asi.at. Climbing gardens are at Axamer Lizum and Igls. **Walkers** enjoy trails through all 15 holiday resorts, along the river at city center, and the scenic Zirbenweg at Patscherkofel.

*The **Innsbruck Alpine School**, in conjunction with the tourist office, organizes a program of free guided hikes offered daily between early June and late September. The program utilizes over 40 different hiking trails, includes lantern-lit walks, sunrise hikes, and music-accompanied pasture strolls. Inquire and make reservations at the tourist office.*

On Water

AUTHOR'S PICK

New in Innsbruck is the rare opportunity to hop aboard a *Floss* raft, here a modern take on an old Alpine tradition. Each of the modern floats incorporates umbrella tables, beer service, and lots of convivial fun. ***Floss* rafting trips** set sail each Thursday from May through October, launching from the Kranebitten district on the western outskirts of town and finishing at the Löwenhaus Inn. €20 includes the ride and bus transfer. For reservations and information, ☎ 052 6355 83, www.flossfahrt.at.

On Snow & Ice

In winter, Innsbruck's resorts – jointly marketed under the name Olympia Skiworld Innsbruck – offer a full spectrum of slopes and snow sports. In all, 64 lifts access 150 km of **skiing** piste across seven regions. **Ice sports** play in the city's Olympic halls, natural **toboggan runs** drop 60 km down local hills, and **cross-country skiers** head out on 300 km of trails. In Igls, daredevils can sample high-speed **bobsledding** on the Olympic run. Ride in an original competition sled accompanied by an expert pilot and brakeman (85 Euro, by arrangement), or take the shorter layman's ride offered January through February each Tuesday from 10 am and Thursday from 7 pm (€30, reservations required). Sliders must be 14 years old to take the short ride; 16 for the long. Inquire and reserve at ☎ 0512 338 38. From May through September, the bob run is made on wheels each Thursday and Friday from 4-6 pm; info and reservations, ☎ 0664 357 86 07, www.sommerbobrunning.at.

On Innsbruck's Doorstep

Innsbruck counts 15 holiday villages with its encircling Alpine terrain, each offering an array of summer and winter trails and a wide range of sporting opportunities. Below, I highlight four of the most popular resorts on Innsbruck's doorstep.

■ Nordpark-Seegrube

All visitors should scale the ridgeline of Innsbruck's northern mountain wall. The **Hungerburgerbahn** funicular chugs its way from the northern edge of town, over the river, past the zoo, and up to the settlement of **Hoch-Innsbruck Hungerburg** at 868 m. From there, the Nordkettenbahn cable car rises to Seegrube at 1,905 m, whence a short cable-car ride delivers guests to the area's highest peak, the **Hafelekarspitze** at 2,334 m. From here, views stretch out to the **Zillertal**, the **Stubaital**, and the **Ötztal Alps**. For more information, contact the Innsbrücker Nordkettenbahnen at ☎ 0512 293 344, www.nordpark.at.

Every Friday from 5 to 11:30 pm, the Nordkettenbahn cable car brings guests to the Seegrube peak for a romantic dinner at the mountain restaurant and spectacular nighttime views over the city lights.

■ Igls

An hour's tram ride south from the center of Innsbruck, Igls is the city's favorite forest playground. The quaint resort village draws recreational hikers, bikers, and skiers, as well as the world's best ice-sliding athletes, who come here to practice and compete on the Olympic bobsled run. The **Patscherkofel** cable car climbs up to the local peak, passing over the bobsled tube and one of Europe's largest stands of stone pines. At the top, summertime visitors enjoy the continent's largest Alpine botanical garden, a plot harboring over 400 plants, and the hike down to the valley is pleasant and not fearfully steep. Between the village and the tram station, a tiny riverside park offers a Kneipp water trail – remove your shoes, and find relief for sore feet. For more information, contact www.patscherkofelbahnen.at.

Igls has a number of hotels, and visitors preferring rural recreation over city sightseeing should consider basing here and day-tripping into Innsbruck.

■ Mutterer Alm

This small-time resort on the southwestern edge of Innsbruck offers gentle slopes for family hiking, biking, and skiing. It's also the starting point for the hike and bike trek that runs south to the Stubai Valley. Recent construction has shut down lifts here, but good things are on the way: Upon re-opening, tentatively planned for winter 2004, Mutters' guests will enjoy a new lift link with Axamer Lizum. For more information, contact www.skiparkmutters.at.

■ Azamer Lizum

The most remote of the resorts highlighted here, Axamer Lizum lies 25 km west of Innsbruck. Its **Kalkkögel** peak affords splendid views over the **Inn Valley**, and a handful of hotels here offer slope-side accommodations. Although famed for its Olympic-caliber ski runs, the resort is popular as well with local snowboarders and summertime hikers. For more information, contact www.axamer-lizum.at.

Where to Sleep

The **Hotel Europa** ($$$$) is the choice of visiting dignitaries, but it's closer to the station than it is to the city's sights. Elegant service, modern amenities, and the city's best restaurant are the draws here. Reserve at ☎ 0512 59 31, www.europatyrol.com.

The **Innsbruck Hilton** ($$$) has rooms in the city's tallest tower, offering a reasonably central location and lovely mountain views. The town casino is next door. Inquire at ☎ 0512 593 50, www.innsbruck.hilton.com.

HOTEL PRICE CHART	
Double room without tax; $$$-$$$$ always with bath.	
$	Under €80
$$	€81-150
$$$	€151-250
$$$$	Over €250

The **Hotel Innsbruck** ($$-$$$) occupies a rambling old townhouse, just steps from either the old town or the Inn River, a location that makes it popular with overnighting bus tours. Its décor is contemporary, there's a small, basement pool, and the accommodations are comfortable enough. Inquire at ☎ 0512 59 86 80, www.hotelinnsbruck.com.

Austria

Goldener Adler ($$) is the most famous of the *altstadt*'s traditional inns; it's directly in the center and boasts a long list of distinguished patrons, of which King Ludwig, Goethe, and Mozart are just a few. Reserve at ☎ 0512 571 11 10, www.goldeneradler.com.

The **Weisses Rössl** ($$), or "white stallion," has welcomed guests since 1410. The simple, traditional inn sits on a snug little alley in the *altstadt* – and is one of my favorite stays in town, both for its hospitable hosts and its delicious food; ☎ 0512 58 30 57, www.roessl.at.

The **Hotel Central** ($$) sits a few blocks east of the old town, yet draws a steady stream of tour groups for its hip interior styling, its grand Viennese café, and its excellent package deals for skiers, bikers, and hikers. Rooms are simple. Reserve at ☎ 0512 59 20, www.central.co.at.

Up the hill in a pleasant neighborhood near the zoo, the **Pension Paula** ($) offers 12 homey rooms, either with bath or without, and free parking, ☎ 0512 29 22 62.

The **Jungendherberge St. Nikolaus** ($) is the most central of the youth hostels here. Simple dorm-bedded rooms are the norm; ☎ 0512 28 65 15.

Where to Eat

 Directly in the center, the **Goldenes Dachl** ($$) has traditional food, lots of beer, and a terrace beer garden at Hofgasse 1; and the cozy **Stiftskeller** ($$) boasts an old-world setting, outdoor seating, and both Austrian and Italian food. It's at Stiftsgasse 1.

DINING PRICE CHART	
Average entrée, with tax.	
$	Under €10
$$	€10-25
$$$	Over €25

The **Weisses Rössl** ($$) at Kiebachgasse 8 serves up good regional specialties in a cheery atmosphere, or try the Gästhaus Gruber's **Das Wirtshaus am Markt** ($$), near the river at Innrain 22. The **Löwenhaus** ($$) has riverside dining on the banks of the Inn and a good selection of traditional dishes. It's at Rennweg 5, along the river walk approximately one kilometer north of the old town; ☎ 0512 58 54 79.

For a romantic meal out and the best traditional food in town, head for the **Europastüberl** ($$$) in the Hotel Europa, directly across from the train station.

For snacks, **Peter's TeaHouse** ($), in an ideal, upstairs location within view of the Goldene Dachl, offers over 250 kinds of tea accompanied by snacks and classical music. Down nearby Kiebachgasse,

Pap Joe's ($-$$) grills up ribs, steaks, and burgers. At Kiebachgasse 11, the **Pizzeria Romantica** ($) does good pizzas and pasta, offering half-portions to boot; and **Thai-Li** ($) has well priced Thai dishes at the corner of Markt Graben and Seilergasse.

To pack an elegant picnic basket, head for Stiftgasse in the old town, where two shops oblige: The **Spezialitäten aus der Stiftgasse** at number 2 and the **s'Speckladele** at number 4. Finally, several inexpensive **food outlets** occupy the new Galleria shopping mall at Maria Theresien Strasse 18.

Where to Party

Being both an Austrian city and a university town, Innsbruck has more than its share of watering holes. In the center, try the **Elferhaus**, in English "11th house," at Herzog Friedrich Strasse 11. The pub features beer, snacks, and, on the 11th day of each month, live music .

Theresienbräu, at Maria Theresienstrasse 51, was the first *wirtshaus* and brewery in Innsbruck, and today it's a favorite beer-hall hangout.

For disco dancing and DJ'd entertainment, head for the **Innkeller**, at Innstrasse 1, the **Café Bar Down Under** at Bogen 24, or the **Hafen** on the outskirts of town – all three stay lively till the wee hours. Live music kicks up frequently at a variety of late-night venues throughout town. Check with the tourist office (or the posters around the university) to see what's playing.

The **Casino Innsbruck** is a dressy affair with blackjack, roulette, slots, and popular dinner packages; it's at Salurnerstrasse in the Hilton Hotel; ☎ 0512 587 040, www.casinos.at. For more traditional evening entertainment, consider the **Tyrolean Evening Show** at the Gästhaus Sandwirt; it runs daily from April through October; ☎ 0512 263 263, www.tiroleralpenbuehne.com.

Where to Play

Children enjoy many of Innsbruck's activities, including **cable car rides**, **outdoor recreation**, and visits to the **Alpine zoo**. In Natters, between the resorts of Igls and Mutters, the **Natterser Lake Children's Program** offers a popular service that's free to holders of the Club Innsbruck Card. Organizers oversee activities such as adventure games, mini-golf, swimming, handicrafts, painting, and pony rides. The program operates from mid-May through mid-October, Monday through Friday, 10 am-5 pm; a shuttle service runs between Natters and the village of Igls. For more information, contact the tourist office.

Festivals & Events

 Innsbruck celebrates the warmer months with the **Innsbruck Summer Festival**, a program of cultural festivals revolving more around art, music, and dance than folkloric tradition. From late June through early July, the **Summer Dance Festival** draws classical, modern, and ethnic dancers to the city's stages; and the **Innsbruck Festival Weeks**, held from early July through late August, features a wide range of classical music concerts staged at various venues, including Ambras Castle and the Imperial Palace. Advent brings the city's **Christmas markets**, the most popular of which crowds the *altstadt* with stalls selling food, gifts, and the hot, mulled wine called *gluhwein*.

New Year's rings in with a party in old town and fireworks on the mountains above, and the **Mullerlaufen Parades** march through the *altstadt* streets each Saturday during the Carnival season. The winter sees world-class **athletic competitions** on Innsbruck's Olympic winter sports venues.

Innsbruck celebrates the spring thaw with the **Solstice in the Mountains Festival**, during which traditional fires are set all across the Nordkette mountain range.

Seefeld

Golf at Wildwoods, Seefeld

Tucked up in a forest-bordered valley 25 km northwest of Innsbruck, near the German frontier and its Zügspitze mountain, Seefeld – or *Sevelt*, as it was called in the 11th century – enjoys an enviable locale midway between Innsbruck and Garmisch-Partenkirchen. The village first became a place of pilgrimage after the "miracle of the host" incident on Easter of 1384, when in the parish church an arrogant knight ate a consecrated communion wafer, causing the ground to shake and his feet to sink. Today's pilgrims, however, come in pursuit of more hedonistic pleasures.

The Seefeld Holiday Region – a conglomerate comprising Seefeld and four neighboring villages – enjoys a Europe-wide reputation as one of Austria's best village resorts. However, the action here is not the turbo-charged, adrenaline-pumping sort found elsewhere; it is instead a low-key, highbrow hum of soothing relaxation. Visitors come here, above all, to *breathe*. Walking, biking, horseback riding, golf, and fishing are the town's most popular pursuits. In the winter, skiers come for easy downhill runs, winter walking paths, and cross-country trails that were twice a venue for the Olympic Winter Games. Active guests also enjoy an expansive sports center, blessed with multiple swimming pools and a lake-top ice rink out front. The elegant little Seekapl church lies across the lake. It was surrounded by water when first erected in 1666.

The Seefeld Cable Car Experience

This package deal is a good option for summertime walkers looking for a half-day outing. The deal includes round-trip cable car rides and a cup of tea or coffee and cake at a mountain restaurant. The excursion starts from town, heading by cable car to the Rosshütte Middle Station for a 20-minute walking loop along the Zirbenweg trail; a second cable car ride goes to the Harmelekopf, a favorite paragliding launch point; and then back down to the Rosshütte at mid-mountain for a coffee-and-cake break. From there, the Jochbahn cable car leads up to the Seefelder Joch peak, where the one-hour Panoramic Trail loop offers sweeping views. Hikers return to town on the lift or hike down the lumber road. Your unused return lift ticket is good for a drink at the Rosshütte on your way back to town.

 Want to stay? Big, modern chalet-hotels dominate Seefeld's lodging scene. Most are expensive. The **Gästhof Batzenhäusl** ($$) has simple rooms, some with balcony, and a nice location at the edge of the pedestrian shopping street. It's next to the Raabach river and near the sports center; ☎ 05212 22 92, www.kaltschmid.co.at.

 The excellent tourist office is in the pedestrian center, just across from the church. For more information, contact ☎ 05212 23 13, www.seefeld.com.

The Ötztal

The Ötz Valley, or the Ötztal, opens up at its northern end near the town of Sautens, just off the A12 Autobahn, and finally peters out at Obergurgl some 41 slow-driving km south. The region's young, energetic clientele comes to climb, ski, hike, and bike – and there's plenty of opportunity for all. Skiers come year-round to the glacial slopes, climbers head up the Klettersteig wall near Langenfeld, and mountain bikers take to a magnificent trail running 80 km along the length of the valley.

Although several stops along the Ötztal road merit year-round tourist attention, our favorite winter bases are **Sölden** – the region's largest, loudest, rowdiest resort – and **Obergurgl**, at valley's end, a quiet little hamlet with a life all its own.

*If you visit in summer and plan to get around a lot, consider the **Ötztal Card**. It offers free access to valley buses, cableways (one per day), toll roads, museums, and swimming pools, and discounts at several other attractions. The card is sold in seven- and 10-day increments – the seven-day card costs €45. Purchase yours at any tourist office or at many ticket desks.*

First, moving south from the northern mouth of the Ötztal, I stop at Umhausen. The Tyrol region's largest waterfalls, the **Stuibenfalls**, rise 150 m in height and are less than an hour's hike east of town. Nearby, the new **Ötzi Dorf** open-air museum takes you for an archeological stroll through the Stone Age. Several huts demonstrate long-dead methods of handicraft, fishing gear, and baking techniques; a herd of farm animals (alive and well) entertains kids; and much is made, of course, of Ötzi, the valley's favorite prehistoric son (see below). The park is open daily, May through September, 10 am-6 pm; ☎ 05255 500 22, www.oetzi-dorf.com, €4.50.

Ötzi

In 1991, hikers above the Ötztal's southern end stumbled upon an interesting find – a man, frozen in ice, with curious tools and an outfit most unfashionable. The man was un-iced, and scientific tests showed that he'd died here during the Neolithic Age, sometime around the fourth millennium before Christ. The world's archeologists and all Austria celebrated the sensational discovery, and the mummified marvel was soon christened "Ötzi" by his beaming hometown fans. Soon thereafter, however, geological surveys showed that the mummy had actually fallen just across the national border, and Italy demanded his remains returned. Today, the mummy rests in a refrigerated box in the South Tyrol Museum of Archaeology in Bolzano, Italy. He still enjoys something of a cult following, however; and there are rumors, too, of women who've petitioned to bear Ötzi's children by means of artificial insemination. Exactly how *that* would work out, I don't pretend to know.

Farther up the valley at Langenfeld, the **Ötztaler Heimat-und Freilichtmuseum** shows off historical buildings, tools, and traditions from a more recent age. It's open June through September, Monday through Friday, 10 am-noon and 2 to 5 pm, Sundays from 2 to 4 pm; ☎ 05253 55 40, www.oetztal-museum.at. An English-language guide to the park is available.

More popular with kids is the nearby **Ötztaler Fun Park**, a climbing, jumping, swinging, skating kind of place – a playground paradise open daily from July through late September, 9 am to 11 pm, on September weekdays closing at 6 pm; ☎ 05253 649 49, www.oetztaler-funpark.at; €4.

Austria

Sölden rocks with a party-hearty beat all winter – one that merely wanes during the summer months – and evenings feature après-ski in all its forms. Whether you like to dance on tables in ski boots or watch table-dancers wearing little more than that, Sölden entertains. Its ski slopes rise immediately above the town toward Hochsölden, the village's high-altitude hamlet. The Tiefenbach and Rettenbach glaciers are connected to town by cableway and to each other via both road and ski tunnels. Glacier skiing is done year-round as conditions allow; access the glaciers by lift or via the toll road that runs the 15 km from town. (The €16.50 toll is waived if you've pre-purchased a ski pass.) Glacier runs here are more varied than most, boasting one fast run that each October stages the World Cup racing circuit's season opener. Winter runs here total 149 km; summer glacier runs, considerably less.

> *If you hit town in mid-April, Sölden's annual production of **Hannibal** is worth the price of admission. Some 500 actors re-enact Hannibal's 200 BC Alpine crossing, when he came across with an ungainly army of 60,000 Africans, Celts, and Spaniards – and their 34 elephant steeds. The Rettenbach Glacier becomes the stage for an unforgettable (if bizarre) display of lights, video, and pyrotechnics alongside action scenes featuring 24 snowcats, numerous snowmobiles, and several paragliders, among others. Contact the tourist office for ticket information.*

Farther south, the valley road climbs steeply to valley end, where the quieter, more traditional hamlet of **Obergurgl** nestles in splendid seclusion. It's among our favorite early-season ski resorts, as its slopes are high enough to have good snow, and as the social ambiance here tends more toward convivial mingling than meat-market melée.

The village largely shuts down in summer, with only solitude-seeking hikers in town; but Obergurgl proves lively in the winter months, with 110 km of high-altitude ski runs, lift links to nearby Hochgurgl, and lots of ski-in accommodations – much of it booked well in advance.

THE OZTAL EXREMISTS

Although we've stuck mainly to mainstream sights in our coverage of the Oztal, visitors wishing to take part in more adrenaline-pumping activities will find no shortage of company in the Ötztal. The valley's youthful clientele comes here for canyoning, bungee jumping, whitewater rafting and kayaking – and two main outfitters help them find the fun. In Sölden, look up **Vacancia Outdoor** at Hauptstrasse 438, ☎ 05254 29 39, www.vacancia.at; farther north, consult the **Kajak & Raftingschule Ötztal**, ☎ 05252 67 21, www.rafting-oetztal.at.

 Want to stay? In Sölden, I'm a fan of the cheery **Hotel Alpina** ($$-$$$). It's near the church, off the busy main road, and a short walk from the Hochsölden lift; ☎ 05254 50 20, www.riml.com. The hospitable Riml family also runs a less expensive house, the **Montana** ($-$$), just across the river; ☎ 05254 50 30, www.riml.com. In Obergurgl, I like the modern chalet-style **Edelwiess & Gurgl** ($$$). Inside, it warms with traiditional hospitality; outside, it fronts the lifts and a popular après-ski café. Inquire at ☎ 05256 62 23, www.edelweiss-gurgl.com.

 Find valley tourist information at www.oetztal.at. For more information on Sölden, stop by the tourist office in the Freizeit sport center or inquire at ☎ 05254 51 00, www.soelden.com. For more info on Obergurgl, contact the tourist office at village center or dial ☎ 05256 64 66, www.obergurgl.com.

The Timmelsjoch Hochalpenstrasse

The Timmelsjoch high Alpine road leads south from Hochgurgl up through the Ötztal's glacier country, over the 2,509-m Timmelsjoch Pass, descending across the border into Italy. The scenic route is open in summer only, from late May through September, and the current toll is €10; for road information in German, contact ☎ 0512 581 970, www.timmelsjoch-hochalpenstrasse. Farther into Italy along the same route is the town of Bolzano, home to Ötzi and the **South Tyrol Archaeological Museum**. For museum information, check ☎ +39 (0)471 320 100, www.archaeologiemuseum.it.

The Stubaital

The Stubai Valley, or Stubaital, stretches southwest from Schönberg, which sits 27 km south of Innsbruck, north of the Brenner Pass on the A13 Autobahn. While neither the most expansive nor the most compact resort around Innsbruck, the long Stubai Valley draws guests for its good hiking and climbing opportunities, for the nearby glacier and its long-season slopes, and for the valley's inexpensive, family-friendly accommodations. Four villages lie along the Stubaital road, or Route 183, and the parallel Ruetz River: **Mieders**, **Telfes**, **Fulpmes**, and **Neustift**. Each village offers accommodations and limited lift facilities, but Neustift, farthest along the valley, by far gets the most attention from tourists.

*The local visitor's card, the **Stubaital Card**, offers a five-day summertime package including free bus transport throughout the valley, travel on the tram between Fulpmes and Innsbruck, admission to four local swimming pools, and pedestrian use of the lifts at the glacier, at Schlick, and the Neustift. Tourist offices throughout the valley dispense cards in exchange for €40, children half-price.*

Neustift centers on the intersection of the Stubaital road and Dorfstrasse, a cramped side-street that loops through the heart of the village. The church, with its lovely cemetery, stands on the corner, and après-ski, nightlife, and dining establishments line the nearby square. Neustift's sporting facilities, however, lie mostly in the pastures on the southeastern edge of town, just across the Stubaital road. Here, visitors take to riverside walking paths, cross-country ski slopes, a paragliding field, the Elfer mountain lift, and (new this year), a lighted nighttime toboggan run.

Although Neustift is the closest developed village to the Stubai Glacier, it is still a 20-km drive south to the glacier base – a commute best made in winter by local bus.

Because the lots fill up early, drivers who attempt the commute by private vehicle may well find themselves on a bus anyway, with their cars parked somewhere down valley in a muddy, makeshift parking field.

The glacier slopes offer skiers 60 km of mostly intermediate and beginner runs and a 4.5-km cross-country loop. Snow sports on the glacier run year-round when condition allow.

*Stubai mountain guides lead daily summertime walks along the Stubai Glacier Trail from the Eisgrat gondola top station to the **Jochdohle**, Austria's highest restaurant. The tour departs at 11 am and takes approximately an hour one-way.*

Want to stay? In a pastoral setting on the outskirts of Neustift, the **Hotel Alpenschlössl** ($$) offers modern chalet-style accommodations and family-style hospitality. Its location is peaceful yet it is central to all sorts of sporting venues: the ice rink, the Elfer lift and its sledding run, the cross-country ski trails, and a riverside walking path. Reserve at ☎ 005226 20 50, www.alpenschloessl.at.

The Zillertal

The magnificent Ziller Valley, or Zillertal, runs 30 km from the A12 Autobahn at Jenbach to Mayrhofen at its southern head. Along the way, the valley links a dozen small villages, many with their own lifts, side-valleys, and lakes. In winter, the all-area ski pass includes access to 150 lifts and 500 km of groomed runs. Climbers come from all around to conquer the region's cliffs and crevasses. In summer, trails wind among the villages and the mountain huts above, drawing hikers and bikers; the Ziller River spills down the valley's center, tempting watersports enthusiasts; and the peaks rise all around, beckoning to paragliders and rock-climbers.

At the southernmost tip of the valley, above the hamlet of Tux, the **Hintertux Glacier** obliges snow-sport lovers with year-round skiing and snowboarding. It also offers some of Austria's best off-season racing camps.

*Summer visitors should consider purchasing the **Zillertal Card**. The all-inclusive arrangement includes a daily ride on one of the valley's cable cars, entry to all public swimming pools, a visit to the Königsleiten Observatory and Planetarium, and free bus transportation. The cards are sold from early June through early October with validities of six, nine, or 12 days – the six-day version runs €39. Purchase cards at any valley tourist office.*

The Zillertal's most happening action – particularly in winter – centers on the village resort of **Mayrhofen**. First settled as an Alpine faming community, the village is today the Zillertal's most popular tourist resort, enjoying a splendid location at the confluence of the Zemmbach and Ziller rivers and at the foot of a magnificent ring of peaks. The train station and the Penkenbahn gondola depart from town center, and attractions include, in winter, several cross-country skiing loops, easy access to local ski slopes, and a lively après-ski scene; in summer, hiking, biking, glacier skiing, watersports, a nice pool complex, and – of course – the extensive sporting opportunities of the extended Zillertal valley.

Zillertal Outfitters

The Zillertal sees frenetic sporting activity during winter and summer season, largely because of its proximity to the city of Innsbruck. Transportation and trail networks are well developed here, as is the army of sports outfitters, which offer adventure tour packages of every imaginable sort. Below are some of the best.

- **Action Club Zillertal** operates the Mayrhofen's most adrenaline-charged outings. Activities include rafting, hydrospeed, canyoning, mountaining, paragliding, a "flying fox" ropes course, and balloon rides. Make arrangements at the office on Hauptstrasse 100, near the Penkenbahn station; ☎ 05285 629 77.

- Some Action Club activities are co-hosted with the **Klettergarten Floite**, a climbing garden with three climbing routes, including one up the 120-m "Brain Wash" waterfall. Arrange climbing activities directly with the Klettergarten in Ginzling; ☎ 0664 214 42 07.

- For hikers and climbers, there's no better guide in the Zillertal than Peter Habeler and his **Mount Everest** mountain sports school. The Mayrhofen native and his friend Reinhold Messner were the first to scale the Mt. Everest summit without the aid of oxygen. Today, the expert guide shares his expertise with visitors to his home valley. Inquire at ☎ 05285 628 29.

■ In Tux, the **Bergsportschule Tux** offers instruction for serious outdoorsmen and guiding across an array of mountaineering disciplines. They also offer climbing courses for children – although I imagine that there aren't many mothers outside of Austria who wish to see their six-year-olds dangling from an ice wall by ice pick and crampon. For more info, contact ☎ 05287 873 72, www.bergsportschule-tux.at.

 Want to stay? Mayrhofen's most luxurious accommodations are at the five-star **Elisabethhotel** ($$$$), a modern chalet with an expansive wellness center, a busy activity program, and a cozy fireplace bar; ☎ 05285 67 60, www.elisabethhotel.com. For less expensive lodging, try the **Berghof** ($$). The rowdy, rambling old chalet sits directly at town center; ☎ 05285 622 54, www.berghof.cc.

 The **Zillertal valley tourist office** centralizes information for the local villages; contact ☎ 05288 87 187 or www.zillertal.at for more information. The Mayrhofen office is in the village center at the Europahaus; contact ☎ 05285 67 60, www.mayrhofen.at. For additional info regarding Hintertux, log in at www.hintertux.at.

THE GERLOS ALPINE ROAD

If you're headed east after visiting the Zillertal, enjoy a scenic drive over the **Gerlos Pass**. The mountain road departs from Zell am Ziller, winding its way up to the Durlassbodensee and the 1531-m pass, then descends to the Salzachtal and the spectacular **Krimmler Falls** (see page 128). The road is open year-round.

■ Kitzbühel

Population: 8,200

Base elevation: 762 m

Mountain Resort Town

Kitzbühel's medieval old town seduces with a flourish of fairytale charm. Brightly painted façades front cobblestone alleys, elegant boutiques beckon, and ancient town walls give an air of seclusion. Cozy as it may be, however, it's also a snobby, hobnobbing sort of place where furs prove more fashionable than ski wear. Nonetheless, stock your wallet well and join the promenading crowd; you'll soon discover the allure that makes Kitzbühel a place worth lingering.

History & Overview

 Kitzbühel grew up along the trade route between Italy and Munich, growing larger and richer when the mining industry moved in and the village was granted market status in 1255. King Ludwig II blessed the village with a town charter in 1271, officially founding the town. Several centuries later, in 1892, Mayor Franz Reisch imported a pair of skis from Norway and liked them so much he created several ski runs, converted a few friends, and launched what would became a winter sports resort phenomenon. Political, film, and military luminaries soon made Kitzbühel their exclusive retreat, and the resort remains the playground of Europe's high society (visitors will note the correspondingly high prices). Unscathed by either of the 20th-century wars, the medieval center of town remains largely intact to this day.

Kitzbühel lies on the northern edge of central Austria's Kitzbüheler Alps. The town spreads along the Kitzbüheler Ache river in a valley flanked by the 1,655-m Hahnenkamm to the west and the 1,996-m Kitzbüheler Horn to the east. The region's small but popular lake, the Schwarzsee, lies just west of town. Train tracks encircle the old town center, running north toward St. Johann and Salzburg and west toward Kirchberg and Innsbruck. Access roads follow much the same routes, with an additional thoroughfare heading south over the Pass Thurn.

The Town

The town of Kitzbühel perches on a hillside terrace below the Hahnenkamm peak. The town's tourism industry banks on its medieval nucleus, where two wide streets, the **Hinterstadt** to the west and the **Vorstadt** to the east, run parallel between the ancient center's walls. From the town gates run **Bichlstrasse** to the southeast, **Josef Herold Strasse** up the mountain to the west, **Franz Reisch**

Strasse to the northwest toward the Schwarzsee, and **Josef Pirchl Strasse** northeast toward the train station. On the western edge of the center, train tracks divide the old town from the ski slopes and lifts, eventually running north toward the main station and west past the Schwarsee.

Hop aboard the **Hahnenkammbahn gondola**, which climbs from the western edge of town up to the Hahnenkamm peak; or, cross the valley to the base of the **Kitzbüheler Hornbahn**, which climbs in two stages to the Kitzbüheler Horn on the east side of town.

Getting Here & Around

 Kitzbühel is well located within reasonable driving distance from several air and train transportation hubs: **Innsbruck**, 100 km to the west; **Salzburg**, 80 km to the northeast; and **Munich**, 160 km to the northwest. Trains pull into the main station on the northern edge of town, a 10-minute walk to the old town center. Local and regional buses hub here, too. The use of local buses is free in both summer and winter to holders of regional lift passes. For taxi service, ☎ 05356 626 17.

Mountain transportation runs in both summer and winter. The main lift access points are the Hahenkammbahn gondola just above town, the Kitzbüheler Hornbahn across the valley, and the Fleckalmbahn gondola, which departs from a station approximately four km west of town. For more information on area lift service, contact ☎ 05356 69 57 15, www.bergbahn-kitzbuehel.com.

LIFT PASS PRICE SAMPLES

Winter

1-day adult €34

6-day adult €160

Round-trip on Hahnenkammbahn. €14

Summer

Round-trip on Hahnenkammbahn. €14

3-day pedestrian pass €35

Getting Connected

 The **tourist office** is at Hinterstadt 18, next to the movie theater in old town. The office has lots of brochures and an electronic hotel reservation board. Contact the tourist office at ☎ 05356 621 550, www.kitzbuehel.at.

Above: Arlberg, Austria

Below: Wilder Kaiser, St. Johann, Austria

Above: Höhe Tauern National Park, Austria

Below: Seefeld, Austria

Val d'Isère, France

Kitzbühel's post office is at Josef-Pirchl-Strasse 11. It's open Monday through Friday from 8 am to noon and 2-5 pm.

 For Internet access, try the **Grieserl** at Im Gries 1, www.grieserl.com; or the **Internet Café Videothek** at Schlossergasse 10, next to the Hotel Schwarzer Adler.

The Sights

 Kitzbühel's tourist attractions are mostly of the sporting or shopping type, and visitors will spend most of their time here simply wandering the cobblestone streets of the charming walled center. That said, several local churches merit a look. The **Katharinenkirche**, now a war memorial, is tucked away in the old town center; the 15th-century **Pfarrkirche**, on a knoll just north of center, has an interesting Baroque interior; and next door, the **Liebfrauenkirche** harbors a showy display of lace-like stucco.

Situated in a 13th-century structure that's Kitzbühel's oldest house, the **Heimatmuseum** displays a collection of photos, crafts, and mining tools that tell the story of the town's history. It's open Monday through Saturday, 10 am-1 pm, at Hinterstadt 32; €6.50.

For those with mechanical interests, the **Bergahnmuseum**, or cable car museum, documents the history and technology of lift construction – and don't miss a simulated run down the Streif ski racecourse. The museum is appropriately located at the top station of the Hahnenkammbahn gondola lift; it's open daily 10 am-4 pm.

For fans of World Cup skiing, the blue house at Bichlstrasse 10 is the birthplace of **Toni Sailer** – who, in the 1950s, became a three-time Olympic champion, seven-time World Champion, and hometown Kitzbühel great.

TONI SAILER

Local boy Toni Sailer grew up on the slopes around Kitzbühel, honing his downhill skills and eventually securing fame as Austria's first skiing superstar. At age 17 he dominated the Tyrolean championships and, four years later, put on a similar show at the Olympic Winter Games at Cortina in 1956, winning three gold medals in the downhill, giant slalom, and slalom events – an Olympic record that today remains unchallenged. He retired at the ripe old age of 22 with an extraordinary career already under his belt. Today, Kitzbühel's favorite son serves as president of the local *Schischule Rote Teufel*, or Red Devil Ski School.

Two attractions outside of the town limits will please kids. The **Wildpark Tirol** is four km south of Kitzbühel along the road to Jochberg. A walking tour winds through enclosures housing deer, boars, yaks, lynx, marmots, ducks, and ibex, among others. It's open summer and winter from 9 am to 5 pm, with feedings (for the animals, not guests) at around 2:30 pm. Contact ☎ 05356 653 51 for more information. Just north of town along the Römerweg, the **Bauernhausmuseum Hinterobernau** offers a look at a 16th-century traditional farmhouse, furnished, operated, and equipped as it would have been some 400 years ago. It's open daily from June through September, 1 to 5 pm, and in winter on request; ☎ 05356 642 15.

The Adventures

On Foot

 Hikers enjoy 187 km of marked **hiking trails** – and no less that 70 marked tour routes. In addition, the tourist office guides a wide selection of outings including our favorite, a hike with Olympic ski champion Ernst Hinterseer along the Streif ski-racing run (see *The Legendary Hahnenkamm* below). For an easy stroll, walkers and botany enthusiasts take the Hornbahn up to 1,800 m for a wander through the **Alpine Flower Garden**. The garden harbors 120 varieties of flora, offers guided tours, and admission is free.

Although I don't usually consider golf and tennis to be Alpine adventures, this is what Kitzbühel's well-heeled clientele seems to do best. So, here goes. Four **golf courses** – two with 18 holes each, two with nine holes each – offer public play. The nine-hole **Golf & Landclub Rasmushof** is nearest the town center; ☎ 05356 652 520 for tee times. The town claims a total of 38 **tennis courts** – 14 of them at the **Tennis Club Kitzbühel**. For more information, ☎ 05356 643 20.

 Recreation opportunities are abundant here. The tourist office organizes guided hiking, biking, and skiing tours, free tennis and golf trials, nostalgic train rides, horseshoe tournaments, community concerts, folklore nights, and barbecues. Check in early during your stay to see what's in the works.

On Horseback

The Gästeiger Family runs the **Henntalhof Reihalle** stable at Unterbrunnweg 21. Offerings include horseback riding and horse-drawn carriage and sleigh rides. Make arrangements in advance at ☎ 05356 646 24.

In Water

The **Aquarena** indoor swimming complex offers several pools, sauna facilities, and spa treatments. The facility is just west of town near the Hahnenkammbahn valley station. Access is free to summer lift pass holders and greatly discounted to winter lift pass holders. For current hours, ☎ 05356 643 85.

Those preferring lake swimming can brave the crowds at the small **Schwarzsee** on the northwestern edge of town. All manner of water fun is available, including boat rentals, floating toys, slides, and swimming platforms. For more information, ☎ 05356 623 81. Fishing is an option at Schwarzsee, but licenses and fees must be squared away in advance with the police station in Kitzbühel. Those seeking whitewater action can make arrangements through **Adventure Club Kaiserwinkl** (see page 92).

On Wheels

Several lifts offer free transport of **mountain bikes**, making high-altitude rides an option even for those who don't want to ride up. Request a bike map at the tourist office. The tourist office also offers free **guided bike tours** from June through September. Several outfitters rent mountain bikes in the summer – the best is **Intersport Kitzsport** at Jochberger Strasse 7, ☎ 05356 622 04. A worthwhile **driving tour** explores the 7.5-km Panorama Road up to the Alpenhaus on the Kitzbüheler Horn. The €3.65 toll is redeemable at the Alpenhaus for food or drink. Get more information at www.kitzbuehelerhorn.com or www.alpenhaus.at.

In the Air

For **tandem paragliding** flights, contact Manfred Hofer at the Hahnenkammbahn mountain station, ☎ 05356 671 94. A unique offering here, the Flight Safari package includes leaps from three mountains in one day. Private **balloon rides** can be arranged through **Ballooning Tyrol** in St. Johann; ☎ 05352 656 66.

On Snow & Ice

 Kitzbühel was a pioneer among European ski resorts, constructing Austria's first ski lift on the Hahnenkamm in 1928. Today's **skiing** facilities include 60 lifts and 158 km of groomed runs rated 50% easy, 42% intermediate, and 8% difficult. Five marked off-piste runs challenge advanced skiers, and mountain guides lead the way into the backcountry. Although local snow conditions are sometimes poor, the sheer extent of skiable terrain here means that decent snow can usually be found, and excellent mountain lodges mean that there's always a cozy place for a drink or snack.

Six local ski schools employ over 350 instructors each winter. We've heard good things about both the **Rote Teufel** and the **Skischule Total** (see page 93).

Snowboarders head for the funpark and boarder-cross course on the Kitzbuhler Horn, and **cross-country skiers** enjoy four groomed loops in the immediate area and a total of 120 km of trails throughout the region. The 3.1-km trail at Schwarzsee has lights and snowmaking facilities. **Tobogganing** fans head for the two-km lighted run on the Gaisberg; rent sleds at the valley station of the lift. **Winter walkers** take to 115 km of trails, joining the tourist office's guided theme, torch-lit, and moonlight hikes.

Ice-skaters head for Schwarzsee and the natural lake ice rink – it normally opens in mid-January and admission is free. An artificial rink at Lebenberg opens daily from 1 to 4 pm; admission charged. *Eisstockshiesen*, or **ice-stick shooting**, is offered both at the Schwarzsee Alpenhotel and at Lebenberg, and an indoor **curling** rink invites reservations at ☎ 05356 710 80; instruction and equipment rental can be arranged.

Sports Services, Outfitters & Guides

- **Intersport Kitzsport** operates no fewer than six sporting good stores and equipment rental outlets. I had good luck at the Jochbergerstrasse store at house number 7, ☎ 05356 625 04 33, www.intersportrent.at.

- **Adventure Club Kaiserwinkl** extends its service to guests of the Kitzbühel region. The outfitter offers a good range of adventuresome watersports, including rafting, canyoning, diving, and kayaking. Contact Mr. Glattner at ☎ 05375 26 07 for more information.

- The **Rote Teufel**, or "red devils," ski school claims as its manager Mr. Rudi Sailer (see box above, page 89). The school has been in operation since 1926 and today offers a wide range of services, including racing, freestyle, and cross-country ski instruction. Contact the school at ☎ 05356 625 00, www.rote-teufel.at.

■ The **Skischule Total**, managed by Ernst Hinterseer, offers a similar range of courses at comparable rates – but in addition features video analyses and a large proportion of British instructors. Contact the school at ☎ 05356 720 12, www.skischule-total.at.

Where to Sleep

 Kitzbühel's accommodations are universally pricey, with soaring rate discrepancies between low season and the winter ski season. If you're in the mood to splurge, this is the place to do it – and several hotels will please guests who are willing to pay steep rates.

HOTEL PRICE CHART	
Double room without tax; $$$-$$$$ always with bath.	
$	Under €80
$$	€81-150
$$$	€151-250
$$$$	Over €250

Five-star options include the glitzy **Hotel Weisses Rössl** ($$$$) just outside the old town walls, ☎ 05356 625 410, www.wiesses-roessl.com; and, across the valley in a pastoral hillside location, the **Romantichotel Tennerhof** ($$$$), which melds country charm and luxury like no other; ☎ 05356 631 81, www.tennerhof.com.

Directly in the old town center, the rustically luxurious **Hotel Goldener Greif** ($$$-$$$$) has been welcoming guests since 1271; reserve at ☎ 05356 643 11, www.hotel-goldener-greif.at.

My favorite town-center splurge, however, is the **Hotel Zur Tenne** ($$$-$$$$), a fetching townhouse hotel decked out in rustic country charm. Inquire at ☎ 05356 644 440, www.bayerischerhof.de/tenne/index_tenne.html. Sports-minded visitors like the **Hotel Rasmushof** ($$$$) for its private nine-hole golf course in summer and for its slopeside location in winter – and in all seasons for its excellent restaurant. Reserve at ☎ 05356 652 52, www.rasmushof.at.

Just above town, the **Hotel Garni Licht** ($$-$$$) occupies an old chalet near the lifts. A fireplace, library, and garden make guests feel at home; ☎ 05356 633 93, www.hotel-licht.com. Also above town, the simple **Hotel Montana** ($$-$$$) is next to the Hahnenkammbahn gondola and near the public pool complex; ☎ 05356 625 26. The **Ho-**

tel Strasshofer ($$-$$$) has comfy-enough rooms directly in the heart of old town on the Vorderstadt; ☎ 05356 622 85.

Those looking for budget accommodations will be hard-pressed in Kitzbühel. A good deal by my estimation is the **Hotel Ehrenbachhöhe** ($$), a comfy old hotel at the top of the Hahnenkamm lift. It's directly on the ski slopes in winter, the starting point for numerous hikes in summer, and splendidly isolated year-round; ☎ 05356 62 15 10. The traditional **Eggerwirt** ($$) offers cozy rooms in the center at Gansbachgasse 12, ☎ 05356 624 55, www.eggerwirt-kitzbuehel.at.

Also near the town center, try the traditional chalet **Hotel Tyrol** ($$), ☎ 05356 666 32; or, in the lower old town at Josef-Perchler-Strasse 60, the friendly **Pension Hörl** ($), ☎ 05356 631 44. The tourist office can also assist in booking private rooms.

Where to Eat

For regional cuisine amid traditional surrounds, try the **Goldener Greif** ($$-$$$) at Hinterstadt 24, cozy up in the **Eggerwirt's Florian Room** ($$), or – our favorite – head down the steps to Bichlstrasse 9 and the old-world gästhof, **Zum Zinnkrug**

DINING PRICE CHART	
Average entrée, with tax.	
$	Under €10
$$	€10-25
$$$	Over €25

($$), ☎ 05356 62613. For elegant evenings out, try the well-regarded dining rooms located in a number of local hotels. The **Romantikhotel Tennerhof** ($$$), ☎ 05356 63 18 10, the **Hotel Zur Tenne** ($$$), ☎ 05356 648 03 56, and the **Hotel Rasmushof** ($$$), ☎ 05356 644 44, each serve award-winning gourmet cuisine.

Several cafés dish out less expensive – but only rarely, *in*expensive – meals. **La Fonda** ($) offers a casual Mexican-themed ambiance and an odd mix of Tex-Mex, Thai, and Indian cuisine. It's open daily on the Hiteerstadt, ☎ 05356 736 73. Try the **Adria Pizzeria** ($-$$) at Josef Pirchl Strasse 17 for good pizzas; the **Huberbräu Stüberl** ($-$$) at Vorderstadt 18 for to-the-point traditional dishes; and, if you're aching for Asian, the **Asian Markt** ($) at Josef Pirchl Strasse 16.

*The Hahnenkammbahn gondola runs late on Friday and Saturday night in winter and Friday night in summer. Don't miss the opportunity for dinner at altitude in one of the candlelit mountain lodges. Reservations for the **Restaurant Hochkitzbuhel** can be secured at ☎ 05356 695 72 30.*

Where to Party

Kitzbühel draws a mixed crowd to party places of varied persuasions. In the winter, for après-ski, The **Londoner Pub** at Franz-Reisch-Strasse is the place to be for rowdy crowds and live music. Crowds gather, too, at the nearby **Stamperl** and, under the Hahnenkamm gondola, at the **Mockingstube**. Later, try the low-key **Highways** bar before hitting the dance floors at the **Olympia** and **Take Five** discos.

Kitzbühel's café culture huddles along the Vorstadt – and the **Café Praxmair** frequently draws a crowd. For elegant evenings out with pricey drinks and posh décor, try the **Gatto Bello**, the piano bar at the **Tenne**, or the bar at the **Goldener Greif**. The Kitzbühel **casino** proves popular as well; it's in the center near the Goldener Greif Hotel and is open daily from 7 pm, with blackjack, poker, roulette, and slot machines. Contact ☎ 05356 623 00, www.casinos.at.

Where to Play

Kids enjoy cable car rides, the **Aquarena** swimming complex, and visits to the **Wildpark Tirol** and the **Bauernmuseum**. **Playgrounds** are near the Mockingstube on Hahnenkammstrasse, northwest of the center at Pfarrau, and near the river at the corner of Jochbergerstrasse and Wagnerstrasse. In the summer, kids four years and up can join the Children's Paradise **day programs** offered by the tourist office; the tourist office also offers a list of local **babysitters**.

Festivals & Events

Kitzbühel's festival calendar is crowded with concerts, folk festivals, and sporting competitions. The winter kicks off in early December with the **Winterstart Party**. New Year's Day brings the **Fire & Music** on-slope show organized by the Rote Teufel, and late January ushers in Kitzbühel's famed **International Hahnenkamm Race**.

Austria

A **Gourmet Festival** highlights early February, and the **Kitzbühel Jazz Festival** swings around in mid-March. The summer season opens in mid-May with the **Alpine Vintage Car Rally**; continues through August with a number of **concerts**, **markets**, and **tennis** and **golf** competitions; and wraps up in late September with the **Alpine Cattle Drive**.

THE LEGENDARY HAHNENKAMM

Since its inception in 1931, the Hahnenkamm Ski Race has marked the height of the annual World Cup racing season. No other event draws more attention in Austria – and only the biannual World Championship and the quadrennial Winter Olympic Games come close. The world's finest skiers rip down the famed Streif Run each January – the men the last weekend of the month, the women a week prior.

Look easy? All but the most dangerous sections of the racecourse are open to the public after the race wraps up in late January. Give it a try. The course does appear somewhat steeper when you're looking *down* it than when you're looking at it on TV. For additional race information and tickets, contact the **Kitzbüheler Skiclub** at ☎ 05356 735 55, www.hahnenkamm.com.

St. Johann

Although just around the Kitzbühelerhorn Mountain from Kitzbühel, St. Johann seems a world away in terms of both atmosphere and cost; and the people, prices, and attractions here are geared more toward family fun than the fashion-conscious. The bustling village sits at the foot of the Kitzbühelerhorn, the mountain up which the local ski lifts climb. Rolling pasturelands stretch north toward the magnificent Wilder Kaiser, offering at once both Tyrolean village charm and striking Alpine scenery.

The village centers on its lovely parish church, a two-towered, onion-domed complex dating from 1723. The church and a wall of frescoed houses dominate the tiny market square, site of this town's many festivals. This pedestrian-only area sits adjacent to the busy Speckbacherstrasse, the narrow main drag that leads up to the mountain lift stations, and the main lift, the Harschbichl gondola, climbs the mountain from the residential area just across the tracks.

Activities in St. Johann run to outdoor recreation and festivals, all family-friendly and all deftly coordinated by the village's tourist office. Hiking, mountain biking, paragliding, ballooning, rafting, climbing, and canyoning – it's all available here. Check in with the **Adventure Center** at ☎ 05352 61422, www.mountain-high.at, to book a guide. In winter, over 100 km of groomed trails keep walkers walking, 60 km of easy and intermediate ski runs please downhill enthusiasts, and the excellent **St. Johann ski school** has a heart (and a great reputation) for serving families and beginning skiers. Book a lesson at ☎ 05352 64 777. Nighttime skiing and tobogganing are offered once or twice each week.

Après-ski and nightlife is rather subdued in St. Johann, but party-minded visitors can see what's on at **Bunny's Pub** or test the latest mix at the local brewery's pub, the **Huber-Bräu-Stüberl**. Look for the brewery's control tower one block east of Speckbacherstrasse.

 Want to stay? The **Gästhof Post** ($$) is one of those few remaining gems – a historical old hotel in a prime location with budget rates. The friendly, family-run guesthouse is over 700 years old, and today offers small rooms decked out in a hodgepodge of furnishings, some antique and some just old. The frescoed façade faces the pedestrian square at Speckbacherstrasse 1, a quiet locale unless one of the village's fests is underway. Parking is free behind the hotel. Dial ☎ 05352 622 30 or click www.hotel-post.tv to book.

 St. Johann's central tourist office sits next to the post office along the rip-roaringly busy Poststrasse. Contact ☎ 05352 633 50 or www.st.johann.tirol.at for more information.

Söll

Nestled between the craggy Wilder Kaiser and the Höhe Salve mountains, the charming village of Söll offers a wealth of recreation, an easily accessed locale, and loads of Tyrolean charm. In the winter, the village is a favorite of British skiers and, in the summer, families flock here for the extensive network of hiking and biking trails. The village clusters around the 1765 landmark church, built on a central hill in Rococo style. A small but lively pedestrian area lies below, lined with hotels, shops, and restaurants.

Söll quite rightly advertises itself as a "walker's paradise." Over 700 km of walking paths wind through the area from village to village, valley to peak, and mountain hut to mountain hut. A favorite day out starts with a hike (or gondola ride) up past the boulder-topping **Stampfanger Chapel** to the mid-mountain hamlet of

Hochsöll, where playgrounds and Hexenwasser (see box below) entertain kids and a handful of guesthouses serve up hearty fare. Farther up the mountain still, wanderers ply through the **Hexenwald**, or Witch's Forest, to reach the peak of Höhe Salve. Here, visitors enjoy panoramic views of 70 Alpine peaks, take photos with cooperative, bell-laden cattle, and peek inside the **Salven Chapel** – at 1829 m, the highest chapel in Austria.

WITCHY WATERS

Kids of all ages can tickle their toes at Hochsöll, a 20-minute gondola ride up the mountain from Söll. **Hexenwasser**, a small water-themed park just below the gondola top station, invites visitors to take off their shoes and wander a 450-m barefoot trail – dipping into Kneipp-therapy basins, maneuvering a water labyrinth, and slip-sliding along wooden flues. But this is no fiberglass-and-chlorine contraption. The course is created of local stones, cut through an Alpine meadow, and irrigated with sparkling clear mountain water. It's a great way to cool off after a hot summer's hike, and German-only signs offer informative *wasser*-related facts, but be forewarned – on August weekends this quiet retreat feels more like an overcrowded city-park playground. (Open May through September; no entry fee; kids should pack their swimsuits.)

Söll offers extensive biking opportunities, a full program of guided walks and activities, and an expansive swimming complex, the **Panoramabad**. Nearby villages are easily reached on foot, bike, snowshoe, or ski, and the Wilder Kaiser challenges climbers with one of the Alps' most difficult climbs. In winter, skiers explore the **SkiWelt**, Austria's largest interconnected ski area, on 250 km of groomed runs and with the help of 93 lifts. Söll enjoys an après-ski and nightlife scene that, for a village this size, is extraordinarily lively; partiers should try **Pub 15**, the **Whisky Mühle**, and the **Salven Stadl**.

*Traveling in mid-September? Don't miss Söll's traditional **Almabtrieb**, or mountain festival. The festival begins at Hochsöll with wood-carving, sheep-shearing, cheese- and bread-making, and lots of music and food. The height of the festival is the cattle parade, when farmers lead their highly adorned cows off the mountain pastures and through Söll's village center to their home stables for the winter.*

Want to stay? The cheery **Hotel Tulpe** ($$) is up the hill from the main village, near the nursery slopes, pool complex, and gondola valley station; Stampfanger 17, ☎ 05333 52 23. For lodging directly at village center, try the homey old **Postwirt Hotel** ($$), Dorf 83, ☎ 05333 50 81, www.tiscover.at/postwirt-soell.at.

The tourist information office is at Dorfstrasse 84 along the main pedestrian street. Contact ☎ 05333 52 16 or www.soell.at for more information.

Salzburg & the Salzburgerland

This section spans a wide chunk of central Austria, wrapping around the southeasternmost corner of Germany and taking in Austria's cultural capital, the city of Salzburg, and the region that shares its name. Known worldwide as home to both Mozart and *The Sound of Music*, conservative Salzburg remains Austria's most toured city. The nearby **Salzkammergut** region draws adventurers for its lovely lakes and forests. Just south, the Europa Sports Region – otherwise known as **Zell am See** and **Kaprun** – offers an admirable docket of year-round sports. Farther south rises the magnificent wilderness of the **Höhe Tauern National Park**, home to Austria's highest mountain, the **Grossglockner**, and the spectacular cascade of **Krimmler Falls**, described on page 128.

■ Salzburg

Population: 146,000

Base elevation: 424 m

Tourist city

The sound of music – Mozart's music – dances through the streets of this charming city, bouncing off onion-domed church towers and echo-

ing off cobblestone streets. With its beautifully preserved old town, its numerous fine arts festivals, and its wealth of cultural history, sumptuous Salzburg should not be missed.

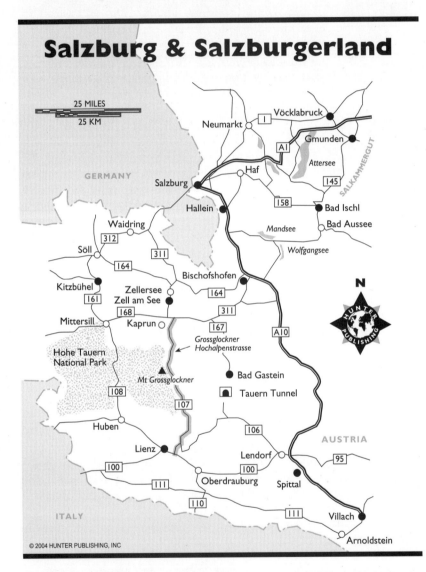

History & Overview

 Although in ancient times Celtic and Roman settlers inhabited the valley, Salzburg's modern history begins with the Bishop St. Rupert, a crusading Franconian who in the late seventh century founded the Abbey of St. Peter, today the oldest Benedictine cloister north of Italy. By the eighth century,

Salzburg was promoted to an archbishopric, and its political and economic rise was underway, eventually affording the archbishops the title of Princes of the Holy Roman Empire. By mining and selling salt from the Salzkammergut, and through their expansive realm, the prince-archbishops amassed the wealth reflected in the grand architecture that marks the *altstadt* today.

The height of Salzburg's development came in the 16th and 17th centuries, when Archbishop Wolf Dietrich von Raitenau employed his power, his Medici connections, and his Renaissance passion for all things Italian to set in motion a century-long building spree that transformed Salzburg into an oddly Italianate city, complete with grand cathedrals, palace courtyards, and large squares. The city became part of Austria in 1816, and today it is the seat of government for the Austrian province that shares its name.

Salzburg occupies a valley in the north of the Salzburgerland, just a few km from the border of Germany. Beautifully sited along the Salzach River, the city lies just north of a magnificent stretch of Alps and just south of a region of rolling hills and small lakes. The Salzkammergut lake region stretches to the east. The region was the historical crossroads of several trade routes, and today is well-served by autobahns: the A10 toward Tauern, the A8 to Munich, and the A1 to Vienna converge just south of town.

The Town

The city of Salzburg unfolds along both banks of the Salzach River – the old town, or *altstadt*, on the left bank to the west; the new town, or *neustadt*, on the right bank to the east. (What's confusing about all this, however, is that the center of town lies along an east-west running bend of the Salzach – so that the old town is actually on the southern bank of the river.) Better landmarks, perhaps, are the center's two hills: the cliff-like **Mönchsberg** stretches to the west, running the length of old town and providing an elevated plot for the **Höhensalzburg Fortress** on its southern end; and, across the river to the east swells the **Kapuzinerberg**, a prominent hill topped off with the **Kupuzinkloster** monastery.

The old town's action revolves around the cathedral and its surrounding squares, which lie 120 m below the cliff-top **Festung Höhensalzburg**. Picturesque, medieval alleys wind between the *altstadt*'s palaces and squares; the most famous of these, the Getreidegasse shopping street, runs roughly parallel to the river from Alter Markt to St. Blasius church. To the north, bridges across the Salzach River lead to the *neustadt* on the northern edge of the Kapuzinerberg hill. **Schloss Mirabell** and its expansive gardens spread out near the riverbank, and Rainerstrasse leads farther north to the main train station.

Getting Here & Around

Salzburg's **W.A. Mozart Airport** receives flights from all around Europe on the western outskirts of the city. The main train station lies to the north of town center, approximately 1.5 km from the *altstadt*. Bus hubs include the Südtirolerplatz directly in front of the train station, the Mirabellplatz in the *neustadt*, and Erzabt Klotz Strasse southwest of old town.

> *If you're driving, finding your way into the vicinity of old town can prove quite a challenge; but in high-season, this irritation is a mere warm-up for the blood-boiling frustration brought on by the city's grossly inadequate parking. If your hotel offers valet parking, accept the service with gratitude – even at upwards of €25 per day, it's a bargain.*

Once in the city center, visitors can reach most of Salzburg's attractions on foot or bike. Those wishing to use public transportation are limited to the local bus network; the service is free to holders of the Salzburg Card (see below). For lack of funds and support, the subway system has seen no development beyond the single stop dug below the main train station. The city's aspirations toward a river transportation scheme sank during the August 2002 flood, when the navigation company's prototype ferry, the *Amadeus*, went down along with its dock just three months after its maiden voyage. (Salvage efforts proved futile, but plans for a replacement vessel are underway.)

Getting Connected

 The train station has a small information kiosk, but the main **tourist office** is in the old town at Mozartplatz. The office – jam-packed during the festival season – doles out a hodge-podge of pamphlets, sells a good town map, and provides a ticket sales service. It's open May through September, 9 am-8 pm, and from October through April, 9 am-6 pm; ☎ 0662 889 873 30, www.salzburginfo.at.

 The city's most convenient post offices are in old town at Residenzplatz and across the river at Dreifaltigasse near the Makartplatz.

WWW For on-line access, head to the friendly **Internet Café Mozartplatz**. It's next to the tourist office and open daily from 10 am-10 pm.

Getreidegasse, Salzburg

The Sights

 Today's Salzburg is one of the planet's most toured cities, and 25% of its GNP is attributable to tourism. Almost seven million visitors arrive each year – that's some 47 guests for every Salzburg resident.

THE SALZBURG CARD

This electronically programmed card offers unlimited transportation on the local bus system and single entries to a long list of attractions. Purchase your card at the tourist office: 24-hour cards run €20; 48-hour cards, €28; and 72-hour cards, €34. Your Salzburg Card can be upgraded, either to Salzburg Plus Light, which includes a three-course meal and two beverages each day at a partner restaurant, or – for those who simply must have a plan – to Salzburg Plus, which includes pre-arranged accommodations, meals, coffee breaks, night caps, and concert or event tickets. Furthermore, any version of the Salzburg Card can be transferred to a Swatch Access wristwatch.

To see it all in a short time, hook up with on of the city's 100 certified city guides. The tourist office can help arrange **tours** by foot, van, bike, and horse-drawn carriage. The best of the organized bus tours is **Panorama Tours**, a Gray Line company that does a variety of regional outings, including the popular **Sound of Music** and **Kehlsteinhaus Eagle's Nest** tours. Reserve at ☎ 0662 88 32 11, toll-free in the US at 1-800-982-7969, or at www.panoramatours.com.

THE SOUND OF MUSIC

The charming story of the Von Trapp family gave the world its image of Austria: lush, rolling hills, elegant palaces, soaring Alpine peaks, and cities full of song. Rodgers and Hammerstein first put the tale to music when they wrote *The Sound of Music*, a musical production staged on Broadway in 1959. In 1964, a film starring Julie Andrews drew international acclaim and forever put Salzburg on the tourist map.

The Von Trapp Story

Georg von Trapp

Baron Georg von Trapp first distinguished himself as a submarine commander during his service with the Austrian Navy in World War I. By 1921, he and his wife, Agathe Whitehead, had seven children: Rupert, Agathe, Maria, Werner, Hedwig, Johanna, and Martina. Upon the mother's death in 1922, the Von Trapps moved from Vienna to Salzburg where, once settled, Georg von Trapp hired a young governess to care for his children. The governess, Maria Augusta von Kutschera, a novice from the Nonnberg Convent in old Salzburg, was soon adored by the children and, eventually, by Baron von Trapp as well.

They were married in the convent's church in 1927, and soon gave birth to two more daughters; but hard times were to follow. During the economic depression, the family lost its fortune, making only enough money to survive by giving family-style choral concerts throughout the region. In the face of Hilter's annexation of their beloved Austria, the Von Trapps defied the Nazi regime and emigrated to America in 1939. The family continued its

Maria

choral pursuits and, even after their last son, Johannes, was born, made concert tours around the world. In 1941, the Von Trapp family settled in Stowe, Vermont, where they still own and operate the chalet-style Von Trapp Family Lodge.

The film version of *The Sound of Music* was largely filmed on location in and around Salzburg, and multiple tour operators here exploit the tourist appeal. The sites can be seen independently, of course, although pre-arranged bus tours do liberate you from transportation logistics. For fans, here's a rundown of the nearby film locations:

- **The Nonnberg Convent** – Maria serves as a novice in this convent. It's here that the nuns sing *Maria*.

- **Residenz Square** – On her way to the Trapp Villa, Maria sings *I Have Confidence*.

- **St. Peter's Cemetery** – The Von Trapp family hides here behind the tombstones.

- **The Festival Hall** – The old riding school. Baron von Trapp here sings *Edelweiss* just before fleeing town.

- **Mirabell Palace and Gardens** – Maria and the children dance in the gardens, singing *Do-Re-Mi* and running up the rose hill steps.

- **Leopoldskron Palace** – This palace was used as the Trapp Villa; Maria and Baron dance and have cocktails on the terrace and balcony.

- **Hellbrunn Palace** – It's now home to the garden gazebo where Liesl and Rolf sing *Sixteen Going on Seventeen.*

- **The Unterberg** – This mountain was the location of both the opening and fleeing scenes.

- **Mondsee Village** – Maria runs across a local hill toward the convent. Several aerial shots were taken here.

- **St. Michael's Church** – This lovely church in Mondsee was the filming location for Maria and the Baron's wedding scene.

AUTHOR'S PICK Dominating the city from the southern end of the Mönchberg, the **Höhensalzburg Fortress**, or *festung*, should rank at the top of any visitor's must-see list. The site first saw construction in 11th century, and that original castle underwent 600 years of reconstruction and expansion thereafter. The complex I tour today dates from 17th century, when local archbishops lost interest and began building palaces in the town below instead. Approach the imposing fortress from the trails atop the Mönchberg, from the steep Festungasse alley leading up from the *altstadt*, or via the Festungsbahn funicular, which depart from near the cathedral's Kapitelplatz. (The train runs on electricity now, but an ingenious operation employing pumps, water-weight, and gravity did the trick when it first opened in 1892.) Funicular ride with fortress entrance costs €6; open daily, 9:30 am-5 pm; in summer, 9 am-6 pm.

At the foot of the Höhensalzburg Fortress, a cluster of churches, squares, and palaces give the *altstadt* its distinctive skyline. Of greatest interest here are the enormous **Dom** cathedral, a 17th-century monument built after the site's original church finally succumbed to its eighth catastrophic fire. The squares surrounding the church are venues for many town festivals, markets, and performances; and the **Glockenspiel** here atop the New Residence sounds its 35 bells three times each day: at 7 am, 11 am, and 6 pm. Nearby, **St. Peter's Cemetery** must rank among the world's most beautiful – and haunting, as I witnessed one Halloween night, with candles flickering and an enormous full moon behind the fortress. Its cliff-side catacombs are open Tuesday through Sunday in summer, Wednesday through Sunday in winter; €1.

Winding through the center's alleys, visitors are bound to discover the **Getreidegasse**, a charming market street decked out with those gilt wrought-iron shop signs that figure prominently in any tourist guide. Fashion, food, and souvenirs – it's all here. Midway down this shopping street, at Getreidegasse 9, stands **Mozart's Geburtshaus**, or birthplace. The yellow house is recognizable for its tourist throngs, all awaiting their turns to visit the museum inside; open 9 am-5 pm, till 6 pm in July and August, €5.50. Across the river, the Linzergasse makes an interesting shopping excursion – it's less expensive than the Getreidegasse, too. Just north sits **Schloss Mirabell**, built in 1606 by the Archbishop Wolf Dietrich for Salome Alt and their children. Today, the palace serves government offices, but the garden and its Mozarteum and Marionettentheater are open to the public.

The City of Mozart

Salzburg's most famous son is Wolfgang Amadeus Mozart. Although born one of seven children, Wolfgang Amadeus, born 1756, and his sister, "Nannerl," were the only two who survived. Leopold Mozart, a vice-director of music for the archbishop, recognized his son's early talent and encouraged him toward music; the prodigy had learned piano at age three, violin at age five, and creative composition at age five. Mozart spent most of his childhood and teenage years touring and playing the courts of Europe. After his adult relationship with the archbishop deteriorated, Mozart moved to Vienna, married Constanze Weber as soon as he arrived, and gradually slid farther and farther into debt. In 1791, Mozart died in Vienna, a pauper; his body was buried there, in an unidentified mass grave at St. Mark's Cemetery.

True fans will want to see all three of Salzburg's Mozart memorials. In the *altstadt*, **Mozarts Gerburtshaus**, offers a look at the house in which the composer was born and the third-floor apartment in which he resided until he was 17. Near the cathedral, Mozartplatz square has as its focal point a **statue** of Mozart that was revealed in 1842 to kick off the city's first Mozart Festival. Finally, across town at Makartplatz 8, the **Mozart Wohnhaus**, or residence, is where Mozart resided between 1773 and 1780, composing 150 works during this time. Much of the house was destroyed during World War II, but the Dance Master's Hall, Mozart's concert hall, was salvaged and his apartment is now a museum. Fans of *The Magic Flute* will want to visit the **Mozarteum**, now an academy of music, for its gardens and the small **summer house** (transported there) in which Mozart composed this score. The grave of Mozart's sister Nannerl lies near that vault of Michael Haydn in **St. Peter's Cemetery**; his mother's grave lies near St. Sebastian's.

Several attractions draw tourists outside of the center. Most popular are day-trips out to **Schloss Hellbrunn**, a Renaissance palace famed for its aquatic gardens, which feature trick fountains, or *wasserspiele*. The fountains were installed by the humor-loving Markus Sittikus, a 17th-century archbishop who'd jovially startle his guests with water fun. (The picnic table's bench-mounted jets must have brought forth particular surprise.)

Schloss Hellbrunn opens for castle and garden tours from April through October; in July and August, the gardens operate at night, too. Contact ☎ 0662 820 37 20, www.hellbrunn.at, €7.50. Nearby, the **Salzburg Zoo** is open year-round, daily from 8:30 am; ☎ 0662 82 01 76, www.salzburg-zoo.at.

West of the city, the **Salzburg Freilicht Museum**, or outdoor museum, displays 60 original farm building, some of them 500 years old. Farmyards, handicraft demonstrations, and a great playground entertain. The park is open 9 am-6 pm, Tuesday through Sunday from April through November; ☎ 0662 85 00 11, www.freilichtmuseum.com, €6.

Farther north, Oberndorf's **Silent Night Chapel** – in German, the *Stille Nacht Kapelle* — and its museum pay homage to the site where the international Christmas carol of the same name was penned in 1818. Particularly popular for its Advent festivities, Oberndorf sits on the border of Germany, in a hilly region approximately 30 minutes from Salzburg; www.oberndorf.co.at.

The Adventures

Salzburg is first and foremost a culture-oriented tourist city, but one that believes itself athletically inclined as well. The city embraces its natural setting – a surrounding wealth of lakes, forests, and mountains. Within the city limits, residents bike along riverside paths, through the city streets, and along the 410-km Mozart biking route. In fact, in this crowded old city, **biking** proves a more efficient means of transport than either private car or bus. Rent your wheels at **Top Bike Salzburg**, either at the main train station or on the old-town side of the Staatsbrücke; ☎ 06272 46 56, www.topbike.at.

Also in town, sportsters **hike** along the forested Mönchsberg, reached via cliff-side elevator at Museumplatz, and **climb** the "City Wall" cliff on the Kapuzinerberg. (The wall is graded E; contact www.akzente.net for access.) Outside of the city, the 1,288-m Gaisberg peak offers a lovely setting for **cycling, hiking,** and **paragliding**. New in 2003, **cross-country skiers** can enjoy 15 km of groomed trails and a 600-m nighttime loop.

The Untersberg Legend

South of the city near St. Leonhard rises the 1,853-m Untersberg, Salzburg's highest peak. According to legend, Charlemagne and his armies have been asleep inside this magnificent mound for the past 1,200 years. Ravens keep watch around the peak; and rumblings within sound the waking grumbles of the great leader. When the time comes that the birds desert the mountain, evildoers beware: Charlemagne and his loyal followers will rise up and come to the aid of all honest men.

Want to check on those birds? A **cable car ride** (or a difficult climb) to the top affords magnificent views. Find more info at ☎ 06246 724 770, www.untersberg.net.

Although the city lost its bid for the 2010 Olympics, its **winter sports facilities** cannot be discounted. Most notably, the city lies within 90 km of several well-known Alpine resorts, including Zell am See, the Gastein Valley, Kitzbühel, Obertauern, Schladming, and Saalbach-Hinterglemm. In all, the Salzburgerland region encompasses some 25 ski resorts with over 600 lifts and 1,700 km of runs.

(Keep in mind, however, that this is an enormous area and that many of the resorts here are small, scattered affairs.)

If you want to ski but not drive, hop aboard the **Salzburg Snow Shuttle**. *The bus departs Mirabell Square at 8:30 am each morning from late December to early March. Destinations vary by day, but include weekly excursions to Zell am See, Bad Gastein, and Kitzbühel. Your host will help arrange ski equipment rental, lift pass purchase, and activities for non-skiers. Bus tickets are €13; contact ☎ 0662 87 17 12 or the tourist office for more information.*

Where to Sleep

For traditional lodging in the center, our favorite is the **Goldener Hirsch** ($$$$), an elegant old house furnished in exquisite, country-style antiques – yes, you're supposed to *use* that 17th-century armoire. It's ideally situated, too; Getreidegasse 37, ☎ 0662 808 40, www.goldenerhirsch.com.

HOTEL PRICE CHART	
Double room without tax; $$$-$$$$ always with bath.	
$	Under €80
$$	€81-150
$$$	€151-250
$$$$	Over €250

Also located in the center, but somewhat more popular with upscale tour groups, the luxurious **Alstadt Radisson SAS** ($$$$) occupies a sprawling plot along the busy riverside road. It's at Rudolfskai 28, ☎ 0662 84 85 71, www.austria-trend.at/ass.

What was once one of my favorite traditional inns is now one of my favorite artsy inns; in the center at Getreidegasse 41, the **Blaue Gans** ($$$) has undergone a dramatic overhaul, splashing bright colors and modern art throughout its ancient halls. Check in at ☎ 0662 84 24 91, www.blauegans.at.

The **Käsererbräu** ($$$) has cozy traditional rooms at Kaigasse 33, ☎ 0662 84 24 45, www.kasererbraeu.at; and the family-run **Hotel Elefant** has been welcoming visitors for 400 years at Sigmund-Haffenergasse 4, just off the Getreidegasee; ☎ 0662 84 33 97, www.elefant.at.

Tucked away on Kaigasse 7, the **Hotel Wolf** ($$) offers basic rooms in a prime *altstadt* locale, ☎ 0662 84 34 53, www.hotelwolf.com; as does the small-and-simple **Trumer-Stube** ($$) at Bergstrasse 6, ☎ 0662 87 47 76, www.trumer-stube.at.

The **Pension Adlerhof** ($) has the least expensive six rooms in the *altstadt*; ☎ 0662 87 52 36. The best-located of the hostel accommodations here is the **Naturfreundehaus Stadtalm** ($), on the Mönchsberg above old town and open from May through September, ☎ 0662 84 17 29.

Where to Eat

For fish specialties and a good wine selection, try the romantic **Alt Salzburg** ($$-$$$), at Burgerspitalgasse 2, behind a gated arch next to the Spielzeugmuseum; reservations at ☎ 0662 84 14 76.

DINING PRICE CHART	
Average entrée, with tax.	
$	Under €10
$$	€10-25
$$$	Over €25

AUTHOR'S PICK The **Stiftskeller St. Peter** ($$) tucks up into the Mönchberg cliff, a cave-like cellar drenched in old-world ambiance – an appropriate setting for the oldest restaurant in Europe. (It's been in service for 1,200 years.) The food is traditional, and the tables line dark, vaulted halls and an ancient courtyard. The restaurant is behind St. Peter's church at Bezirk 4, ☎ 0662 841 268. Our other traditional favorite is the **s'Herzl** ($$-$$$), the elegant Goldener Hirsch Hotel's stüberl. It's less formal than the hotel's gourmet room, but still elegant, and the food adheres to equally high standards. In fall, be sure to sample the game specialties; reserve at ☎ 00662 808 48 89, Getreidegasse 37.

For less expensive traditional fare in the *altstadt*, try **Resch & Lieblich** ($$), near the Festspielhaus at the foot of the Mönchberg. **St. Paul's Stub'n** ($), at Herrengasse 16, offers inexpensive snacks, pizza, and beer to a young clientele; it's on a small side-street below the fortress. Nearby, at Kapitelgasse 11, the tiny **Zum Fleischlaberl** ($) serves up inexpensive Austrian specialties, salads-to-go, and P.J. Tipps tea to a largely British clientele.

The **Sternbräu** ($$) offers a collection of five courtyard restaurants, including an Italian bistro, an Austrian *stüberl*, and a pleasant if busy beer garden. It's an upscale food court, really. To find it, duck down the passage at Getreidegasse 23, ☎ 0662 840 717. In the *neustadt*, try the cozy **Stadtkrug** ($$) at Linzergassse 20, for traditional fare or, for pizza, the nearby **Casanova** ($) at Linzergasse 23.

The simple **Fideler Affe** ($), at Priesterhausgasse 8, has excellent schnitzel and good prices. **Produce markets** set up Monday through Saturday in the old town in front of the Kollegienkirche at

Universitatsplatz; and in the *neustadt* on Thursdays at the Schrannenmarkt near the Andrakirche.

The city's first café, the lovely **Tomasselli** ($$), presides over the Alte Markt, oozing with tradition and the gasps of those patrons who've just received their coffee bill. Another Salzburg tradition, the **Augustiner Bräu** ($) beer garden offers a huge *mass* of house-brewed beer. (Service is of the old-fashioned kind, however – wash off a mug, pay for your brew, then present the receipt at the beer counter.) The beer garden is 750 m north of the old town along the river, at Augustinergasse 4. Another beer garden – this one closer to the tourist trail – lies at Festungsgasse 10 along the path up to the Höhensalzburg fortress; stop in at the **Stieglkeller** ($) for local brews and big views.

Where to Party

 Salzburg's staid, sophisticated reputation is well deserved, and the biggest evening attractions here are musical concerts and, for tourists, a wide range of dinner shows. Check with the tourist office, ☎ 0662 889 873 30, www.salzburginfo.at, to see what **concerts** are in town – there will inevitably be at least a few, some of them in palaces, fortresses, and churches. The tourist office can also make reservations for any of the popular **dinner performances.** The ongoing but seasonal productions include a Mozart Dinner Concert in the Baroque Hall of the Stiftskeller; *Eine Kleine Nachtmusik* at the Höhensalzburg Fortress; and *The Sound of Music* at the Sternbräu.

That said, Salzburg is also a student city with several back-street bar scenes. For casual hangouts, head for the Rudolfskai along the Salzach, where the **Shamrock** flaunts frequent live music, the **Altstadtkeller** does jazz, and the **Barfly** spins up hard rock. Tucked between the river and the Mönchsberg at the northern tip of old town, the Gstättengasse is home to **The Club** disco and **JEXX**, a favorite for beer and chicken wings.

Across the river in *neustadt,* head for the charming Steingasse, where numerous bars, bistros, and cafés converge. Try **Pepe Gonzales** for Mexican snacks, and drink and dance till late at **Saitensprung**. Finally, Salzburg's favorite pop culture venue is the **Rockhouse**. The club books a range of live concerts, including pop, rock, jazz, blues, and metal – anything from punk to funk. It's out past the end of Linzergasse at Schallmooser Haupstrasse 46; dial ☎ 0662 848 78 40 to see what's on.

Festivals & Events

Salzburg hosts 4,000 cultural events each year, so I won't be enumerating them all here, but odds are that you'll find some sort of festival in full swing upon your arrival. The city's festivals are, not surprisingly, almost exclusively musical events. During the last two weeks of January the **Mozart Weeks** take center stage, followed by the **Easter Festival** concerts and the **Pfingstfestspiele** Baroque music festival. The famous **Salzburger Festspiele** packs the town calendar with operas, plays, and concerts from late July through late August, with many performances held in the Festspielhauser, the archbishop's stables of yesteryear.

Kulturtage, or Culture Days, run from mid- to late October. Early November brings a change of key with the **International Jazz Fall Festival.** The Christmas season, too, brings a host of events, including three lovely **Christmas markets** – one at Mirabellplatz, one at Höhensalzburg fortress, and one, the largest, at the Domplatz in front of the Cathedral. The markets run from late November through Christmas Eve.

The Salzkammergut

The Almsee, one of the lakes in the region

The Salzkammergut sprawls east of Salzburg, a hilly region best known for its 76 lakes. Between these lakes, however, are some of Austria's most beautiful forests – and lots and lots of salt. In fact, the salt mining industry made the Salzkammergut the most contested region in Austria, a battle for wealth between the Hapsburgs of Vienna and the prince-archbishops of Salzburg. Today, the Salzkammergut's wealth lies not in salt but in tourism, and the region hosts guests year-round – in winter for the excellent, mostly easy, ski runs; in spring and summer for its lake sports and hiking and biking trails; and in fall, for Austria's most spectacular display of seasonal color.

This book and several others could be filled with only information on Salzkammergut's resorts and attractions. But we'll limit our coverage to a few of the best. Farthest west in the region, the lake closest to Salzburg, the **Mondsee** (and its village of the same name) boast *Sound of Music* connections and a fascinating archeological history. At the Marktplatz in the village, **St. Michael's Church** was the filming site for the Von Trapp wedding scene; and the village and its surrounding landscape features in several aerial shots as well.

More interesting to history buffs will be the **Heimatmuseum**, which documents the discovery of a local community dating from 2500 BC. Farther south, the **Wolfgangsee** lake runs 15 km and is flanked at its middle by the town of **St. Wolfgang**. The village is one of the region's most popular for both water and winter sports, and its parish church and tower museum prove reasonably interesting. Farther east at **Trunsee**, the peaceful Traunkirche gleams, surrounded by water. **Bad Ischl**, the region's most popular spa resort, lies in a valley to the southwest.

AUTHOR'S PICK

The lovely little village of **Halstatt** may very well prove the highlight of any Austrian tour. Its old wooden houses stack up, wedged between the forested mountain and the lake Halstättersee. Cars park in garages outside of town, and trains stop at a station across the lake – passengers, ferried into the village by boat. Most extraordinary here is a visit to the **Pfarrkirche** and its crowded cemetery – a cemetery so crowded, in fact, that burial there is only temporary. After 10 or so years of decomposition time, the bones are cleared out and – after the town gravedigger decoratively paints the skull – filed away in the Beinhaus. Have a look; it's open daily from 10 am-6 pm, €1. If you're up for more, Halstatt also has an interesting history museum that lays out the village's Celtic ties.

THE SALZKAMMERGUT ERLEBNIS-CARD

Although you'd have to work hard to make the €400 savings it's advertising, this card is nonetheless a good deal for those staying and playing awhile. The card offers discounts of up to 30% on rail, boat, and cable car transportation, as well as on admission to cave tours, salt mines, scenic toll road, wildlife parks, museums, and bathing facilities – among others. Cards are valid from May through October, and can be purchased at tourist offices, railway stations, and some hotels; €4.90.

For active visitors, sporting possibilities are ubiquitous throughout the region. Vacationers enjoy hiking and biking between the lakes, paragliding off pleasant peaks, scuba diving in clear Alpine waters, and swimming along grassy shores. Boat rental is offered at numerous outlets, water skiing proves popular at the Wolfgangsee, and sailors and windsurfers catch the breeze at Mondsee. In the winter, cross-country skiers hit lakeside trails, and downhillers enjoy the slopes around the Wolfgangsee and, to the south, in the more extreme Dachsteinguppe.

 Want to stay? Resort hotels, small inns, and cozy pensions abound. In Hallstatt, try the **Gästhof Zauner-Seewirt** at Marktplatz 51, an old, family-run inn squeezed tight in the village center. Its excellent restaurant serves up regional and fish specialties. Reserve at ☎ 06134 82 46.

 Centralized tourist information for the Salzkammergut region is at ☎ 06132 269 09, www.salzkammergut.at. For more info on the Mondsee, contact www.mondsee.at; the Wolfgangsee, www.wolfgangsee.at; the Traunsee, www.traunsee.at; Bad Ischl, www.badischl.at; and for Halstatt, www.halstatt.net.

■ Zell am See & Kaprun

Zell population: 9,900	Kaprun population: 3,100
Zell base elevation: 757 m	Kaprun base elevation: 786 m
Lake resort town	Mountain resort village

In the early 1970s, in a stroke of marketing genius, the lakeside health resort of Zell am See paired up with neighboring Kaprun, a glacier ski resort, to create the Europa Sports Region. Together, the pair offers a well-networked infrastructure and sporting opportunities for all seasons.

History & Overview

 First occupied by early Roman settlers, Zell am See was officially founded in 743 and christened *Cella in Bisontio*. The town grew up as a stop along the trade route from Italy to Germany – the route now followed by the Grossglockner Hochalpenstrasse through the Höhe Tauern National Park. Zell's population exported salt to the south and then returning with Italian wine from the north via the perilous transalpine route. In 1875, the railway came to town – gloriously entering along the banks of the lake, and toting tourism into the region.

Nearby Kaprun got its start as a cattle-farming village and mountain-guiding center. They remain important today. Since the early 1900s, the village has also gained renown in Austria for a couple of technological feats: The **Glockner-Kaprun hydroelectric plant** opened in 1955, integrating a system of reservoirs, rivers, and dams in the manufacture of power; and, a decade, later, the **cable car link**

between the Kaprunertal Valley and the Schmieding Glacier affording Austria its first summer-skiing arena.

The Europa Sports Region sits in central Austria at the southern edge of the province of Salzburg. The Höhe Tauern mountain range to the south and the Steinernes Meer range to the north border the region; its two resorts, Zell am See and Kaprun, lie in the foothills along the shores of the Zellersee. The town of Zell am See flanks the western edge of the lake at the base of the 1,968-m Schmittenhöhe. Across the Salzach Valley, seven km to the south, the village of Kaprun huddles below the 3,029-m Kitzsteinhorn and its Schmieding Glacier.

Zell

The town of Zell am See wedges between the western shore of the Zellersee, or Lake Zell, and the eastern foothills of Schmittenhöhe. The busy B311 now burrows through a tunnel west of town, so Zell's main north-south road, the Brücker Bundesstrasse, is a bit less hectic. Schillerstrasse and Schmittenstrasse run from the center of town up the Schmitten Valley to the west. Action here centers on the Stadtplatz and the pleasant pedestrian town center, a web of alleys clustered between the main road and the train tracks along the lakeshore. The train station anchors the southern edge of town; the Stadtpark and sport center anchor the northern edge.

View of Zell am See

Three main cableways access the mountains west of Zell; each departs from a base along Schmittenstrasse. Nearest the town center, the Zellerbergbahn gondola tugs up in two stages to the Hirschkögel. The Schmittenhöhebahn and the Sonnenalmbahn depart from neighboring bases two km farther up the valley; the Schmittenhöhebahn climbing to the 1,968-m Schmittenhöhe peak, the Sonnenalmbahn climbing up the opposite hillside to the 1,850-m Sonnenkögel peak.

Kaprun

Seven km south of Zell, the village of Kaprun stretches up the Kaprunertal alongside a stream and the busy valley road. The action here centers on the Salzburg Platz – the post office, the tourist information office, and the sports center are all nearby. Kaprun's uplift facilities are also based up-valley from the village. The Maiskögelbahn departs from just south of the village and, several km farther on, the Kitzsteinhornbahn gondola climbs to the glacier for all-season skiing on the 3,204-m Kitzsteinhorn. (The funicular track that enters the mountain near the base station closed in November of 2000, when a horrific tunnel fire killed 155 guests. If the funicular reopens, word is that it will be used only for supply transport.)

Getting Here & Around

 The international airports nearest the Europa Sports Region are Salzburg, 80 km away, and Munich, 210 km away. Trains arrive at the main station on the southern edge of Zell, and the local OBB buses ply the region, well serving both towns and their cable car base stations. Buses are free to ski-pass holders. During the summer months, boats ferry between Zell am See and Seecamp, Bellevue, Thumersbach Kurpark, and Seecamp. For taxi service, ☎ 06542 727 22.

Most drivers will enter town on the B168 Salzach River road, an east-west thoroughfare running from Mettersill in the west toward the A10 autobahn in the east. The B311, which runs perpendicular to the B168, goes north from Zell am See toward Saalfelden and Salburg. Kaprun is up Kaprunerstrasse, south from the B168. Parking is tight in both towns during high seasons; drivers should plan on parking once and using the bus system to explore.

Mountain transportation runs throughout the year with a couple of short breaks for annual maintenance. For information on Zell's Schmittenhöhe area lifts and activities, go to www.schmitten.at; for info on Kaprun's Kitzsteinhorn area lifts and activities, see www.kitzsteinhorn.at.

LIFT PASS PRICE SAMPLES

Winter

1-day adult one-area pass €34.50

6-day adult all-area pass €164

Pedestrian round-trip Kitzsteinhorn €21

Summer

Pedestrian round-trip Kitzsteinhorn €21

Getting Connected

 The tourist office in Zell am See is on Brücker Bundesstrasse near the church. It's open 9 am-6 pm, Monday through Friday; 9 am-noon and 2-6 pm on Saturday. Contact ☎ 06542 77 00 for more information. The tourist office in Kaprun is along the main road at village center. Contact ☎ 06547 864 30, www.kaprun.net, for more information. The resorts share a website at www.europasportregion.at.

 Zell am See's post office is along Brücker Bundesstrasse at Postplatz, just north of the tourist office. Kaprun's post office is in the center at Salzburger Platz.

WWW For Internet access in Zell am See, try the **Stadtcafé Estl** next to the main train station. For Internet access in Kaprun, try the **Sports Bar** at Schlossstrasse 621 or the **Intersport Brundl** at Nikolaus Gassnerstrasse 213.

The Sights

The focus of the Europa Sports Region falls on athletic rather than artistic, sightseeing or academic pursuits. Nonetheless, Zell's lakeside promenade and historical center – now almost entirely car-free – are certainly worth a stroll. Of historical note are the 11th-century **parish church** – peek inside at the 13th- through 15th-century frescoes – and the nearby medieval **Vogtturm**, which now houses the town's museum. In Kaprun, a tour around the reservoirs, dams, and technological works of the local hydroelectric scheme proves more interesting than it first sounds; and the village's namesake **castle** opens occasionally for special events.

Three area museums merit attention. The **Vogtturm Heimatmuseum** in central Zell documents regional history in the intriguing space of the old tower at Kreuzgasse 2. It's open early June through mid-October, Monday through Friday from 2-6 pm (longer on bad-weather days). Kaprun's **local history museum** is on Parkstrasse and open for only an hour on Thursdays and Fridays from 5-6 pm, ☎ 06547 86 43. Finally, Zell's **Vötters Oldtimer Museum** collects cars and memorabilia from the '50s through the '70s – our apologies to those sprightly readers who well remember this era but don't yet consider themselves "old-timers." The museum opens Sunday through Friday from 11 am-6 pm.

Art hounds can visit the **Schloss Rosenberg** Gallery to view its rotating exhibition from regional and international artists; Brücker Bundesstrasse 2, ☎ 06542 726 65. It's open Tuesday through Friday, 4-6 pm. In addition, a year-round **sculpture garden** tops Schmittenhöhe

Mountain, pairing up the attractions of art and landscape in 27 wooden works.

The Adventures

On Foot

 A whopping 400 km of hiking routes wind through the Europa Sports Region. Walkers near Zell enjoy the short 30-minute stroll around the Schmittenhöhe summit, a trail accessible via the cable car; and the ridgeline two-hour Panorama Path connecting the top stations of the Schmittenhöhe and Sonnkögel lifts. (More ambitious pedestrians can start this route with a climb up from town.)

Even on rainy days, visitors can enjoy a **guided walk** on the Schmittenhöhe – raincoats and hot drinks are included. Rainy-day tours depart the car station at 11 am and 1 pm.

At Kaprun, guided 45-minute hikes to the glacier leave the Kitzsteinhorn summit terminal's terrace each summer day at 11:30 am and 1:30 pm. Favorite nearby hikes include treks around the Wasserfallboden and Mooserboden Alpine reservoirs; 1½-hour strolls to the Gletschersee along the circular route from Alpincenter; and adventures through the Sigmund Thun Klamm, a 350-m gorge navigated via a network of wooden steps – it's open from June through mid-September, 9 am-5 pm; www.kaprun.at/klamm.

 Each Monday evening from mid-July through late August, the Sigmund Thun Klamm opens from 8 to 10 pm for nighttime tours. Reserve transfer and entry at ☎ 06547 80 80.

Experienced **rock climbers** head for Kaprun and the Kitzsteinhorn. Two climbing regions are within a 20-minute walk from Alpencenter: the first, the Gletscherseeplatten, has 30 routes and is open from July through October; the second, the Rettenwand, lies across a snowfield and requires a ski traverse, but can also be used in winter when conditions allow. Contact the Bergführer Team for guiding services.

 The Europa Sports Region has a wide range of discounted and combination lift, boat, and tour packages. Before buying a full-price transportation or activity ticket, take a good look at the current money-saving deals. Ask at the tourist offices or boat and cableway ticket counters for more information.

On Horseback

For adventures on hoof, contact the **Porsche Reitanlagen** in Zell am See for **riding lessons**, Iceland **pony rides**, and **horse-drawn sleigh** outings; ☎ 06542 573 62.

In Water

The Zellersee is the focus of the region's water-based activities. The large lake – four km long and over a kilometer wide – is filled by snow run-off rather than by rivers and thus freezes quickly in winter and warms quickly in summer. From late April through October, swimmers enjoy **beaches** at six locations around the lakes, three of which have heated outdoor swimming pools.

Pedalboat and **rowboat rental** is at the **Stadtpark**, and **sailing lessons** are offered at **Wauggi Sailing** on the lakefront at Esplanade 4, ☎ 0664 336 48 50. **Windsurfers, sailboats,** and **catamarans** can be rented from the lakefront near the youth hostel at **Windsurfcenter Seidl Heinz**, Seestrasse 13, ☎ 06542 551 15, www.windsurfcenter.info.

Waterskiing, banana floats, and such, launch from the **Zeller Standbad** along the Esplande between May and October; ☎ 06542 726 50. Try **lake diving** with **Tauchsport Scholz Hugo** at Bahnhofstrasse 13 in Zell, ☎ 0642 726 06, or hop aboard the roundtrip **boat tours** departing the Zell's docks from April through October. **Ferries** are operated by **Schmittenhöhebahn AG**; contact ☎ 006542 78 90, www.schmitten.at for more information.

For year-round **indoor swimming**, both Zell and Kaprun have pool complexes – and both have several pools, children's areas, sauna facilities, and spa services. Zell's **Sport and Leisure Center** is at Steinergasse 3 and is open daily from 10 am-10 pm; ☎ 06542 785, www.freizeitzentrum.at. Kaprun's complex, **Optimum**, is near the center on Parkstrasse and is open daily, 11 am-10 pm; from 10 am in July and August; ☎ 06547 72 76, www.optimum.at.

Fishing is possible in the local area both on the Zellersee and in the Salzach River. Fishing licenses and permits – note the specified rod and bait qualifications – can be obtained at **Intersport Scholz** (see page 122) and at the **Stadtgemeinde** at Brücker Bundesstrasse 2, ☎ 06542 766 27. Local rivers, most notably the Taxanbach Gorge, also accommodate **rafting, kayaking, hydrospeeding,** and **canyoning**; check in with the **Adventure Service** or **Freaks on Tour** (see below). In addition, the specialist school **Kajak Center** offers watersports packages, including a Family Day Tour by **canoe**

for families with kids six years and older. Contact ☎ 06542 470 67, www.kajakcenter-zellamsee.at.

On Wheels

 The Europa Sports Region hosted the Mountain Biking World Championships in 2002, and **mountain biking** is the area's fasting growing sport. No fewer than 14 local shops offer mountain bike rental – for our recommendations, see the listings on page 122. Check in at the tourist office for a good map.

 Mountain biking enthusiasts should inquire at the tourist office regarding the region's outlying biking parks and facilities. The World Games of Mountain Biking in Saalbach, the Mountainbike World Championship runs near Kaprun, and the BikeWorld terrain park is at Leogang.

For kids, free **skate parks** with streetball and a good collection of obstacles open daily from April through September at Zell am See's Sportplatz and at Kaprun's Bauhof; and **steam train** rides depart each Sunday in summer for Krimmler Falls. For adults who think they're kids, the **Trike & Car Center** in Zell am See rents **three-wheeled hotrods**, or trikes. It's expensive – around €105 per day – but there's no better way to cruise the Alps, and these motorbikes only require a car-driver's license. The outlet also rents a variety of luxury and novelty vehicles, including late-model BMWs, road bikes, and Minis. Contact Frank Schumann at ☎ 0664 253 03 81, www.fot.at, for more information.

In the Air

 Fans of airborne sports flock here to ride the excellent thermals rising off the area's south-facing slopes. Want a ride? Several outfitters oblige, offering a good selection of **airplane, glider, parachuting, paragliding,** and **hang-gliding flights**. For airplane rides, glider flights, and parachuting, check in at the local airport at Kaprunerstrasse 7, ☎ 06542 560 41. Other airborne sports are best arranged through either **Adventure Service** or **Freaks on Tour** – both are listed below under *Sports Services*.

On Snow & Ice

 The Europa Sports Region's 57 lifts serve 130 km of groomed **ski trails** – almost 25% of which are assisted by snowmaking machines. Local pistes are graded 43% easy, 38% intermediate, and 19% difficult. More than half the lifts are drags/rope-tows. **Snowboarders** enjoy World-Cup-worthy facilities on the Kitzsteinhorn, and the resort kicks off the World Cup season each year with slalom, parallel slalom, and giant slalom races. A permanent halfpipe at Glocknerwiese on Schmittenhöhe entertains above Zell am See, and the Kitzsteinhorn FunArea draws freeriders to 2,900 m. A total of 10 ski schools vie for business.

SUMMER SNOW FUN

The **FunArea** on the Kitzsteinhorn opens its glacial ice to summertime visitors who have an off-season hankering for snow sports. Oddball equipment, such as snowbikes, snowscoots, zipfelbobs, and skifoxes, are up for rent, as are the more traditional skis, snowblades, and tubes. The **Intersport Kitzsteinhorn** does rentals right from the glacier plateau. The shop has snow-wear for rent as well. Check in at ☎ 06547 84 84, www.kitzsteinhorn.at, for more information.

Hit the ice from early July through early September starting at 10:30 am, glacier and weather conditions permitting.

Cross-country skiers head out on over 200 km of groomed trails, including a 10-km loop on the frozen Zellersee, a three-km glacial track at 2,900 m on the Kitzsteinhorn, and a lighted five-km trail near Kaprun. **Winter walkers** step along 50 km of cleared hiking trails. One route, the panoramic trail from Sonnkögel to Schmittenhöhe, traverses the ridgeline at 2,000 m altitude. Ice sports enthusiasts head for the ice stadium in Zell for **ice-skating, curling,** and **hockey** and to the natural rink on the Zellersee for ice-skating and such fun as **ice-surfing** and **ice-sailing**.

A lighted **tobogganing** run above Zell makes speedsters happy, and the cozy Alpine huts along the way please those wishing to take their time. Some evenings, the lights are left off, and sledders make the slide with torches in their hands; if you do decide to try it, don fire-retardant clothing and forgo the hairspray.

Austria

Sports Services, Outfitters & Guides

■ **Intersport** offers a network of 11 stores throughout the Europa Sports Region – both in town and on the mountain. In Kaprun, head for **Intersport Brundl**, a three-story sporting goods palace in the heart of town at Nikolaus Gassnerstrasse 213, ☎ 066547 83 88. Sports equipment sales and rental, clothing and footwear, internet access, and even an hourly multi-media show; it's all here year-round. In Zell am See, try **Intersport Schultz** in the pedestrian area, the *fussgangerzone*, ☎ 06542 776 06. Reserve rental equipment in advance at the Intersport's website, http://www.servicenetwork.at.

■ The **Bergführer Team** custom-tailors hiking, mountaineering, climbing, and ski outings for athletes of all abilities. Inquire at ☎ 0676 400 79 40, www.alpinsport.at.

■ **Freaks on Tour** runs a wide range of adventure outings, including rafting, canyoning, paragliding, mountain biking, and trekking. The same outfitter organizes the Fridolin children's programs and trike vehicle rentals. For more information, contact ☎ 0664 253 03 81 or www.fot.at.

■ **Adventure Service Outdoorsports** does rafting, mountainbiking tours, canyoning, and paragliding. Check in at the office on Steinergasse 9 next to the swimming complex in Zell, or call ☎ 0664 132 85 52, www.ZellamSee.at/adventure.

Where to Sleep

 The **Hotel Grand** ($$$$) remains Zell's old-world diva, occupying the tiny peninsula at the lakefront. The hotel has a small, lovely garden, a small indoor pool, and easy access to both the ferry docks and the lakeside promenade. Its only downfall: the town's busy train tracks run across its otherwise elegant front porch. Reserve at ☎ 06542 7880, www.grandhotel.cc.

HOTEL PRICE CHART	
Double room without tax; $$$-$$$$ always with bath.	
$	Under €80
$$	€81-150
$$$	€151-250
$$$$	Over €250

Those seeking a relaxing spa stay should consider the luxuries of the **Hotel Salzburgerhof** ($$$$). The hotel is in the town center, just 50 m from the lakeshore, and its exquisite spa includes a heated garden pool (also in winter), a steam grotto, and a natural pond. Ready to unwind? Reserve at ☎ 06542 765, www.salzburgerhof.at.

Families looking for a ski-in property within walking distance of town should consider the **Familienhotel Porschehof** ($$$), a four-star ski-in establishment that's next to a ski school and near the Areitbahn cable car; ☎ 06542 553 55, www.porschehof.com.

The nearby **Hotel Berner** ($$$) also offers a central, ski-in locale. Most of its pleasant rooms have balconies, and the outdoor pool is heated through winter. Inquire at ☎ 06542 779, www.bernerhotel.com.

In the center, the **Hotel Grüner Baum** ($$) rents rooms and apartments, has a central location less than 50 m from the lakefront, and – oddly – an in-house butcher shop; ☎ 06542 77 10, www.gruener-baum.at.

The cheery **Sporthotel Lebzelter** ($$) has central rooms and a cozy basement bar; ☎ 06542 776, www.hotel-lebzelter.at.

Up the hill from town on Schmittenstrasse, along the bus route to the cable cars and a reasonable one-km walk from the center, the **Gästhof Schmittental** ($) offers ski-in (but not out) accommodations on park-like grounds; ☎ 06542 723 32, www.schmittental.at.

Where to Eat

There are some 90 restaurants in the Europa Sports Region. Four km north of Zell, the **Schloss Prielau** ($$$) serves up expensive gourmet fare amid elegant décor – and boasts Austria's Chef of the Year. Reserve a table at ☎ 06542 726 09.

DINING PRICE CHART	
Average entrée, with tax.	
$	Under €10
$$	€10-25
$$$	Over €25

An entertaining summer evening out can also be had by hopping a ferry to the **Strandhotel Bellevue** ($$$) in Thumersbach. The restaurant there specializes in fresh fish dishes; reserve at ☎ 06542 731 04.

For reasonably priced traditional fare in Zell, try the old **Steinerwirt** ($$) on the Schlossplatz, the **Traubenstüberl** ($$) at Kruezgasse, or the **Metzgerwirt** ($$) on Sebastian Hörlgasse.

In Kaprun, the bucolic old **Dorfstadl**, ☎ 06547 7280 ($$), serves up traditional dishes amid farmhouse décor, and both the **Hilberger's Beisel**, ☎ 06547 7246 ($$), at Fazokastrasse and the **Schlemmerstube**, ☎ 06547 8342 ($$), at Schlossstrasse do good Austrian cuisine as well.

Budgeting visitors can try the **Imbiss** ($) and small restaurants that cluster around the Zell train station. A nice **Coop** ($) grocery store near Zell's old tower specializes in wine gourmet treats – the makings of a perfect Alpine picnic.

Where to Party

 More than 35 pubs, discos, and bars vie for attention in the Zell and Kaprun, so no one here should go thirsty. The **Crazy Daisy Restaurant, Bar & So On** beckons: "You're always welcome! Don't eat yellow snow." The bar is Zell's legendary place to party, especially during ski season, when an energetic young crowd fills the bar's narrow corridors. A beer garden accommodates summer crowds. See what's on at www.crazy-daisy.at; Brücker Bundesstrasse 10, ☎ 06542 763 59.

Wedged between the train tracks and a residential street is the **B17**, a tiny shack made of corrugated tin and decked out inside with heaps of military and aerospace memorabilia. Rowdier are the **Viva Disco**, and cozier is the **Lebzelter Keller** basement bar.

In Kaprun, both **Charly's** and the casual **Baum** and **Nindl** are more happening than the rest of the quiet village. The **Pinzgauer Diele** (on Kirchengasse) offers pizza snacks, a rustic ambiance, and late-night disco dancing.

Where to Play

 Children enjoy a good selection of activities, including cable car, boat, and steam train rides, beaches, and indoor pools. Favorite **playgrounds** in Zell are at Steinergasse near the sports center and on the lakefront at the Stadtpark; in Kaprun, at Imbachstrasse across from the Optimum sports center and, at the Kitzsteinhorn, the Alpine Children's funpark. Both tourist offices dole out **babysitters** at a standardized rate – €7.50 per hour plus tip, at last count.

FRIDOLIN CHILDREN'S PROGRAMS

Kids four to eight years old can join Freaks on Tour for their adventure programs, which run daily Monday through Friday, 9:30 am to approximately 3 pm. The changing schedule sometimes includes llama trekking, fishing, crossbow shooting, and skating days. Normal cost is €12 per child per day, but for those staying in Fridolin partner hotels, it's absolutely free. The program provides pick-up and drop-off service from Zell and Kaprun hotels. Check ☎ 0664 253 03 81, www.fot.at, for more information and a list of partner hotels.

Festivals & Events

Both the ski season and the Christmas season kick off in early December with the **Winterstart Snowfestival**, Europe's largest ski opening party. Around the same time, the Krampus, Santa's evil counterpart, is a scary dude that gives bad children what's coming to them. The **Krampus Festival** scares kids into behaving until Christmas with processions of multiple Krampuses (Krampi?), home visits, and lots of coal.

The **Christmas Blowing** takes place at 6 pm on December 24th, and New Year's Day brings the ski school's **Torch Run**. The **Night of the Balloons** takes flight at the end of January, and numerous smaller festivals and snow sport competitions round out the winter months.

The spring concert season starts in May, and July and August bring festivals of some sort almost every weekend. Favorites include the **Sheep Festival** in late July, the **farmer's market and tournament** in September, and **musicals** on a lakeside stage throughout the summer. Pyromaniacs join efforts in mid- to late June for the **Mountains Aflame** and **Lake Aflame** celebrations; one night after the other, these similar events differ only by the location of their fires.

Contact the Kaprun tourist office at ☎ 06547 864 30, www.kaprun.net, or the Zell tourist office at ☎ 06542 77 00, for more information on any of the above events.

Höhe Tauern National Park

Höhe Tauern

Central Europe's largest national park has as its centerpiece the 3,798-m Grossglockner, Austria's highest peak. The immense territory under the national park's watchful care appears positively primeval, with jutting bare mountains, murky glacial run-offs, plus acres and acres of ice. In fact, approximately one-tenth of the enormous park is covered year-round in ice, a glacier bed some 30 m deep – and thickening at a rate of approximately one millimeter per year.

Visitors to this high-altitude wonderland are treated to what many consider Europe's finest nature preserve,

Sheep in Hohe Tauern National Park

and it's hard to argue. A habitat for Alpine species such as ibex, marmots, and the rare white-bearded vulture, the park also protects diverse flora that rebound each spring in a riot of color. Herds of mountain cattle call the park their summer home, too, and Alpine farmers use traditional techniques just as they have in centuries past. Two park attractions merit particular attention: First, the **Grossglockner Hochalpenstrasse**, covered here; second, lovely **Krimmler Falls**, covered on page 128.

Although the Höhe Tauern National Park can be accessed via several roads – and via several hundred footpaths – the most popular route through the park remains the spectacular Grossglockner Hochalpenstrasse, or "Grossglockner High Alpine road" (otherwise labeled state road 107). The road runs south from Bruck and winds its way up past the lovely village of Fusch to the park entrance, where daytrippers pay an enormous fee for the privilege of driving in. (At last count, the fee was €26 per car per day; a fee as stunning as the landscape to which it opens access.)

Information in hand, visitors zigzag upwards in the shadow of the glowering mountain. Along the road are visitors' centers, museums, lookout points, cafés, and nature trails – all worthwhile. Everyone should visit the **Pasterze Glacier** and heartier folk should venture backcountry to one of the park's high Alpine huts. (Consult a ranger for trail and weather conditions.) Once outside of the park's border, the road continues south toward Lienz and Italy.

The Grossglockner Hochalpenstrasse is one of Austria's premier tourist destinations, and buses, bikes, and BMWs clog the road during August's high season. Your best bet? Go early. During high season, the gates open at 5 am. The next best thing? Park, get out, and walk – far, far from the madding crowds.

For more information, see www.nationalpark.at.

Krimml

Krimml is an extraordinarily lovely village and one of nature's most spectacular works. Visitors reach the tiny hamlet of Krimml through either the Salzach Valley (from Zell am See) or the Zillertal Valley and the Gerlos Pass (from Mayrhofen).

The village stacks up a pastoral foothill below the majestic peaks that rise all around. Terrace cafés and cozy *stüberl* beckon, and in summer flowers spill off balconies blessed with magnificent mountain, valley, and waterfall views. In addition to wintertime skiing, and in spite of direct access into the Höhe Tauern National Park, the primary focus in the village is the spectacular **Krimmler Falls**. At their finest on July afternoons, the roaring waterfalls dive a total of 380 m through three segments of forest-ensconced chutes. A steep, asphalt trail hairpins alongside, allowing spectators – and there are many of them – refreshingly misty vantage points from which to experience this natural wonder. The trail continues past all three stages of the falls, eventually petering out into a gravel road and then a narrow dirt path.

Guesthouses serve up drinks, snacks, and souvenirs at prime points along the trail, and taxis ply a small road nearby, offering tired pedestrians an expensive ride back to base. (Check the info placard near Parking Area 3 for time-and-distance trail estimations.) Again, I recommend making the hike early in order to beat high-season crowds. One further note: Near the entrance to the falls trail splashes the new **WasserWunderWelt**, an interesting exhibit that demonstrates the power of water through interactive (read, "wet") displays. Kids like it, and parents do, too. The park is open regularly in summer, 10 am-5 pm, and on Wednesdays only in winter. Contact ☎ 06564 201 13, www.wawuwe.at, for more info.

 Want to stay? I recommend staying the night – primarily to experience the charm of this valley without all the day-tourists. The most prestigious house in town is the **Ferienhotel Krimmlerfälle** ($$-$$$), ☎ 06564 72 03, www.krimmlerfaelle.at. But almost every house here offers rooms to rent, so newcomers need only look for the *zimmer frei* (room free) placards to find a vacation home.

 The tourist office is just below the church and next door to the post office. Contact ☎ 06564 723 90, www.krimml.at for more information.

France

Languages: French
Population: 59,765,983
Phone Country Code: +33
Currency: Euro

History

The original set-
tlements in
France were Celtic in
origin, peoples who
came to "Gaul" between 1500 and
500 BC. The Gauls prospered until Julius Caesar defeated and
captured their leader,

Vercingetorix, and absorbed the Gallic tribes and lands into the Roman Empire. By the third century, the Roman Empire was in decline
and, by the fourth century, Barbarians began invasions from the East.
(One such tribe, the Germanic Franks, gave the country its name.)
During this period, residents aligned themselves with local lords in exchange for protection, thereby giving birth to the feudal society that
would dominate France until the mid-700s.

In 732, Charles Martel defeated a Muslim advance from the south in
the city of Tours. Buoyed by this success, Charles established himself
as king and launched the Carolingian Dynasty. The dynasty's most
famous ruler was Martel's grandson, Charlemagne, who ruled France
for 30 years and greatly expanded the French empire. However, the
dynasty was short-lived. Unable to work out their differences, Charlemagne's three grandsons, Louis the German, Charles the Bald, and
Lothar, divided the French lands once again.

In 1066, William, the Duke of Normandy, invaded England and assumed the British crown. Shortly thereafter, the former wife of Louis
VII of France married Henry II of England and, as a result, much of
the western part of France ceded to England. When Charles IV of
France died, Edward III of England tried to claim the French throne,
a conflict that set in motion the 1337 Hundred Years War – which, in-
cidentally, lasted 116 years. With the help of a French peasant girl by
the name of Joan of Arc, Charles VIII defeated the English, driving
them all the way back to Calais.

Although under the rule of one king, France maintained what was in
effect a feudal rather than monarchal government. Then, in 1715, at
the ripe old age of five, Louis XIV ascended the throne. Louis eventually strengthened the crown, attacking the feudal aristocracy and, fi-

nally, created the first centralized French state. However, after the Seven Years War, and amid France's controversial support for the colonies during the American Revolution, the population grew ripe for its own revolution. The conflict kicked off with an uprising at the Bastille prison, and culminated with the execution of King Louis the XVI and his wife. Finally, in 1799, Napoleon Bonaparte entered Paris, assumed the title of First Counsel, and thereby brought an end to the French Revolution.

Napoleon's subsequent campaign failures led to his downfall, and later 19th-century rulers fared little better. In 1870, France suffered a defeat by the Prussians, losing the territories of Alsace and Lorraine. A year later, the Third Republic emerged in France, signaling the end – once and for all – of the French monarchy. During World War II, Charles de Gaulle entered Paris alongside the liberating Allies, assuming a position as the head of the Fourth French Republic.

Hannibal

Hannibal was a third-century warmonger who had a bone to pick with the ruling Roman Empire. His father had died while fighting against the Romans in Spain – an event that motivated him to plan carefully and long toward the objective of completely destroying Roman power. Hannibal believed the Romans' most vulnerable spot was actually in Northern Italy, given the loose confederation of states and the continual turmoil between Rome and the neighboring Gauls. Hannibal and his army left Spain in 218 BC, trekking north up the Mediterranean coast, fighting much of the way. After securing the help of the Gauls, Hannibal crossed over the Alps somewhere between the Little St. Bernard and Mont Genèvre passes – an unlikely party of some 60,000 men and 34 elephants.

With his superior numbers, strategic tactics, and a little help from the Gauls, Hannibal won several battles, causing the Romans to withdraw the bulk of their army into central Italy. The war continued for several years until the Romans, in a surprise move, attacked and captured Spanish Carthagena, cutting Hannibal's main supply route. Hannibal continued to fight for several more years but, in 204 BC, the Romans finally attacked Carthage itself. The Roman success in Carthage led to a peace treaty between Carthage and Rome, and Hannibal withdrew. Still suspicious, however, the Romans pursued their nemesis; in 183 BC, unable to escape, Hannibal committed suicide rather than surrender.

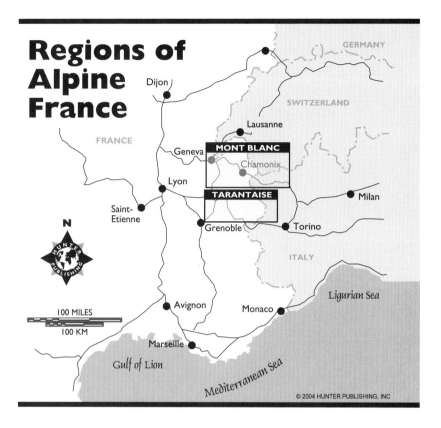

Regions of Alpine France

GERMANY

Dijon

SWITZERLAND

FRANCE

Lausanne

Geneva · **MONT BLANC** · Chamonix

Lyon

TARANTAISE

Milan

Saint-Etienne

Grenoble · Torino

ITALY

Ligurian Sea

N

100 MILES

100 KM

Avignon · Monaco

Marseille

Gulf of Lion

Mediterranean Sea

© 2004 HUNTER PUBLISHING, INC

France

Overview & Government

Today, the French Republic spans 549,183 square km, making it western Europe's largest state. The geography consists of flat plains and gently rolling hills in north and west, and mountainous terrain in the Pyrenees to the south and the Alps in the east. The Alps run the entire length of the eastern border, starting just north of the Mediterranean coast and extending up to the nation's border with Switzerland. The nation shares frontiers with Spain and Andorra to the south; Italy, Switzerland, and Monaco to the east; and Belgium, Luxembourg, and Germany to the north and northeast.

France is composed of 22 administrative regions, or states, and several dependent territories; its capital is Paris. The republic maintains a multi-party system of government, with a president presiding as chief of state and a prime minister operating as head of government. Although the country has long pursued an active policy of integrating immigrants, recent unemployment rates remain among the highest in Europe – and frustration has led to a backlash of anti-immigration sentiment. Youth crime rates have risen dramatically as well, and gang violence is now problematic in the urban low-income housing developments. Unemployment rates now sit at 8.8%.

People & Culture

The population of France is a mix of ethnicities, just as it has been for the past millennium – but some 91% share a Celtic or Latin origin. Approximately 76% of the population claims the Roman Catholic faith; 5% are Muslims; and just 2% say they are Protestants. Three-quarters of France's people live in urban areas, the largest of which are Paris, Marseille, Lyon, Toulouse, Nice, and Strasbourg. The population density is approximately 110 people per square kilometer.

National Holidays 2004

January 1	New Year's Day
	Good Friday
	Easter
	Easter Monday
May 1	Labor Day
May 8	Fête de la Victoire 1945
March/April	Easter
	Easter Monday
May 1	Labor Day
10 days before Whit Sunday	Ascension Day
7th Sunday after Easter	Whit Sunday
Day after Whit Sunday	Whit Monday
July 14	Bastille Day
August 15	Assumption Day & National Day
November 1	All Saints Day
November 11	Armistice Day
December 25	Christmas Day

 For more information, check the website for the French National Tourist Office at www.franceguide.com.

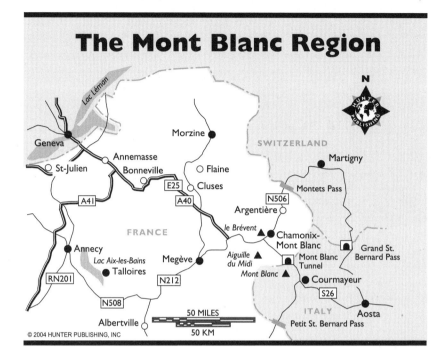

The Mont Blanc Region

Mont Blanc

Soaring to Europe's loftiest heights, the majestic Mont Blanc nestles in eastern France, anchoring the borders between France, the southwestern corner of Switzerland, and the northwestern corner of Italy. The mountain provides a focal point for adventurers in all three countries. In France, the cheerful old town of Chamonix sees a steady, year-round stream of sporting tourists who come to enjoy its legendary mountaineering challenges and skiing terrain. The resort of Courmayeur, Italy, lies at the opposite end of the Mont Blanc Tunnel, while Martigny and Verbier, Switzerland, lie just over the Col des Montes pass. The region's vast wealth of natural sights and cultural diversity make it an outstanding option for a quick, looping tour of the Alps.

■ Chamonix

Population: 10,109

Base elevation: 1,035 m

Mountain resort town

To those who love it, it's simply "Cham" – a bustling mountain town beckoning to international adventurers of all persuasions. Here in the shadow of Mont Blanc, Europe's highest mountain, a dozen villages scatter up the Arve River, majestic peaks line up in rank, and glaciers lick the valley floor. In times past, it was the birthplace of mountaineering and the site of the first Olympic Games; today, few names garner such reverence among in-the-know adventurers. Chamonix is where the big boys come to play.

History & Orientation

 Chamonix popped up on the map in 1786 when Dr. Michel Paccard and Jacques Balmat became the first men to ascend Mont Blanc. Although already known as a center for alpinism, the village quickly became Europe's mountaineering capital, a reputation it maintains to this day. The town's hearty population took to skiing early in the 19th century, and the snow-sporting competitions they staged here in 1924 are considered the first running of the Olympic Winter Games. Today, Chamonix remains an international melting pot; approximately half of its visitors each year come from foreign countries, and the town counts 40 nationalities among its permanent residents. The sporting tradition continues, and athletes across many mountaineering disciplines call Chamonix home.

Nestled in the shadow of the 4,810-m Mont Blanc, in the Upper Arve Valley near the Swiss and Italian frontiers, Chamonix ranks among the most scenic resorts in the Alps. The town sprawls along a rushing river and a long, north-south hollow wedged between the Massif des Aiguilles Rouges to the west and the Mont Blanc Massif to the east. The valley's main roads, the N506 and N205, parallel the Arve River, connecting a dozen far-flung neighborhoods.

The Town

Town center revolves around its lively car-free old town and the Place Blamat, a riverside square memorializing the men who first conquered Mont blanc. From here, the Rue du Paccard heads south, the Rue Joseph Vallot heads north, and a network of smaller alleys web along the Arve's western shore. The tourist office lies on the western edge of the center; the train station, across the river down Avenue Michel Croz. A ring road diverts traffic from the center, and all around, majestic mountain peaks soar.

Getting Here & Around

 Visitors arriving by air should fly into the international airport at Geneva, some 90 km northwest. Trains pull into the station on the center's eastern edge, and buses navigate through town and up-valley toward Argentière. Buses are free to ski-pass and guest-card holders. For taxi service, contact **Taxi Monard** at ☎ 0608 26 84 76, or **Taxi Rousseau** at ☎ 0607 67 88 85. Drivers will use two main roads, the N506 and N205. Past the neighborhoods of Argentière and Le Tour at the northern end of the valley, the N506 runs northeast over the Col de Montets and into Switzerland; past Les Houches at the southern end of the valley, the N205 turns west toward St. Gervais, hooking up with the A40 freeway to Geneva. The newly reopened Mont Blanc Tunnel burrows into Italy; the tunnel entrance lies just south of town. For more info, check www.tunnelmb.com.

Three cable cars climb from the center's outskirts: on the western side of town, two lifts climb to Le Brevent; on the eastern side, a cableway climbs to l'Aiguille du Midi and Mont blanc.

LIFT PASS PRICE SAMPLES
Winter
1-day adult Cham'ski pass €40
6-day adult Cham'ski pass €171
Pedestrian round-trip to l'Aiguille du Midi (& into Italy) €51.30
Pedestrian weekly lift pass €87

Getting Connected

The Chamonix Mont-Blanc Tourist Office on the western edge of the center at 85 Place du Triangle de l'Amitie. For more info, contact them at ☎ 0450 53 00 24, www.chamonix.com.

The post office is directly in the center on the eastern side of the Place Balmat.

The Sights

Visitors to Chamonix should simply enjoy a stroll through the pedestrian center, perhaps stopping by the **Alpine Museum** at 89 Avenue Michel Croz. The museum houses a good collection of mountaineering artifacts as well as exhibits on winter sports history and regional culture. It's open from from 2 to 3 pm in the summer and 3 to 7 in winter; ☎ 0450 55 25 93; €4. Other than that, Chamonix's sights are all at altitude.

*The **Carte d'Hôte Guest Card** brings discounts on admission to a number of public services, including the Alpine museum, swimming pool, ice rink, and cross-country track – in addition to free ski-bus transportation. Cards are issued at check-in without charge to visitors lodging in area hotels.*

Into the Mountains

Activities abound year-round in the mountains surrounding Chamonix. Footpaths, trains, and cableways lead back to adventures on glaciers, lakes, and mountain peaks – the options are overwhelming. Below I've rounded up a few favorite excursions by mountain transport.

- **L'Aiguille du Midi Cableway** – This is the classic tour of Mont Blanc. Cable cars depart the eastern edge of town for the breathtaking two-stage ride up to 3,842 m. From there, visitors can cross into Italy via the Helbronner cableway. On either side of the border, views are spectacular, visitors standing eye-to-spire below Mont Blanc's glacial peak.

- **Train du Montenvers** – First built in 1908, the rack railway chugs from Chamonix to Montenvers and the foot of the Mer de Glace, or "sea of ice." At the top, visitors enjoy views of the 14-km-long glacier, a crystal gallery exhibit, a museum of Alpine wildlife, and the Grotte de Glace, an ice grotto carved out from inside the glacier.

- **Le Brevent and La Flegère Cableways** – These two tours depart the western edge of town for the 2,525-m Brevent Peak and the 2,385-m Index Peak. Rising on the western side of town, the peaks each enjoy spectacular big-picture views across the valley to the Mont Blanc Massif. Both are favorite areas for hiking and climbing; Le Brevent is a favorite paragliding launch site; and La Flegere offers good views of the Mer de Glace.

- **The Grands Montets Cableway** – From the eastern edge of Argentière, a cable car climbs in two stages to 3,275 m at Les Grands Montets. The peak offers a 360-degree panorama of the French, Italian, and Swiss Alps. In winter, the screamingly steep run off backside lures expert skiers from all around the globe.

Above Méribel, France

Above: Val Thorens, France

Below: Méribel

Berchtesgaden National Park, Germany, with Bindalm peak

Neuschwanstein Castle, Füssen, Germany

Upon arriving alongside the area's glaciers, you may well feel envy for those roping up and venturing out onto the ice. Although glaciers can be traversed by any visitor of reasonable fitness, a knowledgeable guide and appropriate gear are absolutely necessary. See guide listing below, and arrange for one before you go.

The Adventures

On Foot

 Mountaineering is both Chamonix's legacy and its passion. **Climbers** head for the Mont blanc Massif and granite cliffs of Le Brevent and Les Aiguilles Rouges. In bad weather, climbers take to the **Richard Bozon Sports Center's** indoor climbing hall; ☎ 0450 53 23 70; entry €3.30, ages 14 and up. Chamonix offers 350 km of trails across a variety of terrain and altitudes – making it the most extensive **hiking** network in the Haute-Savoie region. One favorite walk starts at the mid-station of l'Aiguille du Midi cable car and heads approximately three hours across the Gran Balcon Nord to Montenvers, its mountain restaurant, and the Mer de Glace. To return, walkers can take the Montenvers train or walk another two hours down to town.

The Mont Blanc Ascent

The ascent of Mont Blanc is a difficult climb, not to be taken lightly. If climbing's your thing and you want to give it a shot, consult a qualified guiding service early in your planning stage (see *Sports Services*, page 140). The climb is an expensive outing – I last saw rates upwards of €1,500, and many outfitters require that you arrive early in order to acclimatize and undertake preliminary training. The tourist office can help, too; their booklet, *L'Ascension du Mont Blanc est Affaire d'Alpinisme,* can shed some light on local mountain protocol and safety. Not to discourage, but to inform, here are some facts:

■ Mont Blanc's high-mountain rescue squad assisted 151 climbing parties in 2001 – the figure grows 15-17% each year.

■ More than 30% of those attempting the ascent return injured – whether from frostbite, altitude illness, or more serious accidents.

■ Only 50% of those who attempt the climb with certified expert guidance achieve success; of those who attempt without, only 33% achieve success.

The normal route takes climbers from Chamonix to Les Houches, Bellvue, Nid d'Aigle, the Tete Rousse Refuge, and, finally, to the Aiguille du Gouter Refuge for the first night. The second day culminates with a summit ascent via Vallot; then, a descent via Vallot, Grands Mulets, and Plan de l'Aiguille, where the cable car returns exhausted wanderers to town. Accommodations are in a mountain hut with half-board; lunches are packed in. Barring poor weather conditions, the ascent can be attempted from mid-June through September.

In Water

Chamonix's focus is on mountain sports rather than water, but swimmers enjoy the pool, whirlpool, waterslide, sauna, and hammam (Turkish bath) facilities at the **Richard Bozon Sports Center** at 214 Avenue de la Plage. The center is open daily in season; ☎ 0450 53 23 70, www.sports.chamonix.com, entry €4.10.

On Wheels

Mountain bikers, like skiers, come to Chamonix for its varied terrain and extreme vertical drops. Several trails of varying difficulty line the valley floor, and steep runs descend from Planpraz near Le Brevent, from La Flegere, from Les Mottets, and above Argentière, from Lognan and Let Tour. The tourist office offers maps, and the excellent **Ecole de VTT** operates a rental and guiding service and can advise on trail conditions and closures. Check in at their hut just below the tourist office, open daily in summer 5-7 pm, or dial ☎ 0619 75 69 16.

In the Air

Paragliding is extremely popular here, and several outfitters arrange tandem flights. I like **Les Ailes du Mont Blanc** school, ☎ 0620 46 55 57. It's home to Sandie Cochepain, paragliding World Champion. For **balloon rides** out of Mégève, contact **Ballons du Mont Blanc**, ☎ 0450 21 03 07. **Chamonix Mont-Blanc Helicopters** offers rotor-propelled flights of varying lengths; ☎ 0450 54 13 82, www.helico.fr. And **Parachutisme** in Chambery extends its **parachuting** services to Chamonix guests; ☎ 0479 54 42 93.

On Snow & Ice

 Famed for its extensive off-piste and expert **skiing** and **snowboarding**, the Chamonix area offers over 150 km of marked runs (and many more off-piste routes), all served by some 50 lifts. Scattered across nine resort areas, the marked runs are graded 21% novice, 31% intermediate, 25% advanced, and 13% expert.

At the northern end of the valley, near Argentière, the Grand Montets area beckons to experts, who flock here for its famed vertical drops and snow-sure slopes. Below, Les Chosalets has good slopes for first-timers. Nearby, the hamlet of Le Tour enjoys a sunny position and mostly mild descents popular with intermediate-level skiers. Above the center of Chamonix, Le Brevent and La Flegère offer extensive slopes for skiers of all abilities, lots of sunshine, and spectacular views across the valley toward Mont blanc. Farther south at Les Bossons, Le Glacier du Mont-Blanc is a popular venue for nighttime skiing Wednesday through Saturday.

Le Vallee Blanche

For an up-close-and-personal view of glacial slopes, there's no better run than the Vallée Blanche, or white valley, ski route. Although technically an off-piste route, the run is one of the Alps' classic ski runs and it often attracts crowds. They come for the same reasons you should – spectacular mountain scenery, intimate glacier views, and a 24-km ski run of mostly intermediate difficulty.

 The slopes here are least crowded on weekday mornings – find a guide who'll head up the mountain early.

The route descends from 3,842 m at the top of the Aiguille du Midi cable car, from where there are stunning views of Mont Blanc. Adventurers navigate a steep, sporty ridgeline before stepping into their skis; then, the long run loops down across the Mer de Glace glacier, passing crevasses, icefalls, and forests along the way. The Montenvers mountain restaurant at 1,913 m offers hospitality and, if conditions are poor, a train ride back to Chamonix center. Every mountain guide in town knows the Vallée Blanche well; lest you fall of a cliff or into a glacial crevasse, don't venture onto the ice without one.

AUTHOR'S PICK

Chamonix is one of the few resorts offering visitors an opportunity to sample **dog-sledding**. **Huskydalen** offers an array of full- and half-day outings, including a popular "trapper evening"; ☎ 0450 47 77 24. **Cross-country skiers** enjoy 21 km of loipe, and **winter walkers** head out on 17 km of footpaths; the tourist office offers loipe and walking maps. The **Compagnie des Guides** arranges **snowshoeing** excursions, and **ice-skaters** hit the ice at indoor and outdoor rinks at the **Richard Bozon Sports Center**; ☎ 0450 53 12 36, €4.10 skate rental available.

Sports Services, Outfitters & Guides

16 guiding organizations and a whole mess of related tourism operators take advantage of Chamonix's booming mountaineering market. As the resort is a long-time favorite among British visitors, English is widely spoken. I list some of the best services below.

■ Of the multi-sport outfitters in town, I like **Evolution 2**. The organization runs introductory alpinism courses, Mont Blanc excursions, mountain-bike outings, kids' programs, and rafting, hydrospeed, canyoning, and canoeing trips. In winter, the ski school and guiding program here are excellent, and dogsledding, helicopter flights, and snowshoeing are offered. For more info, contact ☎ 0450 55 90 22, www.evolution2.com.

■ With a similarly diverse array of services, the local chapter of the traditional **Compagnie des Guides** operates **Cham'Adventure**, a daily program of hiking, biking, paragliding, canyoning, hydrospeed, and rafting; ☎ 0450 53 55 70. In the winter and summer, the company arranges private guides; ☎ 0450 53 00 88, www.cieguides-chamonix.com.

■ The **High Mountain Office**, or OHM, is a free public service that documents all mountain activities available in the region and posts up-to-date information on mountain conditions. Check in with the OHM office at www.ohm-chamonix.com. The **Maison de la Montagne**, or Mountain Information Center, near the tourist office, posts weather and condition information as well. Know before you go.

Where to Sleep

Nearer the center, the rustic old **Hameau Albert 1er** ($$$$) has a gourmet restaurant, cozy rooms, and a new indoor-outdoor swimming pool; ☎ 0450 53 05 09, www.hameaualbert.fr. Directly in the center, try the grand old **Hotel Mont Blanc** ($$$$), a throwback from yesteryear that peers down on the pedestrian zone from the Allée du Majestic; ☎ 0450 53 05 64.

HOTEL PRICE CHART	
Double room without tax; $$$-$$$$ always with bath.	
$	Under €80
$$	€81-150
$$$	€151-250
$$$$	Over €250

I liked the large **Park Hotel Suisse** ($$$) for its cozy décor, open fireplace, and view-blessed rooftop deck; ☎ 0450 53 07 58, www.chamonix-park-hotel.com.

The **Hotel Vallée Blanche** ($$-$$$) has long been a favorite for its central location on the river; ☎ 0450 53 04 50, www.vallee-blanche.com. Nearby, the **Gourmets & Italy** ($$) shares a similar position on the river but adds cheery color-coordinated prints and a good restaurant downstairs; ☎ 0450 50 53 01 38, www.hotelgourmets-chamonix.com.

Smack in the center of town, near the tourist office, the old **Faucigny** ($-$$) has homey accommodations and a pleasant staff, ☎ 0450 53 01 17, www.hotelfaucigny-chamonix.com. (Before you book here, however, inquire as to the state of the construction site next door. During my last visit the daytime noise was considerable.)

A central two-star on the river, **L'Arve** ($$) has fresh rooms a short crawl from bar row; ☎ 0450 53 02 31.

For an atmospheric stay outside the center, consider a room ($$) or dorm mattress ($) at the Gîte Réfuge du Montenvers. It's at the foot of the Mer de Glace glacier, and at the end of the Montenvers train line. A popular tourist outing during the day, the lodge takes on a cozier ambiance at night; ☎ 0450 53 87 70.

Where to Eat

Le 3842 ($$$) restaurant is the highest gourmet house in Europe. It's at the top of the Aiguille du Midi cable car and, as you might guess, enjoys spectacular views. Reserve at ☎ 0450 55 82 23.

France

The gourmet room at the **Albert 1er** ($$$) serves exquisite, expensive fare as well; ☎ 0450 53 05 09. And **The National** ($$$) offers an elegant riverside dining room and traditional cuisine in the pedestrian zone at 3 Rue Paccard; ☎ 0450 53 02 23.

The **Maison Carrier** ($$) at 44 Route du Bouchet features regional dishes with an excellence similar to that of sibling Albert 1er but charges lower rates; ☎ 0450 53 00 03. And **Le Monchu** ($$) proves popular for its heated outdoor terrace – in addition, of course, to its grills, raclette, and fondue. It's in the center next to the casino, 1 Rue du Lyret, ☎ 0450 53 04 80.

DINING PRICE CHART	
Average entrée, with tax.	
$	Under €10
$$	€10-25
$$$	Over €25

*The winter-only **Cham'Gourmand** lift pass is a great deal for non-skiers who'd like to lunch at a mountain lodge. The €26 round-trip lift ticket also includes €26 worth of food at any participating restaurant. Check with the ticket office at the base of any area lift for more information.*

L'M ($$), in the pedestrian zone on Rue Vallot, serves up delicious Savoyarde specialties on a torch-lit, terraced balcony; ☎ 0450 53 58 30. Also in the center, **Chez Nous** ($$) serves excellent fondues in a rustic dining room near the river; ☎ 0450 53 91 29. With great fondues as well, but up the valley in Argentière, **Le Carnotzet** ($$) proves itself worth the drive; ☎ 0450 54 19 43. For pizza, head for the **Casa Valerio** ($$).

The **Café La Terrasse** ($) boasts a riverside locale in the center and a charming Art Nouveau façade. Its side windows open to the sound of water, and it's open until 1 am.

La Poya ($), in the center at Rue du Lyret, serves up a long list of tasty crêpes until 11:30 pm. **Midnight Express** ($) has inexpensive grub – sandwiches, hot dogs, crêpes, fries, and such – and stays open till 2 am. It's in the center at Rue Docteur Paccard.

For groceries, head to the **Petit Casino** at 50 Rue Paccard or, for more elegant picnic fare, try **Le Terroir** on Rue Vallot for deli items, rotisserie chicken, and wine. Across the street, **L'Alpage des Aiguilles** stocks a good choice of cheese and salami.

Where to Party

 Evenings in Chamonix revolve around a collection of low-key bars, four discos, and one casino. Afternoon après-ski and teatime is busy in Chamonix's center. Those looking for an early party should simply visit the pedestrian zone; later, for nightclub action, head down the Rue Vallot and its tiny sidestreet, the Rue des Moulins. For a casual drink try **The Pub**, **Wild Wallaby's**, or **Queen Vic's**, a sports bar and pool hall with a popular happy hour. Nearby, the **Bar'd Up** is a good dive for pool and beer. Later, for music and dancing, head for the ever-thumping **Dick's Tea Bar** and **Choucas**, the popular après-ski hangout and late-night disco at 206 Rue Paccard. For a quiet, candlelit drink, try **Le Bourrique** next to Dick's Tea Bar. The dressier **Casino Chamonix** at Place de Saussure spins roulette, slots, black jack, and poker. It's open every day from noon to 3 am; ☎ 0450 53 07 65; free entry.

Where to Play

 Chamonix is a resort crafted for Alpine extremists, and few families make this their vacation choice. That said, the standard children's activities, ski schools, and such are all in place. Kids enjoy the **mini-club activities** operating out of the Richard Bozon Sports Center in July and August, the **outdoor adventures** arranged by Cham'Adventure and Evolution 2 (see *Sports Services*, page 140), **miniature golf**, and the **video arcade** at 30 Rue des Moulins. In summer, there is a **skate park** near the cross-country ski building, a **trampoline** at Place du Mont Blanc, and **playgrounds** at the Mer de Glace, Les Planards, and Argentière.

Festivals & Events

 Like most of this athletic town's activity, Chamonix's festivals and events center on sporting pursuits. The winter kicks off with a **New Year's** celebration, and then the races begin – the biannual **Kandahar** race, the annual **FIS World Cup** events, and a wide range of cross-country, motor racing, and free-ride competitions. Spring brings **Carnaval** and, in early March, the annual end-of-season **Cham' Jam** on-and-off-slope party.

Summer ushers in a whole new schedule of warm-weather sporting competitions, including the **Mont Blanc Marathon** in June. **National Day** is celebrated with fireworks and music in mid-July, and the **Mineral Exchange** exhibition sets up in early August.

AUTHOR'S PICK Each August 15th, Chamonix celebrates the **Fête des Guides**. The festival honors the region's hearty mountain guides with parties, light shows, street fairs, and finally, on Sunday, an outdoor mass that culminates with the blessing of the guides' ice picks and ropes.

For information on any of the above, contact the Tourist Board at ☎ 0450 53 00 24, www.chamonix.com.

La Route des Grandes Alpes

Those traveling from Chamonix to Geneva – or vice versa – should consider skipping the freeway and instead making the more scenic drive along the northernmost leg of the Route des Grandes Alpes, or Grand Alps Route. In its entirety, the route runs the length of the French Alps – a total of some 700 km from Lake Geneva, or Lac Leman, in the north, to Nice on the Mediterranean Riviera in the south. Along the way, drivers pass through three national parks, two regional parks, and a number of smaller reserves. The road scales many high-altitude passes, necessitating the closure of much of the road from October through May.

Argentière

The village of Argentière is an oft-overlooked satellite of Chamonix, which lies eight km southwest. However, I find Argentière in some ways a better base than its more famous neighbor: Argentière is smaller and preserves a more traditional ambiance; it's less expensive, both for food and for lodging; and Argentière is nearer to Les Grands Montets, the legendary mountain experts come here to ski.

The village is based at the confluence of the Arve and Arveyron d'Argentière waterways amid the same spectacular mountain scenery that blesses Chamonix. Lifts rise from its southeastern edge. Summertime guests enjoy hiking, biking, and climbing, while wintertime visitors ski on the Chamonix region's 150 km of groomed slopes. Cross-country skiers find some 16 km of marked trails; inexpensive *ski de fond* passes can be purchased at the tourist office. Shops, restaurants, and cafés line the main road, and small hotels and pensions duck off to the sides. Overall, it's a lovely little village, a quiet alternative for those looking to dodge Chamonix's bustling big-town scene.

*The **Argentière Guest Card**, issued by hotels at check-in, allows free unlimited travel on the Chamonix Bus shuttle, making day-trips down-valley an easy option.*

Want to stay? **Les Grands Montets** ($$$) has a lovely wood-paneled, fireside lounge. Although a short walk to town, the hotel is off the main road and is the closest lodging here to the lifts. Reserve at ☎ 0450 54 06 66, www.hotel-grands-montets.com.

The tourist office is near the river at 24 Route du Village. Like the rest of the village, it's open from June through September and from December through early May. For more information, call ☎ 0450 54 02 14.

Le Col des Montets

Heading north from the village, drivers can make their way around Mount Blanc, entering Switzerland via Vallorcine after about 16 km. It's a lovely drive through the pass, Le Col des Montets, with spectacular terrain, emptying out along the steep hillside vineyard near Martigny, Switzerland. The road frequently closes in winter due to heavy snowfall, so wintertime drivers should have an alternate plan.

The Tarantaise

High in the Savoie region of the French Alps, sharing a jagged border with Italy, the Tarantaise first drew the world's eye when it hosted the 1992 Olympic Winter Games. The small city of Albertville heads the Tarantaise Valley, which stretches back along the Isère River. Side valleys veer off into two enormous mountain recreation regions – the Trois Vallées and the Espace Killy. As you might guess, the Trois Vallées region spans a trio of Alpine valleys, incorporating several resorts, including the very British Méribel, the very posh Courchevel, and the very athletic Val Thorens. Together, the resorts boast the world's largest lift-linked Alpine recreation region. Farther east along the Tarantaise, south from Bourg St. Maurice, the Espace Killy links the lovely old village of Val d'Isère with another enormous hiking, biking, and skiing region – this one backing to the pristine terrain of the Vanoise National Park.

France

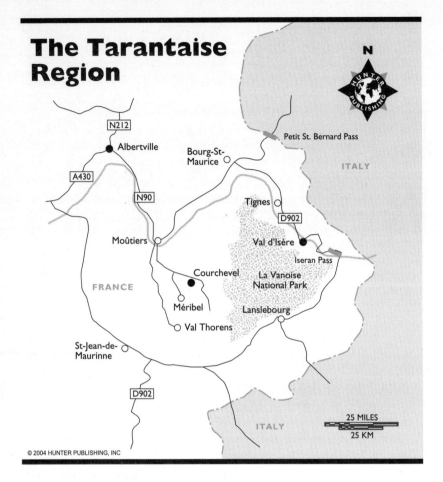

The Tarantaise Region

N

Petit St. Bernard Pass

ITALY

N212

Albertville

Bourg-St-Maurice

A430

N90

Tignes

D902

Moûtiers

Val d'Isère

Iseran Pass

Courchevel

La Vanoise
National Park

FRANCE

Méribel

Lanslebourg

Val Thorens

St-Jean-de-Maurinne

D902

ITALY

25 MILES
25 KM

© 2004 HUNTER PUBLISHING, INC

■ Méribel

Base elevation: 1,431 m

Mountain resort village

Méribel beats strong at the heart of Europe's largest interconnected ski region. A resort first developed and still loved by fun-seeking Englishmen, Méribel retains a distinctly British feel. Its kid-friendly ambiance makes it a favorite with families, and its young-and-lively après-ski scene thumps through the night. Finally, I applaud Méribel's harmonious development scheme; unlike most purpose-built French resorts, the village retains local architectural traditions, employing plenty of wood, stone, and slate.

History & Overview

First settled by Alpine farmers sometime before 428 AD, the sunny Allues Valley first caught the eye of British ski pioneer Sir Arnold

Lunn in 1925. After considerable delay due to the events of World War II, Scottish Colonel Peter Lindsay, took on the development challenge. Early on, farsighted planners initiated an architectural charter mandating the use of the traditional styles and regional building materials. The result, as I see today, is a continually developing yet harmonious village façade.

Set against the border of the Tueda Lake nature preserve, the Méribel and its Les Allues Valley enjoy a prime position at the center of the Trois Vallées region. Courchevel lies one valley east, and Val Thorens lies one valley west; all three are linked by lifts, hiking trails, and ski runs.

Above Méribel

Modern Méribel incorporates 14 small villages all along the Allues Valley, starting with Les Allues down-valley at 1,100 m and heading up the winding riverside road as far as Méribel Mottaret at 1,700 m. The center of today's tourism action is the sprawling hillside village known simply as Méribel.

The Town

The central area of Méribel zigzags up the eastern side of the Les Allues Valley. Lodging is in cheery-named hamlets along the main road, each chalet-style block competing for sun and views. This winding road takes quite an incline, gaining 300 m of altitude before leaving town – a steep walk for those staying in the upper hamlets. The landing strip of Altiport nestles at 1,700 m in the forest above. Most of the village's shopping, dining, and sporting action unfolds in the center along the valley floor. The tourist office complex at the top of Route de la Montée serves as a central axis, and the Parc Olympique, or Olympic Park, anchors the southern end of the strip. To the north, the Hamlet of Mussillon leads down-valley toward Les Allues, and uphill, the hamlet of Rond Point tops off town to the east. Most of the mountain lifts and ski slopes line Méribel's southern, up-valley edge.

Getting Here & Around

Visitors arriving by air should fly into the international airport at Geneva, some 135 km away. Drivers arrive via the A43 Autoroute through Albert, then along the N90 to Moutiers and the D90 up to Les Allues Valley. The village center's figure-eight one-way traffic scheme disorients new arrivals –

park early in the lower lot or garage and go by foot. Travelers arriving by train can get as far as Moutiers, at which point transfer to the regional bus system is required. Local buses ply between Méribel's 14 villages, and free shuttles climb between the hamlets along the main road to Altiport.

LIFT PASS PRICE SAMPLES

Winter

1-day adult Méribel-only pass	€33
1-day adult Trois Vallées pass.	€171
6-day adult Trois Vallées	€193

Summer

1-day pedestrian pass.	€12.50
6-day pedestrian pass	€39

Getting Connected

 The Office du Tourisme is on the village's central square. For more info, contact ☎ 0479 08 60 01, www.meribel.net. For additional information and English-language news, tune a radio to 97.9 FM or 98.9 FM.

 The post office is next door to the tourist office.

 For Internet access, head downstairs at **La Tarverne Bar**. It's in the center, caddy-corner from the tourist office.

The Sights

 Méribel is in general short on tourist sights. Worth a trip, however, is the down-valley village of Les Allues. The lovely Baroque church of **Saint Martin des Allues** has an altarpiece sculpted by Master Jacques Todesco; a museum near town hall documents the valley's history; and ancient communal ovens dot the village, firing up each summer for the **Fanfoue Festival**. Fans of Baroque architecture will want to see the area's many chapels, and museum hounds can check out the small display of natural history at the **Tueda Nature Reserve House**, ☎ 0479 01 04 75. Apart from these minor attractions, however, Méribel sets its sights on sport.

The Adventures

On Foot

Hikers take to 20 marked itineraries winding throughout the valley. Particularly lovely is the forested terrain around Lake Tueda in the **Tueda Natural Reserve** just outside town. Here, rare Cembro pines flourish, and an Alpine botanical trail parades by 80 species of indigenous flora. Additionally, scenic trails along the Saulire and Mont Vallon afford panoramic views of the surrounding Alps.

*The **Meripass Card** offers free summertime access to all lifts in the Trois Vallées region. Also included, entry to the Parc Olympique swimming complex and ice rink. Six-day cards sell for €52 each or €165 per family. Contact the tourist office for more info.*

A variety of **mountaineering** excursions are led by the Méribel Guides, including rock climbing, canyoning, high mountain treks, and hikes (see *Sports Services*, page 151). **Climbers** practice at the Parc Olympique sports center, scale the **Dent de Burgin** with a guide, and play at the **Parc Aventure**, a forest **ropes course** at Bois d'Arbin. The park operates four courses of increasing difficulty. Other oddball activities spring up, too, including **grass skiing** in Méribel-Mottaret. Inquire at the tourist office to see what's on.

On Horseback

For adventures on hoof, the **Riding Club Bois d'Arbin** offers equestrian lessons and rides; ☎ 0479 64 13 50.

In Water

Swimmers enjoy the 25-m pool at the **Parc Olympique** in the middle of town. The center also maintains a children's pool, a whirlpool, and sauna facilities. Call for current hours, ☎ 0479 00 58 21. Rafters take to the Bozel Doron and Isère rivers each day in summer; check with **AN Rafting** at ☎ 0479 09 72 79, www.an-rafting.com. Fishing in mountain lakes and streams is an option for guests with permits. Head for Lake Tueda each Wednesday and Thursday and on weekends; buy your license at the tourist office.

On Wheels

Mountain biking is popular here in the summer, and the French Cycling Federation endorses Méribel as a mountain-biking site. The tourist office has route maps, and all summer gondolas allow mountain bikes on board. For rentals, service, instruction, and guiding, contact **Meribike** at ☎ 0479 08 66 53, or check in at the **Sport Boutique**.

Lionel Laurent offers accompanied tours by **motorbike** and **quads**. All equipment is provided, and anything from two-hour to daylong outings are possible; ☎ 0479 08 50 31.

In the Air

Méribel boasts its own **airport**, a grass/snow landing strip at Altiport. For **scenic flights**, contact **SARL Méribel Air** at ☎ 0479 08 61 33. Flight rates start at €35 per person. Five outfitters offer **tandem paragliding** rides; try **La Saulire Tandem Top** at ☎ 0479 00 45 67. One- to two-hour **balloon flights** are available by **Ski Vol** at ☎ 0479 08 41 72.

On Snow & Ice

Méribel sits at the heart of the Trois Vallées, a legendary **skiing** region claiming the world's largest interconnected ski network – a system of over 600 km of runs and 197 lifts. Méribel itself has 150 km of those runs, and the remaining 450 km are accessible on skis via mountain lifts to Val Thorens in the west and Courchevel in the east. **Snowboarders** head for the funparks, pipes, and boardercross runs at the **Snowpark des Plattières** and **Le Moon Park de L'Arpsson**. Additional freestyle facilities are at Val Thorens.

SORTING OUT THE SKI SCHOOLS

Six ski schools compete for students of the snow sport disciplines. While the **French Ski School**, or ESF, has by far the largest presence in Méribel, I prefer the service of two smaller schools. The **New Generation** school has earned rave reviews for its small groups and expensive but excellent English-language instruction; ☎ 0479 01 03 18, www.skinewgen.com. And **Magic in Motion** enjoys a loyal following for its children's programs; ☎ 0479 08 53 36, www.magicinmotion.co.uk. Both are British-run operations specializing in English-language instruction.

Ice sports play on the Olympic ice at the Parc Olympique in the center. It's open most afternoons and until late on Tuesdays and Thursdays. For a new kick on ice, head for the **ice-karting** sessions that take place here most Monday evenings around 9 pm. **Winter walkers** can enjoy 20 km of maintained paths; the tourist office has maps, and the ski schools offer guided outings. **Snowshoers** plod up to Altiport and along the valley towards Mottaret. **Snowmobile excursions** head out each evening from Mottaret; ☎ 0479 00 33 50, www.snow-biker.com. And **dog-sledders** swish through the forest near Altiport – contact the tourist office to make arrangements. **Cross-country skiers** head for the small loop at Altiport or the trails around Lake Tueda.

*Ski-pass holders are invited to tag along on **snow-cat rides** as operators groom the slopes each Wednesday evening. For information, current prices, and reservations, contact the tourist office.*

Sports Services, Outfitters & Guides

- The **Guides de Méribel**, or the Méribel Guides, offer an all-season program of outings, including high-mountain tours, canyoning, rock climbing, and hiking in summer and heliskiing, off-piste outings, and icefall excursions. Contact the guides at their office in the Parc Olympique, ☎ 0479 00 30 38.

- For equipment rentals, our favorite outfitter is **Freeride.fr**. The small shop is a test center for Salomon and K2 skis, offering try-before-you-buy policies on a wide range of equipment. The boot-fitting center custom-fits your feet, and renters can reserve their preferred gear in advance at the shop's website. Visit the shop at the Tremplin center; ☎ 0479 00 52 21, www.freeride.fr.

- One-stop sport shopping can be had at the **Sport Boutique**, which opened in 1947 as Méribel's first ski shop and recently underwent expansion. All manner of ski and resort wear pack three floors. Stop in at the tourist office square; ☎ 0479 08 63 00.

France

Where to Sleep

Most of Méribel's accommodations are apartments let out on a weeklong, Saturday-to-Saturday basis; rates vary considerably, with high-season periods striking during the Christmas season, at Easter, and during the February French school vacations. The following hotels take nightly guests; seasonal closing periods vary.

HOTEL PRICE CHART	
Double room without tax; $$$-$$$$ always with bath.	
$	Under €80
$$	€81-150
$$$	€151-250
$$$$	Over €250

Le Grand Coeur ($$$-$$$$) is a Relais & Châteaux property with a warm interior and a great in-house restaurant. It's just above center and near the slopes; ☎ 0479 08 60 03, www.legrandcoeur.com.

L'Alba ($$$) has an exquisite, residential-style interior and an excellent location on the slopes at Rond Point; ☎ 0479 08 55 55, www.hotel-alba.com.

Also a good mid-range choice, **La Chaudanne** ($$-$$$) offers three-star facilities in the village center, next to the lift base and across from the sports center. The hotel also has 10 apartments. For more information, contact ☎ 0479 08 89 02, www.chaudanne.com.

In winter, **Les Grangettes** ($$) has well-worn rooms at the central lift base. The Cactus Café is downstairs; ☎ 0479 08 61 86, www.inghams.co.uk. **Doron Hotel** ($) has a town-center locale and simple rooms. Two of the town's most popular bars, Le Pub and Scott's, are just below. Reserve at ☎ 0479 08 60 02.

For other budget accommodations, try **L'Hotel du Moulin** ($) in Mussillon, ☎ 0479 00 52 23; or **Le Roc** ($-$$) up the main road from town, ☎ 0479 08 64 16. Both are simple, chalet-style accommodations.

Where to Eat

For Savoyard specialties, our favorite in-town stop is **La Kouisena** ($$-$$$), a rustic restaurant built in the modern complex across from the sports center. The interior is all charm, with rough-hewn wood and an open grill, and the wide terrace outside

DINING PRICE CHART	
Average entrée, with tax.	
$	Under €10
$$	€10-25
$$$	Over €25

has nice views and lots of sun. If you're with friends, this makes a good place to try a *café de l'Amitie*, a traditional after-dinner drink served in a *grole*, a carved multi-spouted bowl, traditionally shared by several friends; ☎ 0479 08 89 23.

La Taverne ($-$$) serves a wide range of food, from coffee and snacks with TV upstairs to traditional Savoyard specialties in the restaurant below. If you like cheese, this is a good place to sample raclette; ☎ 0479 00 32 45.

In the center across from the sports center, try **Le Tremplin** ($$) for brasserie-style pizzas, sandwiches, and excellent salads. The service gets bogged down around lunch, but the sunken dining terrace isn't a bad place to wait; ☎ 0479 00 37 95.

Slopeside at the top of town, try the **Rond Point** ($$) for lunch. The likable staff serves up a delish Cajun chicken salad. On sunny days, the deck is the best vantage point in town for watching the skiers whiz by; ☎ 0479 00 37 51.

For inexpensive grub, the **Cactus Café** ($) has a cheery interior, multiple TVs, two Internet stations, a big, snow-side terrace, and a young clientele. The food tends toward Tex-Mex.

Across the snow at the sports center, give **Le Méribel Eau** *($) a miss; the service is as biting as the sling-back sun-chairs are enticing.*

Le Gourmandine ($) makes the town's best sandwiches and, nearby, the **Grand Marnier crêpes stand** ($) does a rip-roaring business every afternoon with its selection of French pancakes. (Don't be shy – the big bottle is on the counter so you can douse as you see fit.) For self-caterers, the biggest **grocery store** is across from Dick's Tea Bar in Mussillon.

Where to Party

The party starts early, at least in winter, with après-ski action at the most excellent **Rond Point**, a mid-mountain bar and restaurant with an upbeat British staff, a big, sunny terrace, and live music six days a week. (For a quick warm-up, don't miss the toffee vodka.) The rowdy Doron Hotel pub, known simply as **Le Pub**, slates frequent live bands and event nights just off the tourist office square. Next door, and a bit more mellow, **Scott's Bar** has sofas and snacks. The other hot house in town is **Dick's Tea Bar**, a legendary late-night dance club with DJs nightly and live music on Sundays. Check www.dicksteabar.com to see what's on.

Newly expanded and boasting a big burger, **Jack's Bar** – in competition with Dick's – advertises "Not A Bar, Not a Tavern, Not for Dicks." It's got a sunny terrace, pool tables, and sports on TV. When you tire of clubs named for British boys – or if you're simply seeking a dressier nightlife – head for the disco **Le Loft**.

Where to Play

 Families enjoy Méribel for its **children's programs** – and for the large selection of self-catering apartment lodging here. In the winter, **Les Saturnins daycare** center in the Olympic Park takes babies from 18 months to three years old, a nursery service not found in many Alpine resorts. **Les P'tits Loups Kindergarten** entertains children three to five years of age at three different locales; each has a snow playground with enormous inflatable characters. **Ski schools** teach kids three and up and, additionally, invite kids along on nocturnal show-shoeing excursions in the woods. Six organized **kid's clubs** entertain during the summer with playground, outings, and sports.

Festivals & Events

 Méribel's festivals are few and far between. The village does host several **sporting events**, however, including ice-skating, ski racing, dogsledding, mountain-biking, and horse-jumping events. In early April, Méribel and the other resorts of the Trois Vallées prolong the springtime season with **Musique en Altitude**, a week of varied themed concerts. The valley's most popular folklore festival takes place in August down-valley at Les Allues, where a collection of ancient communal ovens is fired up for the **Fanfoue Festival**.

Albertville

If you're headed north toward Chamonix or Geneva, I recommend a quick stop in Albertville, host city of the 1992 Olympic Winter Games. The town center is an attractive pedestrian shopping zone, and the **Maison des Jeux Olympiques d'Hiver**, or Olympic Winter Games Visitors' Center, will please those interested in sport history. It's at 11 Rue Pargoud, ☎ 0479 37 75 71. On the hill to the east of town is the town's finest attraction, the medieval hamlet of **Conflans**, now a pleasant mix of cafés, museums, and shops.

Courchevel 1850

Courchevel 1850 draws the swankiest of French crowds. Its neighborhoods climb up the easternmost valley of the Three Valleys region at four altitudes: Courchevel 1850, the highest neighborhood here in terms of altitude, price, and reputation; Courchevel 1650; Courchevel 1550; and, finally, La Praz, the valley's original farming village. Resort services descend in price as the hamlets descend in altitude. All hamlets are connected via lift, trails, and ski runs – both to each other and to the rest of the Three Valleys region – but in winter, poor snow cover can close lower-altitude runs.

Courchevel 1850 is what most folks mean when they refer simply to "Courchevel." The resort ranks among the Alps' most expensive – a place where perfectly manicured hands deliver perfectly waxed skis to perfectly groomed slopes. Forests shelter the valley village, and ski-in chalets line the wide runs above. The town centers on **La Croisette**, the lift and service complex at the base of the mountain. Recreation runs to shopping, sporting, and spa-ing. In winter, adventurers enjoy walking, snowshoeing, and skiing on the Three Valleys' 600 km of runs; in summer, visitors hike on 256 km of trails and mountain bike down 17 different itineraries. Numerous shops, an ice rink, and a climbing tower occupy the **Forum** center, and 27 glossy boutiques line the **Espace Diamant**.

AUTHOR'S PICK

*Courchevel has some of the Alps' finest mountain restaurants, and even those lodging elsewhere should sample Courchevel's cuisine. On the mountain, I like the **Restaurant Le Panoramic**, atop the 2,732-m summit of the Saulire, for traditional Savoyard specialties. In the village, stop by the **Moulin du Tremplin** for a snack – delicious crêpes highlight the menu, and décor features an ingeniously incorporated old cogwheel. The pleasant hut stands at the mountain base in the lift complex.*

Want to stay? If you go in knowing that you pay a lot for what you get in Courchevel, then the **Hotel L'Aiglon** ($$$) will feel like a good deal. The two-star hotel is conveniently located in the center at the fool of the slopes, and its pine-paneled rooms are bright and cozy. Inquire at ☎ 0479 08 02 66, www.courchevel1850.com/aiglon.

Courchevel's tourist information office is in the La Croisette lift complex. For more info, check ☎ 0479 08 00 29, www.courchevel.com.

Val Thorens

Val Thorens is all about skiing and was built for that. At 2,325 m, the hamlet crowns the long Bellevue Valley on the western edge of the Three Valleys region. Barren, majestic peaks rise all around. The carefully contrived village clusters around the **Place de Caron**, a snow-covered plaza surrounded by hotels and restaurants and served by a draglift. Large, chalet-style apartment and hotel blocks huddle around the center, creating a village façade more attractive than those of France's other specially built ski resorts. (For an example of the norm, note Les Menuires on your way up the valley.) Cars park in a garage just outside the center. The draw? Snow-sure slopes from November to May and easy access to the Three Valleys' 600 km of runs.

The young clientele comes to this remote village for sport and sport alone. Hiking, snowshoeing, and snowmobiling round out the winter months, and snowboarders come en masse to surf the funpark here. Great snow conditions, lots of ski-in lodging, and an extensive trail and lift network – it all works out rather well unless, of course, bad weather strikes, closing lifts and diminishing visibility. On rotten-weather days, visitors head for the **Centre Sportif**, a newly renovated complex that now offers 9,000 square m of sporting facilities, including swimming pools, saunas, ball courts, and a funpark area for kids. In July and August, hiking, biking, and a small summer ski slope draw minimal tourism.

*If you do turn up here in the summer, consider purchasing the **Carte Sport Valtho**. The card brings free access to the valley's lifts, playgrounds, skate-park, concerts, campfires, and guided walks. The cards go for €25 per person per week and are sold at the tourist office.*

Want to stay? Almost all Val Thorens lodging has ski-in/ski-out convenience, most of it requiring a week-long Saturday-to-Saturday stay. One of the few hotels opening in both summer and winter, **Le Portillo** ($$-$$$) has simple rooms and an excellent gourmet restaurant; ☎ 0479 00 00 88, www.leportillo.fr. Better deals can booked for week-long apartment stays.

The Val Thorens tourist office is on the Place de Caron. For more information, check in at ☎ 0479 00 08 08, www.valthorens.com.

■ Val d'Isère

Population: 1640

Base elevation: 1850 m

Mountain resort village

Val d'Isère is not nearly so cosmopolitan as Chamonix, and it's not nearly so British as Méribel. Val d'Isère is instead the most French of the French resorts I cover here. With a lovely old neighborhood of traditional homes and a modern center refurbished entirely in traditional style, the village is a charming sight. I love it, too, for its enormous winter recreational arena, the **Espace Killy** *– wild terrain wedged in between the Italian frontier and the pristine Vanoise National Park.*

History & Overview

Occupied by Celtic tribes and later settled by their Roman conquerors, Val d'Isère first initiated summer tourism in the early 20th century. The ski resort I know today dates from 1934, when the Rogoney lift was first built on a local slope. Since then, the resort has hosted the men's downhill event for the 1992 Olympic Winter Games and has expanded to include the 97 lifts of the Espace Killy sports region – a recreational expanse named for Jean Claude Killy, winner of three gold medals at the 1968 Olympic Winter Games in Grenoble.

Other Val d'Isère greats have made history as well, from the Goitschel sisters of the 1960s to today's French champion Ingrid Jacquemod. Since 1987, architectural restrictions have mandated the exclusive use of traditional Savoyard building materials for new construction and renovations. The result is admirable; today's visitors enjoy rustic façades of stone and wood, all topped off with the region's characteristic slate roof tiles.

France

Val d'Isère nestles in a remote corner of eastern France, 30 km south of Bourg St. Maurice and only a few km west of the Italian border. The Col de l'Iseran and the Vallée de la Maurienne lie directly south. Val d'Isère sits within the Espace Killy, a recreational area that borders the Vanoise National Park to the south and includes the nearby resort of Tignes.

The Town

Several hamlets make up the village of Val d'Isère. Arriving from the south, drivers first come upon the hamlet of La Daille, a monstrosity of Alpine architecture built to resemble the mountains – avert your eyes, and pass on by. Continuing on, the road passes through Le Cret, Centre Village, Laisinant, and Fornet before entering the national park (or, in winter, simply ending due to park closure). From the center, Centre Village, a secondary road burrows under the lift base area to Rond Point, Le Joseray, Le Chatelard, La Legettaz, and finally, Le Manchet, home to the Espace Sports et Loisirs du Marchet, or simply, the sports center.

The Centre Village, or village center, revolves around the roundabout plaza fronting the tourist office and Town Hall. Two blocks south, the vast expanse of the lift base center anchors the village's sporting venues, playing home to the sports center, the swimming complex, the ice rink in winter, tennis courts in summer, and, of course, the valley stations of several lifts.

Getting Here & Around

 Those arriving by air will have a long drive from the international airport at Geneva, some three hours away by car. The connecting airports and Chambery and Lyon are somewhat closer. If you have money to spare, helicopter transfers are available. For travelers arriving by train, the nearest train station is at Bourg St. Maurice, and bus transfers depart from there. I applaud the village's efforts toward minimizing auto traffic. An underground parking lot serves the center (no fee in summer), and free shuttle buses, or "trains" as they're known here, ply between the outlying hamlets from 8:30 am to 2 am in high season.

Mountain lifts rise from three bases – Le Fornet to the southeast, La Daille to the north, and at the lift base in the village, the most central and well-served of the three. All are connected by a free and efficient shuttle system.

Lac du Chevril

En route from Bourg St. Maurice to Val d'Isère, drivers will emerge from an uphill climb, finding themselves in front of a large dam, the **Barrage de Tignes**, a hydroelectric works erected by the state in the late 1950s. Depending on current water levels, observant visitors may be able to spot some evidence of what once was the valley's small village – a village abandoned by its several hundred inhabitants when the French government submerged it under the lake I see today. The lake is drained every 10 years for dam maintenance, during which time the lakebed and its village remains become a popular tourist draw. The next draining is scheduled for the summer of 2010; until then, look for an oft-exposed, decrepit bridge at the southern end of the lake.

LIFT PASS PRICE SAMPLES

Winter

1-day adult Espace Killy pass €38

6-day adult Espace Killy €181

Summer

Pedestrian Round-trip pass €8.50

Pedestrian 1-day pass €16

Pedestrian 6-day pass €39

Getting Connected

 The tourist office is at the square near Town Hall. For more information, check in at ☎ 0479 06 06 60, www.valdisere.com. Radio 2, broadcasting from inside the tourist office, runs English news and weather segments several times each day in the morning and evening hours.

 The post office hides away in the neighborhood just east of the lift base.

 For Internet access, try **Bentley's**, a dark bar in the center of town, or **Powder Monkey**, in a mall on the northern edge of town.

The Sights

Although the village is short on tourist sights, Val d'Isère begs to be wandered on foot. The most attractive district lies on the southern side of town, between the lift base and the main road. Visitors should stroll up the **Rue Nicolas Bazile** for a look at the traditional architecture and the **Chapel St. Roch**. Note the traditional stone-and-wood materials and the traditional architectural features, such as alternate upstairs entries for times of high snow. Also worth a look is the residential hamlet of **Le Fornet**, up the valley at the entrance to the national park. The tiny old village is a reasonable example of how Val center may have once appeared. On the way to Le Fornet, watch up the northeastern hillside for marmots and chamois.

THE VAL D'ISÈRE SPORTS PASS

During the short summer season – generally from late June through August – the Val d'Isère tourist office offers a debit-card program for use at local sports facilities. Summertime guests can program a card with any denomination of "units" – there's a €50 minimum – and then use the units to partake of a variety of sporting activities. While not attractive for all guests, the cards particularly please families, who can pump up a card and pack the kids off to play without pockets full of cash.

The Adventures

On Foot

Although primarily a winter resort, the Val d'Isère offers an expansive network of some 40 **hiking trails** that wind through the region and into the Vaniose National Park. **Lifts** assist walkers to the surrounding peaks, and numerous outfitters arrange guided outings ranging from local nature walks to multi-day glacier treks. Our favorite operator is **Evolution 2** – see *Sports Services* below. **Climbers** come to the Val d'Isère to scale several sites, including two equipped routes just outside of town. Many guiding services are available – check in with the tourist office or at Evolution 2. In addition, the town caters its athletic programs, including outdoor aerobics and such, to the needs of athletes who come here for **high-altitude cardiovascular training**.

In Water

Swimmers enjoy the indoor pool at the sports center below the Face de Bellevarde, as well as the spa facilities nearby at the **Les Thermes de Christiana**. Whitewater adventures, such as rafting, kayaking, and canyoning are all offered too. See *Sports Services*, page 162. **Jean Sports**, at ☎ 0479 06 04 44, can make arrangements for fishing excursions.

On Wheels

Mountain bikers enjoy local trails and lift service throughout the Espace Killy, but the national park prohibits off-road biking within its bounds. Check in with the tourist office for trail maps. In addition, Val d'Isère offers France's most popular **off-roading** terrain. For more information – and to arrange night outings – contact the **Club 4X4** at ☎ 0479 06 02 06.

In the Air

Although over-flights of the national park are prohibited, **parasailing**, **helicopter tours**, and even **micro-light flights** are available in the vicinity of Val d'Isère. For more information, check in at the tourist office or with Evolution 2 (see *Sports Services*, page 162).

On Snow & Ice

Skiers take to the Espace Killy's 97 lifts and 300 km of groomed runs. Ten free lifts serve beginners, boarders enjoy two funparks, and **summer skiing** slides on the Pissaillas Glacier ice from the end of June through mid August. Val d'Isère is famous for its expert-level skiing, which includes the fabulous Face run, first built here for the 1992 Olympic races. (The slope is so steep that, in order to safely groom it, snow cats are suspended by cables to anchors above. The slope is groomed every other evening – a sight to see if you're in the vicinity.) Heli-skiing into Italy is an option, and expansive off-piste terrain sprawls out around Le Fornet.

Skiers set out on four main areas, La Daille, the Bellevarde, Solaise, and Le Fornet. The La Daille area beckons to beginning skiers with wide, gentle slopes, and the Bellevarde challenges experts. The Solaise includes the resort's original easy and intermediate runs, and Le Fornet draws freestylists for its expansive off-piste opportunities. There are easy runs here, too, near the glacier. Snowboarders head for La Daille and Le Snowpark, a large park with pipes, jumps, obstacles, and a boarder-cross course. Boarder-cross is a snowboarding run with multiple obstacles and stunt ramps.

MOUNTAIN SAFETY

In April of 1996, Ceinwen Faulkner fell to her death while ski-touring above La Grave. A memorial trust was founded in her name with the purpose of training guides and educating the public. To this end, **Henry's Avalanche Talk** (or HAT) offers free educational lectures to recreational skiers in Val d'Isère. English-language talks are held in a casual atmosphere at Dick's Tea Bar each Monday, Wednesday, and Thursday. For more information on the CFM Trust, check www.cfmt.org.uk; for more information on the mountain safety lectures, check www.henrysavalanchetalk.com.

Crosscountry skiers, snowshoers, and **winter walkers** take to local trails – those winding back along the river toward La Manchet are very popular. **Ice-skaters** enjoy the outdoor rink in the center at the lift base, and **ice climbers** scale the two waterfalls flanking the valley's entrance just south of La Daille. Also popular are dog-sledding and, on a track just outside town, **ice-carting, 4X4 ice-driving**, and **snowmobiling**; ☎ 0479 06 21 40.

Sports Services, Outfitters & Guides

■ The British-run **Evolution 2** offers a wide range of instruction and outings, including courses on all snow sports. Ice climbing, ice diving, and dog sledding are all on the winter menu here. In summer, try quad biking, mountain biking, canyoning, and whitewater adventures – and the list goes on. Contact ☎ 0479 06 37 29, www.evolution2.com.

■ **Snow Fun** operates a good selection of year-round adventure outings but are best known for their children's ski courses. Check in at any of their five valley shops; ☎ 0479 41 11 81, www.snowfun.fr.

■ **Precision** sporting goods store ranks among the Alps' best outfitters. The shop rents, fits, and sells all manner of equipment and, as the shop serves a largely British clientele, English is the language of choice here. Check in at ☎ 0479 06 27 54, www.precision-ski.com.

■ **Mountain Masters** is the valley's best specialist school for off-piste skiing. Their courses are expensive but get rave reviews for their effectiveness. The small school operates out of the Killy Sport shop; get more info at ☎ 0479 06 05 04, www.mountain-masters.com.

- **Serial Skieur** offers an attractive service: anything you need, they'll get. The company arranges ski passes, baggage storage and transfer, baby-sitters, housekeepers, catering, dining reservations, and sport outings. Submit your requests at ☎ 0479 41 64 73, www.serial-skieur.com.

Where to Sleep

Val d'Isère offers a good selection of accommodations, although winter rates skyrocket to roughly double the off-season rates. The rates indicated below are for mid-level winter season.

The new **L'Hôtel Les Barmes de l'Ours** ($$$$) promises to be this year's hottest reservation. The four-star house sits in a prime location at the foot of the Bellevarde ski

HOTEL PRICE CHART	
Double room without tax; $$$-$$$$ always with bath.	
$	Under €80
$$	€81-150
$$$	€151-250
$$$$	Over €250

run. The hotel – its name translates as "the bear's cave" – is as cozy as it sounds, with two restaurants, a bar, and a wellness center; ☎ 0479 41 37 00, www.hotel-les-barmes.com. In the same category, directly in the center, the **Hotel Blizzard** ($$$$) has a rustic interior and an indoor-outdoor pool heated year-round; ☎ 0479 06 04 94, www.hotelblizzard.com.

For what may be the warmest hospitality in all the French Alps, head for the **Grand Paradis** ($$$). The three-star block, bland on its exterior, boasts splendid front-side views of the lift base area, its terrace cafés, and the towering Bellevarde. Inside, both the hotel and its management radiate Austrian *gemütlichkeit*, right down to the tole-painted antiques and the old-fashioned tile stoves that brighten each room; ☎ 0479 06 11 73, www.grand-paradis.fr.

Also in the center, the **Hotel Kandahar** ($$$) has a country-cozy interior and a locale convenient for strolling the shops; ☎ 0479 06 02 39, www.hotel-kandahar.com.

I also have a soft spot for the **Chamois d'Or** ($$-$$$), a homey A-frame chalet centered smack in the middle of the lift center's expanse. (As you're ripping down the Bellevarde face, the hotel's enormous "BAR" sign will point the way home.) Once there, the terrace and its blanket-padded chairs may call your name as well. It's not luxurious, but it sure is cozy – kind of like grandma's house (if, of course, grandma lived at the foot of one of the world's greatest ski runs). Inquire at ☎ 0479 06 00 44, www.hotelchamoisdor.com.

Two old hotels offer budget accommodations along the main road a few minutes' walk from the center. The **Hotel Relais du Ski** ($-$$) and the **Hotel La Bailletta** ($$) share a building, differing only by name and room amenities. The one-star Relais has private rooms with shared baths, while the two-star side of the house, La Bailetta, has private rooms with baths and balconies. Breakfast here is better than you'd expect at these low rates; ☎ 0479 06 02 06.

Where to Eat

 The valley's favorite gourmet restaurant is **Le Chalet du Cret** ($$$), a 17th-century stone farmhouse in the hamlet of Cret. Diners receive all of the standard starters, an enormous spread of pumpkin soup, ravioli, foie gras, and salad – and that's before their

DINING PRICE CHART	
Average entrée, with tax.	
$	Under €10
$$	€10-25
$$$	Over €25

entrées arrives. It's pricey, but a superb treat. Reserve at ☎ 0479 06 20 77.

Try as well La **Grande Ourse** ($$$), an old house situated near the church on the lift-base snow. It has a dark, intimate interior and excellent seafood and meat specialties; ☎ 0479 06 00 19.

Les Clochetons ($$-$$$) does gourmet evenings and great lunch specials, all in a splendid riverside setting in Le Chêtelard. It's a great stop along the walking and skiing trails toward Le Manchet. The restaurant's bus offers transportation and, oddly, there's a swimming pool; ☎ 0479 41 13 11.

For traditional Savoyard specialties, head for **La Corniche** ($$) an old stone house in the historic district that does excellent fondue and a mix of fish and beef dishes; ☎ 0479 06 18 75. Try, too, **La Taverne d'Alsace** ($$), a cozy restaurant and wine cellar under the Kandahar Hotel. Reserve at ☎ 0479 06 48 49.

Les 3 Bises ($$) – or "The Three Kisses" – has homey décor and a traditional menu; ☎ 0479 06 04 93. **L'Etable d'Alain** ($$) has the freshest fondue around – it's located in an operating Alpine dairy on the eastern edge of the village. Children like both the cows and the kids' menu; ☎ 0479 06 13 02.

La Casa Scara ($$) serves up elegant Italian dishes in a rustic house across from the old church; ☎ 0479 06 26 21. On the mountain at the top station of the Daille cableway, try **La Fruitière** ($$), a sit-down affair with charming décor and outdoor table service. Next door, **La Folie Douce** ($$) has market-style self-service food, loud music, and a large dining terrace – don't miss the **wafflemaker** ($) in its gazebo.

Chez Nano ($) does good pizzas in the center near Dick's, and **Crêpe Val's** ($) lists on its menu over 60 kinds of crêpes.

The best grocery in town is the **Casino** ($), between the central square and the lifts. It has a great selection of deli foods and wines in addition to a daily hot specialty dish. Valle d'Isère's favorite chocolatier is the **Maison Chevallot**; it has three shops in the valley.

Where to Party

Afternoons pick up on the mountain above La Daille at **La Folie Douce**. In the center near the foot of the Bellevarde, try **Café Face** in the Hotel Christiania or nearby **Bananas**, where it's easy to find a big beer but difficult to find a seat on the tiny deck. Along the main road through town, the deck-fronted **Moris Pub** gets lively during its afternoon happy hour. Later, **Dick's Tea Bar** is the classic party spot in the center. Along the main road, try the **Rodeo Bar** for DJ'd music and a mechanical bull or, for live music and a lounge-like atmosphere, try the **Warm-Up Café** next door. VIP reservations are taken here as well; ☎ 0479 06 27 00.

Where to Play

In addition to the services of the **ski school** and **organized summer programs**, kids aged three to eight enjoy a supervised snow **kindergarten** open daily except Saturday on the nursery slopes at the central lift base. The **Petit Poucet** service picks kids up and drops them off each morning – a blessing for vacationing parents. Floodlights brighten the nursery slopes for evening **sledding**. For **playground** action, try the park near the lift base and the Hotel Blizzard.

In summertime there's no better place than **La Manchet**, the hamlet south of town. Here, playgrounds, **trampolines, sports fields**, and a **skate park** cluster next to the river. The tourist office can assist with **babysitting** arrangements.

Festivals & Events

 Val d'Isère opens its winter season in late November and, in December, opens the European Alpine ski-racing season with the **Criterium de la Première Neige**. In February, the growing reputation of the **Big Day Out** event draws freestylists, snowboarders, and motocross riders from both professional and amateur fields.

April brings **La Scara**, an international skiing competition for the world's best young racers, as well as the **Musicaval** classical music festival. Late April sees the **Adventure & Discovery Film Festival**, and the season ends in early May with the **Spring Supreme** closing party. Summer brings an **International Film Festival** in July and the valley's popular **Exhibition of Leisure Activities and 4X4s** in mid-August.

For more information, contact the tourist office at ☎ 0479 06 06 60, www.valdisere.com.

La Vanoise National Park

(Parc National de la Vanoise)

In 1963, amid growing concerns over the endangered ibex, France drew up the boundaries of its first national park. Today, ibex thrive both here and in Gran Paradiso National Park just across the border in Italy, habitats enjoyed as well by marmots, eagles, and some 5,500 chamois.

La Vanoise now spans 530 square km, covering the glacier-topped massif between the Tarantaise region to the north and the Maurienne Valley to the south. To pacify both established inhabitants and preservationists, the park has adopted two zones, an outer zone where traditional methods of land use are permitted, and an inner zone of virgin land that remains strictly pristine. The park can be accessed by trails all along its edges and by road either from Val d'Isère in the Tarantaise to the north or from Bonneval sur Arc in the Maurienne to the south. The road peaks over the Col de l'Iseran and is open between late May and October.

Some 500 km of trails and 66 refuges keep hikers happy – the classic trek is a seven-day loop around the park's glacier-crowned peaks: **Le Tour des Glaciers de la Vanoise**. Wanderers can reserve beds through the individual hut operators; more information is available at the park's website. When visiting huts that are not guarded, you'll still find blankets, wood, and cooking utensils – deposit your night-charge fee in the provided box. In addition, the park publishes a long list of regulations: No fires, no noise, no dogs, no camping, no flower picking, and no biking. In short, behave yourself.

Each summer in July and August, the park stations host-esses at each of the region's tourist information offices. During this period, you can get information at the Val d'Isère tourist office on your way in. The main park office is in Chambéry; ☎ 0479 62 30 54, www.vanoise.com.

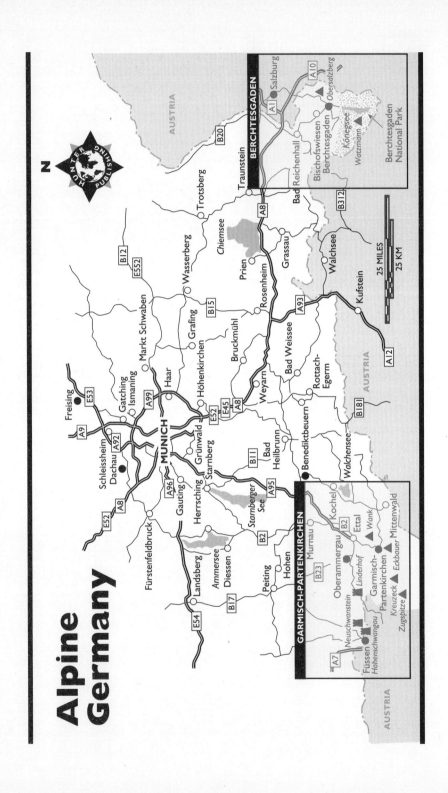

Germany

(Deutschland)
Languages: German
Population: 83,251,851
Phone Country Code: +49
Currency: Euro

History

Although various tribes had wandered the territory for centuries, Germany first found fame in 9 AD with the Battle of the Teutoburg Forest. Here, German tribesmen defeated a Roman force more than three legions strong in a three-day battle. Around 20,000 Roman soldiers were killed in the slaughter and their commander, Publius Quinctilius Varus, took his own life at the end of the battle. The defeat forced the Romans to abandon their dreams of an empire east of the Rhine.

In the fifth century, Germanic tribes wandered west of the Rhine, establishing settlements in what are now France and Spain. The Germanic Franks endured, eventually founding the French Empire of Charlemagne. When Charlemagne's grandsons divvied up France's land, the throne was passed from Conrad of Franconia to Henry the Fowler, founder of the Saxon dynasty. Henry's son, Otto I, reclaimed the title of Emperor in 962. Concurrent with the establishment of the Holy Roman Empire and the rule of the Hapsburgs in Austria, Otto and his line jumped on board and founded the Holy Roman Empire of the German Nation – an empire dissolved by Napoleon in 1806.

After Napoleon's eventual defeat, Germany existed as a loose federation of independent states. However, in 1866, Wilhelm I took control of Bavaria from Austria and, using the Franco-Prussian war as an excuse, unified the former German states under his own rule in 1870. In 1919, Wilhelm II resigned as a result of the First World War. After World War I, Germany established a liberal Democratic government, but the economic hardships of the Great Depression – coupled with a rise in nationalism stemming from the Treaty of Versailles – gave rise to the National Socialist German Workers' Party (NSDAP, or NAZI). In 1932, the NAZI party won a victory in the general election; Adolph Hitler was appointed Chancellor.

In 1934, after the death of president Paul von Hindenburg, Hitler combined the office of chancellor with the presidency and assumed absolute control of Germany, thus establishing the Third Reich. In 1938, he began a campaign to expand the Third Reich and eliminate Jews, among others, from Germany. After annexing Austria and then parts of Czechoslovakia, World War II began with the German invasion of Poland in 1939. By the time Hitler's Third Reich was defeated in 1945, some 11 million Germans had died – over half of them were Jews.

The post-World War II Treaty at Potsdam divided Germany into four occupation zones: The British, French, and Americans controlled the south, central, and west, while the Soviet Union controlled the east. Germany's capital, Berlin, was likewise divided. In 1948, the western powers instituted the Marshall Plan in an attempt to revive the German economy. The Soviet Union opposed and instigated a blockade of Berlin, a move countered with the West's Berlin airlift operation. Ultimately, Germany became the front line of the Cold War between the NATO Alliance and the Warsaw Pact.

In 1989, thousands of East Germans staged peaceful demonstrations demanding access to the west. Hungary allowed East Germans passage to cross into West Germany, eventually leading to the destruction of the Berlin Wall and the German Reunification in 1990. By July of 1990, the German states had united under a single currency. On December 2, 1990, free elections were held for the first time since 1933.

King Ludwig II

 Bavaria's most fascinating character is Ludwig, the fairytale king. Born into the royal family as Prince Otto Ludwig Friedrich Wilhelm, the young boy spent his happiest days in his family's castle near Füssen at the Schwangau. At the age of 16, Ludwig heard his first opera, by Richard Wagner. Two years later, in 1864, Ludwig assumed the Bavarian throne and immediately sent for Wagner. Ludwig set Wagner up in a large villa, and erected the Bayreuth Opera House in his honor. For a time, the two were inseparable – a friendship that inspired much speculation.

However, Bavaria's strong ties to Austria forced Ludwig to support Austria in its 1866 war with Prussia. When Austria was defeated, control of the Bavarian army was ceded to the Prussian King. Then, in 1867, Ludwig became engaged to the sister of the Austrian Empress Sisi, but after several postponements and lots of strategic stiff-arming on Ludwig's part, the bride's father called off the match. Ludwig left Munich for his Alpine retreat, and it was there that he built his cluster of magnificent castles.

Two years later, Prussia went to war with France and, recalling the peace agreement from the 1866 war, called on Bavaria to supply arms. At the conclusion of the war, Wilhelm II "invited" Bavaria into the reestablished German Empire. Although Ludwig maintained the title of king, by 1871 he had lost all power. After a long decline into depression and bankruptcy, the fairytale king was deemed mentally unfit to rule and was removed to the lakeside Schloss Berg. Under mysterious circumstances, in June of 1886, he and his doctor were found drowned along the shallow shore. What happened there remains a mystery.

Orientation & Government

The Federal Republic of Germany encompasses 357,020 square km in north-central Europe. About 30% of its land is forested, and the Rhine, Danube, and Moselle are among its principal rivers. The terrain is a mixture of lowland plains in the north, highland plains in the central lands, and mountains in the South. Germany is bounded by Switzerland to the south, Austria to the southeast, Poland and the Czech Republic to the east, Denmark to the north, and France, Luxembourg, Belgium, and the Netherlands to the west.

Germany is a federal republic composed of 16 states; its capital is Berlin. The chief of state is the president; the head of government, the chancellor. Recent social issues stem from reunification and its costs, as wealth from the west continues to be sucked into modernization projects in the east. Unemployment rates have soared to 9.4%, only recently surpassing those of France. Furthermore, Germany's Basic Law provides for the unconditional citizenship of non-German speakers and for the acceptance of political refugees. Although new laws seek to regulate the influx, the country remains awash in social change, giving rise to racial violence and anti-immigration demonstrations.

People & Culture

Germany's population is just over 90% of Germanic descent; the remainder is of foreign origin, including Danes, Turks, Italian, Greeks, Slovaks, and Serbs. Approximately 50% of the population professes the Protestant faith – predictably, most of those follow the

Lutheran sect. Some 45% are Roman Catholic , and 4% claim the Muslim religion. Over 84% of the population resides in urban settings, with a population density of 222 persons per square kilometer. The largest cities include Berlin, Hamburg, Munich, Cologne, and Frankfurt.

National Holidays

January 1 . . . . New Year's Day
January 6 . . . . Epiphany
January 7 through Shrove Tuesday . . Carnival (Munich)
Friday before Easter . . . . Good Friday
March/April . . . . Easter
. . . . Easter Monday
May 1 . . . . Labor Day
10 days before Whit Sunday . . . . Ascension Day
7th Sunday after Easter . . . . Whit Sunday
Day after Whit Sunday . . . . Whit Monday
Thursday after 8th Sunday after Easter . . Corpus Christi
August 15 . . . . Assumption Day
October 3 . . . . German Unity Day
October 31 . . . . Repentance Day
November 1 . . . . All Saints Day
November 14 . . . . Repentance Day
December 24 . . . . Christmas Eve
December 25 . . . . Christmas Day
December 26 . . . . 2nd Christmas Day
December 31 . . . . New Year's Eve

For more information, visit the German National Tourist Office website at www.germany-tourism.de.

Munich & The Bavarian Alps

Land of fairy tales, fanciful castles, and fabulous Alpine terrain, Bavaria squeezes a wealth of natural and cultural sights into a conveniently compact section of the Alps. The region centers on the bustling metropolis of Munich, a historical city famed for both its grand architecture and its great beer. To the southwest, plains stretch into Alpine foothills fronting Füssen and its famous castles. East of Füssen, mountain byways wind back to the quaint village of Oberammergau and to nearby Garmisch, home of the Zügspitze, Germany's highest peak. Farther east, the Berchtesgaden region towers into Austria, harboring the unspoiled landscape of Berchtesgaden National Park and its pristine Königsee.

■ Munich

(München)

Population: 1.3 million

Base elevation: 530 m

Gateway tourist city

Bavaria's capital bustles with energy, a student city bursting with art, industry, technology, and tourism. The city's tragic, war-torn past is studded with bright eras of royal glory and cultural achievement. Today, cosmopolitan Munich proves a fascinating place, indeed.

History & Orientation

Munich was founded by Henry the Lion (left) on the 14th of June in the year 1158, and became the seat of Bavarian nobility in 1255. The city flourished in the 16th century as the German center of Renaissance culture, nurturing poets, writers, and artists under the rule of Duke Maximilian I. Munich burgeoned between the 18th and 19th centuries, as the population grew. Ludwig I, known as the "Prince of Muses", built the city into one of Europe's premier cultural centers by developing museums, theaters, and universities. King Max II commissioned several architectural gems, and King Ludwig II patronized music masters and craftsmen.

However, turbulent times rocked the early 20th century, as Hitler's National Socialists took control in 1933 and the World War that followed destroyed much of the city. American forces entered the city on April 30, 1945. Munich began to rebuild, and the city hosted the XX Olympic Summer Games in 1972. Sadly, however, the games were forever shadowed when Palestinian terrorists took hostages and killed 11 Israeli Olympic Team members. Today, Munich is Bavaria's political and cultural capital, drawing more domestic tourism than any other city in Germany.

The Town

Munich presides over the southeastern corner of Germany, just west of Salzburg and just north of the Alps and Innsbruck. The Isar River cuts a 14-km swath through the city center, and Munich's "rings" radiate from its banks – the outermost ring looping the city by beltway autobahn, the innermost encompassing the oldest part of the city. Anchoring the outskirts of this sprawling metropolis are several landmarks: **Nymphenburg Palace** to the west, the **Olympic Park** to the north, and the new **trade fair center** to the east.

Munich's tourism centers on the old city center loop and the **Marienplatz**, a pleasant one-km walk east from the main train station. Most of the city's attractions lie within a one-km radius of this square. From the center, the pedestrian shopping streets of Kaufingerstrasse and Neuhauserstrasse run west to Karlsplatz and the train station; Theatinerstrasse heads north to the Residenz, Ludwigstrasse, and the university district; and Sendlingerstrasse runs southwest toward Sendlinger Tor and the Theresienswiese festival grounds. Maximilianstrasse parades a long line of posh shops to the east.

Getting Here & Around

International travelers arriving by air will fly into **Munich Airport**, an ever-growing facility 28 km northeast of the city center. If you're stuck here awhile, the airport museum has a reasonable collection of historical airplanes, and the Visitors' Park and Visitors' Hill are relatively pleasant places to hang out. For more information, check www.munich-airport.de. To reach the city center via public transportation, hop on the S-bahn train for the 40-minute ride into town.

Munich is Bavaria's main bus and train transportation hub. The city-center public transportation system is a tightly woven web of train, subway, tram, and bus routes.

AUTHOR'S PICK I heartily recommend the MVV *Easy Going* brochure, a multilingual guide to sightseeing via Munich's public transportation system. Doled out by the tourist office, the guide offers a helpful description of the various types of public transport, the ticketing system, and the city's fare-determining zone rings.

A simpler way to clear up the issue, however, is to purchase a day pass or, if you plan to cover a few attractions, the München Welcome Card (see below).

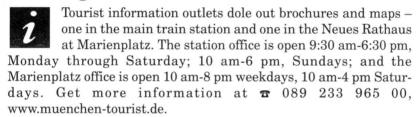

*The **München Welcome Card** offers free transport on all city buses, trams, and subways and discounts on various city tours, attractions, museums, and events. But many discounted attractions don't advertise their discounted rates. Study your Welcome Card booklet and request discounts whenever purchasing tickets. Welcome Cards can be purchased for one or three days; for one person or a group of up to five; and with or without a ride to and from the airport. (A one-day, one-person card without airport transfer costs €6.50). Buy yours at the airport, at your hotel, or at any tourist office.*

Getting Connected

 Tourist information outlets dole out brochures and maps – one in the main train station and one in the Neues Rathaus at Marienplatz. The station office is open 9:30 am-6:30 pm, Monday through Saturday; 10 am-6 pm, Sundays; and the Marienplatz office is open 10 am-8 pm weekdays, 10 am-4 pm Saturdays. Get more information at ☎ 089 233 965 00, www.muenchen-tourist.de.

✉ Two post offices are convenient to the city's tourist center. The first sits directly across the street from the front of the main train station. The second is at Max-Joseph Platz, just across the square from the National Theater.

WWW For Internet access, try the massive **Easy Everything Internet Café** across from the main train station, the **Hard Rock Café** across from the Hofbräuhaus, the **Café Glockenspiel** at Marienplatz or, near the university, the student hang-out **CADU** at 10 Ludwigstrasse.

The Sights

 Much of Munich's original architecture was destroyed during World War II, but some notable structures were either spared or have been rebuilt. In the center, action revolves around the **Marienplatz**, a large square that's been the heart of Munich since its days as a marketplace and jousting tournament venue in the Middle Ages. Dominating the square is the Gothic **Neues Rathaus**, or New City Hall, home to the city's famed **Glockenspiel**, a toy clock that stages a short performance each day at 11 am and noon year-round and, additionally, at 5 pm in the summer.

Between the alleys just south of the square are **St. Peter's** church and Munich's largest outdoor food market, the **Viktualienmarket**. The market is home to a small summertime beer garden, several quick lunch kiosks, and the city's ornate maypole. Stalls are open Monday through Friday, 7 am to 8 pm, and Saturdays till 4 pm. Farther from the Marienplatz, several small chunks remain of what once was the city's fortifying wall – the best sections are at **Sendlinger Tor** to the southwest and **Isartor** to the southeast. Between the Marienplatz and Sendlinger Tor is what must be Germany's most jaw-droppingly ornate interior. For an eyeful, duck inside the tiny **Asamkirche** at Sendlingerstrasse 32.

Head for Heights

Pack a map and gain some altitude to get an orienting view of Bavaria's most expansive metropolis:

■ My favorite vantage point within the city center is **St. Peter's Church**, where ambitious visitors climb 297 narrow scaffolding steps to the catwalk atop the old tower, or *alter turm*. Built in the 11th century, "Old St. Peter's" is Munich's most beloved church.

■ Those desiring a less daunting climb can head for the 15th-century **Frauenkirche**, the city's cathedral and signature landmark. Here, just 86 steps and an elevator ride deliver guests to the highest tower top in central Munich – building restrictions dictate that no structure can stand taller than the church's twin onion-domed towers.

■ Faster, higher, stronger... the elevators in the **Olympic Tower** whisk visitors upward at a rate of seven meters per second. Five floors of indoor and outdoor observation decks (including one revolving restaurant) offer far-reaching views from 192 m above the valley floor. The tower is open daily from 9 am to 11:30 pm; €3.

Bavaria's ruling families dumped mind-boggling wealth into the construction of their palaces, several of which are now open to the public. In the center, **The Residenz** was home to the Wittelbachs and the seat of Bavarian power for 500 years. The complex's 130 rooms show off a splendid collection of antiques and interior design from the successive eras and include the magnificent, barrel-vaulted Antiquarium Hall. Call ☎ 089 290 671 for more info.

West of the city, **Nymphenburg Palace** was the summer residence of Ludwig I and is home to his kingly pin-up collection, the famed "Gallery of Beauties." The Baroque palace's expansive gardens are worth a stroll as well. It's open daily April through September from 9 am-6 pm, and October through March, 10 am-4 pm. For more information, dial ☎ 089 179 080.

Munich's Museums

Thanks in large part to the Wittelsbach royal family's commitment to the creation, preservation, and collection of art, modern Munich's cultural wealth lies in its impressive museums. No fewer than 50 collections vie for attention. Below, we've highlighted a few of the best.

ART

- The **Old Pinakothek** enjoys international renown for its collection of European paintings dating from the 14th through the 18th centuries. Rembrandt, Rubens, and Leonardo da Vinci are well represented here. It's open Tuesday through Sunday from 10 am-5 pm, Thursday until 10 pm; ☎ 089 23 80 52 16, www.alte-pinakothek.de; €5, free on Sundays.

- Nearby, the **New Pinakothek** displays 18th and 19th century art, with particular emphases on English landscapes and the French Impressionist, Biedermeier, and Art Nouveau styles. View the collection Wednesday through Monday from 10 am-5 pm, Thursday until 10 pm; ☎ 089 23 80 51 95, www.neue-pinakothek.de; €5, free on Sundays.

- Newly opened and already immensely popular, the **Pinakothek der Moderne**, is the largest modern art museum in Germany. It shows off contemporary collections across all artistic genres, including paintings, sculpture, design, architecture, and graphics. It's open Tuesday through Sunday from 10 am to 5 pm, Thursday and Friday until 8 pm; ☎ 08923 80 51 18, www.pinakothek-der-moderne.de; €9, free on Sundays.

- The **Municipal Gallery**, housed in the whimsical old Lenbachhaus villa, displays a fine collection of paintings by Kandinsky, Klee, and other artists of the Blue Rider movement. The museum opens daily except Monday from 10 am-6 pm; ☎ 089 23 33 20 00, www.lenbachhaus.de; €6.

HISTORY

- The **Münchner Stadtmuseum**, or City Museum, houses an interesting display of cultural history. Features include historical interiors, a rundown of the city's development, and changing special exhibitions. The exhibits are open Tuesday through Sunday from 10 am-6 pm; ☎ 089 23 32 55 86, www.stadtmuseum-online.de; €2.50, Sundays free.

- The **Bavarian National Museum** houses historical collections focusing on Bavarian art and artifacts. The museum opens Tuesday through Sunday from 10 am-5 pm, Thursdays until 8 pm; ☎ 089 211 24 01, www.bayerisches-national-museum.de; €3.

TECHNOLOGY

- If you're a technology buff, the item topping your don't-miss list should be the **Deutsches Museum**. One of the world's first museums of science and technology (and the largest in the world today), the huge complex occupies an island in the middle of the Isar River and houses a planetarium and an IMAX theater. It's open daily 9 am-5 pm; ☎ 089 21791, www.deutsches-museum.de; €6.

- The **BMW Museum** shows off historical and futuristic propulsion methods, traffic management techniques, and – of course – a dream collection of cars. Look for the Bavarian Motor Works building in the Munich skyline; it's the clover-shaped silver sky-rise designed to resemble a four-cylinder engine. The museum is open Monday through Sunday from 9 am-5 pm, last entry at 4 pm; ☎ 089 382 23 307, www.bmw.com; €3.

- Looking for something a bit more unusual? Check in at the **Center for Extraordinary Museums**, where a handful of "cultural" collections spotlight things like pedal cars, perfume flasks, Easter bunnies, and "potties." It's open daily, 10 am-6 pm; ☎ 089 290 4121, www.zam-museum.de; €4.

Tours

In a city the size of Munich, a short orientation tour can considerably simplify sightseeing logistics. Multiple outfitters oblige: **Panorama Tours**, alternatively known as Stadt-Rundfahrten, offers a varied program of bus and walking tours. Their one-hour city orientation tour departs hourly in an open double-decker bus from in front of the

Hertie Department Store across from the main train station, ☎ 055 02 89 95, €11.

Mike's Bike Tours offers guided city tours by bike from March through October. The four-hour tours stick to easy bike paths and are suitable for young cyclists; ☎ 0651 42 75, www.mikesbiketours.com.

Radius Tours & Bikes does biking tours and bike rental and adds a good collection of themed walking tours under the banner of Munich Walks. Contact ☎ 089 98 60 15, www.radiusmunich.com or www.munichwalks.com, for current offerings and meeting points.

Finally, **Weisser Stadtvogel** guides a variety of irregularly scheduled tours with interesting themes like "Beer," "National Socialism," and – my favorite – "Hangmen, Whores, and Hags." Contact them at ☎ 089 29 16 97 65, www.weisser-stadtvogel.de, to see what's on.

The Adventures

Müncheners play like most city-dwellers, cycling, playing, and **walking** in parks and gardens. Visitors wishing to do the same can join locals in several recreation centers: at the **Schlosspark Nymphenburg** behind the palace, along the central banks of the **Isar River**, at the **Olympic Park** (see below), and at the **English Gardens**.

THE OLYMPIC PARK

The focal point of Munich's athletic prowess is the Olympic Park Munich, a rambling sports complex developed in preparation for the XX Olympic Summer Games in 1972. The park has since staged 30 world, 12 European, and 84 German athletic championships. Today, it regularly hosts soccer, equestrian, swimming, ice-skating, tennis, volleyball, track, cycling, and concert events.

Recreational athletes, too, enjoy the park's facilities. Several small lakes and streams stud grassy grounds, and the sprawling, silvery angles of the tent roof add a modern artsy touch. Visitors enjoy walking paths, playgrounds, and pedal boat rentals. The complex's swimming, ice, and skating facilities are open for public use, and elevators scale the heights of the Olympic Tower. Tourists enjoy the mini-train tours that depart the tower base every 15 minutes and the themed soccer, architecture, and roof-climbing tours offered from April through October. For more information, contact ☎ 089 30 67 24 14, www.olympiapark-muenchen.de.

Bike rental is available at several city outlets, but our favorite is **Radius Touristik**, a British-run operation conveniently located at the main train station from May through October; ☎ 089 98 60 15, www.radiusmunich.com. **DBRent** rents bikes year-round; www.callabike.de.

Several public **swimming** complexes are open for public use. The **Olympia Swimmhalle** at Olympic Park has a 50-m pool, diving boards, and a sauna area; ☎ 089 30 67 21 50. And the traditional **Müllersches Volksbad** boasts lovely Art Nouveau design, ☎ 089 23 61 34 29.

The **Olympic Park's Eissportzentrum** offers **ice-skating** year-round and its Action Area proves a hit for **inline skating** and **skateboarding** from March through October. Skate rental is on-site; dial ☎ 089 30 67 21 50 for more information. Inliners should check out the **Münchner Blade Nights** as well, held once each week from May through September along various routes, www.meunchner-blade-nights.de.

Climbers head for the indoor wall **DAV-Kletteranlage Thalkirchen**, www.kletterzentrum-muenchen.de – or, from April to October, harness up at the Olympic Park for the **Zeltdach Roof Climb** tour. Contact ☎ 089 30 67 24 14, www.olympiapark-muenchen.de for more info.

For more **outdoorsy adventures**, several tour operators run package deals to the Chiemsee, Garmisch-Partenkirchen, and Berchtesgaden recreation areas. Contact **PanoramaTours Gray Line**, ☎ 089 54907560, www.autobusoberbayern.de, for ideas.

Where to Sleep

Munich's most prestigious address is the **Kempinski Hotel Vier Jahreszeiten** ($$$$), The Kempinski Four Seasons, a large, luxurious house on Maximilianstrasse, the city's most expensive shopping street; ☎ 089 212 50, www.kempinski-vierjahreszeiten.de.

HOTEL PRICE CHART	
Double room without tax; $$$-$$$$ always with bath.	
$	Under €80
$$	€81-150
$$$	€151-250
$$$$	Over €250

The **Königshof ($$$$)** at Karlsplatz and the **Bayerischer Hof** ($$$$) on Promenadeplaz also offer plush, traditional accommodations in the city center. Book the Königshof at ☎ 089 55 13 60, www.koenigshof-muenchen.de; the Bayerischer Hof at ☎ 089 212 00, www.bayerischerhof.de.

Also in the heart of the old town, but considerably less pricey, is the **Garni An der Oper** ($$$); ☎ 089 290 02 70. Also the lovely **Hotel Platzl** ($$$), with its charming Pfistermühle restaurant, is conveniently located near the Hofbräuhaus and the Marienplatz. Book at ☎ 089 23 70 30, www.platzl.de.

Near Sendlinger Tor, try the cozy **Garni Acanthus** ($$); ☎ 089 23 18 80, www.acanthushotel.de. The **Englischer Garten Garni** has homey villa rooms near the English Gardens; ☎ 089 383 94 10.

Out near the Oktoberfest grounds, try the friendly **Hotel Uhland** ($$), ☎ 08954 33 50; and, in the heart of old town near the Hofbräuhaus, try your luck at the very basic **Hotel Alcron**, ☎ 089 228 35 11, www.hotel-alcron.de.

For budgeting youth, Munich's **HI Youth Hostel** ($) has its own restaurant, bar, beer garden, and disco; ☎ 089 12 00 60, www.haus-internationl.de. **Das Zelt** ($), or The Tent, offers a memorable (and possibly sleepless) night's stay in an enormous communal tent. It's open June through August, and rates include a pad, a blanket, a shower, and breakfast; ☎ 089 141 43 00, www.the-tent.com. Open from mid March through October, **Campingplatz Thalkirchen** is on the southern side of town, just across the Isar River from the Hellabrunn Zoo. It's 10 minutes by bus and underground to the city center, and the Floss raft landing is nearby. Contact ☎ 089 723 17 07, www.camping.muenchen.de, for reservations and tent rental information.

Where to Eat

 With over 500 restaurants, Munich offers something to please all palates. Best among the city's gourmet establishments are **Am Marstall** ($$$), where traditional Bavarian basics get a French gourmet kick; ☎ 089 29 16 55 11. And, just outside the center at Schwabing, the revered **Tantris** ($$$) serves creative cuisine amid ultra-modern décor; ☎ 089 361 95 90.

DINING PRICE CHART	
For an average entrée, with tax.	
$	Under €10
$$	€10-25
$$$	Over €25

For traditional Bavarian dishes, I like the old, ivy-ensconced **Pfiftermühle** ($$) at Pfisterstrasse 4; ☎ 089 23 70 38 65. Also the **Haxenbauer** ($$) at Sparkassenstrasse; ☎ 089 29 16 21 00. Both are near the Hofbräuhaus.

A trio of traditional restaurants clusters at Dreifaltigkeitsplatz, a tiny square just off the Viktualienmarket – each, of course, serves a different brand of beer. Try the **Balentin Stüberl** ($$) for Paulaner; the **Zum Alten Markt** ($$) for Spaten; or the cheery **Bratwurstherzl** ($) for Hacker-Pschorr and fresh Nürnberger bratwurst. Each has outdoor seating in the summer. **Beer halls** and most beer gardens serve limited menus of reasonably priced Bavarian food in addition to local beers – see *Munich's Beer Halls* below.

The **Olympic Tower Drehrestaurant** ($$) offers continental cuisine in a rotating dining room 181 m above ground. Dinner is served daily; lunch on weekends and holidays. Reserve at ☎ 089 30 66 85 85. For fans of the **Hard Rock Café** ($$), Munich's token HRC outlet stands opposite the Hofbräuhaus. Dial ☎ 089 24 29 49 14, www.hardrock.com.

For dinner out with entertainment included, the **Welser Kuche** ($$$) at the Feldherrnkeller offers a medieval gourmet dinner each evening from 7 pm to 1 am; ☎ 089 29 65 65, www.welser-kuche.de. And the famed **Hofbräuhaus** ($$$) serves buffet Bavarian alongside a variety of traditional acts; ☎ 089 29 01 36 10, www.hofbraeuhaus.de.

For an inexpensive lunch, try the kiosks at the **Viktualienmarket** ($) near Marienplatz. Popular with students are the department store **caféterias** along Neuhauser and Kaufinger streets and the **outdoor cafés** near the intersection of Franz-Joseph-Strasse and Leopoldstrasse. Travelers head for the **snack stands and delis** in, around, and under the main train station. **Dallmayr**, at Dienerstrasse 14, and **Kafer's**, at Prinzregentenstrasse 73, dish out pricey gourmet deli items.

Where to Party

 For artsy evening entertainment, Munich's 57 theaters stage a wide range of performances. Music lovers flock here for performances by the city's three orchestras: the **Munich Philharmonic**, the **Bayerischer Rundfunk Symphony Orchestra**, and the **Bavarian State Opera**. Popular venues include the National Theater, the Residenztheater, the Deutsches Theater, and the freshly remodeled Münchner Kammerspiele.

 *For all event tickets, check **München Tickets**, ☎ 089 54 81 81 81, www.muenchenticket.de.*

Munich's Beer Halls

 Munich's beer halls bring the city international fame, and every tourist should visit at least one. Here, guests share tables (but not necessarily conversation), dirndl-clad maids hoist huge loads of beer, and oompa-bands spout traditional tunes with which crowds cheerfully sing along. Each house serves food and its own brand of Bavarian beer, the latter always in a one-liter mug, or *mass* – a quantity quite generous by international standards.

Most visitors head straight for the **Hofbräuhaus** at Platzl, the city's most famous beer hall and the place most likely to be packed with foreign tourists. It's got a big, vaulted hall, a shady fountain garden, and a multilingual staff. On a nearby corner at Talstrasse 7, just east of the Marienplatz, the **Weisses Bräuhaus** has a more reserved atmosphere, serves up delish Bavarian food, and specializes in white, or *weisses*, wheat beer. Also in the center, at Karlsplatz, the **Augustiner Grossgäststätte** dates from 1328. Today it offers great food, a cheerful little garden and upper terrace, and an elegant painted-and-plastered interior.

From early spring through late autumn, Munich's beer-drinking scene expands into the outdoors. Any time the sun shines, head for one of the city's many beer gardens. Best among them are the **Augustiner Keller** west of the main train station at Arnulfstrasse 52; the friendly **Chinesischer Turm** near the pagoda in the English Gardens; and, also in the English Gardens, the classy **Seehaus**, where sunny lakeside seating, good food, and a nearby boat rental make for a pleasant afternoon.

Germany

Munich's late-night party places open their doors around midnight – about the same time the city's beer halls shut down and theaters let out. Bouncers here are notorious for their snobby selectivity, but the following are some places to try. The **Feierwerk** and the **Nachtwerk** are two separate nightclub complexes. Each houses three dance clubs with DJs and live music. See what's on at the Feierwerk at ☎ 089 769 36 00, www.feierwerk.de. Contact the Nachtwerk at ☎ 089 570 83 80. **Kunstpark Ost**, near the Ostbahnhof, is a concert, bar, and disco complex with over 30 outlets and frequent live performances; ☎ 089 49 00 29 28. For jazz, try **Mr. B's** at Isavorstadt; ☎ 089 53 49 01.

Where to Play

 Families enjoy the several **playgrounds** at Olympia Park and the English Gardens and the interactive exhibits at the Deutches Museum. Just outside the city center, the **Hellabrunn Zoo** is popular for its 440 species, all housed in naturalistic habitats. Kids enjoy a petting area, an infrared bat cave, and a jungle tent. The zoo is open daily April to September from 8 am-6 pm and October to March from 9 am-5 pm; ☎ 089 62 50 90; €6.

Festivals & Events

 After the Carnival parties pass, Munich's breweries stage their **Strong Beer Season** in March. The tradition owes its start to the city's first monks, who created the especially strong brews for nourishment during the Lenten fasting season. (How will you know a strong beer? Look for beer names with an *–ator* suffix; for example, *Triumphator, Maximator,* and *Delicator.*) Other festivals include the **Auer Dulten** markets, the **Summer Festival** at Olympia Park in August and, of course, the world-renowned **Oktoberfest** in late September (see *O´zapft is* below). Munich's popular **Christmas Market** centers on the Marienplatz from late November through Christmas Eve.

AUTHOR'S PICK Three times each year at Mariahilfplatz in the Au District, Munich hosts the **Auer Dulten**, folkloric fairs and markets featuring household gadgets, tableware, flea-market stalls, rides for kids, and lots of food and beer. The **Maidult** takes place from late April through early May; the **Jakobidult**, from late July to early August; and the **Kirchweihdult**, from mid- to late October.

Culture-loving nightowls appreciate the city's Long Night events: **The Long Night of Music** in May, when some 100 venues host a wide range of musical performances from 8 pm to 3 am; and **The Long Night of the Munich Museums** in July. The Bavarian State Ballet hosts **Ballet Week** in late March, and the Bavarian State Opera stages the **Munich Opera Festival** late June through July.

O´zapft is!

 **Oktoberfest**, the world's largest festival, kicks off with the opening of the first keg and the mayor's pronouncement, *"O´zapft is"* (it's tapped)!

The festival tradition began in 1810, when Bavaria celebrated the wedding of Crown Prince Ludwig and Princess Therese von Sachsen-Hildburghausen, shown at left, in a field named the *Theresienwiese,* or Theresa's meadow, in honor of the bride. Both the fairgrounds and the festival itself are often referred to as the "*Wiesn,*" a shortened version of this name.

From that celebration grew the *Wiesn* of today, an international party featuring carnival rides, hearty traditional food, and lots and lots of beer. Fourteen enormous brewery tents reign over the festival grounds, each serving up one-liter mugs of house-proud brew, a specialty roast dish

St. Bartholomä church, Berchtesgaden, built in 1134

One of the painted houses in Oberammergau, Germany

Oberammergau Valley

Above: Weissensee at Füssen, Germany

Below: Cinque Torri, Cortina, Italy

or two, and enormous pretzels – all within sight and sound of an energetic Bavarian band. Statistically inclined? Each year, approximately six million visitors take part in the festivities. In 2002, they consumed some 6,088,071 gallons of beer, 459,259 roast chickens, and 438,810 sausages.

UPCOMING OKTOBERFEST DATES

The festival runs each year for 16 days, always ending on the first Sunday in October:

2004 . . . . 18 September-3 October

2005 . . . . 17 September-2 October

2006 . . . . 16 September-1 October

2007 . . . . 22 September-7 October

The festival grounds are at the Theresienwiese, a 15-minute walk southwest of the main train station. Take subway lines U4 and U5 to Theresienwiese station and then follow the lederhosen-clad crowd to the festival. The brewery tents serve beer from 10 am to 10:30 pm on weekdays and 9 am-10:30 pm on Sundays and holidays; the festival shuts down each night at 11:30 pm. (Want to stay later? Käfers Wiesnschänke and the Wein- und Sektzelt stay open until 1 am – last call for drinks at 12:15 am. After that, the city's bars and dance clubs host "After-Wiesn" parties; look for the advertisements posted around town.)

With in-tent seating for 98,000 available, it's hard to believe but true: Finding a place to sit can be difficult – and *you must be seated to order a beer.* (During the busiest hours in the evening and on weekends, it can get so crowded that security shuts off entry.) Our strategy? Go with a group, stake out a table early, and stay put, sending sightseers off in pairs to explore.

 Table reservations for small groups are advised during the festival's busier hours. Reservations must be made in advance through tent-specific hosts, and some tents require pre-booking of meals and beer vouchers. Two favorite tent hosts take on-line reservations in English: **Hippodrome** *at www.hippodrom-oktoberfest.de, or the* **Hofbräu Festzelt** *at http://www.hb-festzelt.de.*

Several events highlight the festival calendar. If you're in town, don't miss these:

Germany

- The colorful **Grand Entry of the Breweries** takes place at 10:45 am on the first Saturday of the festival. Beer-tent landlords parade through town with their families, staff, and horse-drawn keg wagons en route to the festival grounds and the opening of the festival.

- The **Costume and Marksmen's Parade** runs a seven-km route beginning at 10 am on the first Sunday of the festival. Over 7,000 participants show off brewery floats and wagons, marching bands, and rifle troops – all splendidly costumed in traditional dress.

- The **Concert of the Oktoberfest Bands** sounds off at 11 am on the second Sunday of the festival. Some 400 musicians gather at the festival grounds on the steps beneath the statue *Bavaria* for what must be the loudest oompah-pah-ing known to mankind. (In case of bad weather, catch the outdoor concert the following Sunday.)

Dachau

Crematorium at Dachau

Approximately 20 km northwest of Munich, Dachau is lodged in the world's memory as the location of Hitler's first concentration camp, a complex opened in 1933 to train Nazi officers and to "process" Jews, Poles, homosexuals, welfare recipients, gypsies, and any others deemed unacceptable by the Nazi regime. Visitors to **Dachau Concentration Camp Memorial**, or the *KZ-Gedenkstätte Dachau*, come here to remember and learn – and leave gripped by the same conviction that's inscribed out front: "Never again."

Inside the gates, the main hall exhibits photographs, maps, and models documenting the abuse, exterminations, and scientific experimentation to which Dachau prisoners were subjected. By the time the war ended in 1945, over 206,000 prisoners had been held here, and 32,000 of those had died. To put those numbers into horrifying perspective, however, note that Dachau was merely a work camp and staging area from which prisoners were sent east to die in gas chambers beyond Germany's borders – over a million were killed at Auschwitz alone.

The memorial is open Tuesday through Sunday from 9 am to 5 pm; admission is free. Informative English-language tours depart at 12:30 pm daily from June through August and on weekends, September through May; an English-language film screens at 11:30 am and 3:30 pm, and audio-tours are offered. Be forewarned, a visit here is a sobering experience that will disturb children and many adults. For more information, contact ☎ 08131 99 68 80, www.kz-gedenkstaette-dachau.de.

Although most tourists drop in only for a tour of the Dachau memorial, the town itself makes a worthwhile visit. Most notable here is the hilltop **Schloss Dachau**, which began its existence as a medieval fortress and eventually morphed into an expansive country palace for Munich's 16th-century Wittelsbach court. A wooden Renaissance ceiling, a collection of Wittelsbach coats of arms, and a lovely garden are the attractions here. Visit the palace Tuesday through Sunday, April through September from 10 am to 6 pm, and from October through March from 10 am to 4 pm.

 Want to stay? The **Bräuereigästhof Zieglerbräu** has inexpensive rooms in the center next to town hall. This traditional house is proud of its restaurant, a cozy wood-beamed dining room serving hearty traditional food. For more info, contact ☎ 08131 45 43 96, www.gasthof-ziegler-braeu.de.

 Dachau's tourist office is at Konrad Audenauer Strasse 1, ☎ 08131 752 86, www.dachau.info.de. Guides lead tours from in front of the town hall, May through September, Monday, Wednesday, and Saturday at 3 pm.

Chiemsee

Approximately one hour southeast of Munich by car along the lovely A8 autobahn, Chiemsee draws holiday-makers from all over Bavaria for its beaches, water recreation, and island castle. At 80 square km (31 square miles), the lake is Germany's largest and is endearingly known as the "Bavarian Ocean." Bordered to the south by a magnificent stretch of Alps, the region has through history played host to the region's most influential rulers: It was here that King Ludwig I built his elaborate castle, here that Hitler developed his Rastätte Resort, and here that world political leaders convened to hash out Germany's 1948 constitution.

Tourists come for the islands, **Herreninsel**, or "men's island," and **Fraueninsel**, or "women's island." Although no discrimination amongst visitors of either gender is made today, the islands took their names from the monastery and convent, respectfully, which once occupied their shores. On the larger of the two islands sprawls

Schloss Herrenchiemsee, "Mad" King Ludwig's late 19th-century replica of French King Louis XIV's Versailles. The smaller of the two inhabited islands, Fraueninsel, is home to a Benedictine convent and a tiny fishing community.

Along the southwestern lakeshore cluster the lake's primary recreational facilities. At both Bauern/Felden and Prien/Stock, rental services offer bikes, boats, windsurfers, and surreys; beer gardens serve up frothy brews; and grass-and-sand beaches beckon to sunbathers. Kids of all ages hop aboard the Chiemseebahn, a steam tramway running an original 1888 locomotive between Prien's main rail station and the lakeshore docks at Stock. In Prien, a large, attractive village, visitors can ogle the elaborate ceiling within the parish church, shop in glossy boutiques, and dine in high style at a wide variety of restaurants, many with outdoor garden seating.

ISLAND HOPPING BAVARIAN STYLE

While the two- to three-hour drive around the lake is a worthwhile excursion, I prefer a day out by ferryboat. Starting early from the Prien/Stock dock, head for Herreninsel, wander the gardens, take a castle tour, and stop off in a shady beer garden. From Herreninsel, hop a ferry to Fraueninsel. Stroll the fishing village's flower-festooned alleys, hike around the shoreline, take a swim at an island beach, and don't miss a chance to sample the smoked fish at the alley stalls near the northern end of the island. Pottery collectors should seek out the **Insel-Töpferei Klampfleuthner**, a family-run pottery workshop that's been turning its wheels since 1609. Longing for more? Venture around the lake by boat on the "Grosse," or grand tour, or head back to shore and rent a boat of your own.

AUTHOR'S
PICK

Book rooms on the islands and sample life here without all the day tourists. Try the simple **Schlosshotel** *in the old monastery grounds on Herreninsel or, on Fraueninsel, cozy up at the* **Gästhof Zur Linde**. *Book the Schlosshotel ($$) at* ☎ *08051 60 90, www.schlosshotel-herrenchiemsee. com, and the Gästhof Zur Linde ($$) at* ☎ *08054 903 66. Both houses have seasonal closing periods; call for more information.*

The **Chiemsee Schifffahrt Company** has been operating ferries here for 116 years, and they're quite good at what they do. Most boats converge at Prien/Stock and Herreninsel island and then fan out from there. (Passenger ferries en route to the islands also stop in at Bernau/Felden.) Boats run year-round, although service is most frequent during the June-through-September high season – check http://translate.google.com/translate?hl=en&sl=de&u=http:// www.chiemsee-schifffahrt.de for more info. Day-trippers choose between several ticket plans including one or more islands, a "grand" round-trip, or single-trip tickets. Those seeking a special night out should consider the themed pleasure cruises taking float during the high season and weekends; features include dancing, jazz, fairy-tales, and specialty dining.

 Chiemsee's tourist information center is at the Bernau/Felden recreation area at the lake's southwestern shore. Dial ☎ 08051 22 80 or surf www.mychiemsee.de for more information.

■ Garmisch-Partenkirchen

Population: 28,000

Base elevation: 720 m

Mountain resort town

At the foot of the Zügspitze, near the border with Austria, Garmisch-Partenkirchen remains Germany's favorite climatic health and recreation resort. With an Olympic history and an encircling ring of mountains, the twin towns offer a bustling ambiance, two quaint pedestrian areas, and a range of outdoor recreation to suit all tastes.

History & Orientation

 Garmisch-Partenkirchen and the Werdenfelser Land got its start as an intermediate stop on the Roman trade route between Italy's Brenner Pass and Augsburg to the north. The regions's name, the Werdenfels, derives from the castle now in ruins at the edge of the Kramerspitz. Local citizens enjoyed a prosperous 14th century but lost much during the Thirty Years War. New wealth poured into the region in the mid-19th century, as students, painters, and musicians found inspiration in the surrounding hills. Adventuresome mountaineers, climatic health seekers, and wealthy landlords arrived soon after, and Alpine tourism took hold.

The valley was one of Europe's preeminent winter sports resorts, founding Germany's first ski club in 1905, bobsledding made its first run here in 1911, and Bavaria's first hockey players took to local ice in the 1920s. In 1936, in preparation for the Olympic Winter Games, Hitler declared the two villages of Garmisch and Partenkirchen a single town.

Today's Garmisch-Partenkirchen spreads out along a Werdenfels valley, encircled by mountains and split by the Partnach and Loisach rivers. Along the southern edge of town, the magnificent Zugspitz and its Wettersteingebirge range forms the border of Austria; the Wank rises to the east; and to the north rests the sunny, peaceful Kramerspitz area. The quieter hamlet of Grainau lies west of town, near the Eibsee at the foot of the Zügspitze.

The Town

Today, Garmisch-Partenkirchen forms what is politically one town – but culturally two separate centers. Garmisch lies to the west and Partenkirchen to the east, the railroad tracks and Parnach River separating the two. From Garmisch, the Zugspitzstrasse heads west toward the Zügspitze, Reutte, and Füssen; and from Partenkirchen, the Hauptstrasse runs north toward Oberammergau and Munich and south toward Mittenwald and Innsbruck.

In Garmisch, tourism centers on the pedestrian-only stretch of Am Kurpark, the road running between the Kongresshaus and the Marienplatz. The old residential district lies just north, across the Loisach River at Fruhlingstrasse. The somewhat quieter historical and tourist district of Partenkirchen spans Ludwigstrasse, a cobblestone street to the east of, and parallel to, Hauptstrasse.

Getting Here & Around

 Garmisch sits approximately 1½ hours south of Munich and one hour north of Innsbruck, Austria. Both cities have international airports. Garmisch's train station is in the center directly between the two old villages, a 15-minute walk from Partenkirchen's old town, Garmisch's old town, and the Hausbergbahn lift station. Transportation around town is via the local bus system. For taxi service, dial ☎ 00821 16 16.

 *The **Garmisch-Partenkirchen Visitor's Card** offers overnight guests free access to the bus system and a single entry to the Alpspitze Wellenbad wave pool, the spa gardens, and casino. Other discounts apply as well. Ask for the card on arrival at your hotel.*

Mountain transportation includes a total of 38 lifts spanning, from west to east, the Zügspitze, Alpspitze, Kreuzeck, Hausberg, Eckbauer, and Wank areas. Only the Kramerspitz to the north lacks lift service. For more information, contact the Bayerische Zügspitzbahn at ☎ 08821 79 70, www.zugspitze.de.

LIFT PASS PRICE SAMPLES

Winter

1-day adult Classic Pass €28

6-day adult Happy Ski Card. €168

Pedestrian round-trip to Alpspitze €19

Pedestrian round-trip to Zügspitze €35

Summer

Pedestrian round-trip to Alpspitze €19

Pedestrian round-trip to Zügspitze €44

Getting Connected

 The main branch of the Garmisch-Partenkirchen Tourist Office is housed near the Kongresshall at Richard Strauss Platz 2. Visitors reserve accommodations, purchase event tickets, arrange guides, and gather brochures and maps. For more info, check in at ☎ 08821 180 700 or www.garmisch-partenkirchen.de.

 The most convenient post offices are at the train station and in Garmisch at Marienplatz 8 near the Pfarrkirche St. Martin.

 For Internet access in Partenkirchen, try the **Computerhaus** at Ludwigstrasse 69; in Garmisch, head for **Hobi's Internetcafé** – it's got a great bakery, and there's even a small computer station for kids.

The Sights

In Garmisch, shoppers stroll the pedestrian-only **Am Kurparkstrasse**, and history buffs seek out old-world Garmisch along **Frülingstrasse**, where municipal restrictions ensure that the residences appear just as they did 200 years ago. The quaint, cobblestone street parallels the north bank of the Loisach River, just north of Marienplatz and the Pfarrkirch St. Martin. Nearby at Fürstenstrasse, look for the Hungarian soldier in the *Lüftmalerei* window on the façade of the **Bräustubl** restaurant, the town's first *gästhaus*. Beyond the old building façades, duck inside the 11th-century **Alte Kirche**, where meticulous work continues in efforts to unbury newly discovered frescoes from beneath centuries of over-paint.

Across town in Partenkirchen, tourists wander the shops and restaurants along scenic Ludwigstrasse, one of the valley's original Roman roads and a route used by King Ludwig II on his way to the Sachen mountain lodge. Of note are the **Post Hotel**, where King Ludwig stayed; the **Gästhof Frauendorfer**, fronted by a fanciful Lüftmalerei of a Bavarian wedding party; and at house 54, Partenkirchen's own **Goldener Dachl**, a miniature copy of Innsbruck's golden roof. Nearby, the **Werdenfelser Heimatmuseum** covers 2,000 years of local history with its folklore and cultural displays. The museum is at Ludwigstrasse 47 in Partenkirchen, open Tuesday through Friday, 10 am-noon and 3-6 pm, and Saturday and Sunday, 10 am-1 pm; ☎ 08821 21 34, €1.50.

For those interested in music, the **Richard Strauss Institute** documents the life and work of hometown son Richard Strauss. The museum includes multimedia displays, a musical museum, and a library. It's open Tuesday through Friday from 10 am to 5 pm and Saturday and Sunday, 2-5 pm; ☎ 08821 910 950, www.richard-strauss-insitut.de, €2.50.

The Zügspitze

The Zügspitze, Germany's highest mountain, draws busloads of international tourists to its peak each day. The views from the top are spectacular on a clear day, and the trip up is half the fun. Ride the Bayerische Zügspitzbahn from Garmisch-Partenkirchen station past Grainau to Lake Eibsee. The old track railway, first opened in 1930, ascends up and through the mountain to the Schneefern Glacier and the cozy Sonn Alpin restaurant. From there, the Gletscherbahn cable car makes the quick trip up to the 3,000-m Zügspitze peak.

At the top, visitors can enjoy views across four nations, search out the Austrian-German border cut into the forest far below, and cross into Austria – the Alte Zöllhütte snack stand was once passport control. The scrappy, wooden Münchner Haus is interesting for two reasons: First, because its self-service grill offers a refreshing *mass* of beer; second, because it was built here in 1897, well before the railway was in place. Daredevils will want to make the short, sporty climb up to the *gipfelkreuz*, or peak cross.

After visiting the peak, descend via the Eibseeseilbahn cable car back down to Eibsee. (Before boarding, make sure you're on the right cable car: The Gletscherbahn brought you here; the Eibseeseilbahn will take you back down to the valley; but the *third* cable car will strand you in Ehrwald, Austria, far, far from where you want to be.) The Zügspitzbahn and cable cars run daily except during the two-week fall and spring maintenance periods. For more information, log on to www.zugspitze.de.

The Adventures

On Foot

A 300-km network of **mountain paths** winds around the resort. Valley paths meander along the base of the Wettersteingebirge from Partenkirchen through Garmisch and on to Grainau and the Eibsee. At altitude, the Wank, Eckbauer, Kreuzeck, and Alpspitze area offer opportunities for lift-served hiking, and each area is scattered with inviting mountain restaurants. On the north side of town, the Kramerspitz does not have lift service but is popular for its easy Plateauweg walk and its scenic Almhütte and St. Martin mountain restaurants.

AUTHOR'S PICK

If you can only take one hike, head for the **Partnachklamm**, or Partnach Gorge, for a fascinating look at the power of water. To reach the gorge, start from the west side of the Olympic Ski Stadium (worth a quick look, particularly if ski-jumping practice is in session) and take the 20-minute walk or horse-drawn carriage ride up the Wildenau Valley to the gorge base. From the base entry booth, walkers navigate the gorge via a narrow gallery path cut into the gorge walls. The gorge is open year-round – and is at its most beautiful in the winter, when enormous icicles add a surreal ambiance to the already spectacular rock formations. To return, walkers can either head back down the gorge or, from the upper end of the gorge, take the steps uphill toward Graseck and back to the ski stadium via the trail or the Eckbauerbahn cable car.

Yet another favorite hike ascends two-three hours from the Partnach Gorge up to **Schachen**, King Ludwig II's private hunting lodge. Royal views extend to the Zügspitze, and the house's upper floor is decked out in splendid Oriental style. Here, in the Turkish room, the eccentric king celebrated special occasions in isolation, joined only by servants dressed in lavish Oriental robes. The lodge and restaurant open in late May or early June (depending on when the snow melts) and close in early October. Guided lodge tours run at 11 am and 2 pm, €2.

In Water

Garmisch's public **swimming complex**, the **Alpspitz Wellenbad**, offers indoor and outdoor pools, wave and children's pools, a whirlpool, and a sauna area. It's open throughout the year; contact ☎ 08821 753 313, www.gw-gap.de, for more information.

Although Garmisch has several lakes to call its own, they are all tiny, each offering little more than a bathing area and some pleasant trails. The best of the local lakes is **Eibsee**, a small azure lake at the foot of the Zügspitze, surrounded by forests, and with both a **bathing area** and a dock renting **row boats**. In the summer, the **Freizeitpark Loisachbad** maintains a **riverside bathing area** and a **Kneipp therapy** trail on the banks of the Loisach River. **Thomas Sprenzel's Wildwasser & Kajakschule** offers **kayaking** instruction and trips, ☎ 00821520 33. **Fly-fishing** is possible from May through September in the **Loisach** and **Partnach rivers**, but completing the required paperwork is time-consuming and expensive. For more information, contact the **Landratsamt** at Olympiastrasse 10; ☎ 08821 7511.

On Wheels

In the summer, **skaters** enjoy the small park near the Ice Sports Center, and a **wheeled toboggan run** thrills kids at Eckbauer. **Mountain-biking** is extremely popular, and trails of all levels of difficulty wind up, around, and through the local mountains. A favorite easy trek runs from Garmisch to Grainau and around the lovely Lake Eibsee, where a restaurant offers refreshments. The tourist office's map *Radln & Mountainbiken* offers additional ideas. For bike rental – in both city and mountain styles – the best place in town is **Trek Bikes** at Rathausplatz 11 in Partenkirchen; ☎ 00821 548 44, www.trekproshop.de.

In the Air

Paragliders leap from several local launch points, including Wank, Hausberg, and the Alpspitz. Want to try? The **Gleitschirmschule Michael Brunner** offers lessons and tandem flights. Contact ☎ 00821 742 60, www.gleitschirmschule-gap.de, for more information. **Climbers** enjoy the **Hochseilgarten ropes course** near Eibsee, and climbing gardens challenge at Breitenau in Garmisch and on the Alpspitze.

On Snow & Ice

Garmisch-Partenkirchen is Germany's premier Alpine sports resort, boasting 118 km of groomed ski runs, 38 lifts, and the hallowed Kandahar piste, site of Germany's only World Cup ski race. In the local area, **skiers** enjoy early- and late-season runs at Zügspitze on the Schneefern Glacier. Beginners head for the Zügspitze plateau and the Eckbauer family area, intermediates enjoy runs of the entire mountain, and advanced skiers head for Kreuzeck and Hausberg and the Kandahar racing run. A funpark and halfpipe entertain **snowboarders** on the Zügspitze plateau, facilities maintained into the early summer for the mountain's popular **GAP1328 snowboarding camps**; for more info check www.gap1328.de.

> *The **Happy Ski Card** lift pass combines access to 111 lifts and 250 km of runs at 11 resorts in Germany and Austria, including Garmisch-Partenkirchen, Mittenwald, Seefeld, and Ehrwald. Passes can be purchase for a minimum of three days.*

Cross-country skiers take to 40 km of loipe in the local area and near Grainau and day-trip to the additional trails winding through the Loisach and Oberammergau valleys. **Specialist Ski School Thomas Schwinghammer**, at the east entrance of the Olympic Ski Stadium, offers Nordic ski instruction in English; ☎ 08821 556 32. **Wintertime walkers** enjoy 100 km of cleared or groomed paths, while **snowshoers** head out from the Alpspitz-Wellenbad or, for a more difficult challenge, from the Wand middle station to the peak and back.

> *The tourist office sells a good winter trail map with information (in German) entitled Sport & Wintergaudi.*

Fans of **ice sports** head for the **Olympic Ice Sports Center**, the largest complex of its kind in Europe. Five rinks make space for ice hockey, skating, and both indoor and outdoor curling. To see what's on, contact ☎ 08821 753 291. For **tobogganing**, rent sleds in town and hike up to the two-km Hornschlittenrennen run at Parnachklamm or the popular 1.6-km trail below St. Martin's at the Kramerspitz. Try also the fast four-km run at the Hausbergbahn lift – it's open and lit from 5 to 10 pm, Monday and Friday evenings. The bottom of this run is good for kids, too. **Horse-drawn sleighs** await at the ski stadium or by reservation at ☎ 08821 94 29 30.

Sports Services, Outfitters & Guides

- ■ The **Garmisch-Partenkirchen Ski School** offers multi-lingual lessons from the base of the Hausberg area. Contact ☎ 08821 742 60, www.skischule-gap.de, for more information. The school rents equipment, too.

- ■ For multi-sport equipment rental, try **Welt des Sports** at Fürstenstrasse 20, and at Marienplatz, **Sport Total.** Ski rental is available at the Hausbergbahn valley station and at on the glacier at the Zugspitzplatt mountain station.

Germany

- The **Wildwasserschule and Bike Verleih Center** at Alpspitzstrasse 16 team up to offer rafting, kayaking, and mountain-bike outings in the summer. In the winter, ski rental and service is available at the same address. Contact ☎ 08821 14 96, www.ww-gap.com, www.bikeverleih.de.

- **The Werdenfelser Mountain Guides** run a wide range of all-season outings. The bureau offers private guiding services and maintains several mountain huts as well. Contact ☎ 08821 180 744, www.bergfuehrer-werdenfels.de, for more information. Alternatively, meet a representative at the tourist office Monday or Thursday from 4 to 6 pm, between Christmas and Easter and from late May through mid October.

Where to Sleep

 Best among the upscale traditional houses here is the **Hotel Zügspitze** ($$$), a large, cozy chalet brimming with geraniums in summer. The proprietors are most hospitable, and there's an indoor pool and sauna to boot. Book at ☎ 08821 90 10, www.hotel-zugspitze.de.

HOTEL PRICE CHART	
Double room without tax; $$$-$$$$ always with bath.	
$	Under €80
$$	€81-150
$$$	€151-250
$$$$	Over €250

The creeky, old-world **Reindl's Partenkirchner Hof** ($$$) encompasses three sprawling houses in the center, the first built in 1911. World War II history buffs should consider a stay here, as Hitler used the hotel for a hospital before occupying Americans housed a headquarters here; ☎ 08821 943 870, www.reindls.de.

Outside the center, the **Reissersee Renaissance Hotel** ($$$), a businesslike convention hotel, has a romantic forest location adjacent to a small lake that makes it a vacation option as well. Reserve at ☎ 08821 75 80, www.renaissance-riessersee-hotel.de.

Both **Clausings Post Hotel** ($$$) and the **Post Hotel Partenkirchen** ($$-$$$) offer traditional accommodations at midrange rates. Clausings Post Hotel is in the center of Garmisch near the Marienplatz, ☎ 08821 70 90, http://www.clausings-posthotel.de; the Post Hotel Partenkirchen, in the center of Partenkirchen's old town at Ludwigstrasse, ☎ 08821 936 30, www.post-hotel.de. Cozy, traditional accommodations is also found at Partenkirchen's **Gästhof Fraundorfer** ($$), home to the town's favorite Bavarian dinner show; ☎ 08821 92 70, www.gasthof-fraundorfer.de.

The **Alpina** ($$), on a busy corner in the center of Garmisch at Alpspitzstrasse 12, offers modern chalet accommodations within easy reach of the Garmisch old town and the Hausburgbahn lift. Get more info at ☎ 08821 78 30, http://www.alpina-gap.de.

The **Hotel Garmischer Hof** ($$) has low rates despite its central location at Chamonixstrasse 10; ☎ 08821 91 10. Around the corner from the train station, fronting the Partnach River at Partnachauenstrasse 3, the friendly **Hotel Schell** ($-$$) offers homey, modern accommodations at boardinghouse budget rates; ☎ 08821 957 50.

Finally, conveniently located at the train station, the **Hotel Vier Jahreszeiten** ($-$$) is more cheerful than its low rates and pragmatic locale might convey. Check in at ☎ 08821 91 60, www.vierjahreszeiten.cc.

LODGING FOR US MILITARY

The **Edelweiss Lodge and Resort** ($$) opens in September of 2004 to serve US military members and their families. Well located near the Kreuzeckbahn lift and a Zügspitzbahn train station, the new recreational resort offers 330 rooms and suites, a conference center, and a wellness center. The slope-side Hausberg Sport Lodge serves skiers, and a full range of regional tours is available. For more information, ☎ 08821 729 81, www.AFRCEurope.com; proper ID required upon reservation.

Where to Eat

Traditional dining options abound in Garmisch-Partenkirchen. In Garmisch's old residential area, the **Bräustüberl** ($$) at Fürstenstrasse 23 swarms with Bavarian charm, as does the more elegant and modern **Restaurant Alpenhof** ($$$) at the casino on Am Kurpark. Reserve a table at ☎ 08821 590 55, www.alpenhof-garmisch.de. Also in the center near the Kurpark, try the **Hofbräustüberl** ($$) on Chamonixstrasse for an odd mix of Yugoslavian and Bavarian cuisine.

DINING PRICE CHART	
Average entrée, with tax.	
$	Under €10
$$	€10-25
$$$	Over €25

For dinner and entertainment under one roof, the cozy **Gästhof Frauendorfer** ($$) in Partenkirchen stages nightly folklore dinner shows, including an immensely popular Bavarian slap dance. Make reservations at ☎ 08821 92 70, www.gasthof-fraundorfer.de. Nearby, at Ludwigstrasse 58, the **Gästhof Werdenfelser Hof** ($) often features live music and dance alongside its traditional cuisine; ☎ 08821 36 21, www.werdenfelser-hof.de. If it's a sunny day and you're in the Wank area, hike or drive up past the old Wankbahn to the **Panorama Restaurant** ($$) for outdoor dining, and splendid views of the valley and its surrounding mountains.

For café dining in Garmisch, try the **Conditorei Café Krönner** ($) at Am Kurpark and Achenfeldstrasse. It's got a high-visibility street-side patio and a cheering upstairs dining terrace. The valley's best ice cream is at **Eis 2000** ($) at Marienplatz 7, across from the Kathe Wohlfart shop. Budgeting diners should look for the morning market stall, either at Mohrenplatz on Friday or Rathausplatz on Thursday.

Where to Party

Garmisch-Partenkirchen's party scene hinges more on quiet cafés than late-night clubs. That said, the town's youngest, hippest disco is the **Musik Café** on Marienplatz. Nearby, the **Peaches** and **Zum Holzwurm** prove popular as well.

Near city hall, try the popular **Irish Pub** at Rathaus 8, and check in at **John's Club** at Rathaus 7 for cocktails and dancing. The **Spielbank Garmisch-Partenkirchen** casino spins roulette, poker, blackjack, and slot machines daily from 3 pm. It's off the Garmisch pedestrian area at Am Kurpark 10, ☎ 08821 959 90.

Where to Play

In the summer, kids enjoy the **Freizeitpark Loisachbad**, a riverside playground and park on the banks of the Loisach. Additional **playgrounds** are between the Rathaus and Wettersteinstrassein Partenkirchen, at Gartenstrasse in Garmisch, and near the Hausbergbahn mountain station. Cable car and carriage rides, the Alpspitze Wellenbad, and the summer toboggan run at Eckbauer all prove popular, too. The tourist office can help with **babysitting** arrangements, and the office's *Ortsplan* map conveniently marks the outlying walking paths suitable for wheelchairs and strollers.

Festivals & Events

A local tradition, **New Year's Day Ski Jumping** kicks off each January, and the **International Sports Weeks** offer cultural and sporting events for two weeks beginning the day after Christmas and continuing through early January. A variety of World Cup **sporting competitions** highlight the winter months, and mountain biking competitions take to the trails in summer.

Mid-June brings the **Richard Strauss Festival** in celebration of the composer's birthday. Garmisch hosts its **Folklore Festival** at the end of July; Partenkirchen, in early August. From August through September, the **Culture Summer** festival highlights a wide range of theater, cabaret, fine art, and concert events.

Mittenwald

Mittenwald is famed for its 140-year-old violin-making school, a working classroom that ships out some of the world's finest instruments to some of the world's finest concert halls. From its pleasant central square, Mittenwald shows off a Baroque 18th-century church, fanciful Lüftmalerei frescoes, and balconies spilling over with blooms. Add a penchant for age-old customs, traditional costumes, concerts, and arts and crafts, and this colorful town seems the best of all things Bavarian.

Well worth a musician's time is a visit to the **Geigenbau Museum**, Ballenhausgasse 3, for an excellent presentation of violins and violin-making. Typical regional home décor, the work of masters Jakobus Stainer and Mathias Klotz, and violin-making demonstrations highlight attractions here. It's open December through October, Monday through Sunday, 10-11:45 am, and Monday through Friday, 2-4:45 pm. The small **Schnapps Museum** at the Alte Hausbrennerei Penninger, Obermarkt 37, displays a good collection of antique schnapps-making equipment, offers tastings of its schnapps and vinegars, and keeps a good stock for sale as well.

Surrounded by lakes, edged by the Isar River, and shadowed by the Karwendel mastiff, Mittenwald makes a great destination for **outdoor adventure**. In summer, hikers and bikers wander paths around the Kranzberg, walkers venture up the misty Leutäschklamm, and mountain climbers take to the Mittenwald Steep Path, a difficult trail linking eight 2,000-meter-plus peaks. In winter, beginner and intermediate skiers love the Kranzberg's easy slopes, and families flock here for low-key ski holidays. Cross-country skiers head for the nearby Leutäschtal, winter walkers enjoy over 60 km of groomed trails, and view-seekers hop on the Karwendel cable car for a ride to the top – thrill-seekers hop off the Karwendel peak for the seven-km ski run to the bottom.

 If you'd like to stay, try the **Hotel and Gästhof Post**. It's in the center of town at Obermart 9 and offers rooms in both rustic and modern style. For reservations, ☎ 08823 10 94, www.posthotel-mittenwald.de.

For more information, check with the tourist office at ☎ 08823 33981, http://www.mittenwald.de/indexdt.html.

Oberammergau

 In a tight little valley just a 20-minute drive north of Garmisch, the village of Oberammergau huddles along the banks of the Ammer River in the shadow of the 1,343-m Kofel peak. The old town center clusters around the beautiful Baroque church, a web of alleys lined with woodcarving workshops, *gästhofs*, and fancifully frescoed façades. Anchoring the east side of town, near the base station of the Laber cable car, are the WellenBerg swimming complex and a NATO officers' school (which, by the way, explains the hodgepodge of military uniforms in town around lunchtime). The two sides of town are connected by both Ludwig Lang Strasse and Am Kreuzweg, streets ideal for drive-by sightings of Lüftmalerei façades.

LÜFTMALEREI

 Although the custom of painting house façades was well developed by the 18th century, Oberammergau local Franz Zwinck took the tradition to new heights, developing the art of *Luftmalerei*, or "airy painting." The trompe l'oeil technique entertains the eye with false architectural features and fanciful representations of folk tales, historical events, and religious stories. Luftmalerei façades are common throughout Bavaria and the Austrian Tirol and Oberammergau, the tradition's point of origin, positively abounds with fine examples. For a look at Zwinck's original work, head for the Pilatus House at Verlegergasse.

Although the true joys of Oberammergau are best encountered by simply wandering around, there are some sights of note. First, the **Heimatmuseum Oberammergau**, a reasonable documentation of the history and culture of the village, opens each Satuday from 2 to 6 pm. The museum includes an excellent display of woodcarvings and nativity sets. One of Bavaria's finest examples of Lüftmalerei, the **Pilatushaus** on Verlegergasse also serves as a summertime workshop for local artists – barrel painters, woodcarvers, and potters. Come watch them work May through October, Monday through Friday from 1 to 6 pm. Want to give woodcarving a try? The town's masters offer several week-long **woodcarving courses** each April and September; contact the tourist office at ☎ 08821 180 700 or www.garmische-partenkirchen.de for more information.

The Oberammergau Passion Play

Oberammergau's "Play of the Suffering, Death, and Resurrection of our Lord Jesus Christ" got its start in 1634 after the region was hit hard by both the plague and the Thirty Years War. The villagers vowed to perform this play every 10 years if the village was spared, a bargain the powers-that-be saw fit to oblige.

So, to this day, every 10 years, 2,000 locals participate in the staging of the world-famous Oberammergau Passion Play. The play relives the final five days in the life of Jesus, a story that lasts six hours on stage. In the months prior to opening night, the mayor declares preparations in effect: Men forgo shaving (what would a passion play be without beards?), women grow their hair, barbers become costumers, and woodcarving shops turn into set-building studios.

If you won't be here in 2010 when the next play is scheduled, you can see the facility, costumes, and photos on a theater tour. The playhouse is open daily in the winter, 10 am-4 pm, and summer, 9:30 am-5 pm. Occasional operas take the stage, too. Check with the tourist office at ☎ 08821 180 700 for more information.

Adventurers head into the hills on the Kolbensattel chairlift and on the Laber cable car. Both operate in the summer – accessing over 100 km of hiking and mountain biking trails. In winter, the former takes you to easy hikes and downhill ski runs; the latter, to an expert off-piste ski descent and the town's favorite paragliding launch site. Oberammergau's loipe are some of the best in Bavaria, and cross-country ski trails wind along the river, past cozy inns to Ettal and, for those with considerable stamina, all the way to Linderhof's castle. Mountain climbers conquer the Kofel, and swimmers enjoy the WellenBerg swimming complex, which offers indoor, outdoor, and children's pools.

Oberammergau makes a reasonable base from which to explore the sights of the Bavarian Alps. Besides being within easy day-tripping distance of Garmisch, Füssen, and Mittenwald, Oberammergau sits between the **Ettaler Benedictine Abbey** to the east, (www.kloster-ettal.de) and the lovely **Wieskirche** to the north (www.wieskirche.de).

Germany

Want to stay in Oberammergau? I liked the **Hotel Garni Fux** ($-$$) for its variety of simple rooms and its central locale. Reserve a room or apartment at ☎ 08822 930 93, www.firmafux.de.

The tourist office is at Eugen Papst Strasse 9a. Contact ☎ 008822 923 10, www.oberammergau.de, for more information.

Schloss Linderhof

Some 12 km southwest of Oberammergau along the Alpine road that runs from Graswang toward Reutte and Füssen, nestles what I consider the finest of King Ludwig's castles. Completed in 1878, the castle is small and manageable, easily covered in an hour or two; it's eccentric, with features like a hidden cave grotto, a trap-door dining table, fanciful fountain gardens, and eye-popping Rococo decor; and it's *real* – the only one of the king's castle's that was actually finished and where he actually spent considerable time. Visit the castle April through September, 9 am-6 pm, and October through March, 10 am-4 pm. Open daily; €9.

Füssen

First a stop on the third-century Roman route between Italy, Austria, and Augsburg, Füssen is today a stop on the route of most Bavarian bus tours. The modern draws here are a quaint pedestrian center; nearby lake, mountain, and spa retreats; and – most significantly – a pair of famous castles just for km outside of town in nearby Schwangau.

AUTHOR'S PICK

Schloss Neuschwanstein remains many tourists' quintessential image of Germany and the Alps. The most ambitious of King Ludwig's palace projects, the fairy-tale castle perches dramatically above the Pöllat Gorge, high on a forested hill near Füssen. Built between 1869 and 1886, the castle was designed as a fanciful replication of medieval grandeur, but it was never completed and the king was in residence here only a few days.

To reach the castle, follow the road signs to the Königschlosser, or royal castles; park at Höhenschwangau; and make the 25-minute up-hill climb or hire one of the waiting horse-drawn carriages. At the top, join thousands of other international visitors for a guided tour. The castle opens daily April through September from 9 am to 6 pm (Thursdays to 8 pm) and October through March from 10 am to 4 pm; ☎ 008362 810 35, www.schlossneuschwanstein.de; €7.

And by the way, do those turrets look familiar? Walt Disney modeled his Disneyland castle and logo after Neuschwanstein.

The "other" castle in town is **Höhenschwangau**, a yellow palace below Neuschwanstein. This was the much more practical summer home of the Wittelsbach royal family, and King Ludwig I spent much of his time here – possibly gazing up the mountain dreaming up the fairytale castle he eventually constructed there.

The 700-year-old **town center** of Füssen is worth a stroll as well. Visitors enjoy shopping in the old town, tours of the Town Hall **history museum** in the former monastery of St. Mang, views of the exquisite Lüftmalerei in the **Höhe Schloss** courtyard, and visits to the **Mangfall**, a ravine waterfall cut by the River Lech. The Königswinkel region of the Ällgau is known throughout Germany as a low-key health and **recreation** center, and local villages take full advantage of their lakes, rivers, and mountain attractions. Visitors can hop aboard the Tegelberg cable car, rent boats and enjoy ferry rides on Lake Forggensee, and wander the 180-km trail network through local mountains. Ballooning, cycling, and snow- and water-sports keep visitors in town year-round.

LUDWIG II: LONGING FOR PARADISE

Fans of musical theater may want to check out this rendition of the tragic life of "mad" fairy-tale king: his early ascent to the throne, his passions for art and technology, and his relationship with Richard Wagner. Performances take the stage north of Füssen in a lakeside facility encompassing restaurants, a beer garden, and gardens. Shows play Tuesday through Thursday and Sunday, and backstage tours are available. For reservations, contact ☎ 08362 93 90 70, www.ludwigmusical.com, tickets from €45.

 Want to stay? The **Hotel Hirsch** offers lovely accommodations directly in the pedestrian center at Kaiser-Maximilian-Platz 7. All rooms have modern amenities, some with Bavarian antiques and frescoed walls. Reserve at ☎ 08362 939 80, www.hotelhirsch.de.

Germany

The tourist office is at Kaiser-Maximilian-Platz 1; ☎ 08362 938 50, www.fuessen.de.

■ Berchtesgaden

Population: 8,100

Base elevation: 571 m

Mountain tourist town

Spectacular natural beauty surrounds Berchtesgaden. Crystal rivers run through steep-peaked valleys, rustic mountain huts offer fresh Alpine milk, and a national park harbors rare flora and fauna. Nonetheless, international bus tours tend to blow through town, affording only a single day to visit Hitler's "Eagle's Nest" and the World War II documentation center – though these historic sites certainly merit attention. For independent travelers with the freedom to do so, I suggest a longer stay.

History & Overview

 Legend maintains that Berchtesgaden's once ice-locked landscape was first inhabited by fierce dragons and wild beasts – an unruly crowd that was inexplicably scared off when a group of Augustiner monks moved in during the early 12th century. For seven centuries, the archbishops ruled the region from a monastery on the site of today's palace, gaining wealth and power from the harvesting of salt, or "white gold," from local mines. In the early 19th century, rule passed from Napoleon to Austria and then Germany, and Berchtesgaden eventually became a favorite Alpine retreat of the Wittelsbachs, Bavaria's ruling family. In the 20th century, the town caught the fancy of Hitler, who overran the nearby village of Obersalzburg, built his Mt. Kehlstein mountain retreat – and escorted World War II to the Berchtesgaden's doorstep.

Berchtesgaden lies in the Bavarian Alps in the southeastern-most corner of Germany on a politically defined peninsula jutting into central Austria. Shadowed by the 2,713-m Watzmann Mountain, the town enjoys a wealth of natural splendor, including lakes, rivers, dramatic peaks, and a neighboring national park. Several towns are easily reached via the network of valley roads that intersect at Berchtesgaden: **Ramsau** to the west, **Bad-Reichenhall** to the north, **Salzburg** to the northeast, and **Hallein** to the east. Just south of town gleams the lake of **Königsee**, a long narrow stretch of pristine Alpine water – it's covered separately below.

The Town

The modern town of Berchtesgaden sprawls along the B305 valley road between Ramsau ad Hallein, centering on the train station and Königsseerstrasse, which heads south to the lake. Above this intersection, Bahnhofstrasse climbs the hillside toward the old town, marked on maps as Markt Berchtesgaden, or "market town" Berchtesgaden. The old center radiates from the modern Kurpark and Alter Friedhof. To the north, a web of shopping streets leads to Marktplatz square and Schlossplatz, the castle complex's quiet courtyard. To the west, a network of old alleys hides a collection of mundane shops and cafés, and Maximilianstrasse traverses the hillside to the south and west.

Getting Here & Around

 Berchtesgaden sits approximately 30 km southwest of Salzburg and 150 km southeast of Munich. Drivers will find the town along Route B305 between Ramsau and Hallein. Parking is difficult here; your best bet for a central spot is the garage under the Kurpark.

Trains pull in to the main station below the center of town, and the regional RVO buses hub there, too. Mountain transportation is limited to the few lifts scattered outside of town at the ski areas – see *Adventures* below. For taxi transfer, dial **Radio Taxi** at ☎ 08652 40 41.

 The Berchtesgaden Holiday Bus Pass offers five days of unlimited local bus transportation. (A few restrictions apply.) The tourist office, the convention center, and the RVO bus ticket office sell the pass for €15.

Getting Connected

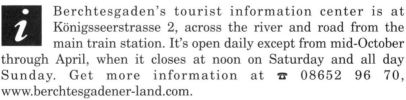 Berchtesgaden's tourist information center is at Königsseerstrasse 2, across the river and road from the main train station. It's open daily except from mid-October through April, when it closes at noon on Saturday and all day Sunday. Get more information at ☎ 08652 96 70, www.berchtesgadener-land.com.

 The post office is at Marktplatz 24 in the old town center's pedestrian area.

The Sights

In the old town center, the chief attraction is the **Schloss Adelsheim** castle complex, a combination monastery, palace, church, concert venue, and museum. The castle got its start in the 11th century as a monastery before Bavaria's royal Wittelsbach family came in 1803 and morphed it into the more luxurious palace I see now. In the Schlossplatz courtyard, visitors should note the **war memorial** spanning the western side of the square and should at least take a glance inside the **Stiftskirche**. The castle **museum** itself includes a reasonable collection of art, furnishings, and armour; tours are offered from Easter through mid-October, 10 am-12 pm and 2-4 pm, closed Saturdays; and from mid-October to Easter, Monday through Friday at 11 am and 2 pm. Call ☎ 0852 94 79 80 for more information.

Berchtesgaden's most notorious resident was Adolf Hitler, and most tourists come here to explore this most unfortunate era of the region's history. Hitler's southern headquarters complex grew up around his original **Obersalzburg** vacation home, the Berghaus, just east of town. In the process of expansion, the Nazi party incorporated or destroyed all of the pre-existing structures, forcing local farmers and their families out of their homes and off their land.

AUTHOR'S PICK

World War II saw extended bombing raids on Obersalzburg, and little of either the original village or Hitler's complex remains. What's left is now the **Dokumentation Obersalzberg**, a museum documenting the Nazi takeover of the Obersalzburg village, the coercion of local citizens, and the construction of the Kehlsteinhaus. Exhibitions include chilling accounts of Nazi tactics and travesties; and visitors are invited to explore part of the massive bunker network tunneled below the Obersalzburg area. The center is open Tuesday through Sunday, 9 am-5 pm from May through October and 10 am-3 pm, November through April; ☎ 08652 94 79 60, www.obersalzburg.de.

The Eagle's Nest

The Kehlsteinhaus – nicknamed the "Eagle's Nest" – perches at 1,834 m atop Mt. Kehlstein and enjoys sweeping views of the Berchtesgaden region. The architectural feat was undertaken as a gift for Hitler's for 50th birthday but, after 3,000 laborers completed the task in just 13 months, Hitler didn't much like the place; he claimed it aggravated his vertigo and subsequently held meetings there on just 10 occasions. It was, however, well appreciated by Hitler's mistress, Eva Bräun, who visited much more frequently.

The Kehlsteinhaus was spared bombing during World War II, and its capture became the culminating quest of the 101st US Airborne Division – a story popularized in author Stephen Ambrose's *Band of Brothers*.

Today, the Kehlsteinhaus is open to tourists, who brave the trip up for astounding views from the terrace and refreshments from the dining room. From the Hintereck parking area at Obersalzburg, buses climb the narrow, winding road up the Kehlstein. Passengers alight at the base of an elevator shaft, whereby visitors ascend into the Kehlsteinhaus. The house is open only in summer, mid-May through October; guided tours in English start from the mountaintop at 10:30 am and 11:30 am or from the tourist office at 1:30 pm. Contact ☎ 0852 96 70 for more information.

Dating from 1517, the **Salzbergwerk** salt mine offers fun 90-minute tours through odd salt formations on foot and across an underground lake by raft. To enliven the experience, visitors don old-fashioned miners' overalls and slide down the mineshaft on a pair of parallel banisters. The mine is open daily, May through mid-October, from 9 am to 5 pm, and daily except Sunday, mid-October through April, 12:30 to 3:30 pm. Contact ☎ 08652 600 60, www.salzbergwerk-berchtesgaden.de, for more information.

Bertchtesgaden's sights are scattered throughout the region, and **guided tours** can ease the hassle this creates. Best among the tour operators here – particularly for English-language tours – is **Berchtesgaden Mini Bus Tours**. They offer a range of tours, including Obersalzburg, the Eagle's Nest, and the popular *Sound of Music* Tour, which highlights a number of filming locations in Bavaria and Austria. Reservations are required; check in at the tourist office desk or dial ☎ 08652 649 71.

The Adventures

On Foot

 While most international visitors consider Berchtesgaden a place of mainly historical interest, German residents come here with recreational pursuits in mind as well. In summer, **hiking** options abound in and around the National Park (see below). For a refreshing, cool stroll, take the bus out to the Kugelmühle, or marble mill, and the base of the Almbach Gorge. It's a 1½-hour walk over 27 bridges to the

Theresienklause dam and, from there, a two-hour hike back to Berchtesgaden; gorge entry is €2.50.

> **Health-minded** visitors consider this: The tourist office rents pulse-rate testers for use during your stay. Wear the watch-like device while hiking to monitor your pulse rate, and compare the average rates of your first and last holiday hikes to measure the heart-healthy improvements you've made.

Experienced **climbers** make pilgrimages here to scale the east wall of the Watzmann.

On Wheels

 Mountain bikers take to an extensive trail network; request the tourist office's map, *Mountainbiken Zwischen Bergen und Seen*. Bike rental is available at **M & R Brandner's** at Bergwerkstrasse 52 in Berchtesgaden, ☎ 08652 14 34, and at the Jennerbahn valley station through **Treff-Aktiv** in Königssee, ☎ 08652 667 10. **Drivers** seeking a scenic route can head up the Rossfeld Ring Road. The 16-km road traverses the mountains between Rossfeld to Obersalzberg, with numerous hiking opportunities along the way; €5 toll.

On Water

 Swimmers head for the **Watazmann Therme**, a muliple-pool, spa, and waterworks complex at Bergwerkstrasse 54. It's open year-round; ☎ 08652 946 40, www.watzmann-therme.de. For **ballooning** and **parasailing** trips, contact the **Outdoor Club** (see *Sports Services* below). Those seeking **mountain-top views** can choose from among several year-round lifts. Most popular are the eight-cabin Obersalzberg cable car departing from Berchtesgaden's center and the Jennerbahn gondola, which climbs from Königssee to 3,320 m for spectacular lake and mountain views.

LIFT PASS PRICE SAMPLES
Winter
1-day adult pass at Jenner €21.50
5-day adult all-area pass €109
Summer
Pedestrian round-trip to Jenner €18
Pedestrian round-trip to Obersalzberg €7.50

On Snow & Ice

 In the winter, Berchtesgaden turns ski town, offering a total of 21 regional lifts and 50 km of groomed **downhill runs**. Ski bums beware, however, as lift areas are small and scattered throughout the region. Each lift area operates under separate management (read, "separate lift pass"); and there are few slopes here to challenge any skier with more than early intermediate skills. That said, Berchtesgaden is a view-blessed, low-key place to ski, and its nursery slopes will certainly please beginners. **Cross-country** skiers enjoy a good network of trails, and the **Cross-Country Center Rostwald-Aschauerweiher** offers specialist instruction; contact ☎ 08652 33 66. **Winter walkers** step out on 120 km of groomed hiking trails.

Fans of ice sports can try **curling** on the Berchtesgaden rink at 13:30 pm each Thursday, and daredevils can race by **luge** or **bobsled** down the frozen track at Königssee. For more information and reservations, contact ☎ 08652 94 78 60, www.rennbob-taxi.de. Berchtesgaden's ice rink opens for **skating** daily when special events aren't occupying the ice; check free skate times at ☎ 08652 614 05. A new **ice-climbing** tower at the Jennerbahn cable car challenges climbers, and the Outdoor Club offers lessons (see *Sports Services* below). Several **toboggan runs** draw speedsters – favorites include a 3.3-km track from the top of the Obersalzberg cable car and, at Ramsau, a 3.2-km run from the Hirscheck cable car down to Gästhaus Schwarzeck.

Sports Services, Outfitters & Guides

- The **Alpenverein Alpine Association** has a desk at the Kurgarten in the town center at Maximilianstrasse 1. It's open Tuesday, Thursday, and Friday from 3 to 5:30 pm, offering information on the surrounding mountains.

- The **Bergschule Berchtesgadener Land** has a range of professionally guided mountain and ski outings. Contact the Bergschule at ☎ 08652 53 71.

- The **Outdoor Club Berchtesgaden** offers ski and mountain guiding in addition to a wide range of outings, such as ballooning, kayaking, rafting, and climbing. For more information, ☎ 08652 977 60, www.outdoor-club.de.

Germany

■ **Bergsport Geistaller**, at Griesstätterstrasse 8, sells and rents all manner of mountaineering equipment; ☎ 08652 31 86.

Where to Sleep

Berchtesgaden's hotels haven't modernized much over the years, and as a group they're dark, creaky places with reasonable rates and often adorned with of hunting décor. Locations scatter throughout the valley, with few hotels directly in the center. Hotels are outnumbered by small guesthouses, private rooms, and long-stay holiday apartments.

HOTEL PRICE CHART	
Double room without tax; $$$-$$$$ always with bath.	
$	Under €80
$$	€81-150
$$$	€151-250
$$$$	Over €250

The old **Hotel Vier Jahreszeiten** ($$-$$$) is the priciest place in town, with a four-star rating, nice views, and a location reasonably close to the old town's pedestrian area. It's at Maximilianstrasse 20; ☎ 08652 95 20, www.berchtesgaden.com/vier-jahreszeiten.

Near the center, try the country-style **Hotel Bavaria** ($$). It's 400 m uphill from the train station, 400 m downhill from the town center, and offers a selection of accommodations, including family, apartment, and romantic whirlpool rooms. Check in at ☎ 0852 966 10, www.hotelbavaria.net.

The cheery **Wittelsbach** ($$) sits at Maximilianstrasse 16, just below old town and the Kurpark; ☎ 0852 963 80, www.hotel-wittlesbach.com.

On a sunny hillside directly above the town center, the **Gästehaus Mitterweinfeld** ($) offers homey, farmhouse accommodations; contact ☎ 08652 613 74, www.mitterweinfeld.de. On the hillside 10 minutes outside the center, the **Hotel Krone** ($) welcomes guests to cozy rooms, many with pine-paneling and balconies; Am Rad 5, ☎ 0852 946 00, www.hotel-krone-berchtesgaden.de.

Budgeting guests arriving by train might consider the **Gästhof Schwabenwirt** ($). It's at Königsseerstrasse 1, next to the train station and tourist office; ☎ 08652 20 22, www.schwabenwirt.de.

Where to Eat

Plenty of traditional food is available in Berchtesgaden, much of it served from hotel dining rooms. In the center just below the castle, try the **Gästhof Neuhaus** ($$) for shady seats and beer-garden fare. Around the corner, the dark, smoky **Brotzeit Stüberl** ($) serves up traditional plates of salami, cheese, and bread; and the best beer hall in town (and well worth a visit for the traditional food, too) is the cheery **Bräustüberl Berchtesgaden** ($) below the old town center at Bräuhausstrasse 13, ☎ 08652 97 67 24.

DINING PRICE CHART	
Average entrée, with tax.	
$	Under €10
$$	€10-25
$$$	Over €25

For a nice meal out, try the **Restaurant Vier Jahreszeiten** ($$) at the hotel of the same name; reserve at ☎ 08652 95 20. The Kurpark's bistro, **Café Restaurant Am Kurgarten** ($$), offers traditional and continental dishes all day; ☎ 0852 94 87 55. And the **Echostüberl** ($$), a lakeside *gästhof* with a big terrace, is worth a drive out to Königssee.

For budgeting diners, **Restaurant s'Platzl** ($) at Nonntal 8 cooks up good Mediterranean fare, and **Schnitzel-Paradies** ($) is everything you might expect, offering a range of schnitzel in simple surroundings on Bahnhofstrasse.

Café cuisine and snacks are best at the **Hofbäckerei-Konditorei Kruis** ($) at Rathausplatz 2, just above the palace square; or, for a quick bite, at the **Grillstüberl** ($) imbiss on the Marktplatz. **Market stalls** cluster nearby.

Where to Party

Although Berchtesgaden is a fairly reticent town, each of its neighborhoods does have a disco. In Berchtesgaden, try the **Beverly** at the Bahnhof; in Schönau, head for the **Viva Dance Hall** at Panorama Park; and in Königssee, cut loose at the **Käser Bar** on Seestrasse 2. Other evening outlets huddle in the center along Maximilianstrasse – try the **Pilspub**, the **Sound Café**, or **Heidi's Abend-Café**.

Folk music, and **dancing** are on order at several evening locales. In Berchtesgaden, try the **Gästhof Bräustubl**, the **Gästhof Neuhaus**. In addition, frequent **concerts** take place at the Kurpark and at various venues throughout town; check with the tourist office to see what's playing.

Where to Play

 Kids enjoy tours of the **salt mines**, **boat trips** on the lake, **cable car rides**, and the **birds of prey zoo** at Obersalzberg near the Hintereck car park. In addition, the tourist office can help arrange hiking trips and visits to a local farm. In winter, kids can attend the **ski schools**.

Festivals & Events

 The **Christmas season** features several Buttnmandl parades, Klockl singers, and a Christmas market on the Schlossplatz. **Christmas and New Year's shootings** – both non-violent rifle troop salutes – fire away at 11:30 pm on both Christmas and New Year's eves in an effort to scare off the bad spirits lurking at these hours. On January 6th, the **Dreikönigstag**, or Three Kings Singers, go from door to door blessing each house.

The **May Pole Celebration** kicks off spring on May first, and June brings the summer solstice and **St. John's Day**, when fires are lit in the mountains. Local residents dress in traditional *tracht* for the **Christmas Shooters Festival** on 14 July and, in August, around 1,000 pilgrims trek from Saalfelden, Austria, to the chapel at St. Bartholomew.

In late September, for **Whitsuntide**, a fun fair comes to the Triftplatz, and around St. Michael's Day, between the middle of September and the end of October, farmers bring their herds down from the Alpine pasture with all the pomp and décor of the Transhumance, **Almabtrieb Festival**.

Berchtesgaden National Park

Berchtesgaden National Park encompasses 210 square km of rugged, high-mountain terrain along the border of Austria. Founded in 1978, the park strives to preserve the course of nature, allowing much of its territory to grow, decay, and burn without intervention wherever possible. Other sections of the park – those inhabited before its formation – are set aside for traditional uses, by the old electric boats on the Königssee and the cattle herds grazing on high Alpine fields each summer, for example.

The park's other missions are environmental education and research. To these ends, the park maintains an exhibit in the Nationalpark Haus, and offers guided theme hikes including walk-and-talks about nature, friendship, bird calling, herbs, and geology – as well as walks in the company of a doctor or a priest. The park also supports research efforts toward the understanding and preservation of the region's land, flora, and fauna. Chamois, golden eagles, and marmots now number among the residents here.

Adventurers access the park at Hintersee, at Wimbachbrücke, and by boat over the Königssee; from these points of departure, 230 km of hiking, biking, and climbing trails explore the region, many passing by Alpine farmers' huts that serve drinks, snacks, and fresh dairy products. One favorite 2½-hour hike leads from the shore of the Königssee to the Eiskapelle, or "ice chapel." Take the Königssee boat as far as St. Bartholomew, and then follow the trail past the chapel, up through the woods to the avalanche field below the Watzmann. Part of the ice chapel's charm is that it's always changing by season, snowfall, and temperature. If you find the ice cave, don't enter – it's prone to collapse and has, in the past, been the site of tragedy.

 The Nationalpark Haus information center is at Fraziskanerplatz 7 in Berchtesgaden; it's open Monday through Saturday from 9 am-5 pm. Other info desks are at St. Bartholomew, Königssee, and Ramsau. Contact ☎ 08652 968 60, www.nationalpark-berchtesgaden.de.

Königsee

The village of Schönau am Königsee sits just a few kilometers south of Berchtesgaden and is oft written off as "just a suburb" of the larger market town. However, there's one little corner of Schönau that rates its own coverage here – a little corner that's one of my favorite places in all of Europe.

At the southern end of the Königseerstrasse lies the tiny neighborhood of Seefeld, a lakeside retreat hugely popular with tourists, yet still possessed of its natural tranquility. The handful of buildings huddles around the northern shore of the Königsee, or "king's lake," a two-mile swathe of turquoise wedged between steep, forested peaks on all sides. The pristine lake is among the few in Germany to remain undamaged by human use, as its steep walls prohibit excessive development. In addition, early efforts at preservation were successful here, and the Königsee's fleet of ferries continues to use clean electric power.

AUTHOR'S PICK

Tourists understandably adore the Königsee, and crowds overrun the little village during the high summer season. Travelers visiting in the early spring and late fall shoulder seasons, however, will be blessed with a truly tranquil lake – and a scene largely all to themselves.

You'll know you've hit town when you reach the parking toll booth and gargantuan lot to the northwest. (Guests not staying the night will have to leave their cars here.) The Jennerbahn lift climbs up the hill just beyond. Walking down Seestrasse toward the lake, visitors will find some interesting rock shops, along with a mix of kitchy souvenir stands, beer gardens, traditional dress outlets, and ice cream stands.

The lakefront road leads past the ferry docks and along the old boat huts to the east and, to the west, along the lakeshore and across a covered bridge to the Od neighborhood, home to the world's first refrigerated bobsled track – a track still in use today as both a training and World Cup competition venue.

AUTHOR'S PICK

Hungry? The **Echostüberl** on the western edge of the lake is, in my estimation, one of the finest little guesthouses in the Alps. The service is friendly, the food is hearty and traditional, and the long, lakeside terrace makes summer dining a treat. (Parents love its proximity to the tiny swimming beach: Envision happy, entertained kids within watching-and-rescuing distance of a beer garden.) In wintertime, dining moves indoors to the cozy, wood-paneled dining room.

Adventures around the Königsee span the seasons. From January through March, skiers come for the Jenner slopes, and sledders rip down the **bobsled** track at 120 km per hour. Visitors can try, too, from October through March. For more info, contact ☎ 08652 94 78 60, www.rennbob-taxi.de; €77.

Summer brings hikers, swimmers, and rowers to the area. Over 100 km of trails wind through the Schönau am Königsee area, and boat tours run year-round – although service is cut considerably during the winter (and occasionally stops altogether when the lake freezes over). Check www.bayerische-seenschifffahrt.de for current schedules.

The Königsee by Boat

A great day on the lake starts with an early departure from the docks in front of the century-old Schiffmeister Hotel. The electrically powered boats move past the tiny isle of Christlieger, then silently cross the deep, glassy lake, passing below sheer cliffs with only the wake waves audible in a scene of sublime beauty. At the far end of the lake, day-trippers can stop to look at the tiny St. Bartholomew Chapel, grab a bite to eat at the local *gästhof*, and head off by foot into the Berchtesgaden National Park.

Want to stay? The rickety old **Hotel Schiffmeister** ($$) remains my lodging of choice whenever I'm in the Berchtesgaten area. The 100-year-old hotel fronts the ferry docks at the northernmost end of the lake. The homey furnishings range from antique to just plain old; and the staff is low-key and friendly. Reserve a room at ☎ 08652 963 50, www.jowi.de/schiffmeister.

 The nearest tourist information office is down-valley in the town of Schönau; for more information, contact ☎ 08652 645 26.

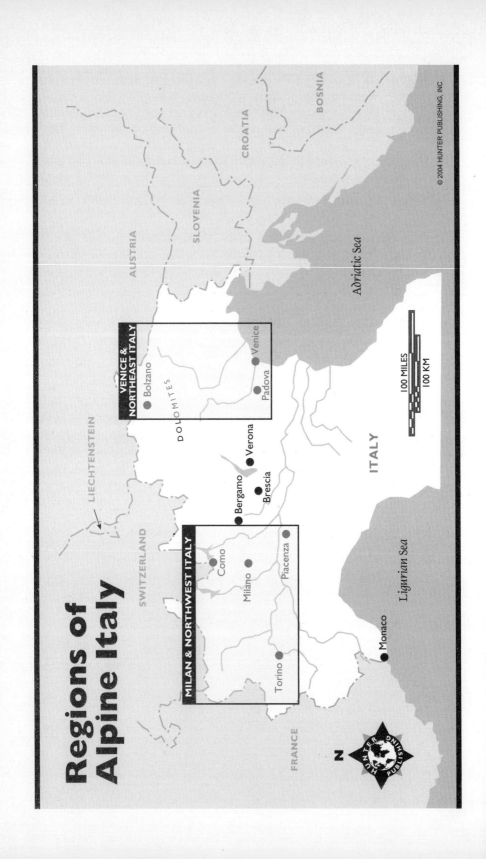

Regions of Alpine Italy

VENICE & NORTHEAST ITALY

MILAN & NORTHWEST ITALY

FRANCE

SWITZERLAND

LIECHTENSTEIN

AUSTRIA

SLOVENIA

CROATIA

BOSNIA

ITALY

DOLOMITES

Bolzano

Venice

Padova

Verona

Bergamo

Brescia

Como

Milano

Piacenza

Torino

Monaco

Adriatic Sea

Ligurian Sea

100 MILES

100 KM

N

HUNTER PUBLISHING

© 2004 HUNTER PUBLISHING, INC

Italy

(Italia)
Languages: Italian
Population: 57,715,625
Phone Country Code: +39
Currency: Euro

History

 Originally, three distinct groups occupied the peninsula: the Greeks on the southern tip, the Etruscans in the north, and the Romans in the central regions. Rome got off to a shaky start, aligning with the

Etruscans against the Celts, who sacked the city in 390 BC. But Julius Caesar drove the Celts out, and he kept right on going. In the end, they had control of almost all the Mediterranean region.

After the Roman Empire fell, Italy fell into a governmental system of independent feudalisms. City-states such as Venice, Pisa, and Milan grew in power and wealth, but never unified. Control of northern Italy bounced back and forth between empires, including those of Charlemagne and the Hapsburgs, and the rise and spread of the Roman Church and the Holy Roman Empire made the area a battleground.

Despite its war-torn hardships, Italy produced some of the world's greatest Renaissance leaders. Many of the era's explorers hailed from Italian cities, including Marco Polo, Christopher Columbus, and Amerigo Vespucci. The Renaissance brought a great rebirth of art and science, and the push for a single Italian nation strengthened. Finally, in 1860, the nationalist movement succeeded in creating a unified Italy – only Venice and Rome refused to join. A year later, Victor Savoy was proclaimed king. In 1866, following a conflict with Austria, Venice joined the Italian nation and finally, in 1870, Rome was added, too.

The new nation of Italy plunged into trouble alongside the rest of Europe during World War I. Abandoning its historical ties with Germany and Austria, Italy sided with the Allies in this conflict. While victorious, the war propelled the popularity of Benito Mussolini who, upon entering power, initiated an aggressive program of repression, eliminating political parties, stifling liberties, and initiating a fascist dictatorship he called the Corporate State. (Although the kingship continued in name only, the position had very little real authority.) Then, after signing the Tripartite Pact with Germany and Japan, Italy was bound to fight against the Allies in World War II. Mussolini was fired and imprisoned in 1943, and the new Italian leader, Marshal Pietro Badoglio, declared war on Germany – whose army quickly and easily occupied the southern state. But, the occupation was short-lived, and the Allies liberated Italian territory, starting in Sicily in the summer of 1943. Italy established its constitution in 1948, a document that, among other things, forever prohibits the reinstatement of the Fascist Party and forever banishes from Italy all male heirs to the once-powerful Savoy throne.

Marco Polo

Marco Polo's legendary trip to China began without him.

He was born in 1254 either in or near Venice – no one knows for sure – the son of a wealthy merchant explorer. Just six years later, young Marco watched his father sail off toward the Orient on a trip that would last nine years. When his father finally returned, he did so with a golden tablet one foot long and three inches wide – a symbolic ticket guaranteeing safe passage by the fearsome Kublai Khan. During his earlier travels, the elder Polo had fascinated the Khan with tales of the Pope and European culture, and the Khan had sent the Polos back to Italy with a letter addressed to the Pope. The letter requested that Pope Clement IV send other westerners who could teach the Chinese about Christianity and European technology. In 1271, the Polos set out for China with 17-year-old Marco, a trip that took 3½ years.

Upon arriving in the Mongol capital, Marco's mastery of languages earned him favor with the Khan. The ruler appointed Marco Polo to his court, and Marco was sent on a variety of missions to China, Burma, and India. During this time, Marco Polo was exposed to many new things, among which were the concepts of paper money and multi-class mail delivery. During his 17-year stay in China, Marco Polo served in a variety of positions, ranging from a seat on the Privy Council to a thug tax collector. Marco Polo returned to Venice in 1295, 24 years after his departure. (What treasure did he bring back from the far-off lands? The *noodle*! But don't tell your pasta-proud Italian friends.)

Three years after returning home from China, Captain Marco was captured from his war ship and imprisoned by Genovese. While in prison, he met the writer Rustichello of Pisa. During their stay, Marco dictated his book to Rustichello and, upon its release, the book became an immediate bestseller. Few, however, believed that the stories were anything more than fiction, and the tome was nicknamed *Il*

Milione, or *The Million Lies*. Indeed, much cultural and anthropological evidence suggests that the stories were heavily fabricated. Despite these suspicions, however, the book was popular and remained in publication for a century after his death.

Overview & Government

Italy encompasses some 301,255 square km of primarily mountainous terrain. The Alps peer down from the north, and the Appennines run down the center. Less than one third of the country is plains – the largest portion of that being the Po flats in the north of the country. Major rivers include the Po, Tiber, Arno, and Adige. Italy shares its borders with France to the northwest, Switzerland and Austria to the north, and Slovenia to the northeast. Two tiny states within the country, San Marino and Vatican City, maintain their independence. Italy's boot dips into the Adriatic, Ionian, and Mediterranean seas, kicking the small islands of Sicily and Sardinia.

Italy is a democratic republic of 20 regions; the capital is Rome. Its chief of state is the president, who is elected to a seven-year term. Its head of government is the prime minister, who is appointed by the president and confirmed by parliament. The country enjoys a lively political scene, and some 50 governments have been in place since the establishment of the republic's 1948 constitution. Multiple parties vie for attention, including one of the largest Communist parties in Western Europe.

Ongoing issues concern the social disparity between the wealthy industrialized north and the poor, rural south. Two-thirds of the population now lives in the upper half of the country and the migration continues, as southerners move to the north's large cities in search of work. Further complicating matters, industry has been slow to develop in the south, for reasons of low investment capital and the influence of the Mafia crime groups. Unemployment rates have steadily declined over the past several years but still remain high at 8.7%.

People & Culture

The population of Italy is 99% Italian, an ethnic mix that includes the Germanic ancestry of the north, the Greeks, Spaniards, and Saracens in the south, and a large influence of Latin and Etruscan cultures in the central regions. Today, although Italian is the official language, other dialects are widely spoken in pocket regions of the Alps and its foothills – languages including German, French, Ladin, and Friulan.

Approximately 83% of the population is Roman Catholic, although only about a quarter of those attend mass regularly. The government eradicated the custom of an official state religion in 1985, and religious education is no longer mandated in public schools. Some 70% of the Italian population resides in urban settings, many of them in the large cities of Rome, Milan, Turin, and Naples. The average population density is approximately 192 persons per square km; however, the population is much sparser in the south than in the industrialized north.

National Holidays 2004

January 1	New Year's Day
January 6	Epiphany
The 10 days prior to Shrove Tuesday	Carnival (Venice)
47 days prior to Easter	Shrove Tuesday
March-April	Easter
	Easter Monday
April 25	Liberation Day
June 3	Anniversary of the Republic
June 24	St. John's Day
June 29	St. Peter & St. Paul's Day
July 15	St. Rosalia's Day
15 August	Assumption Day
19 September	St. Gennaro's Day
November 1	All Saints Day
November 4	World War I Victory Anniversary Day
December 7	St. Ambrogio's Day
December 8	Immaculate Conception
December 25	Christmas Day
December 26	St. Stephen's Day

 For more information, check with the Italian National Tourism Office at www.italiantourism.com.

Milan & Northwest Italy

The plains of northwestern Italy rise steeply into Alpine terrain. Our coverage spans the westernmost section of the Alps' arch, from the Mediterranean in the south, along the French border to Mont Blanc, and then east along the lakes and the Swiss frontier. Activity here centers on the enormous city of **Milan**, which sprawls out below the Alps and the spectacular scenery surrounding **Lake Como**. Across the plain to the south of Milan, **Turin** bustles with industry – and hustles to prepare for its stint as host of the 2006 Olympic Winter Games. The city's mountain resorts rise to the east, and the **Val d'Aosta** juts off to the northwest. Here, at the foot of Mont Blanc, steep valley walls harbor the Roman town of **Aosta**, the barren peaks of the **Gran Paradiso National Park**, and the delightful mountain resort of **Courmayeur**.

■ Milan

(Milano)

Population: 1,500,000

Base elevation: 122 m

Gateway city

Bustling, hustling, cosmopolitan Milano delights city-folk with its couture, a hoard of artistic treasures, and a cultural calendar jam-packed with opera, theater, and concert events. However, if urbanite frenzy is not your thing, Milan may just get on your nerves.

History & Overview

Milan grew up in the heartland of the Lombardy Plains, populated by Gauls and then conquered by the Romans, who named the city "Mediolanum," or Middle Land. With the growth of Roman trade, Milan became an important center of the Roman Empire, eventually falling to the Goths and coming under Longobard rule. The city rose again in 1176 to defeat Barbarossa and gain its independence as a recognized city-state, an event followed by great growth and prosperity under the rule of the Visconti and Sforza dynasties – and much of Milan's visible splendor arose from this period.

Today, Milan is the capital of the province that shares its name; and, truth be told, many Italians consider it the capital of all Italy. Its economic influence on the country's finance, fashion, and trade convention industries is unmatched, yet plenty of problems still exist. The population has fled the city center for more comfortable and less expensive housing in the suburbs. But, because the public transportation network inadequately serves these new areas, the exodus at once exacerbates traffic congestion and reduces the tax revenues that might be used to alleviate the problem. All that said, once tourists get settled in the center, they shouldn't feel too much of the crunch.

The Town

As the ancient city of Milan expanded, the walls ringing it were moved outward in steps. Although no longer walled, those rings remain discernible on modern maps; the outer rings are made up of streets beginning with the name *Viale*; the inner ring encircles the old city center. The **Piazza del Duomo** lies roughly at the center of this inner ring – and the city's heart beats here. On the outskirts of the inner circle are the Public Gardens and the Stazione Centrale, or central train station, to the northeast. To the northwest stretches the Castello Sforzesco complex; the wide boulevard Corso Sempione continues off toward Malpensa Airport in the northeast.

Getting Here & Around

 Visitors arriving by air will fly in to either **Linate International Airport**, seven km east of the center, or **Malpensa International Airport**, 45 km northwest of the center. Malpensa services most intercontinental flights. For more information on either airport, click to www.sea-aeroporti.it. From Malpensa, take the Malpensa Express train to the North Station at Cadorna, just south of the Castello Sforzesco; from Linate, hop a bus or taxi.

Those arriving by **train** should enter the city via the Milano Centrale, Milan Central Station. Some trains, mostly short-distance commuters, use the smaller stations around the outskirts of the center.

For travel in the center, use the city's public transportation network, a reasonably efficient web of **bus** and **subway** lines. Tickets cost €1 per ride and are good for 75 minutes on any line. (They can't, however, be used again once you've left the subway.) For more information, check www.atm-mi.it.

For **taxi** service, call ☎ 02 69 69 or 02 85 85. The city's traffic woes are legendary, and rush-hour jams will send taxi fares soaring. Drivers of private vehicles should use hotel parking or one of the park-and-ride garages near outlying train and subway stations.

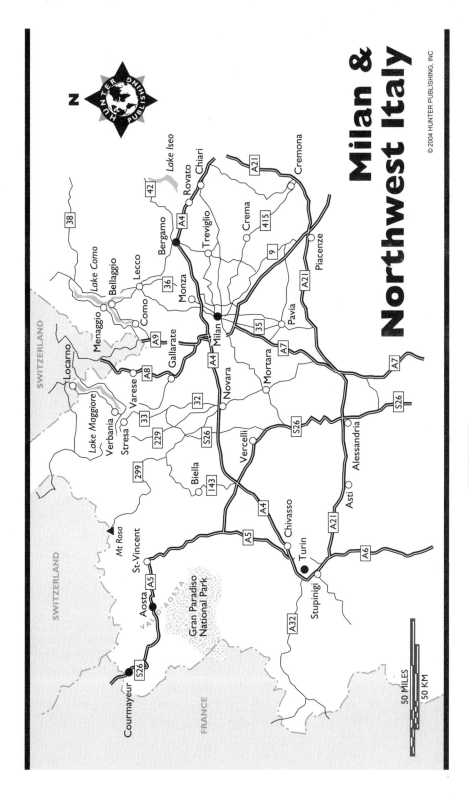

Milan & Northwest Italy

© 2004 HUNTER PUBLISHING, INC

Italy

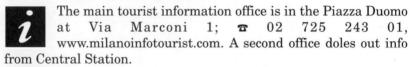

The convenient Tourist Day Pass offers 24 or 48 hours of public transportation for €3 and €5.50, respectively. It's a good deal if you'll travel three or more legs each day. Purchase the pass at newsstands, tobacco shops, tourist offices, or from automated ticket machines.

Getting Connected

The main tourist information office is in the Piazza Duomo at Via Marconi 1; ☎ 02 725 243 01, www.milanoinfotourist.com. A second office doles out info from Central Station.

The central post office is at Piazza Cordusio 2, but the post office in the Central Station may be more convenient.

WWW For Internet access, head to Central Station and the **Internet Café Gr@zia** at Piazza Duca d'Aosta 14.

The Sights

Spires jut, buttresses fly, and gargoyles loom all around. Like some ancient stalagmite cluster rising from city-center floor, the Gothic **Duomo** stands proud as Milan's most recognizable landmark. Built over four centuries, beginning in 1386, the cathedral is the third-largest church in the world after St. Peter's and the Seville Cathedral. Visitors shouldn't miss the chance to climb to the roof for a pigeon's-eye view of the city. Surrounding the **Piazza del Duomo**, or cathedral square, are the administrative buildings that were once the seats of the city's religious and civil leaders.

The **Galleria Vittorio Emanuela II** rises behind the church square. Constructed in 1877, the glass-enclosed Galleria was among the world's first mega-malls. Today, its arcades are home to a mix of shops and fashionable cafés – all atop a colorful mosaic tile floor.

The **Sforza Castle**, or Castello Sforzesco, dominates a lovely park on the northwestern edge of the old center. The fortress was built by the ruling Visconti family in the mid 14th century, then reconstructed by the Sforza family when it took power. Attractions inside include several museums, including a sculpture collection with Michelangelo's *Pietà Rondanini*, which was left unfinished when the artist died. The museum is open Tuesday through Sunday, 9 am-5:30 pm; ☎ 02 884 637 00; admission is free.

The **Brera Art Museum**, or the Pinacoteca di Brera, is home to many great Italian masterpieces dating from the 14th to the 20th centuries, including Raphael's *Marriage of the Virgin* and Bellini's *Pietá* and *Virgin and Child*, and a number of works by other European artists as well. The collection is housed in the Palazzo di Brera, 17th-century palace constructed for Richini. It's at Via Brera 28 and is open Tuesday through Sunday from 8:30 am to 7:30 pm; ☎ 02 72 26 31; €5. Devotees should also see Leonardo da Vinci's *Last Supper*, known in Italian as the *Cenacolo Venciano*. The mural adorns a darkened wall of the St. Maria delle Grazia Monastery – travelers must call ahead to book a visit; ☎ 02 894 211 46. For more information on all of Milan's museums, check www.mimu.it.

Opera City

Milan and opera harmonize so well that the city's sophisticated audiences have become a veritable testing ground for new works by the world's greatest composers, premiering operas by Rossini, Verdi, Puccini, and Bellini, among others.

The original **Teatro alla Scala**, or La Scala Theater, first opened its curtain in 1778, and since that time has come to rank among the world's finest opera houses – and one of Milan's most treasured institutions. In fact, after much of the city had been bombed during World War II, the theater enjoyed top priority for reconstruction and reopened its stage just a year later in 1946. Today, the interior of the horseshoe-shaped auditorium gleams in splendid red velvet and gilded carved wood.

La Scala closed in 2002 for renovations; officials estimate the reopening of the original theater for 2005, but this is Italy, so don't count on it. In the meantime, La Scala relocates its performances to the new **Arcimboldi Theatre**, a larger, modern auditorium north of the city center.

Opera buffs should check out **La Scala Theater Museum**; it displays a large collection of artifacts depicting the theater's history. During restorations, the museum is in the Palazzo Busco at Corso Magenta 71 and is open daily, 9 am-6 pm; ☎ 02 469 12 49, €5. The original theater is just north of the Duomo along the Via Manzoni. For more information on all things La Scala, check in at ☎ 02 720 037 44, www.teatroallascala.org.

Where to Sleep

Interestingly situated in a 15th-century convent, the **Four Seasons** ($$$$) remains our favorite luxury house here. Its peaceful arcades, light beige color schemes, and excellent dining create a perfect place to unwind; ☎ 02 770 88, www.fourseasons.com/milan.

HOTEL PRICE CHART	
Double room without tax; $$$-$$$$ always with bath.	
$	Under €80
$$	€81-150
$$$	€151-250
$$$$	Over €250

Much more businesslike and overtly grand is the **Principe di Savoia** ($$$$), famed both for the stained-glass ceiling over its lobby bar and the exquisite presidential suite occupying its penthouse; ☎ 02 623 01, www.luxurycollection.com.

Hotel Spadari al Duomo ($$$-$$$$) rates highly among Milan's art-loving set. The hotel is set in an early 20th-century palazzo and decked out with all manner of modern art, much of it contrived by local artists; ☎ 02 720 023 71, www.spadarihotel.com.

The **Hotel Manzoni** ($$$) enjoys a quiet location near the gardens, tucked off a side street just one block away from the Four Seasons. Inside, the residential décor is homey enough; ☎ 02 760 057 00, www.hotelmanzoni.com.

At a busy location, but a great choice for environmentalists, the **Hotel Ariston** ($$$) is Milan's greenest hostelry. Clean-cut and fresh, the Ariston features lots of natural materials, a meticulous recycling program, a bio-breakfast buffet, and loaner bikes; ☎ 02 720 005 56, www.brerahotels.com.

Hotel London ($$) sits in the center just a short walk from the Piazza Castello and La Scala Theater. Its small lobby features a cozy fireplace nook; ☎ 02 720 201 66, www.traveleurope.it/hotellondon.it.

The **Hotel Gritti** ($$) has simple, residential décor and a good, if busy, location along the Via Torino; ☎ 02 890 109 99, www.hotelgritti.com.

The local youth hostel is the **Ostello Piero Rotta** ($), a dingy, unfriendly place that no one much likes. It's near the QT8 Metro stop; ☎ 02 392 670 95.

Where to Eat

Milan offers diners the same wide-ranging options as do other cities of this size.

DINING PRICE CHART	
Average entrée, with tax.	
$	Under €10
$$	€10-25
$$$	Over €25

The venerable **Cracco Peck** ($$$) tops the city's charts for gourmet fare. The chef here specializes in original approaches to Italian cuisine; book a table at ☎ 02 876 774. Also on the upscale list is **Savini** ($$$), a grand gourmet house first opened in 1867. It's found under the glass dome of the Galleria Via Emanuele; reserve at ☎ 02 720 034 33.

Literary folks should stop in amid the antique dealers at **Bagutta** ($$) at via Bagutta 14. The historic trattoria was once patronized by a group of writers and publishers that created the Bagutta Literary Prize there. Tuscan food is on the menu, and there's summertime seating in the garden; reserve at ☎ 02 760 009 02.

Al Mercante ($$) serves up traditional fare amid the medieval ambiance of Piazza Mercanti; ☎ 02 805 21 98. At Umbria 80, the **Trattoria Masuelli** ($$) – also known as the San Marco – dishes out delish regional specialties amid simple traditional décor; ☎ 02 551 841 38.

Near Central Station, the **Osteria del Treno** ($$) offers hearty authentic fare in an old workman's tavern. The décor is simple – long tables in a long hall – and the atmosphere busy and loud; ☎ 02 670 04 79.

For a wide range of pizzas, try **Pizza Big** ($), also near the station at Vialle Brianza 30; ☎ 02 284 65 48. The **train station** itself has several fast, inexpensive options, too.

Where to Party

In addition to the highbrow cultural performances staged at La Scala and the city's many other playhouses, cosmopolitan Milan offers a predictably lively and diverse nightlife. For general revelry – bars, cafés, discos, and such – try the **Brera district** just north of the center. Lots of good hang-outs line the streets. For a low-key artsy ambiance, try **Jamaica** at Via Brera. For late-night disco action, head to **La Banque**, near the La Scala – it has a modern interior and was once actually a bank; the massive weekend-only **Alcatraz**; or the always fashionable **Shocking Club** at Porta Nuova.

Italy

For live concerts and shows, try **Binario Zero** at Lambertenghi or the **Magazzini Generali**, an old warehouse on Via Pietrasanta. The **Blues House** posts a solid schedule of live blues performances, and **Zelig** offers cabaret-style entertainment featuring some top names in comedy.

Festivals & Events

As one of Europe's premier trade fair cities, Milan sees many more convention events than festivals. The city kicks off winter with the **Carnevale Ambrosiano**, a masked pre-Lenten celebration with a number of related balls and events.

In March, the **Milano-San Remo** cycling races depart, and the **MODIT Fashion Fair** presents designers' new fall fashion lines. April brings the **Fiera dei Fiori**, or the Festival of Flowers, to Via Moscova in an explosion of spring color.

The **Festa del Naviglio** market and folklore fest comes to town on the first Sunday in June and, in September, the auto racing world's eyes turn to the **Gran Premio di Monza**. October sees two famed trade events, the **Smau Technology Fair** and the **MODIT Fashion Fair** with its presentations of spring and summer couture. In December the **Oh bej Oh bej Festival** draws market stalls to Sant' Ambrogio on the 7th, and **La Scala** launches its opera, ballet, and theater season.

Lake Como

Several lakes glisten along the foothills of the northern Italian Alps. Lining up from west to east are lakes **Orta**, **Maggiore**, **Varese**, **Lugano**, **Como**, **Iseo**, and **Garda** – and many smaller lakes scatter among these. Every one has its own distinct allure, and each draws crowds from the lower Italian plains during the hot summer months. Although the region's attractions could alone fill a book, we'll tease you with just one adventure here.

Lago di Como, or **Lake Como**, has long been Milan's backyard beach. With steep mountain walls rising all around, its enticements are many. The long body of water stretches into the Alps in an inverted 'Y' shape, anchored at its southern end by the towns of **Como** and **Lecco** and at its northern end by **Sorico**. Midway up the lake, at the intersection of the 'Y', rests lovely **Bellagio**. The drive around Lake Como totals 170 km, much of the eastern shore through tunnels. From the town of Como, a nice day-trip can loop by either boat or car around the southwestern leg of the lake. I follow that route below.

The town of **Como** lies at the lake's southwestern tip, approximately 50 km north of Milan. The bustling town boasts a lovely lakefront square, the Piazza Cavour; a 14th- century Gothic church; and a ferryboat hub whence boats zigzag up to Bellagio and beyond. Traveling north alongside the western shore of the lake, **Cernobbio** is home to the fabulous Villa d'Este, a 16th-century villa that's now the region's most famous hotel – an ideal locale for a memorable lunch. Farther north still is the picturesque village of Tremezzo, site of the **Villa Carlotta**. Lovingly tended gardens srround the 18th-century villa, its beds harboring some 500 species of plants – over 150 types of rhododendrons and azaleas alone. From here, day-trippers should cross by ferry to Bellagio, "pearl of Lake Como." The old village nestles below the northwestern tip of the Punte Spartivento, its villas stacking up the hillside, its cobblestone alleys winding between. Visitors enjoy sweeping lake views and a number of touristy shops, but "sights" here are meager – just two outstanding villas, the Villa Melzi d'Eryl to the south and the Villa Serbelloni to the north.

The Grand Dames of Lake Como

Two famous villa hotels face off across the southwestern leg of Lake Como.

First opened as a hotel in 1873, the neo-classical **Villa Serbelloni** ($$$$) enjoys an enviable position on a lakefront promontory. It's the kind of place where marble pillars support coffered ceilings, French tapestries adorn walls, and Persian carpets muffle squeaky wooden floors. The hotel is open from April through mid-November. For room or restaurant reservations, contact ☎ 031 95 15 29, www.villaserbelloni.

Across Lake Como at Cernobbio, the **Villa d'Este** ($$$$) is the most famous of the lake district hotels. Built in 1568 by Tolomeo Gallio, Cardinal of Como, the villa changed hands several times before becoming a hotel in 1873. The  luxurious villa rests in 25 acres of gardens, fronting the lake and Italy's only floating swimming pool. The cuisine is excellent; the ambiance purely formal. For reservations, contact ☎ 031 34 88 35, www.villadeste.com.

Italy

Want to stay? If you don't wait to shell out the bucks for either of the grand hotels above – or if you simply prefer low-key accommodations – book a room at the **Hotel Florence** ($$-$$$) in Bellagio. The 18th-century hotel has an open fireplace, rustic décor, and a central location near the waterfront. Reserve at ☎ 031 95 17 22.

 For more information on Lake Como, contact the tourist office at Piazza Cavour 17; ☎ 031 26 97 12, www.lakecomo.org.

Turin

(Torino)

Turin got its start as a capital of the Taurin, a Celtic tribe, but in the 11th century passed under the control of the House of Savoy for what was to be almost 900 years. The city's heyday came in the early 1700s, when that ruling family erected many of Turin's most magnificent buildings. In the years that followed, the House of Savoy was instrumental in the unification of Italy, patriarch Victor Emmanuel II was named king in 1861, and the family ruled all of Italy until 1946, when the Italian Republic was born.

 Today, Modern Turin is home to a dynasty of another sort – the Fiat car company thrives here, supporting many of the city's nearly one million residents. The city continues to bask in the memory of its royal heritage, as well, its vast cultural wealth apparent in its rich Baroque architecture and 18th-century monuments. Visitors stroll the 14th-century **Piazza Castello**, nucleus of the old city and home to many cafés, shops, and museums. Several palaces and squares embellish the center, and the 15th-century cathedral, the **Duomo di San Giovanni**, rises to the north. The **Mole Antonelliana**, above, the city's favorite landmark, climbs lacily toward the sky in the east. For a lovely view of the city, ride the elevator to the top.

The Shroud of Turin

While many cathedrals house religious artifacts, Turin's Duomo di San Giovanni holds claim to Christendom's most notorious relic, The Shroud of Turin. Passed down for centuries through the House of Savoy, the 4.43-m strip of cloth shows a faint image of the corpse it once wrapped, a corpse believed by many to be the dead body of Christ. Photographic negatives taken in 1898 made the image on the burial cloth clearer, revealing a crown of thorns and wounds to the hands, feet, side, and head.

The shroud officially passed into the hands of the church upon the 1983 death of Umberto II of Savoy, at which point it was carbon-dated by a worldwide team of experts. Disappointingly, they concluded that the cloth was made sometime between the 13th and 14th centuries. Nonetheless, examination continues, and the burial cloth and its mysterious image remains an icon of veneration. The shroud rests in the cathedral but only rarely is it displayed to the public. When it is on display, you'll know it – thousands of pilgrims throng the city.

 Want to stay? The cheery **Hotel Victoria** ($$-$$$) remains the front-runner of the mid-priced houses here. Popular with international visitor, the central city hotel offers reasonable comfort amid considerable charm, each room individually decorated. Inquire at ☎ 011 561 19 09, www.hotelvictoria-torino.com.

 For more information, check in at the tourist office at the Piazza Castello or contact ☎ 011 53 59 01, www.turismotorino.org.

Torino 2006: Sampling the Sites

 Turin will host the XX Winter Olympic Games in 2006 from 10-26 February. During these 17 days, 2,550 athletes from 80 nations will compete in 15 sporting disciplines. More than a million spectators and 9,600 journalists are expected to attend. The games will revolve around 13 competition venues and three Olympic Villages, one each in Turin, Sestrière, and Bardonecchia. Although construction around the event and village sites continues in preparation for the big event, each is worth a look if you're in the area.

Much of the venue development is taking place in the **Turin Olympic District** at Lingotto, which lies southeast of Turin's center, between the Corso Unita d'Italia and the Via Ventimiglia on the left bank of the Po River. Turin's Olympic Village will make its home in the General Market, a now-defunct wholesale market first opened in 1934. The converted complex will span 100,000 square m, house 2,500

Italy

athletes and shopping, logistics, and athlete recreation centers.

The Alpine village of **Sestrière** will play host to one of the three Olympic Villages and will stage the Alpine Skiing events. Around 100 km west of Turin, Sestrière's skiing facilities are linked with the Milky Way region and currently include 92 lifts and 400 km of runs spanning the border of Italy and France. Long known as an Alpine eyesore, it's now seeing aesthetic improvements in preparation for the games. If you ski at Sestrière, be sure to check out the two racing sites: Mount Sises will host the giant slalom course, and Borgata will run the men's super-G, downhill, and downhill/slalom combined. Test events began in March of 2004. For more info on Sestrière, contact www.sestriere.it.

Snowboarders should head for **Bardonecchia**, 96 km west of Turin, site of the third Olympic Village and host of all snowboarding events. The small town lies along the French-Italian border and offers access to 23 lifts and 140 km of mostly easy runs. Course 23 will be extended for use as the racing run, and a halfpipe will be constructed on Course 24. Construction on Bardonecchia slopes will end by October of 2004, and test events will run in February of 2005. Contact www.comune.bardonecchia.to.it for more info.

 For more information regarding the 2006 Olympic Winter Games, the events, tickets and a map, visit www.torino2006.org.

■ Courmayeur

Population: 3,000

Base elevation: 1,224 m

Mountain resort village

Mont Blanc beckons at the end of the Val d'Aosta, the ancient village of Courmayeur nestling at its foot. Once a roadside rest stop on the Roman map, Courmayeur is today the winter-weekend playground of northeastern Italy's elite. They come to socialize, shop, ski, and dine – but there's a less frivolous crowd here, too. Today, as in days past, Courmayeur welcomes heartier adventurers, those here to conquer mountain summits, trek glacial ice-beds, scale granite walls, climb frozen waterfalls, and heli-drop into some of Europe's most extreme wilderness. It's a different crowd, indeed.

Above: Canalside market in Venice

Below: Bardonecchia, Italy, site of snowboarding competition in 2006 Winter Olympics

Above: Pariol-Greniere, Italy, 2006 Olympic site of luge and bobsled competitions

Below: Torno, on Lake Como

Above: Santa Maria Rezzonico, Lake Como

Below: Pona, Lake Como

Above: Argegno, Como

Below: Cremia, Como

History & Orientation

Courmayeur got its start as a thoroughfare along the Roman transalpine trade route between the regions that are now Italy and France. After its first church was built around the eighth century, the area saw continued growth and eventually fell under the rule of the House of Savoy. Courmayeur gradually morphed from a 14th-century iron-mining center to an 18th-century spa town, and from there, to a 19th-century mountaineering center. Skiers first took to local slopes in the early 1900s and by mid-century had erected the first lifts, successfully transforming Courmayeur from a summer-only playground to a year-round mountain resort.

Courmayeur nestles at the foot of **Mont Blanc**, Europe's highest mountain. The **Val d'Aosta** stretches southeast toward Milan and Turin, and to the north, **Val Ferret** and **Val Veny** split off at **Entrèves**, running a short distance along the white mountain's southeastern base. To the south, the **Vallée de la Thuile** leads to the resort of **La Thuile** and, in the summer, up and over the **Petit St. Bernard Pass** into the **French Tarantaise**.

The Town

The village of Courmayeur sprawls along the eastern riverbank of the Dora Baltea. Across the river, the hamlet of Dolonne climbs up the western foothills. Courmayeur centers on the Piazzale Monte Bianco – a busy traffic circle fronting the main valley road, the bus station, and the tourist office. The old center is just up the hill, running north and south along the Via Roma on either side of the old church. This pedestrian zone is home to the valley's most inviting shops, restaurants, and bars. Anchoring the outskirts is the Courmayeur Cable Car to the south, the sports center in Dolonne to the west, and the hamlets of Larzey and La Saxe to the north.

Getting Here & Around

Those arriving by **air** should fly in to Geneva, 100 km away via the Mont Blanc Tunnel; Turin, 150 km south; or Milan, 190 km east. **Bus** transfers run Saturday and Sunday from Milan's Malpensa Airport; contact ☎ 0165 773 240 for reservations. **Train** travelers can get as far as Pre-St. Didier on rail but must transfer to bus to get to Courmayeur. The main bus station hubs near the tourist office at Piazzale Monte Bianco. For **taxi** service, dial ☎ 0165 842 960.

The quickest **driving** route to Courmayeur is via one of three tunnels that access the valley year-round: the new Val d'Aosta autostrada tunnel from Milan and Turin, the newly reopened Mont Blanc tunnel from Chamonix, France, or the Grand St. Bernard Tunnel from Switzerland. Those wishing to take their time can meander into the valley via three scenic, winding routes: the old road up the valley, which remains open year round; the Grand St. Bernard Pass road from the Swiss Valais; and the Petit St. Bernard Pass road from the French Tarantaise. These final two routes are open during summer only.

Mountain transportation departs for Plan Checrouit from two bases, one at the southern side of town and the other from Entrèves, just up-valley. The cable car to Punta Helbronner and France departs from the village of La Palud, one hairpin curve before the entrance to the Mont Blanc Tunnel. For more information on Courmayeur's cableways, see www.courmayeur-montblanc.com; for more information on the Mont Blanc Cable Car, go to www.montebianco.com.

LIFT PASS PRICE SAMPLES

Winter

1-day adult €34

6-day adult €175

1-day off-piste day pass at Helbronner €31

Pedestrian round-trip to Helbronner €30.50

Summer

Pedestrian round-trip to Helbronner €30.50

Getting Connected

 The **Monte Bianco Tourist Information Office** is at the Piazzale Monte Bianco 13, just behind the traffic circle (possibly still a construction zone) when you first enter town. For more info, contact ☎ 0165 842 060, www.comune.courmayeur. ao.it.

 The post office is near the tourist office at the Piazzale Monte Bianco.

 For Internet access, try **Planet Discobar** at the sports center or, in town, the **Bar Tavola Calda Ziggy** at Via Marconi 15.

The Sights

 Courmayeur is a resort town with lots of beauty to gaze at but very few "sights" to see. **Mont Blanc** is, of course, the village's primary draw. For more information on how to explore it, see *Adventures* below. Alpine enthusiasts should check out the small **Alpine Museum** at Piazza Henry 2, and all visitors should spend some time exploring the **Via Roma**, the village's oldest street and now its primary entertainment district. Wondering what it might have been like before all the shops set in? Head across the valley to **Dolonne**, where the oft-ignored **Via della Vittoria** retains its old-world residential charm.

The Adventures

Mont Blanc

■ One Mountain, Two Countries, Six Cableways & a Bus

AUTHOR'S
PICK

Both tourists and adventurers come to Courmayeur to experience Mont Blanc – no visitor should miss a trip up. The mountain has much to offer at each of its cableway stages, and travelers can choose among a variety of lift tickets ranging from a quick trip up Mont Frety to a full day's excursion into France. Below, I tell you what's where on Mont Blanc.

The Mont Blanc Cable Car departs from 1,370 m at La Palud, a village at the head of the valley just north of Entrèves, approximately four km north of Courmayeur. (Local buses make the trip.) The first stage of the Mont Blanc ascent is to Mont Fréty at 2,173 m. Here, visitors can enjoy a *prosecco* or a hearty meal at the Pavillon Restaurant – or sunbathe in a rented lounge chair on the panoramic terrace. In summer, hikers enjoy several paths, and botanists stroll through the Saussurea Alpine Garden, home to more than 800 species of plants.

From Mont Fréty, a second cable car climbs to Réfuge Torino at 3,375 m, and a third cable car – this one rather small – ascends to 3,462 m at Punta Helbronner, the last mountain station on the Italian side of the border. Visitors enjoy the Rock Crystal Museum; marvel at the mountain's jutting needles, or *aiguilles*; or rope up and trek across the glacier with prearranged mountain guides. (In winter, experienced skiers and snowboarders venture off-piste from here, down the mountain toward Toula or down the Vallée Blanche into France.)

In summer, visitors can opt to cross from Punta Helbronner into France via the Panoramic Mont Blanc Gondola, a triple gondola that dangles its way across the glacial ice and up to the Aiguille du Midi at 3,842 m. The trip takes 30 minutes and covers five km. From there, the magnificent Aiguille Cable Car descends via the Plan de l'Aiguille at 2,137 m into the outskirts of Chamonix. Buses depart Chamonix for Courmayeur, making the 40-minute trip through the newly reopened Mont Blanc Tunnel. Buses run daily; be sure to check the current schedule before you go.

Italy

> **TIP:** If you'd rather go with a package deal and a pre-arranged return bus, inquire at the tourist office about the Trans Mont Blanc Excursion. It currently runs €78 for adults.

On Foot

 The Courmayeur area enjoys around 300 km of maintained hiking trails, and a good collection of mountain restaurants and refuges offer trailside hospitality. Favorite valley hikes include trails along the Val Ferret, the Val Veny, and Mont Blanc foothills, and numerous trails are easily accessed via the region's summertime cable car service.

One lovely, short walk leads from Arnouva at the end of the Val Ferret road around the Pré de Bard. The two-hour route loops by the Combette Gorge, takes in glacier views, and passes by the cozy Elena, a mountain refuge open mid-June through mid-September. In addition to a good hiking map, pick up the tourist office's brochure, *Mountain Huts and Bivouacs in Aosta Valley,* before you set out.

For more extreme mountaineering action, such as climbing, glacier-trekking, and canyoning, contact the **Courmayeur's Alpine Guides Association** – see *Sports Services* below.

> **TIP:** The cable cars in the Courmayeur area close at lunchtime for approximately one to 1½ hours, normally from about 1 pm. But, if you have to wait it out on the mountain, there are in most cases restaurants open at the upper lift stations.

In Water

 In summer, swimmers hop a lift or hike up to the **Alpine swimming pool** at Plan Chercrouit. Here, there are big valley views, a restaurant, and a playground. The pool is open daily from late June through late August, 10:30 am-4:45 pm; entry is €10, or €16 with roundtrip lift ticket. **Canyoning** excursions are organized by the Alpine Guide Association (see *Sports Services* below).

Fishing is technically an option, but the steep rates will make it prohibitive for most. For those wanting to give it a try, the Val Ferret Fishing Club has more information regarding sites, seasons, and regulations. Several hotels and *refugi* sell the pricey permits – a single day permit is €36, and the season runs from May to November. For more information, contact the **Val Ferret Fishing Club** at ☎ 0348 604 65 05, www.valferretfishingclub.com.

On Wheels

Mountain biking trails wind through each of the local valleys, and steeper technical routes slice down the mountainsides from the upper lift stations. The place to go for more information is M.B. Adventure, a specialist mountain-biking operation in La Salle on the northern side of town. They offer advice, maps, and organized outings, including some rip-roaring biking adventures involving helicopters, rafts, and snowy trails. For more info, contact **M.B. Adventure** at ☎ 0347 241 76 67, www.mbaventure.it. For mountain bike rental in the center, head for **Lo Caraco** at Via Roma 150, ☎ 0165 844 152.

On Snow & Ice

Courmayeur operates 23 lifts and grooms 100 km of **skiing** runs graded 20% easy, 70% intermediate, and 10% difficult. These numbers deceive, however, as experts find plenty of off-piste activity. The resort is small but offers a nice selection of trails. Beginners enjoy two free lifts, the Chiecco and Tzaly lifts, and intermediates have run of most of the mountain. Advanced skiers and snowboarders head for the long off-piste routes below Crest d'Arp – and venture farther backcountry by helicopter. Both the ski school and the Alpine Guides Association offer off-piste guiding and instruction, including the popular day-trip from Punte Helbronner, down the Vallée Blanche, and into Courmayeur, France.

Helicopter Drops

The Val d'Aosta is one of Europe's premier heli-skiing and heli-boarding destinations – the region's steep, inaccessible terrain and Italy's laidback laws combine to make it so. A wide range of drops is offered, including extreme excursions to Mont Fortin and less demanding tours to the Pyramides Calcaires. Participants must have advanced skills and be comfortable skiing on off-piste terrain, and a guide or instructor must accompany each group.

For more information and reservations, contact **Mr. Massimo Rey** at ☎ 0338 679 06 36 or the **Alpine Guides Association** in Courmayeur; ☎ 0165 842 064, www.guidecourmayeur.com. Reservations must be confirmed no later than 6:30 pm the evening prior to your excursion.

Italy

In addition to skiing and boarding, wintertime visitors **walk** on maintained trails, **ice-skate** at the sports center, and **snow shoe** between cozy mountain huts. **Cross-country skiers** enjoy groomed loipe along the river at Val Ferret, including loops from three to 11 km in length. The Alpine Guides Association runs high-mountain **Alpine treks**, snowshoeing excursions, and **ice climbing** courses (kids can start from age seven). For more information, see *Sports Services* below.

Sports Services, Outfitters & Guides

The **Courmayeur Alpine Guides Association**, or the Societá delle Guide di Courmayeur, has been leading excursions on rock, dirt, and ice since 1850. Summertime options including glacier treks, free and equipped climbs, and mountaineering courses. In winter, the guides run ski tours all over the region, including popular off-piste runs down the Vallée Blanche in France. For more info, contact ☎ 0165 842 064, www.guidecourmayeur.com.

The **Forum Sports Center** offers a wide range of year-round sporting activities and frequent special events. Its attractions include an ice rink, tennis, indoor golf, ping-pong, video games, a nursery, and even a disco. It's across the river in Dolonne; for more info contact ☎ 0165 844 096, www.sportcourmayeur.com.

The **Monte Bianco Ski School** operates a good range of courses – from first-timer classes to off-piste guided excursions. For more information and reservations, contact ☎ 0165 842 477.

Where to Sleep

Courmayeur has a good selection of hotels, although most tend to be pricey for what you get. At the upper end of the luxury scale, I remain a fan of the **Gallia Gran Baita** ($$$-$$$$). Although a long walk from the center, the hotel has a professional staff and an excellent wellness center. The décor is country-cozy fresh, and the views from every balcony are astounding. Inquire at ☎ 0165 844 040, www.sogliahotels.com.

HOTEL PRICE CHART	
Double room without tax; $$$-$$$$ always with bath.	
$	Under €80
$$	€81-150
$$$	€151-250
$$$$	Over €250

Also on the outskirts of town, the **Hotel Villa Novecento** ($$$-$$$$) offers a romantic villa atmosphere and creaky old residential décor. For reservations, contact them at ☎ 0165 843 000, www.villanovecento.it.

The **Hotel Les Jumeaux** ($$$-$$$$) has a location right at the Courmayeur cable car. The large chalet has nice views from its balconies as well. For more information, check in at ☎ 0165 844 122.

The **Hotel Courmayeur** ($$-$$$) has cozy rooms 200 m from the central cable car – and a fireplace in its lounge. Reserve at ☎ 0165 846 732, www.hotelcourmayeur.com.

The old **Hotel Crampon** ($$) has inviting décor and small rooms just behind the tourist office, a short walk to the center; ☎ 0165 842 385, www.crampon.it.

Hotel Edelweiss ($$) has a great location at the back of old town. Rooms are basic, but each has its own bath, and the private hotel garden makes a fine summer retreat; ☎ 0165 841590, www.albergoedelweiss.it.

The **Hotel Laurent** ($-$$) is an old, flower-fronted chalet just below the center, with good parking and thoughtful décor, ☎ 0165 846 687, www.meublelaurent.com.

In the center of La Palud, approximately four km north of Courmayeur, the **Albergo Delle Funivia** ($) shares a square with the Mont Blanc cable car valley station. The chalet is a simple, homey affair, with residential décor and a restaurant downstairs. Book at ☎ 0165 899 24, www.hotelfunivia.com.

Where to Eat

Courmayeur boasts restaurants of a generally high caliber, a collection well suited to the village's discerning city crowds. At Via Marconi 54, the **Pierre Alexis 1877** ($$$) does good set menus, with creative takes on traditional cuisine. Book a table at ☎ 0165 844 403.

DINING PRICE CHART	
Average entrée, with tax.	
$	Under €10
$$	€10-25
$$$	Over €25

The classy restaurant and café **Cadran Solaire** ($$) has a short menu of pricey fare and a narrow, shady patio; ☎ 0165 844 609.

For traditional specialties, try the characteristic **Leone Rosso** ($$). Its stone and wood house is down an ally at 73 Via Roma – look for the red lion sign out front; ☎ 0165 846 726.

Also good, particularly for a summer lunch, is the **Mont Fréty** ($$) at Strada Regionale 21. Garden dining proves a treat, with tables scattered on the lawn around a cheerful little fountain. Pizzas and other traditional dishes fill the menu; ☎ 0165 841 786.

AUTHOR'S PICK

*If you're looking for a memorable night out and are willing to drive or cab it a bit, head for the **Maison de Filippo** ($$$) in Entrèves, three km up the valley. It's a set-menu affair, but with 36 courses on the way, you're bound to find something you like. It's popular; reserve at ☎ 0165 869 797, www.lamaison.com.*

For pizza, try **La Terrazza** ($-$$) at Via Circonvallazione 73 or, at Via Roma 86, the cozy **Ancien Casino** ($-$$). I liked **Pan Per Focaccia** ($), both for the focaccia and the crêpes as well. It sits charmingly on Via Rue Dei Giardini, a tiny passage off Via Roma.

For **groceries**, head to the **Margherita Market** – it's set back from the road at Via Circonvallazione 23. Or pick up more glorified picnic fare at one of the **gourmet delis** along Via Roma; I liked the **Ortofrutta Santino** at Via Roma 6 for its mushrooms and delish marinated veggies. If you're lucky enough to have someplace to cook, don't miss the fresh pasta at **Pastifico Gabriella**, Passage del Angelo 2. **Crème et Chocolat** has the old town's best gelato; it's on the Piazza Brocherei.

Where to Party

For a town this small, Courmayeur offers a good selection of nightlife. In winter, the evening begins with low-key après-ski in the cafés along the Via Roma. The **Caffe della Posta** at Via Roma 51 draws a casual crowd around the fireplace in its back room; the nearby **Café Bar des Guides** is comfy, too, with sofa chairs and sports on TV. The **Bar Roma** offers drinks and snacks, the **American Bar** gets lively, and the Spanish **Le Prive**, just above, has a good selection of both drinks and *tapas*.

For late-night action, try the **Planet Discobar** in the sports center, **Poppy's** at town center, or **Jimmy's Night Café** at the Hotel Astoria.

Where to Play

Courmayeur provides more **childcare** opportunities than most Italian resorts. The **Plan Checrouit** nursery accepts children from six months of age, the **Kinderheim** at the sports center accepts children from nine months of age, and the tourist office can help arrange

babysitters. In addition to the winter activities arranged by the **ski school**, families enjoy **organized summer programs** and the area's hiking, biking, and cable car rides. Children love the Plan Checrouit **Alpine swimming pool**, and there's a **playground** there as well.

The Two Saint Bernards

Two mountain roads climb out of the Val d'Aosta, each pass confusingly known as the St. Bernard. The Petit St. Bernard heads into France; the Grand St. Bernard climbs into Switzerland.

The route differentiated as the ***Petit*** or ***Piccolo*** **St. Bernard** – in English the Little St. Bernard – heads southwest toward France and the Tarantaise region. Since ancient times, this road has been a hotly contested strategic trade route through the high Alps; even Hannibal saw it as fit for his elephants. From just south of Courmayeur, the road climbs through La Thuile Valley and out of Italy, passing by the **Cromlech,** or "Hannibal's Circle," an ancient Celtic monument of carefully laid stone that remains an object of much archeological inquiry. The 10th-century **Pilgrim's Hospice** and the **Chanousia** botanical gardens lie farther along. For a lunch break, try the **Bar Ristorante San Bernardo** at 2,200 m; it has good traditional food, including fondue and raclette. Six simple guest rooms offer accommodations.

The route called the ***Grand*** **St. Bernard**, or the Great St. Bernard, climbs from the town of Aosta north into Switzerland and the region of Valais. While a tunnel keeps the route open throughout the year, the more interesting summer option is the Col du St. Bernard mountain road. The pass has long been an important north-south transalpine route – as early as 58 BC, Julius Caesar ordered an army legion over the trail, and the first automobile path opened in 1905. Aside from the stunning scenery, the route's main attraction is just across the Swiss border. The **Great St. Bernard Hospice** offers Christian hospitality amid some of the Alps' most inhospitable terrain. Since the 11th century, the monks here have sheltered Alpine travelers, on many occasions rescuing stranded walkers with the help of the hospice's enormous dogs, a canine breed we know as the St. Bernard. Visitors should tour the hospice museum for its fascinating documentation of local history – and, of course, walk through the kennels, summer home of the legendary hospice dogs. Fancy a pup? Plunk down €2,000 to put your name on the waiting list.

Italy

AUTHOR'S
PICK

It's worth planning lunchtime around a stop at **Praz d'Arc**, *up above the tree line on the Italian side of the Grand St. Bernard route. Here, an Alpine dairy offers farm-made cheese, bread, salami, and honey. At the bar inside, requesting* piatti misti *for the number of people in your party will net you a communal basket of fresh bread and a plate heaped with a mix of cheese and meats. It's all ideally accompanied with a pitcher of red wine and glasses of water from the trough fountain out front.*

Aosta

With a 5,000-year history and some of Italy's finest Roman ruins, Aosta deserves more attention than it gets. Most tourists blow by the town en route to the more famous sights beyond – and I suspect that of those few who do drive in, many leave in frustration after unsuccessfully seeking the old town and/or a place to park. Our advice is this: If at all possible, arrive by train, as the station sits flush against the old town's southern wall. If arriving by car, follow the signs to the train station, or *stazione*, where there are several lots nearby.

A bustling town of over 11,000 people, Aosta lies at the foot of Mont Emilius and at the intersection of the Aosta, Grand St. Bernard, and Cogne valleys. Its walled, rectangular old town has a roughly east-west orientation, parallel to the train tracks on the western bank of the Torrente Buthier River. The **Piazza Chanoux** and its grand **Municipio** palace comprise the old town's nucleus and the center of the car-free shopping area. From here, cobbled alleys lead off in several directions. Pick up a map from the square's tourist office before you set out; it has detailed information in English.

From the northeast corner of the Municipio on Piazza Chanoux, tourists head down the tiny Via Charrey – past the trash dumpsters along a residential back alley – and, amusingly, stumble upon the magnificent first-century ruins of the **Roman Theater**. Excavation and preservation work continues (and they're fairly serious about all those posted rules).

South along the town wall is the massive **Porta Pretoria** and, beyond, the charming Via Sant Anselmo, which leads east to the **Roman Arch**. The **Roman Amphitheater** occupies the northeastern corner of town. Farther west along the northern wall are the Renaissance-era **Palazzo Roncas**, the **Regional Museum of Archeology**, and – slightly south – the **Cathedral of the Assunta** with its splendidly ornate central portal.

Want to stay? Aosta's accommodations are less than enticing. The best thing going is the **Hotel Europe** ($$-$$$), a business-oriented establishment at the heart of the old town. It's reasonably close to the train station, at Piazza Narbonne 8; ☎ 0165 23 63 63, www.ethotels.com/hoteleurope.

 For more information drop by the tourist office in the old town center at the Piazza Chanoux; ☎ 0165 333 52, www.aostaturismo.com.

Gran Paradiso National Park
(Il Parco Nationale del Gran Paradiso)

 The Gran Paradiso National Park is up in the northwestern-most corner of Italy, straddling the provincial borders of Aosta and Piemonte, and edging the French frontier and La Vanoise National Park just west. At its center, the Gran Pardiso Massif rises 4,061 m, the highest peak to fall entirely within Italian borders. The region was for centuries an ancient transalpine crossroads and, in the mid-19th century, the land here became the royal hunting grounds of the House of Savoy. The Gran Paradiso National Park was established in 1922 with a royal land grant donated to protect the rapidly disappearing ibex.

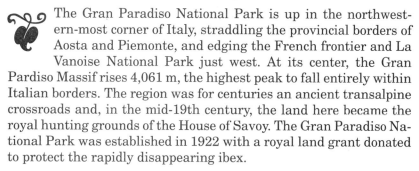

Ibex are both skittish and fast, so many visitors leave the park without ever spotting one. The best time to view them is during evening hours, when they slow down to graze along the high-Alpine pastures.

Within the park's bounds, climbers explore rock faces and summit the Gran Paradiso, riders take to equestrian trails, and walkers enjoy routes ranging from a few hours to a few days. In winter, cross-country skiers tour high glacier trails or take to the loipe along the valleys, and snowshoers venture into the woods and up mountain paths. Observant visitors are likely to see ibex, chamois, marmots, and eagles. The park is accessed via the Val d'Aosta and any of three side-valleys, **Valgrisenche** to the west, **Rhemes** in the middle, and **Valsavarenche** to the east.

We prefer to explore the park from the Valsavarenche. The valley centers on the small community of **Degioz**, where the National Park Information Center makes its home. Museum entries here document the predators living inside the park, with particular focus on the lynx. The Valsavarenche offers excellent cross-country and easy downhill skiing in winter; good climbing, hiking, and biking in summer; and a reasonable tourism infrastructure year-round.

Italy

Want to stay? The **Hostellerie du Paradis** ($$) in Valsavarenche offers mountainside accommodations at the park's doorstep. Walking trails depart directly from the hotel, maps and mountain bikes are available, and the food's darn good as well. To inquire, contact ☎ 0165 905 971, www.hostellerieduparadis.it.

 For more information on the park, stop by the National Park Information Center at Degioz or click on www.granparadiso.net.

Venice & Northeast Italy

Northeastern Italy claims some of the Alps' most majestic terrain. Our coverage spans the region from the Adriatic Sea to the high Alpine terrain along the Austrian frontier. To the south, Venice glistens at the heart of a large lagoon, rich with ancient architecture and untold mounds of gilded art. The serene city's shimmering waterways, tiny shops, and sidewalk cafés entice the international crowds to linger. From here, the northern plains quickly give way to the southern wall of the Dolomiti Alps.

Farther on, the resort town of Cortina courts a wealthy Italian clientele with upscale hotels and pricey boutiques – but makes room, too, for an international mix of adventuring tourists who come to marvel at the craggy peaks that soar all around. Beyond, the Val Gardena offers a wealth of dramatic hiking, biking, and skiing terrain at the foot of stalwart Sella Massif.

■ Venice

(Venezia)

Population: 64,076

Base elevation: Sea level

Gateway tourist city

Like a crumbling old dame grieving the lost bloom of her youth, Venice races against the indomitable powers of time, erosion, and pollution; of late, and sadly, vandalism scars her as well. Yet the city once known as La Serenissima Repubblica, "the most serene republic," remains elegant, an alluring mix of dilapidation and exotic glamour. Today, as in days past, the name conjures up shimmering visions of palaces reflected in water, narrow webs of cobblestone alleys and squares, and classical music echoed off narrow canal walls.

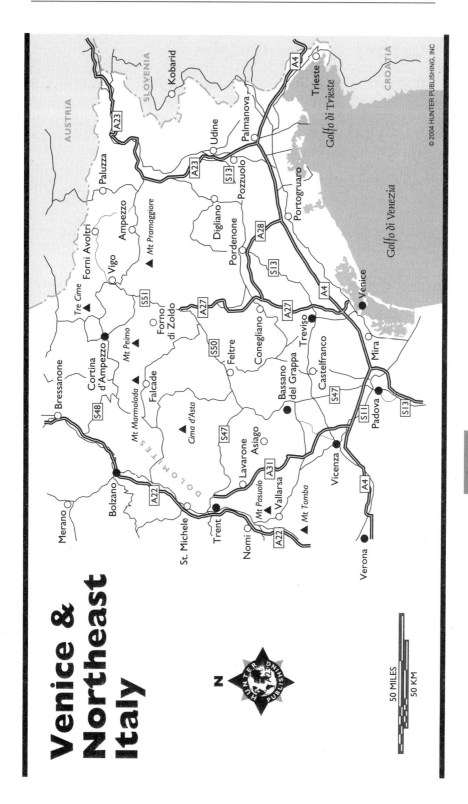

Venice & Northeast Italy

© 2004 HUNTER PUBLISHING, INC

Italy

History & Orientation

 Settlers first fled into the Venetian Lagoon some 1,500 years ago, when barbarians attacked the Roman towns of the Veneto. The island settlements soon formed an alliance, their bonds gradually strengthening and culminating in the joint election of their first leader, or *doge*, in 697. Venice's merchants quickly became the world's wealthest, importing the finest spices, fabrics, and wares from the east; fattening the city's coffers; and inspiring young Ventians such as Marco Polo to even greater exploits. With its wealth grew envy, and with envy, enemies; yet Venice protected herself. The Venetians sacked Constantinople in 1204 and, after a 127-year war, won dominance over Genoa, the city's primary competition in Mediterranean trade.

The height of Venetian empirical power peaked during the 15th century, yet her party-town reputation continued and, at one point during the 16th century a local tourist guidebook boasted 11,654 registered prostitutes. So, although Venice's power had faded, her stowed riches carried her grandly through 1791, when the last Venetian *doge* abdicated power to Napoleon. The city was tossed back and forth between Vienna and Italy, finally joining the Kingdom of Italy in 1866.

Tourism grew in the 19th century, yet the city saw a drastic population exodus, as its residents left in search of greater economic opportunity – a trend that continues alarmingly. Today, the city that once claimed over 174,000 residents now has just 64,000.

The Town

The city of Venice is comprised of some 120 islands connected by over 400 bridges, only three of which span the Grand Canal. Six *sestieri,* or districts, make up the city – Cannaregio, San Marco, and Castello to the east of the Grand Canal; Santa Croce, San Polo, and Dorsoduro to the west. Houses are numbered by *sestrieri* rather than streets, a system that newcomers find more hindering than helpful. In fact, most visitors spend their time in Venice dizzyingly disoriented, wandering a tangled maze of dark alleys without the aid of any predominant landmark.

Now, I realize the following orientation method will seem a bit silly; scoff, if you must. But, I've been getting around Venice with it for years, and it might just work for you, too. Picture Venice's *Centro Storico*, or old center, as a whale riding the wave of the Giudecca, the island to its south. The whale's nose points west at the ship dock; its tail forks toward the east with the gardens at its downward tip. Cars and trains enter the city via the spout; the Grand Canal marks a backwards 'S' down the whale's center; and the Dorsorduro district forms its lower fin – at its tip, the Dogana da Mar and the Santa

Maria della Salute church. And finally, if our whale had a belly button, the Piazzo San Marco would be it.

Getting Here & Around

 Travelers arriving by air will fly in to the **Marco Polo Airport** on the northern edge of the lagoon, some 13 km by car from Venice. **Buses** make the trip to Piazzale Roma in about 30 minutes. More interesting, however, is transfer by **boat**. Public waterbuses leave the docks just outside the terminal to make the 50-minute trip to the Piazza San

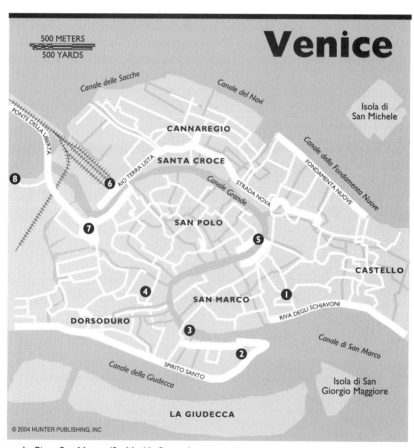

Italy

1. Piaza San Marco (St. Mark's Square)
2. Santa Maria della Salute
3. Accademia Bridge
4. Campo Santa Margherita
5. Rialto Bridge
6. Santa Lucia Ferrovia Train Station
7. Piazzale Roma (bus stop & parking)
8. Tronchetto (parking)

Marco, or St. Mark's Square. Bus and boat tickets are sold inside the airport's arrivals terminal.

Trains pull in on the northern edge of the city, and waterbuses depart from the docks just out the station's front doors. As Venice is a traffic-free city, drivers must cross the lagoon bridge and park their cars in the enormous garages at Tronchetto and Piazzale Roma. The slightly more central Piazzale Roma lots are more expensive and fill quickly in high season – I suggest the Tronchetto garage. Both parking areas are well-served by waterbus.

Venice is most efficiently navigated by boat. **Water-taxis** are both the most convenient and most excruciatingly expensive means of travel. (If you're going to splurge, at least bargain a bit.) Public waterbuses, or *vaporetti*, offer a more affordable means of travel, making the rounds through the Grand Canal and to the outer lagoon islands. The Grand Canal *vaporetti* stops most frequented by tourists are Tronchetto and Piazzale Roma for parking; Ferrovia for the train station; Rialto for its bridge and shopping area; Accademia for the museums; and either San Marco Giardinetti or San Zaccaria for St. Mark's Square.

Grand Canal Vaporetti Routes

To the Grand Canal, from Tronchetto, Piazzale Roma, or Ferrovia:

Route 1 – the slow boat; stops at every dock.

Route 82 – the boat stops several times, including Rialto, Accademia, and San Zaccaria; also loops via the Giudecca Canal along the southeastern edge of the city.

Route 3 – the express boat; stops only at San Samuele, Accademia, and San Marco; then loops back to Tronchetto.

If you plan to make more than two rides each day on the *vaporetti* waterbuses, purchase a 24-hour (or more) pass. For more information on routes, check www.actv.it.

Many, many books have been written on Venice – and many, many films have been shot here. Thomas Mann's 1971 Death in Venice *stirred local sentiment; but our favorite Venice-set saga is the film version of Henry James' novel,* The Wings of the Dove.

Getting Connected

 The main tourist office is Piazza San Marco 71, in front of the San Marco Giardinetti waterbus stop. There's a smaller, less useful office in the train station as well. For more information, contact ☎ 041 529 87 11, www.turismovenezia.it.

 The main post office is in the Fondaco di Tedeschi on the eastern side of the Rialto Bridge. The train station has a convenient post office, too.

 For Internet access, head to the **Net House** on Campo Morosini, near San Stefano, just north of the Accademia Bridge.

The Sights

 Venice harbors more tourist "sights" than any city I know. Every alley begs to be explored; every shop, browsed; every church, entered. If you must attempt it in a single day, I suggest a boat ride from the parking and station area down the Grand Canal to Piazza San Marco, and then a walk back via the Rialto Bridge. In any case, you can't see it all. With this in mind, we've narrowed the city's infinite attractions down to several must-see sights.

Perhaps the most famous waterway in the world, the **Grand Canal**, or Canale Grande, is Venice's biggest boulevard. The canal winds 3½ km through the city center, clogged the entire way with waterbuses, motorboats, water-taxis, and slow-moving gondolas. (Although expensive water-taxis offer excellent tours, a more affordable version comes by way of a waterbus ride – preferably in one of the coveted seats at the boat's bow.) Some 200 palaces flank the Grand Canal, most of them built between the 12th and 18th centuries; I won't attempt to describe them all here, but if you're interested, excellent maps and canal guides are available at the kiosks near the station. On the way south, do note the locations of the canal's three bridges, the **Ponte Scalzi** near the train station, the famed **Rialto** about midway down the canal, and the wooden **Accademia** just before the canal opens into the basin.

Italy

AUTHOR'S
PICK

Most tourists go ashore at Vallaresso or Giardinetti, the first stops near Piazza San Marco. I suggest continuing on by boat a bit, in order to get your first view of the square from the water. Stay on the boat as it moves along the San Marco Basin – at least one more stop to San Zaccaria. If you stay aboard to Arsenale or Giardini, you'll have a nice walk back to the square and big views of the Venetian Lagoon.

St. Mark's Square, or the Piazza San Marco, is Venice's living room, the administrative and religious center of the city. It's the largest open space in the city and the only square to bear the title of *piazza* – other smaller squares are called *campo*, *piazzeta*, or *piazzale*. Cafés and shops line the arcades encircling the square. St. Mark's basilica lies at the eastern end, fronted by the Campanile tower, and flanked by the Palazzo Ducale to the south and the 15th-century clock tower to the north. Visitors shop for souvenirs, climb the Campanile for views, and await the striking of the hour by the clock tower's two Moors.

A Tale of Two Cafés

Caffeine-consumers unite, and thank Venice for introducing coffee to Europe. In 1640, Venetian ships began importing coffee beans, or *kahve*, from Turkey to be used as medicine, a precursor to Prozac, if you will. Some 80 years later, on the 29th of December in 1720, a Venetian named Floriano Francesconi threw open the doors of Europe's first coffee house: it was called the **Venice Triumphant**, and it sat on St. Mark's Square. The café drew such illustrious visitors as Lord Byron, Goethe, and Charles Dickens. Casanova found the female-friendly coffee house a prime hunting ground. In the decadence of the 18th and early 19th centuries, the whole of St. Mark's Square became a solid ring of cafés – houses of hedonism that saw in one week more intrigues and infidelity than 10 seasons of *Friends*.

During the Austrian occupation of the 19th century, Austrian soldiers frequented the **Gran Caffé Quadri** on the northern side of the *piazza*. Proud Venetians boycotted the place, sitting and sipping elsewhere around the square. Today, only two of the original cafés remain: **Florian's**, originally the Venice Triumphant, and the once-traitorous **Quadri** across the square. Although tourists are likely to note no difference save the color schemes of the elegant interiors, true Venetians remember where their loyalties lie.

AUTHOR'S PICK

> *Both cafés host live music on the square during summer evenings, each house dueling for the biggest crowds. It's a delightful, if expensive, way to while away a Venetian evening.*

St. Mark's Basilica, or the Basilica di San Marco, is the city's most enduring landmark. First built as a doge's chapel in the ninth century and reconstructed in the 11th, the magnificent church has been gradually adorned with all manner of glorified loot, from the remains of St. Mark (stolen from Alexandria in 828) to the much-touted Four Bronze Horses (swiped from Constantinople in 1204). The exterior of the church puts the "busy" in Byzantine, with five domes, a gaggle of 13th-century carvings, and several splendid mosaics – the one to the right depicts the pilfering of St. Mark's body. Inside, admire the exquisite mosaic floors and pay a nominal fee to see the Pala d'Ora, an altar piece made of 250 gold panels and encrusted with jewels.

The **Doge's Palace**, or the Palazzo Ducale, was the nucleus of Venetian life from its founding in the ninth century. A pale pink, lacey façade fronts the Gothic structure, hiding within a richly ornamented interior that served at once as residence of the *doge* rulers, seat of the government, and home to both the courts and the prison. The famous Ponte dei Sospiri, or **Bridge of Sighs**, links the palace courts to the prison cells, a place of great horror, indeed. (Although you can walk through it here, the bridge is best seen and photographed from the outside of the palazzo, along the waterfront at Rio di Palazzo della Canonica.) Tours are offered in English; the "Secret Itineraries" tour is particularly recommended. The palace is open daily from 9 am to 5 pm, till 7 pm in summer; ☎ 041 271 59 11; €11.

Italy

Venice Under Water

Each winter, occasional high tides flood the low-lying areas of Venice, particularly those around the Doge's Palace and St. Mark's Square. On several occasions we've witnessed the piazza under water; it's a tragic yet magical sight, the splendid Basilica seeming to float above a continuous sea.

These high waters, or *acque alte*, have grown more frequent over the years, as Venice sinks and tides rise. The population copes with *acque alte* by erecting elevated wooden walkways, rearranging waterbus docks, and sounding warning sirens. However, none of that stops the floods from hastening the erosion of the city's foundations. So, a massive rescue effort is underway; the installation of huge drainage pipes beneath the city will relieve the flooding – and, unfortunately, make a construction-zone mess of St. Mark's Square over the next several years.

The **Rialto Bridge**, or Ponte Rialto, was the first to span the Grand Canal, a valuable link between the mercantile centers on either side. First constructed as a wooden drawbridge, the stone version that stands today was built in the late 16th century based on a design by Andrea da Ponte. (He beat Palladio out for the gig.) Today the bridge's arcades are home to a collection of expensive touristy shops. The alleys down its steps lead northwest toward Piazzale Roma and the train station and southeast toward Piazza San Marco – this latter route through the city's most exclusive shopping district. Follow the yellow signs to the square; when two *San Marco* signs point in opposite directions, choose one, and you'll get there eventually.

For museum hounds, three museums stand out. The **Gallerie dell'Accademia**, or Accademia Gallery, is the city's most famous museum and home to the globe's most extensive collection of Venetian art. Housed in a former church, the exhibit displays works from the 14th through the 18th centuries, including paintings by Veneziano, Carpaccio, Tintoretto, and Veronese, among many, many others. The museum is open from Tuesday through Sunday, 8:15 am-7:15 pm, Monday from 8:15 am-2 pm; ☎ 041 522 22 47; €6.50.

The nearby **Peggy Guggenheim Collection** invites visitors into the neo-classical Palazzo Venier dei Leoni for a look at one of the world's greatest private collections of modern art. The museum is open 10 am-5 pm daily except Tuesday, April through October, and till 10 pm on Saturdays; ☎ 041 240 54 11; €8.

One *vaparetto* dock north, the Ca' Rezzonico houses the new **Museo del Settecento Veneziano**, or the Museum of 18th-century Venice. The fascinating collection features art and interior design exhibits, all well-displayed within the 17th-century palace walls. It's closed temporarily for restoration. ☎ 041 522 54 95; www2.regione.veneto.it/cultura/musei/inglese/pag446e.htm €6.50.

*Venice's cramped alleys may well feel a bit claustrophobic, particularly for those travelers now accustomed to panoramic Alpine views and wide, open spaces. If you feel the need to climb something – or just want a big-picture perspective – hop a boat for **Isola di San Giorgio Maggiore**, the island directly across the basin to the south of Piazza San Marco. From there, enjoy wide water views, and ascend the church tower for panoramic lagoon vistas. Although the San Marco Campanile is taller, this tower remains my favorite vantage point in Venice.*

The Adventures

Venice's adventures are simple: long wanders through the city, and long boat rides through the lagoon. The most popular outings by boat are gondola rides through the center's narrow canals and waterbus excursions to the outer islands of Murano, Burano, Torcello, and the Lido.

The Gondolas

Gondolas have plied Venetian canals since the 11th century; in the 18th century, some 14,000 gondolas rowed through town. Each boat adheres to traditional specifications, constructed using 280 separate parts and eight kinds of wood; each weighs approximately 400 kilograms; and, in adherence with the luxury laws of 1562, each is glossed with seven layers of black lacquer paint. The boats are flat along the bottom and are asymmetrically framed, listing to the right in order to counteract the effect of the gondolier's single oar. Each gondola sports a *forcola*, or oar rest, toward the back; and on the bow, a *fero*, a decorative six-pronged fork symbolizing the six *sestieri* districts of Venice.

Today, the city's 400 remaining gondolas corral at several locations to await tourist fares; some of the most popular docks are near the Doge's Palace, behind St. Mark's Square at Orseolo, and near the Rialto Bridge. Rides are pricey – expect to pay €80 for a 50-minute evening jaunt, day rates somewhat less. Bargaining is most appropriate.

Italy

AUTHOR'S PICK

*The city's least expensive gondola rides are via the **traghetti**, stationed at strategic crossing-points along the Grand Canal. Gondoliers oar straight across the canal, ferrying pedestrians for a small fee – at last count, €1.40. When a traghetto gondola fills up, passengers stand rather than sit, giving the ride an extra-sporty touch. (Widen your stance for balance; you don't want to swim in this water.)*

Lagoon excursions depart by waterbus from the San Zaccaria dock near Piazza San Marco. The island of **Murano** is famed for its ornate glasswork, examples of which can be purchased throughout the city. Visitors can watch master craftsmen at work in shops around the islands, and learn about the history of glassmaking at the **Museum of Glass Art**.

The island of **Burano** is renowned for is elegant lace, and tourists come here to visit the lace-making school. I love Burano, too, for its brightly painted fishermen's houses, a legacy of the fishing industry that once thrived here. Take time, if you can, for a meal in one of the island's small seafood restaurants.

Nearby, the island of **Torcello** rests peacefully in the northern lagoon. First settled between the fifth and seventh centuries, the island was the birthplace of Venice and was once home to some 20,000 people. Today, fewer than 100 residents remain. Torcello draws tourists for the mosaics inside its elegant cathedral, the **Santa Maria dell-Assunta**, a church built in the seventh century and reconstructed during the 11th.

The Lido, at the eastern edge of the lagoon, is Venice's beachside community. The long, narrow strip stretches between the Adriatic and the Venetian Lagoon, a land bar first popularized around the turn of the 20th century and today cluttered with paid-entry beaches and cabana bars.

Venice Off-Hours

We hope you'll spend a night in Venice. Most of the city's guests – and, indeed, its workers, too – day-trip into the city then flee to the mainland at night in search of less expensive lodging. While it's true that local hotels post outrageous rates, a splurge here buys you a look at the off-hours city that most never see.

- **Late-night** Venice is quiet; deathly, delightfully so. Wander through the deserted alleyways, stroll along the splashing canals, and sit silently on a bridge a while – a homebound gondola might just pass under, the gondolier singing only for himself.

- **Nighttime boats** run up the Grand Canal, allowing riders the opportunity for a wee bit of palace-peeping. Although most palaces remain dark, some illuminated interiors tease with glimpses of Murano-glass chandeliers, luxurious draperies, and ornately carved ceilings.

- **Sunrise** is most spectacular from the banks of the San Marco Basin. The sun climbs up behind the Lido and the Isola di San Giorgio Maggiore, throwing a warm glow over the Gothic arches of the Doge's Palace and the dome of the Santa Maria della Salute church. Photographers gather at the Doge's Palace for that classic gondolas-in-the-foreground shot.

- The **morning market** sets up on the northwestern side of the Rialto Bridge, its colors, sounds, and smells giving rise to some most memorable moments. Come either by gondola, via the Santa Sofia *traghetti* across the Grand Canal, or on foot. The authentic action here takes place beyond the Rialto tourist stalls; wander north to the covered markets at Campo Battisti and Campo Pescaria, where fresh fish and produce is hauled in each morning by boat.

TIP: Tourists and workers flood into the city in the morning and out of the city at night, cramming boats beyond comfortable capacity. If you stay in the city, you have the opportunity to sightsee opposite the current crowd flow. In the evenings, ride south from the station toward San Marco; in the mornings, ride north instead.

Where to Sleep

Venice hotels post notoriously high rates for rooms that are notoriously scruffy. Nonetheless, occupancy and turnover rates in the city are so high that owners understandably claim that there's no good time to renovate. I've looked for hotels with good locations and indicated average rates; rooms facing any type of water will be more expensive.

If you have the cash, there is no better stay in the lagoon than the legendary **Cipriani** ($$$$). The hotel sits in an isolated position at the western edge of the Giudecca, one island south of the old city center. The rooms are luxurious, the views mesmerizing, and the canal-side garden pool a pleasant retreat. A private motorboat ferries guests between the hotel and St. Mark's Square. Inquire at ☎ 041 520 77 44, www.hotelcipriani.com.

HOTEL PRICE CHART	
Double room without tax; $$$-$$$$ always with bath.	
$	Under €80
$$	€81-150
$$$	€151-250
$$$$	Over €250

For luxury along the Grand Canal, head to the **Gritti Palace** ($$$$), the most genteel of the traditional palace hotels in the center. Book at ☎ 041 179 46 11, www.luxurycollection.com. The staff at the basin-front Danieli, a sibling of the Gritti, has been rude on both of our last two visits; at these rates, we'd expect better.

Travelers preferring the predicable luxuries of commercial chains will appreciate the **Sofitel Venezia** ($$$-$$$$). The hotel fronts a canal in a pleasant location near the station, and its rooms are among the city's most modern. Inquire at ☎ 041 71 04 00, www.accor-hotels.it.

The **Romantik Hotel Metropole** ($$$) fronts the wide basin, just east along the waterfront from St. Mark's Square and flanks a smaller canal to one side. Inside, loads of antiques and homey touches warm fancifully decorated rooms. Reserve at ☎ 041 520 50 44, www.hotelmetropole.com.

Also near St. Mark's Square, try the **Flora** ($$-$$$), a small hotel with a fetching little garden and rooms of variable comfort; ☎ 041 520 58 44, www.hotelflora.it.

Near the Fenice Theater, the quaint **La Fenice et des Artistes** ($$-$$$) draws applause from its artsy clientele; ☎ 041 523 23 33, www.fenicehotels.it.

For a waterside view near the Rialto, try the **Locanda Sturion** ($$-$$$). It has Venetian-style rooms up a steep flight of stairs; ☎ 041 523 62 43, www.locandasturion.com.

I've long had a soft spot for the charming **Accademia Villa Maravege** ($$$). It's in Dorsoduro, housed in a small villa with a pleasant canal-side garden; ☎ 041 521 01 88, www.pensioneaccademia.it. Just around the corner, the similarly named **Accademia Bed & Breakfast** ($$) occupies the top two floors of a villa just one lot back from the Grand Canal – a few steps from the Accademia museum and boat stop. Guests enter via a locked courtyard and relax on a garden terrace with pleasant views. Some rooms have a bath, others share, but all enjoy the hospitality of Mr. Luca Bigozzi; ☎ 041 522 11 13, www.bbaccademia.com.

Farther south, two hotels front the Giudecca Canal and a floating waterside café. The **Seguso** ($-$$$) is the less expensive of the two, with some rooms sharing baths; ☎ 041 528 68 58. Next door, **La Calcina** ($$-$$$) trades on the fact that Ruskin once spent time here; ☎ 041 522 70 45.

Farther to the north in the direction of the station, the squat **Antizo Capon** ($) resides in the "real" Venice, on the café-lined Campo Santa Margherita, the city's most authentic residential square; ☎ 041 528 52 92.

Where to Eat

Venetian cuisine, like its lodging, is pricey, yet not particularly good. But, I do have a few favorites to share. The best thing going for a romantic summer night out is **Cip's Club** ($$$), a Hotel Cipriani endeavor. The restaurant floats atop a barge along the

DINING PRICE CHART	
Average entrée, with tax.	
$	Under €10
$$	€10-25
$$$	Over €25

Giudecca, with enormous views of the city and St. Mark's Square stretching out across the water. Candlelit, tables with white linens provide an elegant décor. Reserve at ☎ 041 520 77 44; also inquire about boat transfers.

North of St. Mark's Square, try **Da Arturo** ($$$), a small restaurant with good regional cuisine and a quiet location on a *calle* near Campo Manin. Reserve at ☎ 041 528 69 74.

For fish, head to the market area at Rialto and the restaurant **Ai Mercanti** ($$$). Here, creative seafood specialties highlight the traditional Venetian tasting menu. Book a table at ☎ 041 523 8269.

For mid-range fare near the Rialto, try my favorite pizzeria, **Aquila Nera** ($$), home to a delish arugula pizza. It's been down a narrow alley off of Campo S. Bartolomeo since 1505. There's a small terrace in summer and homey décor inside; ☎ 041 522 47 69. Nearby, the **Ristorante Da Mario** ($$) has traditional cuisine and a large summertime dining terrace; ☎ 041 528 51 47.

At the northeastern corner of St. Mark's Square, across a canal, is the Campo Santi Filippo e Giacomo, a small square that's home to

Trattoria Aciugheta ($), or "little anchovy." The simple restaurant does pizzas and other traditional food.

Venice has a booming **café culture**, and visitors should spend a little time just sitting, watching the world go by. At St. Mark's Square, **Florian's** and **Quadri** are the most famous cafés in town. Cozy little bars dot the shopping streets behind the square, and sidewalk cafés line the **Riva** along the basin's waterfront. On sunny days, join the good mix of locals and tourists at the cafés along the **Zattere**.

> **TIP:** For groceries, follow the locals and head for either the **morning market** near Rialto, the picturesque **produce boat** near Campo San Barnaba, or the **Billa grocery store** on the Zattere near the Basilio boat stop.

Where to Party

 As both tourists and workers exit the lagoon *en masse* each evening, Venice sees very little nighttime action. To simply soak up the ambiance of the city, park yourself in a café along the **Riva waterfront** or join the Venetians sitting out at **Campo Santa Margarita**. **Il Doge** has the best gelato there.

In summer, **Florian's** and **Quadri** (see *A Tale of Two Cafés*, above) both host live music outdoors on **St. Mark's Square**, offering an ideal way to spend an evening amid the grandeur of the square. The piazza inspires less formal performances, too; I once watched a group of Austrian tourists break into to splendid, spontaneous song – it turns out they were an off-duty touring choir. **Harry's Dolci** sometimes hosts jazz out on the Giudecca, and **Casanova**, near the station along the Lista di Spagna, has occasional live music as well.

The **Gran Teatro La Fenice** has once again risen from ashes, as we go to press reopening its curtain after a devastating fire in 1996. See what's playing at the opera house at www.teatrolafenice.it.

The **Interpreti Veneziani** ensembles perform several times each week at various venues around the city; if you can catch a **classical concert** in one of the city's old churches, the ambiance alone is worth the price of a ticket. For more information, check current listings or www.interpretiveneziani.com. The elegant **Palazzo Vendramin Calegari** is home to the city's **casino**. It's along the Grand Canal and can be reached either on foot or by boat. Shuttles leave St. Mark's Square at regular intervals; ☎ 041 529 71 11, www.casinovenezia.it; jacket required.

Where to Play

All of Venice is an adult playground, but children won't find much specifically designed for them. That said, kids enjoy feeding the pigeons at St. Mark's Square, boat rides along the Grand Canal, and trips out to the Lido beaches.

Festivals & Events

Venice is busy all year – but come festival time, the old city packs in tourists by the busload. **Carnivale** is the city's most renowned festival, drawing tourists from around the world during the 10 days prior to Lent, during which time fabulously costumed revelers adorn bridges, doorways, and squares. (If you want to visit during Carnivale, book far, far in advance.)

On Ascension Sunday, the **Vogalonga**, or "long row," regatta takes oarsmen some 32 km through the lagoon, finishing up on the Grand Canal. The regatta celebrates the doge's historical *Bucintoro* ceremony, when he would row out to the Lido, throw a ring into the Adriatic, and thereby reaffirm Venice's "marriage to the sea."

Summer brings the **Festa del Redentore,** held on the third Sunday in July, a festival marking the passing of the 1576 plague. A bridge of boats crosses the Giudecca to the church, and fireworks light up the sky.

For the three months of summer during even-numbered years, the **Biennale** brings to Venice the world's largest festival of modern art. Each September, on the first Sunday of the month, the **Regata Storica** on the Grand Canal features a parade of rowers dressed in historic costumes. Finally, the festival season closes on the 21st of November with the **Festa Della Salute**, a celebration marking the passing of the 1630 epidemic of the bubonic plague. Today's festival includes a candlelit procession over the pontoon bridge crossing the Grand Canal to Santa Maria della Salute.

■ Cortina d'Ampezzo

Population: 6,500

Base elevation: 1,224 m

Mountain resort town

Cortina draws a glamorous crowd – boutiques gleam, cell phones ring, and socialites strut their ritz and glitz. It's a fascinating display, really, but one that regretfully obscures the greater riches here. So stop. Step back. Pull your eyes away from the pompous parade.

Italy

And look up. The scenic splendors there are some of the most magnificent of all the Alps. Jagged peaks soar all around, their forested foothills networked with paths, their crags made cozy in hospitable mountain huts. And it's all just a few steps away.

History & Orientation

 Although evidence shows that prehistoric hunters once wandered the Ampezzo Valley, Cortina remained a quiet backwater until access roads brought transalpine travelers its way. In the 1860s the region was discovered by budding mountaineers, wealthy adventure travelers from England and Germany in search of new sites to practice their newfound sport. Their influential accounts popularized tourism in the area. Winter tourism took hold in the early 20th century, and in 1956 Cortina took the world stage as host of the VII Olympic Winter Games. Today, this little town of 6,500 people swells to over 60,000 in high season.

The village of Cortina sits in natural splendor in the basin of the Ampezzo bowl, a valley surrounded by some 23 peaks of over 2,000 m. The valley rests in the north of the Veneto region and in the province of Belluno. Jutting mountains rise all around, including the Faloria to the east, the Cristallo to the northeast, the Tofana to the northwest, and the Cinque Torri to the west.

 Many films have been shot in Cortina and its majestic Dolomites, both Italian and foreign. For a big-screen look at the region, check out the following flicks: the James Bond film For Your Eyes Only, Peter Sellers in The Pink Panther, Elizabeth Taylor and Henry Fonda in Ash Wednesday, and Sylvester Stallone in Cliffhanger.

The Town

Cortina centers on its old town, now a pedestrian zone crammed full of expensive boutiques and cafés. The old town flanks a river and fills a rectangular area created by four one-way roads: **Via Franchetti** loops up the hill, **Via Marconi** runs the long leg north, **Via Grohmann** heads downhill to the west, and the main road squares off the area (and goes by changing names including **Via Battisti**, **Via Mercato**, and **Via Olimpia**). This old-town pedestrian area revolves around the **Piazza Venezia** and its lovely church. The main pedestrian drag, **Corso Italia**, runs the length of the center, and several smaller alleys veer off uphill.

Getting Here & Around

 Those traveling by **air** will fly in to the international airports at either **Venice** or **Innsbruck**. Cortina is just 44 km south of the Austrian border, 162 km north of Venice and 156 km south of Innsbruck – about a 2½-hour drive from either city. **Train** travelers arrive at the station in **Calalzo di Cadore**, some 35 km away, and transfer to a connecting bus. **Drivers** will find the center a frustrating place to navigate – and curse the town's lack of parking. Several lots lie below the town along the river.

 From December through March, direct buses run between Cortina and the airport at Venice, eradicating the need for a private vehicle or complicated train transfer. The service operates only on Saturdays and Sundays – the start and end days of local hotel package weeks. Reserve a seat on the bus when you book your hotel.

Public **buses** hub at the **Via Marconi** station on the northern edge of the center. Local buses ply through town and well serve the outlying lift bases. Buses are free to lift-pass holders.

Mountain transportation is scattered on the outskirts of town. Only the Faloria cable car departs from the town center. (However, buses run between the lift stations at reasonable intervals.) Lift passes run the gamut from single-lift rides to the winter-only Dolomiti SuperSki Pass, a ticket covering 460 lifts and 1,220 km of runs.

Italy

LIFT PASS PRICE SAMPLES	
Winter	
1-day adult local area	€27
1-day adult SuperSki.	€37
6-day adult SuperSki	€182
Pedestrian round-trip to Helbronner	€30.50
Summer	
Pedestrian round-trip to Cinque Torri	€10.50

Getting Connected

 The tourist information office is in the center at Corso Italia. For more information, check ☎ 0436 27 11, www.cortina.dolomiti.org.

 The post office is in the center at Largo Post.

The Sights

 Sightseeing in Cortina must include a see-and-be-seen stroll along the **Corso Italia**, the main drag of the pedestrian zone shopping area. Over 50 shops clog Cortina's old alleyways, offering antiques, fashion, and jewelry. (Sports shops, on the other hand, are hard to find.)

Tourists should visit Cortina's lovely **parish church** in the center of town, an 18th-century rebuilding of the original 13th-century chapel that once stood here. Inside are several worthwhile frescoes, carvings, and altars. The **bell tower** next door is an 1858 reconstruction of a 12th-century original. Nearby, the **Ciasa de Ra Regoles** houses three small museums, including a collection of modern art, an ethnological display of folkloric art and costumes, and a paleontology exhibit of fossils gleaned from the Dolomite region. For more information on the museums, contact ☎ 0436 22 06, www.musei.regole.it.

> **TIP:** Several interesting day-trips are possible from Cortina. **DynamicTour** does a good range of outings to far-off destinations such as Venice, Innsbruck and Salzburg – and even into Germany for visits to King Ludwig's castles and Hitler's Eagle's Nest. See Sports Services below, page 265.

The Adventures

On Foot

 Cortina's network of footpaths winds some 300 km through the local mountains. Cableways assist **walkers** in reaching the area's 56 mountain restaurants and *refugi*, and the Cortina Mountain Guides organize daily excursions for both families and more experienced hikers. The guides also arrange a wide variety of outings for **climbers**, including free-climbing and trips to the region's excellent *vie ferrate* (see *Sports Services*, page 265).

In addition, the **Parco Naturale Regole d'Ampezzo**, or Natural Park of the Ampezzo, shelters some 20,000 acres of the Dolomites just north of Cortina. Strict preservation laws protect the environment here in order to cultivate a habitat in which the region's rich flora and fauna can thrive. Visitors wander the park on over 500 km of trails, along the way spotting chamois, marmots, and even golden eagles. For more information on the park, contact ☎ 0436 22 06, www.dolomitiparco.com.

World War I & Cortina

From the 16th through the 19th centuries, while under the rule of Austria's Hapsburgs, the region enjoyed a peaceful prosperity. That peace shattered in dramatic fashion, however, when Italy declared war on Austria in 1915 and World War I brought fierce fighting to Cortina's mountains. The Austrian lines stretched along the Stelvio Pass, at Lagazuoi, and across the Valparola Pass; Italian troops fought from Cinque Torri. Over the course of the war, both armies tunneled into the mountains, digging trenches and fortifying their positions.

Today, war-history hounds can tour the **Great War Museum in the Dolomites**, a collection of three preserved sites just west of Cortina, all with explanatory markers in English. Farthest west is the Austrian fort at **Tre Sassi**; for a nominal entry fee, its interior is open for exploration. Above the Valparola Pass to the east tower the **Lagazuoi peak** and its open-air war museum, a collection of galleries, tunnels, and trenches enhanced with exhibits, model figures, and commentaries. The area can be reached on foot or via the Lagazuoi cable car. Nearest to Cortina is the **Cinque Torri**, or "five towers," mountain region. Here, visitors ride a chairlift or hike up to the Italian defense lines, where several easy itineraries lead through entrenchments and artillery emplacements. Look for uniformed soldiers in the woods, and don't miss the fresh pasta at the Refugio Scoiattoli.

In Water

 Watersports in Cortina are limited to **swimming** in the old pool complex, ☎ 0436 86 05 81, and the **whitewater** day-trips arranged by the Cortina Adrenaline center (see *Sports Services* below). Trips include rafting, kayaking, hydro-speeding, and canyoning.

On Wheels

Mountain bikers love Cortina for its wide variety of long, looping trails. Easy trails meander along waterways, and intermediate trails head up side-valleys. Advanced riders take to more technical trails. One favorite difficult itinerary takes bikers from Cortina's center up the Faloria cable car, then down a winding path to Rio Gere. From here, a lift mounts the Cristallo, where a long trail speeds from Rifugio Son Forca down to Ospitale. An easy trail loops along the river from there back to Cortina. The tourist office has trail maps, and Due & Due rents gear (see *Sports Services*, page 265).

On Snow & Ice

Cortina has 51 lifts and 140 km of local **skiing** runs, which are graded 33% easy, 62% intermediate, and 5% difficult. The groomed trails span five fragmented mountain areas, each served by local buses. In addition, holders of the legendary Dolomiti SuperSki Pass have choice of an enormous area, including 1,220 km of runs and some 460 lifts.

Favorite runs include the secluded trail off the back of the Faloria area and a long run from the Passo Falzarego and the top of Lagazuoi down to San Cassiano – and even beyond to the Sella Ronda circuit. Along the trail, don't miss a stop at the tiny memorial chapel and a warm-up in the cozy Scontoni Refuge. If you're lucky, teams of ski-joring horses will be waiting to pull you across the run-out. (Buses head back to Cortina from San Cassiano; and the Dolomiti SuperSki Pass is required for lifts beyond Lagazuoi.)

Olympic Trails Tour

The new Olympia ski itinerary loops through all of the slopes on which racing competitions were held during the 1956 Olympic Winter Games. The route crosses the Tofana, Monte Cristallo, and Monte Faloria, among other areas, and can be accomplished in one or two days. The ski ticket office has maps and information. True followers of the Olympic Torch should also check out the Duca d'Aosta hut, where the torch was stored prior the opening ceremonies; do a lap on Olympic ice at the local rink; and race down the Olympic bobsled track at the Cortina Adrenaline Center (see *Sports Services* below).

Snowboarders take to the new funpark at **Faloria**, and **cross-country skiers** enjoy the new **Fiamesport Nordic Center** in the Fiames neighborhood. A 30-km loop runs between Cortina and Dobbiaco and, from there, loipe (trails) continue into Austria, some 200 km away. **Dogsledding** is available, as are **high-mountain treks** and **ice-climbing** at no fewer than seven frozen falls. The ice rink, on the northern outskirts of town, offers **skating, hockey**, and **curling**.

In the Extreme

The **Cortina Adrenaline Center** advertises their odd activities as "everything that doesn't in any way resemble your grandmother's cookies, or a stuffed armchair with you sitting in it...." In addition to popular TaxiBob **bobsled rides** on the Olympic ice track, winter visitors can hop aboard a rubber boat for **snow-rafting** on the ski jump slope; **toboggan** down a moonlit run on a "very aggressive sledge," miner's lamp strapped to their foreheads; or **luge** without breaks down the Olympic ice tube over "the most personal 400 m of your life." Summer activities include **hydro-speeding, kayaking, rafting**, and **canyoning** on nearby whitewater runs and **wheeled bobsled rides** on the concrete TaxiBob course. For contact info, see *Sports Services* below.

Sports Services, Outfitters & Guides

Dynamic Tours arranges an array of outings and adventures in both summer and winter. For example, the operator coordinates dog-sledding, wine tasting, and day-trip tours to destinations in Italy, Austria, and Bavaria. For more information, stop by the DynamicTour office at the northern end of the Corso Italia; ☎ 0436 23 63, www.dynamictour.it.

The **Gruppo Guide Alpine Cortina**, or the Cortina Mountain Guides, maintains a century-long tradition of education, training, and guiding. In addition to scheduled group outings, the guides lead private excursions, including rock and ice climbing, multi-day treks, and even nature walks. Contact ☎ 0436 86 85 05, www.guidecortina.com.

The **Due & Due** sports shop specializes in two things – bikes and skis – but stocks climbing kits, snowshoes, sleds, and baby joggers, too. The outfitter offers equipment rental, sales, and service and can arrange shuttles for bikers, mountain excursions, and ski lessons. Stop in at Via Roma 70 or check ☎ 0436 41 21, www.dueduecortina.com.

The **Cortina Adrenaline Center** spikes heart rates with a range of extreme activities you probably won't find at home. See *In the Extreme* above, and contact ☎ 0436 86 08 08, www.adrenalincenter.it.

Italy

Where to Sleep

Cortina offers a good range of accommodations, much of it in creaky old buildings, and much of it closing in shoulder season. The castle-like **Miramonti Majestic** ($$$$) has long been Cortina's grand dame. In a forested park setting outside of town, the elegant old house offers formal luxury, an indoor pool, and a private nine-hole golf course. Book at ☎ 0436 86 70 19, www.geturhotels.com.

HOTEL PRICE CHART	
Double room without tax; $$$-$$$$ always with bath.	
$	Under €80
$$	€81-150
$$$	€151-250
$$$$	Over €250

For rustic luxury, try the **Hotel de la Poste** ($$$-$$$$), directly in the town center. The large yellow chalet has been welcoming guests since 1835. Reserve at ☎ 0436 86 84 35, www.delaposte.it. Also along the Corso Roma, the **Hotel Aquila** ($$-$$$) offers homey accommodations and a lovely wine bar and lounge. Inquire at ☎ 0436 86 73 15, www.aquilacortina.com.

The **Hotel Olimpia** ($$) is a friendly, family-run lodge popular with budget travelers and tour groups. It's directly in the center at Largo delle Poste 37, and some of its rooms offer balconies; ☎ 0436 32 56, www.hotelolimpia.com.

The **Villa Resy** ($$) has homey accommodations on the village outskirts. Alberto de Stefani and his English wife Susan welcome guests from around the world. The small hotel sits on the footpath into town, offers its own shuttle service to the slopes, and boasts lovely views from its back garden. Reserve at ☎ 0436 32 56 or vresy.cortina@dolomiti.org.

The **Hotel Montana** ($-$$) has a good position on the main pedestrian street; reserve at ☎ 0436 86 82 11, www.cortina-hotel.com.

Where to Eat

Diners seeking gourmet cuisine should head to the outskirts of town for several epicurean treats. **Tivoli** ($$$) is the most celebrated gourmet house here, serving up regional cuisine with a creative kick. Book a table at ☎ 0436 86 64 00. Nearby **El Toula** ($$$) occupies a ramshackle barn on a northwestern hillside in Ronco; in summer, the terrace and garden are lovely open-air dining rooms. Make reservations at ☎ 0436 33 39.

For grilled meats, head to the rustic **El Zoco** ($$$), a few km up the road toward Dobbiaco; ☎ 0436 86 00 41. (The pumpkin gnocchi here ranks among the best we've tasted.) Also special for regional fare is the **Lago Pianozes** ($$), a chalet situated on a small lake at the base of the Croda da Lago; ☎ 043656 01.

DINING PRICE CHART	
Average entrée, with tax.	
$	Under €10
$$	€10-25
$$$	Over €25

For somewhat less glorified fare in the center of town, head to the reliable **Cinque Torri** ($$), a large restaurant with pizza, pasta, and meat dishes and a terrace overlooking the Largo della Poste; ☎ 0436 86 63 01.

Our favorite pizza place – and that of many others – is the **Porto Rotundo** ($$). It's just off the main square below the church tower; ☎ 0436 86 77 77. Try also the **Croda Café** ($) at Corso Italia 163 or the **Il Passetto** ($) near the bus station. **Ai Due Forni** ($), in an alley off Via Battisti, offers pizza to take away.

For groceries head for **La Coopertiva** department store or, more interestingly, the **Da Giacomo** fruit stand, the adjacent **wine shop**, and the **Panifico Alvera** down the block. All three are north of the Café Royal along the Corso Italia.

AUTHOR'S PICK

*On Cortina's mountains, several refugi offer hearty regional fare amid cozy surroundings. At the top of the Cinque Torri chairlift is the **Scoiattoli** mountain restaurant, where fresh pasta is made in-house – my favorite is a rich ravioli dish called Cansuziei all'Ampezzana – little pasta packages filled with seasoned beets, served in a browned butter sauce, and topped with poppy seeds and parmesan cheese.*

Where to Party

Cortina afternoons begin with coffee and cake in any of the town's many cafés, and evenings commence with a pre-dinner stroll, or *passeggiatta*, along the Corso Roma – a tradition offering ample opportunity for flaunting furs and haute couture fashion. Dinner starts late and runs long, and the best bars don't really get going until well after midnight. Hearty partiers rock on until daylight.

At tea-time, try the **Café Royal** on the Corso Italia, just uphill from the Piazza Venezia, or the **Rubens** at the Corso Italia's northern end. A younger crowd hangs out under the umbrella at the **Cristallino** on the Largo della Poste. The **Hacker-Pschorr Haus** pub just off of Largo della Poste offers good beer and food just across the alley.

Wine bars are a popular afternoon and pre-meal stop, particularly for a glass of sparkling Prosecco wine. I suggest making the rounds. Try the dark, wood-paneled **Enoteca** at Via Mercato 5, the **Bar Becalen** at Via Battisti 22, or the **Villa Sandi** at Largo Poste 1. **L'Osteria** offers a good selection of wine, local ham and bread, and outdoor seating on a garden deck. It's tucked away just off of the Corso Italia.

Later – much, much later – dance through the night at one of the town's five discos. **Ciarlis** is at the site of the old Hyppo bar, Largo Poste 35, and promises to be just as popular. The **VIP Club** draws a lively crowd, and the **Discotecha Belvedere** is often worth the taxi fare out to Pocol.

Where to Play

In winter, **ski schools** take kids from four years of age, and the new Kinderheim Babypark **nursery** service offers care for children three months to three years of age. It's in the Pocol skiing area and is open daily from 9:30 am to 4:30 pm. During the summer months, children enjoy **walks, bike rides, mini golf,** and any of the several **organized outings** arranged by the local mountain guides. For play areas, try the **park** on the northeast corner of the old town, or head for the **snow playgrounds** at several lift-base huts.

Festivals & Events

Cortina's festivals and events include many sporting competitions. The winter opens with a festival **Christmas Market** along the Corso Italia. **Snowboarding, bobsledding, curling,** and **sled-dog events** punctuate a schedule dominated by **ski racing** events including the **women's World Cup races** in mid-January and the **Dobbiaco-Cortina cross-country race** in February.

Summer brings a number of cultural, musical and sporting events, including **mountain-bike races** and the **Cortina-Dobbiaco Marathon**. The town's traditional folklore festival, the **Feste Campesetri dei Sestrieri**, draws crowds of colorfully costumed locals; the **Festival of the Bands** gathers regional musical groups; and the **Dolomites Golden Cup** shows off vintage cars.

For more information, contact the tourist office at ☎ 0436 27 11, www.cortina.dolomiti.org.

The Val Gardena

(Gröden)

The Val Gardena tucks away in the Dolomites in the heart of Ladin country, 250 km north of Venice and 120 km south of Innsbruck, Austria. The valley runs 25 km from the A22 Autostrada at Chiusa in the west to Selva at its head in the east. The magnificent pillar of the Sella Massif rises just beyond. To its north, the valley is bordered by the Parco Naturale Puez-Odle; to the south, the Alpe di Siusi and the Sasso Lungo.

Three small villages line the Val Gardena, each confusingly known by two names: **Ortisei** (or St. Ulrich) at 1,236 m, **Santa Cristina** (or St. Christina) at 428 m, and **Selva Gardena** (or Wolkenstein) at 1,563 m. All three serve as reasonable bases from which to explore the valley in both summer and winter. Ortisei is the largest and most developed of the three villages, home to numerous shops, museums, and sporting facilities. Up-valley, Santa Cristina is the smallest hamlet, ideal for families and those looking for a peaceful holiday. Our favorite base, Selva Gardena, lies at the heart of the region's hiking and skiing trails. It has a nice sports center and a good tourism infrastructure.

The valley is known first for its green tourism – the **Sella Massif**, the **Parco Naturale Puez-Odle**, and the **Alps di Suisi** all beckon to hikers, climbers, and skiers. It's known as well for its adherence to traditional customs, including its craftsmanship and woodworking, its colorful festivals, and its Ladin culture and language. (The valley uses three languages: Italian, German, and Ladin.) Visitors interested in learning more about the Ladin culture should visit the **Val Gardena Local Heritage Museum** in Ortisei at Rezia 83; ☎ 0471 79 75 54. Also of cultural note are several churches, including the **Church of St. Giacomo**, reachable by foot from Ortisei. It was first built in the 12th century and is the oldest in the valley today.

> **TIP:** The **Gardena Card** offers free summertime access to the entire valley's bus and lifts. Another one, the **Sella Ronda Card** offers summertime access to the lifts and buses around the Sella Massif, allowing experienced hikers to complete the Sella Ronda loop in approximately eight hours The cards can be purchased at the tourist office.

Adventurers set out on foot across the valley's numerous trails, linking paths with summertime lifts along the way. From Selva, climb to ruins of **Wolkenstein Castle**, follow the old line of the Val Gardena Railway on an hour's stroll to **Santa Cristina**, or take on an over-

Italy

night excursion to one of the natural park's refuges. Mountain guides lead organized and private excursions; ☎ 0471 79 41 33. And climbers check in with Catores, Ortesei's climbing guides; ☎ 0471 79 82 23. In winter, snow sport fans take to the valley's 81 lifts and 175 km of local trails or, purchase the more expensive Dolomiti SuperSki Pass, which opens up 464 lifts and some 1,100 km of groomed runs.

The Sella Ronda Ski Circuit

 Selva Gardena sits on the doorstep of the Sella Ronda – and the world's only opportunity to ski on groomed runs *around* an entire mountain. The region's network of lift-linked trails encircles the Sella Ronda group, allowing skiers to circumnavigate the massif like a snow-sporting merry-go-round. Along the way, travelers cross several passes and enter four villages: Selva, Canazei, Arabba, and Corvara.

The 40-km circuit requires stamina rather than any great skill, as the pistes here are mostly intermediate level. The loop can be made in either direction, but the clockwise runs employ fewer draglifts. Some long run-outs create minor issues for snowboarders, and poor snow conditions sometimes interfere along the lower-altitude runs. In any case, start early to allow time to enjoy the mountain huts and spectacular scenery along the way. Done in its entirety – with no lift-line waits and no rest stops – the circuit takes approximately four hours. Inquire at the tourist office for a route map.

 Want to stay? The **Hotel Aaritz** ($$-$$$) has a good position near the Ciampinoi chairlift. Its interior warms with lots of wood paneling, elegant arches, and an enormous open fireplace. Inquire at ☎ 0471 79 50 11, www.val-gardena.com/hotel/aaritz. Rates vary dramatically by season.

 Each village has its own tourist office. Contact Ortisei at ☎ 0471 79 63 28; Santa Cristina at ☎ 0471 79 30 46; or Selva Gardena at ☎ 0471 79 51 22. All three share a website at www.valgardena.it.

Liechtenstein

(Fürstentum Liechtenstein)
Languages: German, local dialects
Population: 33,525
Phone Country Code: +432
Currency: Swiss Franc (CHF)

History & Government

Although both the Rhaetians and the Romans held ancient rule over the territory, Liechtenstein's cur-

rent monarchy began in 1699, when Prince Johann Adam bought from the local population the Lordship of Schellenberg and later, in 1712, the County of Vaduz. The wily count thereby earned himself a vote in the Diet of Princes, and Liechtenstein was inaugurated as a principality of the Roman Empire in 1719. It's since been both overrun by Napoleon and absorbed by the German Confederation, but finally gained its independence in 1866.

The fledgling state dissolved its army in 1868, adopted a constitution in 1921, and has been moseying along under its current monarchy ever since. Although it has long political and social ties with Austria, Liechtenstein today aligns itself more closely with Switzerland. (It wasn't until 1872 that a bridge was built over the Rhine into Switzerland.) The countries partnered up in 1923 to jointly use the Swiss Franc (CHF) as currency, and no border regulations exist between the two.

Prince Franz Josef II died in 1989, officially passing the monarchy to his son, Prince Hans Adam II. Today's nation operates as a constitutional hereditary monarchy with a democratic and parliamentary foundation. In theory, the monarch and the people govern together. An elected parliament represents the people, but the prince can issue Princely Orders – and thereby disband parliament if need be. The prince also represents the people as Head of State, entering into international agreements as he sees fit.

Liechtenstein

The Royal Family

Liechtenstein's royal family has resided inside the country's borders only since 1939, when Prince Franz Josef II moved his family into the hillside castle and sent his son, current ruler Prince Hans Adam II, off to be educated at the local school. Today, silvery ladies still whisper over white-wine spritzers regarding his schoolboy antics. One such tale tells of the day that two playground bullies – both girls – pushed the prince to the ground. He responded calmly, as only a young royal could, that when the day came for him to take the throne, all females would be banned from Liechtenstein *forever*. He hasn't yet made good on the threat.

Orientation, Economy & People

Measuring only 25 km long and six km wide, Liechtenstein squeezes its 160 square m between Switzerland to the west and Austria to the east. Half of the principality's territory is mountainous; the other half, pasturelands reclaimed with dikes from the once-unruly Rhine. The principality is divided into two sectors, the Unterland to the south and the Oberland to the north, and a total of 11 communities. The largest communities – **Vaduz**, **Triesen**, **Schaan**, and **Balzers** – line the Rhine at the foot of the mountains toward the south end of the small country. Up the steep mountain road from Triesen are several smaller villages: **Triesenberg**, **Steg**, and **Malbun**.

Liechtenstein joined the United Nations in 1990 and the European Economic Area in 1995. Today it enjoys a prosperity founded largely on tourism, wine production, and manufacturing.

> **Did You Know?** Liechtenstein is the largest exporter of dentures in the world. Its other claim to fame is as a self-described "liberal" international banking center.

The banking business has boomed in the past several years, doubling total deposits between 1995 and 2001 and increasing the number of banks here from three to 17. Liechtenstein remains an attractive haven for tax-avoiding businesses (both real and paper), and boasts an unemployment rate of just 1.2%. The country's population is 80% Catholic, 7% Protestant, and 13% of other religious orientations.

National Holidays

January 1	New Year's Day
January 2	Berchtold's Day
January 6	Epiphany
February 2	Candlemas
47 days prior to Easter	Shrove Tuesday
March 19	St. Joseph's Day
Friday before Easter	Good Friday
March/April	Easter; Easter Monday
May 1	Labor Day
10 days before Whit Sunday	Ascension Day
7th Sunday after Easter	Whit Sunday
Monday after Whit Sunday	Whit Monday
Thursday after 8th Sunday after Easter	Corpus Christi
August 15	Assumption Day & National Day
September 8	Nativity of Our Lady
November 1	All Saints Day
December 8	Immaculate Conception
December 25	Christmas Day
December 26	St. Stephen's Day
December 31	New Year's Eve

The very helpful Liechtenstein Tourism Office is in Vaduz, Städtle 37; ☎ 239 63 00, www.tourismus.li. The office is open daily from 9 am-12 pm and from 1:30-5 pm in season; from mid-April through May, closed Saturday and Sunday. For more information on Liechtenstein, see www.liechtenstein.li; for more information on the royal family, go to www.fuerstenhaus.li

Liechtenstein

■ Vaduz

Population: 4,949

Base elevation: 455 m

Tourist town

The average tourist blows through Liechtenstein seeking only a glance at its castle and a stamp in his passport. But stay a while; there's really much more to see than that. Concentrated in this compact country are a number of worthwhile attractions – a cheerful town center, a prince's art collection, a royal wine cellar, and an all-season wilderness playground.

The Town

Although it was probably first settled in fifth century, Vaduz (or *Faduzes*) is first mentioned in historical texts dating from the 12th century. Today's city, the capital of the country, spreads out along the Rhine Valley between the eastern riverbank and the western foothills of The Alps. One major road, Route 16, runs through Vaduz and the length of Liechtenstein. However, Route 16 is rarely marked as such. Instead, the street signs change names every few blocks: Landstrasse, Herrengasse, Aulestrasse, Heiligkreuz, Austrasse, etc. You get the idea. In the text that follows, we'll refer to Route 16 as the "main road." When you're in town, it's hard to miss.

Visitors' first stop should be the small pedestrian area at the town's center. Wander along the Städtle between the art museum, the tourist office, and the many surrounding shops. Gazing down from the hill above is Liechtenstein's landmark castle, which, because it's the private residence of the royal family, is not open to the public.

Liechtenstein's national flag shows two equal horizontal bars – one blue and one red – with a crown emblem in the upper left corner. The royal family's flag, however, shows simply two equal bars – one gold and one red. From Vaduz, look up the hill toward the castle: If the gold and red flag flies there, the royal family is in residence.

Getting Here & Around

Liechtenstein has no airport. Those traveling by **air** should fly into Zürich, 110 km west. Liechtenstein does have some **train** service, but the rail system is Austrian owned-and-operated, and two issues complicate travel:

first, no international trains depart the country, and travelers must change trains before continuing into Switzerland or Austria; second, the tracks don't reach to Vaduz. Passengers headed for the capital must take a bus from the nearest train station in Schann. (It's easier, really, to disembark at the border and bus in from Feldkirch, Buchs, or Sargans.) The **bus** terminal is in the town center within easy reach of hotels, the art museum, and the tourist office, and the Liechtenstein Bus Anstalt (LBA) runs efficient service between all local communities. For **taxi** service, try **Castle Taxi** at ☎ 0 423 777 00 77.

Two roads run the length of the country: Route 16, from Balzers in the south to Feldkirch in the north; and A13, the Swiss Autobahn on the western bank of the Rhine River. A third route, the mountain road, winds from Route 16 east, through Triesen, Triesenberg, and Steg to Malbun. Parking can be troublesome – in the center, try the underground garage below the museum.

Getting More Info

 The very efficient Liechtenstein Tourism handles tourist information issues for Vaduz. Drop by Städtle 37 for assistance, or contact ☎ 0 423 239 63 00, www.tourismus.li. The central office is open daily from 9 am-noon and from 1:30-5 pm in season; from mid-April through May, closed Saturday and Sunday.

 The post office is in the center near the tourist office.

WWW For Internet access, try the **Telecom Shop** on the main road Austrasse 77.

CURRENCY CONVERSION		
I CHF	$0.79	€0.66
$I	1.27 CHF	€0.832

The Sights

For a town this tiny, in a country this small, Vaduz has far more than its share of **museums**. Several collections stand out. The **National Art Museum Liechtenstein**, housed in a striking modern building in the center, houses the substantial Collections of the Prince. Exhibits include works by diverse masters, including Rembrandt, Rubens, and Picasso. The museum is open Tuesday through Sunday 10 am to 5 pm and Thursdays until 8 pm; www.kunstmuseum.li, 8 CHF. The **Liechtenstein Landesmuseum** should open its historical collections as we go to press. Check in at ☎ 0 423 236 75 50. Winter-sports fans should visit the **Ski Museum Vaduz**, a lovingly cared-for collection assembled by Noldi Beck. Mr. Beck was equipment manager for Hanni Wenzel, a skier who found herself Liechtenstein's darling after bringing home the gold medal from the 1980 Olympic Winter Games in Lake Placid. His collection is considerable, and his connections apparent.

Liechtenstein Postage Stamps

 Philatelists know Liechtenstein for its coveted postage stamps – tiny little elegant works of art perfectly suited to this tiny little elegant nation. The **Briefmarken Postmuseum** houses a collection of postal stamps that together tell the story of the principality. The museum is upstairs from the tourist office at Stadtle 37 and is open daily, 10 am-12 pm and 2 to 6 pm; ☎ 0 423 236 61 05; free admission.

In the **Hofkellerei des Fürsten von Liechtenstein**, otherwise known as the prince's wine cellars, visitors can sample and purchase local wines. (If you do the first, the latter is customary – even if you just buy one small bottle.) The surrounding vineyard is planted with 9.9 acres of Pinot Noir grapes and, yes, it is actually owned by the royal family; ☎ 0 423 232 10 18, www.hofkellerei.li. A path through the vineyard leads to the Restaurant Torkel (see *Where to Eat* below).

In summer, the **Vaduz City Train** departs the main bus station each day at 4:30 pm for a 30-minute tour of town; www.citytrain.li; 9 CHF. The tourist office also arranges **guided tours** through Vaduz and around Liechtenstein. Regularly scheduled, hour-long walking tours depart Monday through Friday at 2 pm from the bus terminal desk (summer only, 10 CHF). Private guides can be arranged through the tourist office.

> **TIP:** Still want that stamp in your passport? Although the border-patrol no longer takes interest in the comings-and-goings of Liechtenstein visitors, the tourist office doles out a souvenir passport stamp for 2 CHF each.

Those seeking outdoor recreation in Vaduz hike, bike, and ride into and along the nearby mountains. **Bikers** and **skaters** enjoy 90 km of posted trails, rolling the length of the nation in an easy stretch along the Rhine. More difficult mountain-biking trails climb at altitude, and the **Dreamteam** offers guided tours; ☎ 423 392 29 92, www.dreamteam.li. The **Bike Garage**, on the main road in Triesen, rents mountain bikes; ☎ 0390 03 09, www.bikegarage.li. **Bernhard and Sabine Tschol** offer a variety of guided, single- and multi-day **horseback rides**; contact ☎ 0392 29 85, www.westerntrekking.li.

While Vaduz is very much a tourist town, Malbun and Steg – its mountain neighbors – are the local centers for **outdoor play**. There, adventurers head into the mountains on a 400-km network of hiking and biking trails and ski on 21 km of groomed runs. For more information, see the entries below for *Malbun* and *Steg*.

An Interesting Deal

AUTHOR'S PICK

Liechtenstein's adventure pass, the **Erlebnispass**, offers free and discounted admission to 21 of the principality's summertime attractions. (The marketing scheme claims you'll "save up to 400%," but I might question that math.) You can, however, save plenty – if you make good use of the card. It sells for 24 CHF (or half that for kids) and is good for two days. Partner attractions include the National Art Museum, the Ski Museum, the chairlift at Malbun, CityTrain Tours, and Liechtenstein Bus. Purchase your card at the tourist office, the post office, partner attractions, or at many hotels. Six-day passes are also available.

Where to Sleep

Fresh and new in 2003, the **Hotel Residence** ($$$) is Lichtenstein's undisputed forerunner for business travelers and tourists looking for a friendly staff and modern amenities. The hotel has a suburb town-center locale and rooms outfitted with high-tech gadgets like security doors and flat-screen TVs with integrated Internet access. Its slick, artsy kick ideally suits visitors to the art museum just across the street. Reserve at ☎ 0 423 239 20 20, www.residence.li.

HOTEL PRICE CHART	
Double room without tax; $$$-$$$$ always with bath.	
$	Under 120 CHF
$$	121-225 CHF
$$$	226-375 CHF
$$$$	Over 375 CHF

Also in the center – but more renowned for its restaurant than its guestrooms – is the **Hotel Restaurant Real** ($$$); ☎ 0 423 232 22 22, www.hotel-real.li. Don't miss dinner.

The **Gästhof Löwen** ($$$) is the oldest hotel in Liechtenstein; it's been welcoming guests since 1388 and, if practice makes perfect, it certainly has the hang of it now. The back rooms have lovely vineyard views; ☎ 0 423 238 11 44, www.hotel-loewen.li.

Another traditional house, the **Park-Hotel Sonnenhof** ($$$$), sits high on the hill near the castle. Prices here are as lofty as the address, but for those with the budget, an elegant, residential feel makes this villa worth its rates; ☎ 0 423 239 02 02, www.sonnenhof.li.

Halfway between Vaduz and Malbun – with spectacular views of the Rhine Valley – the **Hotel Restaurant Kulm** ($$) in Triesenberg welcomes vacationing families with great food and friendly hospitality; ☎ 0 423 237 79 79, www.hotelkulm.li.

For budget accommodations near the center in Vaduz, try the simple **Landgästhof Au** ($). Some rooms have baths, others don't, but all are within a few minute's walk of the town center; ☎ 0 423 232 11 17.

Where to Eat

Liechtenstein has no shortage of expensive restaurants. In a lovely vineyard setting, the romantic **Torkel** ($$$) specializes in freshwater fish dishes; ☎ 0 423 232 44 10, www.torkel.li. Farther up the hill, the **Hotel Sonnenhof** ($$$) spoons up Continental gourmet

DINING PRICE CHART	
Average entrée, with tax.	
$	Under 15 CHF
$$	16-37 CHF
$$$	Over 37 CHF

grub; reserve a table at ☎ 0 423 239 02 02. The **Hotel Real** ($$$), too, is well-known for its international take on haute cuisine; ☎ 0 423 232 22 22. For regional specialties and a traditional atmosphere, try the old **Gasthof Löwen** ($$$); ☎ 0 423 238 11 44.

For less costly fare, sample the regional specialties at the **Old Castle Inn** on Aulestrasse; ☎ 0 423 232 10 65. Or, for cheesy dumpling käseknofle, head for the cozy **Landgästhof Au**; ☎ 0 423 232 11 17. The art museum's **Café am Kunstmuseum** ($$) serves up Vaduz's best sushi and, at Kirchstrasse 2, the **Restaurant Linde** ($$) does an odd mix of Chinese, Mexican, and Spanish food.

Where to Party

Vaduz is a pretty staid town, and those looking to party may find themselves partying alone. For social lounging, try the piano bar at the **Hotel Löwen**, the less elegant **Crash Bar** in the center, or **B'eat** at Städtle 5.

For a cultural evening out, check what's playing at the **Theater am Kirchplatz** (better-known as TAK). The schedule highlights a variety of performers, several international acts each year, and summer concerts in a mountainside fortress; www.tak.li. The **Kino Movie Theater** is on Aeulestrasse – check the newspaper, or call ☎ 0 423 232 12 18 for current shows.

Where to Play

Each of Liechtenstein's communities maintains a **playground** and swimming center – both popular activities with kids. Favorites include the **Adventure Playground** at Triesen, the **bird park** at Mauren, and the **Vaduz City Train Tour**. Malbun runs a variety of **children's programs** during the summer and a ski kindergarten in winter, and the Vaduz tourist office can make suggestions regarding babysitters.

Festivals & Events

Vaduz starts its year with a town-center **New Year's Eve** party and a festive **Mardi Gras** carnival season. Spring brings a slew of art, film, and music festivals that pack the calendar through summer. Favorites include the **Rhine Park Stadium Film Festival** from late June through mid-July; **Guitar, Jazz, and Classical Music Days** throughout July; and the five-day **Meeting of the Artists** in early August.

AUTHOR'S PICK

If you happen to be in town on the evening of August 15th, you're cordially invited to the castle garden for cocktails with Prince Hans Adam II. Each year, in celebration of **National Day**, the royal family opens its castle grounds to the public for drinks, food, and a fireworks show. It's a fun party, and a rare opportunity to see Liechtensteiners let loose.

Vaduz to Malbun

The trip up to Malbun from Vaduz can, of course, be made in the most direct fashion – going there and back via the steep road from Triesenberg. However, when snow closures don't prevent it, I suggest making a circular tour via the lesser-known castle road just north of Vaduz. North of town along the main road, head up the hill through the vineyards and up past the castle's back door. Continue along the narrow, forested, one-way path to Triesenberg, but beware of emergency vehicles headed *down* this "one-way" uphill road. In Triesenberg, you'll intersect the main drag near the church and can head for Malbun from there. After your mountain visit, continue downhill in the direction of Triesen, turning north on Route 16 to get back to Vaduz.

Malbun

Up the mountain 15 km from Vaduz, below the Three Sisters massif, Malbun is Liechtenstein's outdoor playground. Popular in winter with families for its traffic-free center and easy, centralized ski runs – and popular in summer for its cool temperatures and good trail network – the quiet hamlet draws crowds from June through September and from December through March.

Malbun grew up in the 1960s after completion of the tunnel and road from Steg. Today's village includes several hotels, a handful of shops, and a cluster of privately owned holiday cabins, all centered on Malbun's original hotel, the brightly painted Alpenhotel Malbuner. Worth a quick look is the **Friedenskapelle** just up the hill at the entrance to town – a stone chapel built in 1945 as a war memorial in pious gratitude for Liechtenstein's non-participation in the war.

AUTHOR'S PICK The Falknerei Hotel Garni Galina puts on a small **falconry show** that will delight kids and all those fascinated by wildlife. From the hotel's dining terrace, visitors get an intimate look at aerial acrobatics by several of the falconry's 19 birds of prey. Don't stand up during the show – flight paths run within a few feet of spectator tables. The standard show is presented in German, of course, but the handler, Mr. Rot, speaks English well and will answer any questions you have might have about his flock. Catch the 40-minute presentation at 3 pm every day except Monday, from May through October. (6 CHF, drink and snack service additional.)

Winter-season adventurers enjoy a wide range of sports, including ice-skating, ski touring, winter hiking, snowshoeing, tobogganing, and downhill skiing, with six lifts and 21 km of mostly easy pistes. Snowboarders enjoy a funpark, bikers test their skills on snow-scoots, and skaters take to the ice on a natural rink. Cross-country skiers head for Steg, three km down the mountain. For snow sport instruction, contact the **Malbun Skischule** at ☎ 0 423 263 97 70, www.schneesportschule.li. For equipment rentals and sales, contact **Malbun Sport** at ☎ 0 423 263 37 55.

> **TIP:** The **Sareiserjoch** moutain restaurant stages raclette dinners every Thursday during high season. The chairlift from Malbun operates late on these evenings for transport to the inn. Reserve ahead at ☎ 0 423 263 46 86.

In summer, lift-assisted hiking is popular – try the **Fürstin-Gina-Weg**, a view-blessed trail that hugs the Austrian border as far as the Bettlerjoch hut and then drops down through Gritsch for the return to Malbun. Need a more difficult challenge? Step out

Above: Landwasser viaduct, just before Filisur, Switzerland

Below: Front compartment on the Swiss Golden Pass Panoramic train

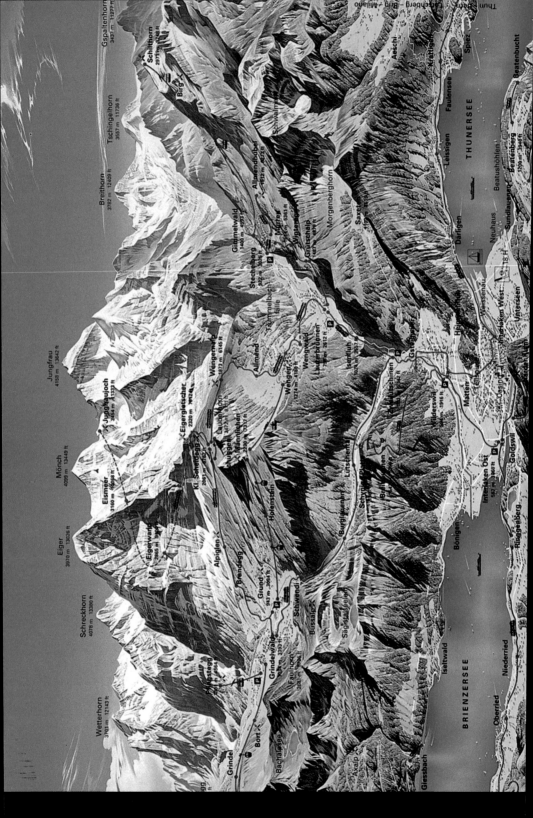

Map of the Jungfrau

Above: Ringgenberg-Goldswill on Lake Brienz, Switzerland

Below: The Eiger, in the Jungfrau

Above: Interlaken across the Lake of Thun

Below: Lake Lucerne

onto the **Fürstensteig**, a narrow, cliff-hugging trail cut into rock of the Three Sisters massif. Hold on tight – to the cableway *and your soul*. Local lore alleges that the mountains here steal human spirits.

LIFT PASS PRICE SAMPLES	
Winter	
1-day adult pass	37 CHF
6-day adult pass	155 CHF
Round-trip to Sareiserjoch.	10 CHF
Summer	
Round-trip to Sareiserjoch	11.70 CHF

Malbun can be reached by car or hourly bus from Vaduz, Treisenberg, and Steg. Want to stay the night? Try the creaky old **Alpenhotel Malbuner** ($$); ☎ 0 423 263 11 81. Or the family-friendly **Hotel Gorfion-Malbun** ($$) next to the ski school; ☎ 0 423 264 18 83, www.gorfion.li. The **Falknerei Hotel Garni Galina** ($$) offers a falconry show in summer and well-regarded cake specialties year-round; ☎ 0 423 263 34 24, www.galina.li. Reserve accommodations early in winter.

 For more information, check with the Tourist Office Malbun at ☎ 0 423 263 65 77, malbuninfo@liechtenstein.li. For lift openings, check www.bergbahnen.li.

Steg

The tiny hamlet of Steg is made up of pre-World War II Alpine farmers' huts, the summer residences of the Triesenberger farmers who once brought their herds here in search of greener pastures. The huts circle around a well-fertilized grazing field and today create a rustic little holiday village for vacationers in search of peace, convenient hiking trails, and fresh dairy products. In winter, the main attractions in Steg are a groomed winter walking trail and Liechtenstein's finest cross-country ski loops, 19 km in all, including a lovely trek along the Valünerbach stream in the shadow of the Kirchlespitz peak. (Check in at the Malbun Tourism Office for an inexpensive loipe pass.)

Barring the road traffic en route to and from Malbun, Steg is an extremely quiet place – the village claims a population of just 50 residents and, by the look of things, even that may be exaggerated. However, buses stop here hourly, and a couple of hotels are on hand. Try the **Hotel Restaurant Steg** ($$), ☎ 0423 263 21 46, or up the mountain, the **Berggästhaus Sücka** ($), ☎ 0 423 263 25 79, a remote inn with shared baths, a dormitory, and several private rooms. Treats here include house-produced cheese, milk, butter, and yogurt – goodies that make the hike up worthwhile even for non-guests. In winter, ask about the guesthouse's fondue dinners and nighttime toboggan run.

 Steg has no tourist office. Check with the Liechtenstein Tourist Office for more information; ☎ 0 423 239 63 00, www.tourismus.li.

Switzerland

(Schweiz, Suisse, Svizzera)
Languages: German, French, Italian, Romansch
Population: 7,301,994
Phone Country Code: +41
Currency: Swiss Franc (CHF)

History

Switzerland is today renowned for its staunch neutrality. However, a look at Swiss history reveals that Swiss non-aggression is actually a relatively new policy. Located at the crossroads of the Alps, the most significant natural barrier

of Western Europe, the people of Switzerland have weathered several major conflicts.

■ The First Tribes

The first identifiable groups to settle in the Swiss Alps were the Celtic tribes, who eventually migrated south and west. However, around the first century, Julius Caesar started Rome's great expansion, and the Celts were driven from France back into Switzerland, where the Romans established several towns. As the Roman Empire began to wilt, the eastern half of Switzerland fell under the control of German tribes while the western half was reclaimed by the remaining Celts.

■ Charlemagne & the Hapsburgs

Shortly thereafter, the land of Switzerland became part of the Kingdom of Charlemagne. As Charlemagne's kingdom was divided, the tribes of Switzerland enjoyed years of relative independence. Then, the Hapsburgs began their expansion beyond Austria, attempting to seize control of the Swiss Gotthard Pass. Thus provoked, three Swiss tribes – the Uri, the Schwyz, and the Unterwalden – fought the Hapsburgs to maintain their independence. Their "pact of defensive alliance" is considered the foundation of the Swiss Confederation. Because of Schwyzer excellence in a series of battles with the Hapsburgs, the entire confederation became known as the Schwyz – today, *Schweiz*, or Switzerland.

■ The Expansion

The Swiss confederation continued to expand and, by the late 16th century, encompassed 13 cantons. However, this expansionist policy led to the Swiss' next significant defeat, when 12,000 soldiers were killed in a campaign on the Po Valley of Northern Italy. Nonetheless, the Swiss soldiers were renowned as great fighters, and many nations (including the Vatican) employed their mercenary services.

■ Neutrality

In the 17th century, Switzerland established itself as a land for asylum when it allowed many French Protestants to immigrate into the country. Several wars between Catholic and Protestant factions ensued, culminating with Napoleon's introduction of a new Swiss constitution. The policy eventually led to the Vienna Congress (in 1814) and to the establishment of the Swiss cantons. Although the regions skirmished for several years over religious differences, a new constitution was ratified in 1874, and the modern day Switzerland was born.

It was also during these early years that Switzerland launched its policies of neutrality and asylum. In this vein, Henri Dunant founded the Red Cross in Geneva in 1863 (see box below). Switzerland maintained its neutrality through both World Wars, although emergent evidence indicates that the nation may have bent a bit to the Nazi regime in order to do so. Recently, however, Switzerland has begun to back away from its strictly neutral policy and, in 2002, the country voted to join the United Nations and has since enrolled in NATO's Partnership For Peace Alliance.

Henri Dunant

 Henri Dunant was born in 1828 to a family with staunch religious, civic, and humanitarian convictions. When he was 26, he began traveling for business and, in 1859, he went to Solferino to discuss a business proposition with the French ruler, Napoleon III. At the time, France and Italy were at war with Austria, and it was during this trip that Dunant witnessed one of the bloodiest battles of the 19th century. The images would haunt him for the rest of his life.

In 1862, Dunant authored a book telling of the carnage at Solferino, *Un Souvenir de Solferino*, or *A Memory of Solferino*. After describing the battle and its aftermath,

Dunant used the last third of his book to propose an organization of relief societies to provide care for wartime wounded. The proposal interested Gustave Monyier, a prominent lawyer in Geneva, who then helped Dunant establish *The Permanent International Committee of the Red Cross*. In October of 1863, delegates from 16 nations met and approved the resolutions of the Geneva Committee – the First Geneva Convention. The attending delegates agreed to create private societies in their own territories to complement the work of their military's medical services; workers were to be universally identified by the large red cross on their equipment – a symbol taken from the Swiss flag.

Through the years, the Red Cross flourished; Dunant, however, did not. Focusing his energies on his organization rather than his business, Dunant went bankrupt in 1867. As such, Dunant was no longer welcome in Geneva society groups, and from 1875 to 1895 he lived in relative seclusion. In 1895, Dunant was at last recognized for his contributions with honors and a large monetary award. Dunant died in 1910, having spent almost none of the award money. At his death, as during his life, Dunant gave his wealth to the sick and poor.

Orientation & Government

The Swiss Confederation spans some 41,293 square km in west-central Europe. Bounding Switzerland are Germany to the north, France to the west, Italy to the south, and Liechtenstein and Austria to the east. Around 70% of Switzerland's terrain is mountainous, much of its land rippling along the Bernese, Rhaetian, and Pennine Alps. The mighty Rhine River drains 68% of the land here, and some 60% is either pastureland or forest.

Switzerland is a federal republic made up of 26 cantons; its capital city is Bern. Its chief of state is the president, who also serves as the head of the government. However, states' rights are of extreme importance here, and the federal administration allows great cantonal autonomy. Many political issues revolve around perceived threats to this autonomy; other ongoing issues include questions of immigration and asylum policy. Switzerland enjoys a high standard of living, with among the world's lowest unemployment, highest income, and longest life expectancy rates. Recent unemployment rates rose to 3.1% – still not bad, given Europe's 8.6% average.

Switzerland

Regions of Alpine Switzerland

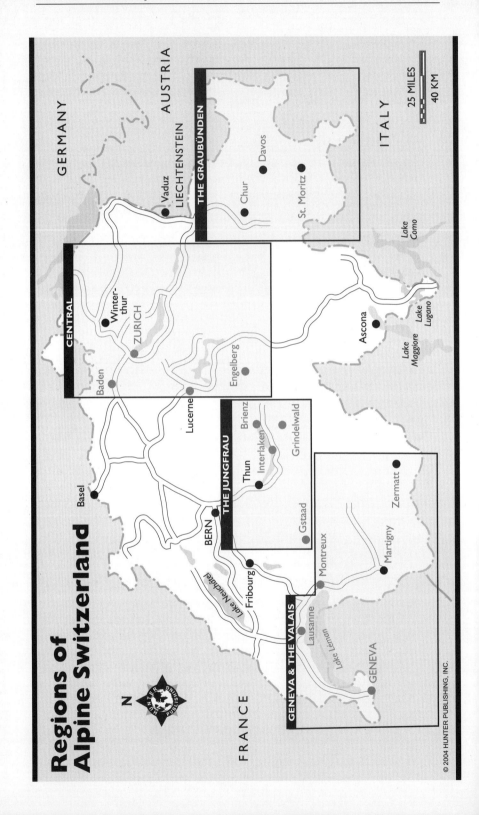

People & Culture

Switzerland's official name is *Confoederatio Helvetica*, a Latin term that translates as Swiss Confederation – and explains both the "CH" stickers you'll see on cars and the "CHF" abbreviation for the Swiss Franc currency.

The country has three widely spoken official languages, each practiced in the corner of Switzerland nearest its origin – and each with its own slang term for Switzerland: in **German**, *Schweiz*; in **French**, *Suisse*; in **Italian**, *Svizzera*.

 Sign postings and publications often include text in all three languages.

The fourth official language is **Romansch**, an ancient dialect practiced today by just one percent of the population. Further befuddling the situation is the common use of both regional dialects and *Schweizerdeutsch*, or Swiss German. However, even with four official languages and a babble of traditional dialects, Swiss communication works out better than you might expect. Public schools enforce rigorous language studies, and thus most Swiss are multilingual. Better still for readers of this guide, more English is spoken here than in any other corner of the Alps.

The Swiss population includes four main ethnic groups: German, French, Italian, and Romansch. Some 65% of the population is German, 18% French, 10% Italian, and 1% Romansch. Most of the population claims to be Christian – 48% Roman Catholic and 44% Protestant. Six in 10 live in urban settings, with the remaining 40% in smaller villages. Major cities include **Zürich**, **Basel**, and **Geneva**. Switzerland's population density hovers at about 177 persons per square km.

National Holidays

January 1 . . . . New Year's Day

January 2 . . . . Berchtold's Day

The 6 days prior to Shrove Tuesday . . Carnival (Lucerne)

47 days prior to Easter . . . . Shrove Tuesday

Friday before Easter . . . . Good Friday

March/April . . . . Easter; Easter Monday

May 1 . . . . Labor Day

10 days prior to Whit Sunday. . . . . Ascension Day

7th Sunday after Easter	Whit Sunday
Monday after Whit Sunday	Whit Monday
Thursday after 8th Sunday after Easter	Corpus Christi
August 1	Confederation Day
August 15	Assumption Day
November 1	All Saints Day
December 8	Immaculate Conception
December 25	Christmas Day
December 26	St. Stephen's Day
December 31	St. Sylvester's Day

 For more information, check in with Switzerland's National Tourism Office at www.myswitzerland.com.

Geneva & The Valais

50 MILES

50 KM

Geneva & The Valais

The Valais region encompasses Switzerland's most rugged terrain. Our coverage extends from the gateway city of Geneva to the upper reaches of the Walliser Alps along the Italian frontier. Visitors are apt to enter the region in **Geneva**, a small, cosmopolitan city between the border of France and the western end of Lake Geneva, known in French as *Lac Leman*. The city bustles with the business of international organizations, plays along a garden-lined lakefront, and harbors a pleasant pedestrian old town.

The city of **Lausanne** lies across the lake, drawing visitors for its own pleasant lakefront and the Olympic Games History Museum. Beyond, south of the Berner Alps, the Valais region is home to the Roman town of **Martigny** and the trendy mountain resort of **Verbier**. Farther east still protrudes the magnificent **Matterhorn Peak**, with famed **Zermatt** at its foot and secluded **Saas-Fee** just over the hill.

■ Geneva

(Geneve)

Population: 178,476

Base elevation: 374 m

Gateway city

While Geneva's cuisine, language, and fashion sense reveal its French heritage, the city's people are today a cosmopolitan mix of over 200 nationalities. As home to some 250 international organizations and host to thousands of conventions, trade fairs, and meetings each year, Geneva enjoys a reputation as the world's neutral ground. Over the years, it has also garnered nicknames such as "the world's smallest big city," "city of parks," "city of peace," and even the lofty "capital of human knowledge." I call Geneva the ideal gateway to the Alps.

History & Orientation

 Geneva got its start under Roman rule, when Julius Caesar passed through in 58 AD, and the city came under Rome's rule. Development during the first century focused on the little knoll we know as old town – its central Bourg-de-Four square was in those days a Roman forum. Geneva saw continued growth under the rule of Burgundy, eventually becoming an important market town under the Holy Roman Empire.

In 1536, Jean Calvin moved to town, ushering in the Reformation, founding an academy, and turning Geneva into the "Rome of the Protestants." The 18th century saw an influx of Europe's elite artists, businessmen, and scientists into the city, including rivals Rousseau and Voltaire. In the 19th century, after brief occupation under Napoleon's French troops, Geneva joined the Helvetic Confederation on 12 September, 1814.

Geneva rests at the western end of Lake Geneva, or Lac Leman, 75 km long and Switzerland's largest Alpine lake. The Alps rise to the south, the Jura Moutains stretch north, and vineyards roll along the foothills all around. The city is conveniently located within striking distance of several Alpine resorts, including Verbier, Courmayeur in Italy, and Chamonix in France.

The Town

Geneva sprawls out from the western tip of Lake Geneva, at the mouth of the Rhône River. Tourists will visit three districts: the **city center**, the **old town**, and the **Place des Nations**. The city center splits along the Rhône into two sections, the right bank to the north and the left bank to the south. On the right bank clusters the train station and a number of hotels and restaurants; on the left bank, the bulk of the city's business and upscale shopping zones. The hilltop old town sits to the south of the center, and the Place des Nations sits to the north. Here, many international organizations make their homes near the city's pleasant gardens.

Getting Here & Around

 Geneva's international **airport** lies just four km from the city center, and a new railway terminal allows air passengers to transfer to the main **train station** in only six minutes. Trains pull into the Gare Cornavin at the Place de Montbrillant. It's on the right bank, on northern edge of the city center. **Buses** gather around a dwarfed church at the Square du Mont Blanc, just north of the Rhône River mouth, and **trolleys** ply the city streets. For **taxi** service, contact ☎ 022 331 41 33, www.taxi-phone.ch. Traffic conditions are dismal in the city center, and **drivers** are likely to have difficulty both navigating and parking.

> **TIP:** If you can take your eyes off the traffic fray for a moment, digital parking signs indicate the number of free spaces in each garage.

Getting Connected

 Check in at the very helpful tourist office at Rue du Mont-Blanc 18 or, at the second office, on the Pont de la Machine bridge. For more information, contact ☎ 022 909 70 00, www.geneva-tourism.ch.

 Two post offices are convenient, one at Rue des Gares 16 near the train station, the other at Rue du Mont Blanc 18 next to the tourist office.

 For Internet access, head to **Charly's Multimedia Check Point** at Rue de Fribourg 7; it's near the train station off the Rue des Alpes.

The Sights

 The **City Center** is home to Geneva's modern rush – shops, businesses and banks dominate. On the left bank, or south side of the river, is the commerce and banking center. Café tables and flowers enhance the **Place Molard**. Between the Rue du Rhône, the Rue de la Confédération, and the Rue du Marché, pricey shops at street level prop up the banks that tower above. But the city center is also the location of Geneva's elegant lakeside, a garden-lined promenade at the mouth of the Rhône River. You can relax along the lakefront, admire the **Jet d'Eau**, and wander north along the right bank toward the **Perle du Lac Park** and the **Botanical Gardens**.

The Jet d'Eau

 In 1886, Geneva had a problem. Each night, when the city's craftsmen closed their workshop faucets, the water pressure at the Coulouvrenière Hydraulic Factory rose to alarming levels. An ingenious plan created the solution – a pipe downstream along the Rhône would empty the excess water pressure. When installed, however, the valve blew with such force that it soon became a tourist attraction. In 1891 the Jet d'Eau was relocated from the Rhône to the Rade, where it now stands.

Today, the fountain is Geneva's most recognizable landmark, hurling 500 gallons of water each second to a height of 140 m. The jet reaches speeds of 200 km an hour. Except in times of high winds, it operates from early March through the second Sunday of October, 9:30 am-11:15 pm.

Switzerland

The **Old Town**, or *Vieille Ville*, sits on a knoll behind the city center, comprising the most fetching little corner of town. Antique shops, cafés, and art galleries gather around the **Place du Bourg-de-Four**, Geneva's oldest square. The 12th-century **Cathedrale St. Pierre** tops town – climb to the top of the tower for far-reaching views over the city, mountains, and lake. Below the cathedral, an **archaeological site** exposes fourth-century ruins and the lifestyle of the Roman era. Around the corner is the 16th-century **Ancien Arsenal**, or old arsenal, and the **Hotel de Ville**, or Town Hall, where the Alabama Room saw the founding of the Red Cross in 1864 and the signing of what we know today as the original Geneva Convention. Nearby the **Maison Tavel**, first built in 12th century, is Geneva's oldest house and home to the **Museum of Old Geneva**; open Tuesday through Sunday 10 am-5 pm; free entry; ☎ 022 418 37 00.

The **Place des Nations** district is home to many of the city's more than 200 international organizations. Best known on the international scene is the Palais des Nations, house of the **United Nation's European Headquarters**. Built in 1936 in exemplary Art Deco style, the massive complex enjoys lovely views and offers tourists a look inside from April through October, daily from 10 am-noon and 2-4 pm; from July through August, daily 9 am-6 pm; from November through March, Monday to Friday from 10 am-noon and 2-4 pm. It's closed the second half of December. Book a tour in any of 15 languages at ☎ 022 917 48 96, www.unog.ch; 8.50 CHF. Nearby, the **Red Cross and Red Crescent Museum** offers a wealth of historical documentation in relation to the Geneva-based humanitarian organization; open Wednesday through Monday, 10 am-5 pm; ☎ 022 748 95 25, www.micr.org; 10 CHF.

Henry James set his classic story of *Daisy Miller* against the backdrop of Geneva's lakeshores. It's a good short read on a sunny day. Mary Shelley's *Frankenstein* was also penned near here – a great spooky story for stormy nights in Old Town.

Several **guided tours** are offered from Geneva Tourism, including a 2½-hour self-guided audio tour through the old town. Recordings rent for 10 CHF, plus a 50 CHF refundable deposit; check in at the tourist office for more info. In the summer, mini-train tram tours chug along three routes: the old town, the lakefront, and the parks and residences district. Each tour runs 30-45 minutes and costs around 8 CHF per person.

Geneva with the Cathedrale St. Pierre

The Adventures

Boat excursions depart the city center's docks for a wide variety of **lake cruises**, including everything from a one-hour harbor tour (12 CHF) to a full-day Lake Geneva loop (74 CHF). Evening and theme cruises are available as well. For more info, check www.cgn.ch or www.swissboat.ch.

Genève Mouette boats run **river cruises** up the Rhône and short **water-taxi transfers** between the lakeside parks. **Boat rentals,** including sail, pedal, and motor models, are offered at Quai Gustave-Ador. Contact **Les Corsaires** at ☎ 022 736 25 66, www.lescoursaires. Miniature electric ships are a hit with kids; they're for rent from April through October.

In the summer, **lake swimmers** enjoy two strips of lakeside land. The first, the Paquis Baths, is little more than a jetty stretching into the lake from the right bank. The second, Genève Plage, has a heated, Olympic-size **swimming pool**, playgrounds, windsurfing, and a restaurant. In addition, several outfitters run **whitewater excursions** to destinations outside the city. Try **Rafting Genève Adventure Center** for kayaking, hydrospeeding, canyoning, and rafting; ☎ 079 213 41 40, www.rafting.ch.

Where to Sleep

 Some 125 hotels welcome Geneva's guests, 14 of them with five full stars – a highly disproportionate percentage, but one highly suited to a town that draws so many high-level visitors to so many high-profile events. Hotel rates tend to be as lofty as the names of the people paying them, and *the entire town* can book out during popular trade fairs.

HOTEL PRICE CHART	
Double room without tax; $$$-$$$$ always with bath.	
$	Under 120 CHF
$$	121-225 CHF
$$$	226-375 CHF
$$$$	Over 375 CHF

Of the five-star palaces here, I like best the **Beau Rivage** ($$$$), a family-run establishment built in 1865 and still gleaming along the lakefront; ☎ 022 716 60 60, www.beau-rivage.ch.

In the old town, head for the **Hotel Les Amures** ($$$$), an intimate townhouse with wood beams and residential decor – elegant but neither stuffy nor pretentious. It's on the square at Rue du Puits St. Pier 1; ☎ 022 310 91 72, www.hotel-les-amures.ch.

The **Tiffany** ($$$) welcomes with bright colors and cheery Art Nouveau décor. It's near Plainpalais at Rue des Marbriers 1; ☎ 022 708 16 16, www.hotel-tiffany.ch. Also on the left bank, at Place Longmalle 13, the **Hotel Touring-Balance** ($$$) offers a relatively quiet location in the heart of the city. Public areas are inviting, as is the small terrace; ☎ 022 818 62 61.

For modern accommodations at the train station, try the **Hotel Cornavin** ($$$). It has streamlined rooms and sweeping views from the restaurant; ☎ 022 716 12 12, www.fhotels.ch.

Also near the station, the **Hotel Strasbourg** ($$-$$$) offers commercial rooms and three-star comforts such as hairdryers and Internet connections; ☎ 022 906 58 00, www.strasbourg-geneva.ch.

Budgeting visitors can try the **Hotel Central** ($-$$). It's just below the old town and has variable rooms with balconies; ☎ 022 818 81 00, www.hotelcentral.ch.

The creaky old **Hotel Beau Site** ($) has homey accommodations near Plainpalais on the left bank; ☎ 022 818 37 37. And the **De la Cloche** ($) offers clean rooms in an old apartment block, reasonably close to the station, and just off the lakefront near the Paquis jetty; ☎ 022 732 94 81, www.tbh-ge.ch/cloche.

Where to Eat

With over 1,100 restaurants, 10 of those with Michelin stars, Geneva dines well. Visitors enjoy the international mix of cuisine, French gourmet influences, and wines from the local vineyards – many growing dry white Perlan and Pinot Gris or red Gamay and Pinot Noir. Several of the most renowned gourmet houses are slightly out of the center, taking up more attractive residences outside the city. Of the stars here, Chef Philippe Chevrier heads up the **Domaine de Chateauvieux** ($$$), a 16th-century stone house in the vicinity of Satigny Station. The hotel boasts a menu of seasonal cuisine, a cellar with over 900 wines, and menus starting at €118; book at ☎ 022 753 15 11, www.chateauvieux.ch.

DINING PRICE CHART	
Average entrée, with tax.	
$	Under 15 CHF
$$	16-37 CHF
$$$	Over 37 CHF

Joseph Righetto guides the **Hostellerie de la Vendée** ($$$) on Lacey Hill, offering a choice of two creative menus, each coordinated with wines, and encouraging wine tasting by the glass. Check in at ☎ 022 792 04 11, www.vendee.ch. In the city, Chef Jean-Paul Goddard shines with creative French cuisine at **Le Béarn**, the city's premier dining room; ☎ 0321 00 28, www.lebearn.ch.

For fish specialties, head for **Le Cigalon** at Thonex ($$$), a tavern-cum-bistro with a good selection of local wines; ☎ 022 349 97 33. **Le Perle du Lac** ($$$) is popular for its fish specialties and its park-side, lakeside locale. It's at Rue de Lausanne 128; ☎ 022 909 10 20. Fans of entrecôte should try the **Café de Paris** ($$$), where it's the only thing on the menu. The beef dish is served with the café's signature butter; Rue du Mont Blanc 26, ☎ 022 732 84 50.

For traditional Swiss cuisine, try the touristy **Chalet Suisse** ($$) at the Place du Cirque, ☎ 022 328 58 20, www.chaletswiss.ch; the **Café Au Petit Châlet** ($$) at Rue de Berne 17, ☎ 022 732 69 79; or the **Auberge de Saviese** ($$) at the Rue des Paquis, where warm cheese dishes are served until midnight, ☎ 022 732 83 30.

For fresh pasta and pizza, head for **Molino** ($$). It's in the center at Place du Moldard 7; ☎ 022 310 99 88. V**esuvio** ($-$$) in Eaux-Vives at Rue Cherbuiliez does good pizzas and homemade pasta, too. For budget fare, head for the inexpensive cafés around the station, or check in at any of the city's department stores – most have groceries in the basement and quick caféteria food.

Switzerland

Where to Party

Geneva is known for its work ethic, but it does relax – quietly, elegantly, and above all, with great sophistication. A typical evening starts with an aperitif and a long, expensive meal. Later, some 40 **theaters** stage a good range of **classical music** and **opera** performances, although more than likely the most exciting thing to happen after dinner will be the distribution of nightcap digestifs. For stage and ticket information, check in at **Ticket Corner**; ☎ 0848 800 800.

For a pub atmosphere near the station, try **Big Ben's** at Rue Grenus 7. Nearby, at Rue du Temple 5, **Café Bizarre** caters to an artsy student crowd with trendy house music and tapas for snacks. In old town, **Café La Clemence** has a big terrace on the Bourg de Flour. Later, English-speakers congregate at the old **Shaker's Club** at Rue Boulangerie 7 or nearby at **Flanagan's Irish Bar**. Both are in old town. Several disco venues dot Geneva's outskirts, but for dancing action in the city center, try **l'Inderdit** or drag-show-driven **Le Loft**; both stay open until dawn.

Festivals & Events

Best known for massive trade shows and conventions – its **PALEXPO** convention center can seat 6,500 people – Geneva hosts a multitude of annual events. Several renowned trade fairs are open to the public. Check out the **International Motor Show** in March, the **International Exhibition of Inventions** in April, the **Book Fair** in May, and the **Geneva Fair Ideal Home Exhibition** in November. To see what's on at the PALEXPO, check www.palexpo.ch.

Carnivale comes to town during the pre-Lenten season, and **Le Bol d'Or** draws over 500 crews for a prestigious sailing regatta. Geneva's **Musical Summer** takes center stage from June through September, **Swiss National Day** is celebrated at Bastions Park on the 1st of August, and the **Fêtes de Geneve Summer Festival** brings shows, concerts, parades, and food to the city's shoreline in early August.

Oddly, Geneva holds the world's largest foreign celebration of **American Independence Day** each 4th of July – fireworks and all. When Christmas rolls around, festivities include a month-long **International Christmas Market** at Fusterie Square, a **Christmas Tree Festival**, and **La Coupe de Noel,** a nippy lake-swimming competition. Finally, in the midst of the holiday season, comes the **Escalade**, Geneva's favorite party.

The Escalade Escapade

In the fall season of 1602, the Duke of Savoy set out to overthrow his ally Geneva. The duke's troops toiled in secret, crafting and hauling wooden ladders with which they planned to scale the city walls. On the night of December 11th, 1602, the army mounted its assault. While many heroic acts transpired that night, one tale tells of the daring deeds of Mère Royaume. Upon spying an invading Savoyard soldier outside her kitchen window, the cook sacrificed her family's dinner, attacking the invaders with a cauldron of boiling stew. With daring acts such as these, Geneva's townsfolk united – and together repelled the traitorous Duke of Savoy.

Four hundred years later, Geneva continues the victory celebration with an annual festival, The Escalade. For one weekend in mid-December, mounted brigades, fife and drum parades, and torchlight marches bring the old quarter to life. Kids trick-or-treat through the local cafés, alarm bells clang, and a bonfire roars in the Cathedral's square. Around the corner at the Ancien Arsenal, shivering revelers line up for a freshly prepared bowl of Mère Royaume's soup.

Lausanne

Although Lausanne figures prominently on few tourist itineraries, its pleasant lakeside location, its connections to the Olympic Movement, and its accessible small-city feel make it a worthwhile stop. The lake-set, vineyard-ensconced town revolves around Ouchy, a lakeside community bustling with parks, cafés, and the ferry docks. Climbing uphill, visitors shop along the Rue de Bourg, visit the city's 13th-century Gothic cathedral, and wander through the old center around the Place de la Palud and its imposing Town Hall.

Want to stay? Although the **Beau-Rivage** ($$$$) down the lakefront is the grandest hotel here, I like the **Château d'Ouchy** ($$-$$$). The neo-Gothic 19th-century château sits on the lakefront at the site of a 12th-century castle. The hotel has a glassed-in terrace lounge, a good restaurant, and an Internet café. Its deluxe rooms are worth the small jump in price. To book, ☎ 021 616 74 51, www.chateaudouchy.ch.

For more information, contact the Lausanne tourist office at ☎ 021 613 73 73, www.lausanne-tourisme.ch. Offices are at Ouchy and at the central train station.

THE OLYMPIC CAPITAL

Lausanne is the world's Olympic capital – home to the International Olympic Committee, 17 international sporting federations, and the renowned Olympic Museum. This museum, the Musée Olympique, occupies a sprawling modern complex at the Ouchy lakefront. Sculpture-studded parks step down to the water and views stretch to the mountains beyond. Inside, interactive exhibits depict the history, culture, and art of the Olympic Movement, ranging from equipment of interest to computer and film presentations of the Olympic Games' most memorable moments. The museum is open daily from May through September, 9 am-6 pm; from October through April, closed on Mondays; 14 CHF. For more information, contact ☎ 021 621 65 11, www.museum.olympic.org.

■ Verbier

Population: 2,500

Base elevation: 1,500 m

Mountain resort village

Verbier is the kind of winter resort where skiers access the mountains by helicopters rather than chairlifts. Here, ski instructors give morning briefs using topographical rather than mere piste maps – briefs that often employ the phrase, "Don't fall here or you'll die." This is Europe's premier free-riding, free-styling resort; all manner of alternative equipment is for hire, and all manner of off-piste guiding is available. Have fun. Be safe.

History & Orientation

 From the early 1900s, Verbier consisted of little more than a summertime cattle pasture and a cluster of farmers' huts. Its ski history got off to a late but quick start when, in 1925, several hearty sportsmen made the 15-km hike up from Sembrancher with the sole purpose of skiing down. In 1927 the village opened its first hotel and, in 1945, its 27 residents hired a federal expert to study the resort's potential development. The findings weren't encouraging. The village could supposedly support a maximum of only 2,500 tourists. Today, the resort's 2,500 residents support some 25,000 tourist beds.

Verbier Grows

Although Verbier got off to a relatively late start, the little resort saw explosive expansion from the 1950s. What a difference 50 years can make:

- In 1951, the lift company hired its third employee; today, it employs more than 300.

- In 1951, the lift company counted 50,000 passenger trips; in 1996, 12 million.

- In 1950, Verbier had 10,000 overnight stays; that number grew to 60,000 in just one year. By 1968, the resort saw 600,000 visitors, and today welcomes around one million.

Verbier nestles in the southwestern corner of the Swiss Valais region, near the borders of both France and Italy. Geneva sits 170 km to the west; Milan, 270 km to the south; and Zürich, 300 km to the north. Martigny lies 27 km southeast, and the Grand St. Bernard Pass into Italy lies directly south; the smaller ski resorts of the Four Valleys region scatter sparsely around.

The village perches above the Val de Bagnes, soaking up the sun from its southwest-facing position, and a bowl of mountains rise up above the tree line all around.

The Town

Visitors enter Verbier from its southern edge, along the Rue de Verbier up from Le Chable and the "suburb" of Verbier Village. The center of Verbier proper is Place Centrale, the traffic circle at the end of Rue de Verbier. From Place Centrale, the town fans out and up the mountainside bowl, a homogenous, sprawling mass of mostly modern chalets. (There is no quaint pedestrian center here.) Three main roads finger out through town from the palm of the Place Centrale traffic circle. First, the Rue de Médran runs up the hill to the east, passing through the shopping zone and ending at the Médran lift station. The Route des Creux runs uphill and north from Place Centrale traffic circle, eventually passing by the Savoleyres gondola base. Finally, running west from the Place Centrale traffic circle, the Rue de la Poste quickly becomes the Rue du Centre Sportif.

Getting Here & Around

Travelers arriving by **air** will fly into Geneva, Milan, or Zürich. Those traveling by **train** should disembark the main Simplon line at Martigny, change to the Martigny-Le Chable line as far as Le Chable, and then climb the mountain via bus or cable car. **Drivers** will arrive along the Grand St. Bernard main road, either from Italy in the south or from Martigny in the north. From Sembrancher, follow the valley road through the Val de Bagnes to Le Chable, where a dozen hairpin turns leads steeply up the mountain to Verbier.

Once in town, four **bus** routes network the village. Buses are free to lift-pass holders. For **taxi** service, try **Alpentaxi** at ☎ 027 771 71 96 or **Taxi Rosset** at ☎ 027 771 12 66.

Mountain transportation climbs from the town's outskirts up in two main directions – to Savoleyres to the north and to Les Ruinettes and beyond to the east. One gondola descends to La Chable in the south. For more information on local lifts, check in at www.televerbier.ch.

LIFT PASS PRICE SAMPLES	
Winter	
1-day Four Valleys	59 CHF
1-day Verbier only	52 CHF
6-day Four Valleys	306 CHF
Summer	
1-day pass for Mont Fort	34 CHF
Biker lift pass for Verbier	16 CHF

Getting Connected

The very helpful tourist office fronts Place Centrale. For more information, check ☎ 027 775 38 88, www.verbier.ch.

The post office is on the Rue de la Poste, a few doors west of Place Centrale.

Internet access is at **Harold's** above Place Centrale, **Pub Mont-Fort**, and at **Verbier Beach** in the Sports Center.

The Adventures

Aside from a small museum up at Le Hameau, Verbier lacks any real sights, and there's not even a pedestrian center in which to stroll. For those interested in history, the **Musée Espace Alpin** documents life in the Alpine regions from the 18th through the 20th centuries. It's open December through Easter and from mid-June through October; ☎ 027 771 65 39, www.lehameau.ch. Beyond that, Verbier is all about adventure.

On Foot

Snowshoe trekking in Verbier

Some 400 km of **hiking paths** wind through the region, so summertime visitors have no shortage of ways to wander. Hikers enjoy the area's rich flora, which includes several species of orchids and rhododendrons, and a wealth of fauna, including chamois, ibex, and marmots. The Verbier tourist office offers a program of **guided hikes** in July and August. Many, such as walks to an Alpine dairy, are particularly suited to kids. Several **multi-day hiking routes** converge at Verbier; inquire at the Maison du Sport or the tourist office about the Tour du Val de Bagnes, the Tour des Combins, and the Tour des Quatre Vallées. More difficult mountaineering routes depart Verbier as well, including the six-day Haute Route to Chamonix and Zermatt.

Each Thursday morning in summer, visitors can hop an early morning lift to Mont Fort for a spectacular sunrise and a hearty breakfast in a mountain restaurant. Contact the tourist office for more info; adults 47 CHF, children 37 CHF.

Climbers enjoy many sites throughout the Val de Bagnes region, including opportunities for free climbing, ice climbing, and practice on man-made walls. The **Médran Adventure Park** has a rock-climbing wall in summer, an ice-climbing wall in winter, and a suspended trail **ropes course** year-round. This course is comprised of hanging bridges, ladders, and ropes all suspended from trees and poles – the perfect place for young climbers to tie their first knots. For more information on climbing or the ropes course, contact **La Maison du Sport** (page 304).

On Wheels

Mountain bikers enjoy 200 km of trails. Bikers' lift passes are a good deal, lifts carry bikes free of charge, and the tourist office offers route maps. Downhillers speed off from Ruinettes to Verbier, and endurance riders head off to conquer the 131-km Verbier-Grimentz racecourse (see *Festivals & Events* below). Several shops along the main road offer bike rental, and each of the outdoor adventure outfitters runs guided excursions. In addition, the tourist office guides free outings each week; contact ☎ 027 775 38 88 for more information. Finally, **Quad Aventure Verbier** offers summertime outings on four-wheeled **quad motorbikes**. Check the offerings at ☎ 078 707 37 04, www.quads.ch.

In the Air

 Exceptional flying conditions make Verbier an ideal **paragliding** center, and the village has even hosted the Paragliding World Championships. Visitors who wish to take flight can book tandem flights or licensing course in both the **hang-gliding** and paragliding disciplines. For more information, contact the **Center de Parapente** at ☎ 027 771 68 18 or the **Maison du Sport** at ☎ 027 775 33 63. **Bungee jumping** and **balloon ride** excursions are also available; book a flight with **No Limits**, the **Maison du Sport**, or **La Fantastique** (see page 304).

On Snow & Ice

 Verbier enjoys access to the **Four Valleys Ski region**, a conglomeration of 11 smaller areas for a total of 410 km of runs and 94 uplift facilities. Verbier itself boasts 38 lifts and 150 km of **skiing** and **snowboarding** runs graded 32% easy, 33% intermediate, and 35% advanced or off-piste. These numbers are misleading, however. Beginners have it tough, as runs here are notoriously under-graded, and the piste marking is notoriously poor. Skiers and snowboarders of all abilities frequently find themselves looking uphill at the intersecting run they *meant* to take – a problem not so serious for experienced skiers but one that lands beginners on steeps unsuited to their skills. (Verbier does so many things so splendidly – you'd think that piste marking would be a fairly easy thing to fix.)

Intermediate skiers enjoy a wide range of runs, and free-stylists enjoy the halfpipe at Col des Gentianes and the two freestyle areas, at La Chaux and La Tournelle. Experts rave over the Mont Fort Glacier run, a banging, bumpy ride under the cable car; grow giddy over the extensive off-piste; and wax lyrical about heli-drops and powder bowls.

Snowboarders for Safety

In late March, the **Red Bull Xtreme Freeride Contest** slams Verbier with the year's biggest bash. Snowboarding's most renowned off-piste competition invites the globe's top 20 men and seven women boarders to show off their skills. The event runs on the Bec des Rosses, where gradients of up to 55° propel each boarder across a self-determined route of deep powder, narrow couloirs, and rock cliffs.

Paradoxically, all this extremist adrenaline flows in the name of safety awareness. Participants must carry the equipment every freerider should pack: a bulky list, including helmet, harness, back protector, avalanche victim detector, rucksack, shovel, and probe. Much is made, too, of avalanche education, rescue techniques, and the mountain's safety features. Viewed live, the competition is a delightfully mind-blowing showcase of snowboarding talent – take binoculars to the Gentianes Pass for the best view. And yes, *as if* there were any question, the slope-side party is a hoot, too.

For more information, surf www.xtreme-snowboard.com.

Cross-country skiers have a four-km trail near the sports center and a five-km trial at altitude in Ruinettes. Down the hill, more than 45 km of trails wind through the Val de Bagnes. **Winter walkers** head out on 25 km of marked and groomed tracks, and local guides lead the way to the back-country on skis and **snow shoes**. Fans of ice sports congregate at the Sports Center for **ice skating**, **ice hockey**, and **curling**. **Tobogganing** runs span 10 km from Savoleyres to Tzoumaz.

In the Extreme

Several operators run extreme sports adventures, but my favorite is **No Limits**. (While the other outfitters focus on winter sports, No Limits is all about the alternative.) The company organizes outlandish activities on snow, dirt, air, and water. The all-season outings include **snow scooting**, **snow carting**, **bungee jumping**, bridge **pendulum swings**, and – my favorite – **mud biking**. No Limits runs whitewater activities in the summer, including high-energy canyoning, tubing, hydrospeed, rafting, and **air-boat** outings. For more information, reservations, or private guiding services, contact ☎ 027 771 72 50, www.outdoor-activity.ch.

Switzerland

Sports Services, Outfitters & Guides

■ The **Sport Center**, or Centre Sportif, is open year-round, offering two indoor and one outdoor swimming pools, an indoor ice rink, curling rinks, tennis, squash, sauna, whirlpool, solarium, and a restaurant. Massages and Internet access are available here, too. To see what's on, check in at ☎ 027 771 66 01, www.verbier-sport.ch.

■ **No Limits Outdoor Activity** – see *In the Extreme* above.

■ **La Maison du Sport** is home to the traditional Swiss Ski and Snowboarding School. Its offerings, however, run a much wider range, including all-season mountaineering, paragliding, summer whitewater outings, and the ropes course at the Médran Adventure Park. La Maison du Sport also offers a summer program and a winter kindergarten for kids. For more info, check ☎ 027 775 33 63, www.maisondusport.ch.

■ **Adrenaline Ski School** is a winter-only operation offering what we've been told is the best snowboarding instruction in town. Their real passion, however, is guiding: off-piste, heli-drops, or winter mountaineering, Adrenaline's guides will get you there – and back. Contact ☎ 027 771 74 59, www.adrenaline-verbier.ch.

■ **La Fantastique** is the third ski school option here. They run a decent selection of winter instruction and guiding packages and dabble in the summer market with mountain treks and climbing. Like No Limits and La Maison, they can arrange paragliding trips. For more information, contact ☎ 027 771 41 41, www.lafantastique.com.

Where to Sleep

Around 90% of Verbier's visitors stay in private chalet or apartment accommodations, meaning that there are relatively few hotels. Below are a few of the best. The 25-room **Châlet d'Adrien** ($$$$) is the only five-star house in town. Its fresh rooms are country cozy and its location is good, right next to the Savoleyres gondola in the upper reaches of town. It is, however, a long haul to the shopping and restaurant zone. Inquire at ☎ 027 771 62 00, www.chalet-adrien.com.

The time-honored four-star favorite in town is the **Rosalp** ($$$-$$$$), an elegant hotel in the center on Rue de Médran. Its professional service and excellent dining room keep guests coming back year after year; ☎ 027 771 63 23, www.rosalp.ch.

South of the Médran lift station in a peaceful location, the new **Verbier Lodge** ($$-$$$) touts an American-style log-cabin façade, an outdoor whirlpool, and a fireplace within. Its rates vary dramatically by season; ☎ 027 771 66 66, www.verbierlodge.ch.

HOTEL PRICE CHART	
Double room without tax; $$$-$$$$ always with bath.	
$	Under 120 CHF
$$	121-225 CHF
$$$	226-375 CHF
$$$$	Over 375 CHF

The **Hotel Farinet** ($$-$$$) has an excellent corner location at Place Centrale and balconies outside most of its color-coordinated rooms. Contact ☎ 027 771 66 26, www.hotelfarinet.ch.

Across the traffic circle at Place Centrale, rooms at the **Hotel de Verbier** ($$-$$$) are cozy rather than color-coordinated. I loved the homey décor, the inviting fireplace lounge, and the helpful young staff. Book at ☎ 027 775 21 21, www.hotelverbier.ch.

Up the hill toward the Médran lift station, on the main road, the **Hotel Garbo** ($$) offers relatively inexpensive rooms in a great location – great, that is, if you like rather than loathe the après-ski bar scene on the terrace out front. Book at ☎ 027 771 62 72, www.hotelgarbo.com.

Less expensive and more bare-boned is **Les Ruinettes** ($); its enviable location, however, places it next door to the Médran lift base and just around the corner from Pub Mont Fort; ☎ 027 771 19 79.

The **Bunker** ($) hostel has beds out near the Sports Center; ☎ 027 771 66 02, www.thebunker.ch. And on the mountain, the isolated and basic **Cabane du Mont-Fort** ($-$$) warms with hearty food and a convivial atmosphere; ☎ 027 778 13 84.

Where to Eat

If you have a hankering for gourmet cuisine, get your epicurean thrills at **Le Rosalp** ($$$), where Roland Pierroz and his team pull in an enormous 19-point score from Gault Millau. It's a special night out, and expensive to prove it; dinner starts at 175 CHF per person. The restaurant is in the hotel of the same

DINING PRICE CHART	
Average entrée, with tax.	
$	Under 15 CHF
$$	16-37 CHF
$$$	Over 37 CHF

name, in the center along Rue de Médran. To book a table, contact
☎ 027 771 63 23, www.rosalp.ch.

One of Verbier's loveliest places to dine is up at **Le Hameau** ($$-$$$)
conference center, in a modern chalet built in rustic style, with big
windows overlooking the valley outside. The traditional fare is well
complemented by a nice wine selection; reserve at ☎ 027 771 45 80.

Although the gourmet royalty in town gets all the applause, we'd just
as soon settle down to a cozy meal at **Le Caveau** ($$-$$$), a rustic lit-
tle room specializing in traditional Bagnes cheese fondue and
raclette – the latter made over an open fire in the middle of the dining
room. It's small and popular; they'll tell you what time to come. Book
a table at ☎ 027 771 22 26.

Near the Médran lift station, try **Au Vieux Verbier** ($$); they have a
big deck and reasonably priced traditional fare; ☎ 027 771 64 02. Just
below, the **Fer de Cheval** ($) has been doing pizzas and après-ski
since 1969. We had good pizza as well at the homey **Borsalina Piz-
zeria** ($-$$) off the Place Centrale toward Savoleyres.

The **Offshore Café** ($), just below the Médran lift station, has a
short menu, a pink VW Bug, and big mugs of hot chocholate.

Harold's ($) draws a crowd of young resort workers for its burgers,
beer, and Internet stations, and **Verbier Beach** ($) has good snacks
out at the Sports Center. Don't miss a stop at **Le Monde des Crêpes**
($) down Rue de la Poste.

Finally, self-caterers should check out the fine selection of local
cheese and wines available at **La Chaumière**. The shop is tucked
away below the Milk Bar on rue de Médran.

AUTHOR'S Dining on the mountain at Verbier is a hit-or-miss affair,
PICK but one of the Alps' classic ski lunch breaks awaits at the
Cabane du Mont Fort ($-$$). Once tiny but recently en-
larged, the stone hut has simple, self-service fare – not
something I'd normally recommend. But the treat here is fondue, a
delicious mix of cheeses best paired with bread and a pitcher of wine,
and best served outside on the sunny deck. Go early to get a table; the
astounding views lull diners into lingering.

Where to Party

Over a quarter of Verbier's dining outlets are pubs, bars,
or discotheques; there's no shortage of places to party.
Après-ski begins on the lower slopes at the **Chez Dany**
mountain hut. After sliding back to town, revelers spend
the afternoon in one of the several bars and cafés lining the Rue de
Médran. The **Fer à Cheval** is popular for its corner deck and its
pizza – if you're lucky you'll get there when they're passing out free-

bies. **Big Ben's** just across the street has good people-watching seats outside and pool and fussball inside. A bit farther down, crowds congregate at **Garbo's** outdoor bar – it offers sun chairs and Verbier's largest terrace.

Later, British partiers congregate at the **Pub Mont Fort**, a two-story bar that glows green and blue from up behind the Médran lift station. There's food and drink here from après-ski on, and the shots bar in the basement is legendary – although it's hard to reason why, since few who've experienced it properly remember much about the experience. See what's on at www.pubmontfort.com.

Murphy's offers a good pub atmosphere, as well. Just up the Savoleyres road from Place Centrale, **Le Crok No Name** has live music and cocktails, and the upscale **King's Lounge** boasts a fireplace and sofas. The ever-popular **Farm** was under renovation last time I visited; but it should be up and dancing again soon.

> **TIP:** Many late-night clubs reserve tables; ask at your hotel if you should call ahead.

Where to Play

More a town for adults who play like kids than for actual, bona fide children, Verbier offers minimal attraction for families. **La Maison du Sport** runs **ski schools** in the winter and **children's programs** in the summer; and **Les Schtroumpfs** (The Smurfs) offer daytime **childcare** near the center. Contact ☎ 027 771 65 85 for more info. There's no pedestrian area to stroll, and the ski slopes here are a rotten place to learn, but the Sports Center does draw kids for its indoor and outdoor pools.

Festivals & Events

Verbier is legendary for its festivals and events – in particular, for those extreme sporting competitions that taunt athletes with both great danger and greater prestige. Many of Verbier's big events add the attraction of *mindful purpose*, sponsoring charities and supporting awareness efforts. One such occasion, the **24-Hour Freeride**, kicks off the winter season. In early January, some 120 teams take to the mountain, skiing laps to raise money for charity. The proceeds? They go to the Swiss Aid Foundation for Landmine Victims – those who no longer have the privilege of skiing on two legs.

In March, **Verbier Ride** features big-air, skier-cross, and mountain freeride events, and the **Red Bull Extreme Freeride Contest** (see *Snowboarders for Safety* above) brings the world's best to town. April closes out the season with the **Carlsberg High Five**, a combination event allowing all comers to test their skills across four disciplines: giant slalom, mogul, boarder-cross, and triathlon. For more information – or to register for the race – check in at www.carlsberghighfive.ch.

During the winter of each even-numbered year, the biannual **Patrol of the Glaciers** brings ski mountaineers from around the globe to compete in the world's toughest winter endurance event. Military, police, and civilian participants in teams of three cross 53 km from Zermatt to Verbier — over glaciers, rock summits, and mountain passes. The record was set in 2000 by a Swiss border guard patrol unit. Their time? Just seven hours, three minutes, and 44 seconds. For more info, click to www.pdg.ch.

In summer, the **Verbier Golf Pro-Am Schroeder**, the **Grand Concours Hippique National** equestrian competition, and the **4X4 Verbier** show come to town. In late August, Verbier hosts the **Grand Raid Cristalp**, the world's longest one-day mountain bike race. Some 4,500 riders take part, covering 131 km and crossing six valleys with a total vertical climb of almost 4,700 m. For more information, check www.grand-raid-cristalp.ch.

Rounding out all this sporting prowess is the **Verbier Festival & Academy**, held each year for 17 days from mid-July through early August. This well-regarded music festival brings together great singers, musicians, and directors in order to inspire collaboration, education, and performance. For more information on the Verbier Festival, check www.verbierfestival.com.

Martigny

First home to Celtic tribes, then a Roman settlement called Octodorum, Martigny has long enjoyed a prominent position at the Alpine crossroads of the St. Bernard, Forclaz and Simplon routes. The town sits near a bend in the Rhône River; all around, vineyards climb up the steep valley walls, spilling over with the Gamay, Fendant, and Arvine grapes that feature prominently in local wines.

Although most tourists blow on by en route to France or Italy – each less than an hour's drive away – Martigny's few sights do merit a short stop. The town stretches north and south along the Avenue du Grand St. Bernard, a busy boulevard paralleling the Rhône to the west. At the road's southern end is the old town center; at its northern end is the Place Centrale, today's modern hub; and in the east, along the mountains, dot the town's archeological sites and sport center. To the west, in the crook of the river's bend, the 13th-century **La Batiaz Tower** dominates the valley as it has for seven centuries, offering nice views to those who choose to drop in.

The **Place Centrale** is the nucleus of modern Martigny, a large, tree-lined square bustling with traffic, pedestrians, shops, and cafés.

Cow fights are now held in Martigny's Roman amphitheater

The Place Centrale is home, too, to the town's tourist office. Also worth a stroll is the **Rue du Bourg** in the old quarter, a small web of cobblestone streets at the southern end of the Avenue du Grand St. Bernard. Today, the ancient way enjoys a low-key social scene, with a small but pleasant mix of antique shops, studios, and cafés.

Martigny's oldest attractions range up against the mountain to the east: the **Roman Amphitheater**, which once seated 5,000 people, and the **Fondation Pierre Gianadda**, a museum complex that is itself centered over the ruins of a Celtic temple. The foundation museums include collections of cars, paintings, numerous antiquities, and a sculpture garden; the foundation is named for the deceased brother of the ruins' discoverer, local landowner Leonard Gianadda. The museums are open November through June from 10 am to 6 pm, and June through November from 9 am to 7 pm; ☎ 027 722 39 78, www.gianadda.ch.

AUTHOR'S PICK

If you're hungry, head up the hill to the **Plan-Cerisier** *($$). The restaurant nestles in the hillside vineyards, serving hearty Valaisian dishes such as raclette, fondues, and grills. Thirty regional wines are available. For more info, contact ☎ 027 722 25 29; open daily 9 am-10 pm.*

Switzerland

Want to stay? There's really not much to recommend in Martigny. The **Hotel du Parc** ($$-$$$) is the freshest face in town – a modern convention hotel with bright commercial rooms and pleasant grounds. It's north of the center at Avenue des Prés-Beudin 20. Inquire at ☎ 027 720 1313, www.hotelduparc.ch.

 The Office du Tourisme is at Place Centrale 9. Dial ☎ 027 721 22 20, www.martignytourism.ch.

■ Zermatt

Population: 5,500

Base elevation: 1,620 m

Mountain resort town

In southeastern Switzerland next to the border of Italy, Zermatt reclines amid a cluster of 38 4,000-m peaks. Above the town towers the distinctive hook of the Matterhorn crest. Curiously, few here seem to notice. In this glamorous, clamorous town, electric taxis tear through the alleys, moving shoppers, sightseers, and skiers at a frantic pace. For this jet-setting clientele, Zermatt isn't a place to relax; it's a place to play, and play hard.

History & Orientation

 Zermatt was first known as **Pratobornum**, under which name records exist from as early as 1280, and the first use of its current name dates from the 15th century. Its sovereign, the Bishop of Sion, largely ignored the little valley, and by 1691 the three local hamlets voluntarily united under a single village constitution. British climbers discovered the area in the late 18th century; in 1838, a local surgeon opened the village's first guest house. It was called the Hôtel Mont Cervie, and it accommodated up to three people. Today, this little village of 5,500 can house some 14,000 guests per night.

The Matterhorn

 Its very name conjures up fairy-tale images of high-Alpine grandeur. The fascination began early, when British adventurers first discovered the climbing potential of the region's peaks. In 1792, Horace Benedict scaled the Klein Matterhorn and trigonometrically estimated its larger sibling to be 4,501.7 m high. Thus, the gauntlet was thrown down.

Climbers thronged to the region. And finally, on July 14th, 1865, after seven previous attempts and a 32-hour ascent, Edward Whymper and a party of six others became the first to summit the Matterhorn: Edward Whymper, the two Peter Taugwalders (father and son), Michel Croz, Reverend Charles Hudson, Lord Francis Douglas, and Robert Hadow had made history. However, early in their triumphant descent, one member of the roped party slipped over the North Wall, dragging with him three other climbers. A weak roped snapped, and all four fell 1,200 m to their deaths. Whymper and the Taugwalders returned to Zermatt alone.

The Town

Zermatt streches along the Mattervispa River, up the valley toward the imposing Matterhorn. Anchoring its northern end is the train station, where most visitors arrive. Across Bahnhofstrasse, the street running in front of the station, the Gornergrat Railway chugs up the mountainside to the southeast. Bahnhofstrasse, the main road in town, heads south toward the Matterhorn, paralleling the river and its waterside road. The road travels past the church at Platz, and several cross-streets lead east over the river.

Confusingly for visitors, houses are numbered, but street names are rarely used; learn districts and landmarks instead. The Matten district is home to the railway station and the sports fields, and Hinterdorf, Hof, Am Bach, and Oberdorf lie south on the same side of the river. Across the river to the east, on the extreme northern end of town, is Wiesti. Oberhausern, Steinmatte, and Winkelmatten lie south. At the valley's northern head, the Schluhmatten district is home to the Matterhorn Express cableway stations.

Getting Here & Around

 Travelers arriving by **air** should fly in to either Geneva or Zürich, both approximately 3½ hours away by car. Helicopter transfers are possible, for those willing to part with substantial amounts of cash. **Drivers** head up a southern valley from Visp, or park their cars and hop a **train** for the 90-minute ride to Zermatt. (Park-and-ride spaces are free for Zermatt visitors.) Motorists can drive as far as Täsch, park in paid lots, and catch the train to Zermatt from there. Convenient luggage carts are available – they can be taken aboard the train, strapped in for the ride, and deposited on arrival in Zermatt. New arrivals from Zermatt's train station move in a muddle of taxis, carriages, and luggage carts. (Before you pay, check with your hotel to see if they offer a complimentary shuttle.)

Once settled, visitors get around town on foot, via electric bus or taxi, or in a horse-drawn carriage. For electric **taxi** service, contact ☎ 027 967 77 77 or 027 12 12. For **horse-drawn carriage** and **sleigh** service – either as a taxi or a round-trip tour – contact **Imboden Werner** at ☎ 079 436 76 12.

Mountain transport rises in three main sections: the **Matterhorn Express** from the southern edge of town to Furi, Trockener Steg, Schwarzsee, and the Klein Matterhorn; the **Alpen-Metro train** to Sunnegga from the northeastern corner of town; and the **Gornergratbahn railway** from its base near the main train station to Riffelalp and beyond.

LIFT PASS PRICE SAMPLES	
Winter	
1-day all-area	72 CHF
6-day adult	362 CHF
Pedestrian round-trip on Gornergrat Railway	67 CHF
Summer	
1-day Matterhorn ski pass	60 CHF
1-day Matterhorn & Schwarzsee	78 CHF
2-day all-area Panoramic Pass	119 CHF
6-day all-area Zermatt Peak Pass	220 CHF

Getting Connected

 The excellent tourist office is near the train station at Bahnhofplatz 5. For more information, contact ☎ 027 966 81 00, www.zermatt.ch.

 The post office is on Bahnhofstrasse directly in the center.

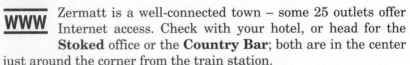 Zermatt is a well-connected town – some 25 outlets offer Internet access. Check with your hotel, or head for the **Stoked** office or the **Country Bar**; both are in the center just around the corner from the train station.

The Sights

 In town, Zermatt's sights are limited. Visitors stroll and shop along Bahnhofstrasse and through the narrow village lanes, stopping at cafés and perhaps at the church cemetery, where many famous climbers are buried. The most interesting **old lanes** wind just beyond the church and, as well, between Bahnhofstrasse and the river in the Hinterdorf district.

The **Alpine Museum** draws history enthusiasts for its collection of climbing memorabilia and geology exhibits. Life in the Alps is covered, too, including a mock-up of an 18th-century kitchen. The museum is open in winter, Sunday through Friday from 4:30 to 6:30 pm; in summer daily, 10 am-noon and 3-6 pm. For more info, contact ☎ 027 967 41 00, €8.

Several peaks draw tourists as well as sports enthusiasts, but no visitor should miss a trip up to the **Klein Matterhorn Peak**. A glacier grotto sits just below the top lift station; inside the cave, enjoy sculptures and exhibits on glaciers, geology, and climbing sports. For a panoramic view of the Matterhorn, however, no vantage point compares to the top station of the old **Gornergratbahn** across the valley – sunsets are particularly memorable from here.

The Adventures

On Foot

About 400 km of **hiking** paths wind through the mountains above Zermatt, most areas well-served by cableway or mountain train. The most spectacular of the trails tangle through the Sunnegga and Rothorn areas, winding around several lakes, skirting glaciers, and all within view of the Matterhorn across the valley. One of these, the **Marmot Trail**, leads from mid-mountain Rothorn at Blauherd down to Sunnegga via a path lined with several marmot family groups.

Walkers wanting a closer look at the majestic mountain should try the new **Matterhorn Trail**. It drops from the lift station at Schwarzsee, along the foot of the Matterhorn to Stafel, to the lake at Zmutt, and then down to the lift station at Furi – passing several inviting mountain huts along the way.

Zermatt is one of the few high-mountain resorts to remain open into the late fall season. Autumn wanders are enhanced with colorful views of blue sky, icy peaks, red pasturelands, and variable green larch trees. When weather conditions allow, footpaths remain open through October.

Zermatt cut its tourism teeth on the earliest mountaineers, and opportunities for **climbing** still abound. Visitors head out with moun-

Switzerland

tain guides to climb rock faces, scale glacier crevasses, and trek to remote mountain huts. Outdoor and indoor climbing walls and an ice-climbing tower are available, the climbing school offers instruction, and an excellent equipped route traverses the Gorner Gorge. For experienced climbers, a number of summits beckon – not least the legendary Matterhorn. Check in with the **Alpin Center Zermatt** to join a group or to hire a private guide. For more info, see *Sports Services* below.

Memorable Moments

Zermatt has a knack for creating fond memories. Check in with the tourist office regarding the following adventures.

- Fondues under the full moon at the **Rothorn** restaurant and a moonlit ski run down.

- Friday-evening winetasting in the glacier grotto at Klein Matterhorn.

- Evening snowshoeing to dinner in a mountain hut.

- Sunrise excursions to the Rothorn, Klein Matterhorn, and Gornergrat.

- Open-carriage train rides on the Gornergrat Mountain Railway.

- Fire-and-ice ski descents by torchlight from the Gornergrat.

On Horseback

The **Zermatt Mule Trekking Company** runs mule-trekking excursions varying in length from one hour to several days. Check in at ☎ 027 967 64 59, www.rhone.ch/zermatt-mule-trekking. **Llamas** plod along the Gornergrat at Riffelberg from July to September; www.zermatt-tours.ch. And **horse-drawn carriage** and **sleigh rides** are offered from **Imboden Werner,** ☎ 079 436 76 12.

On Wheels

Zermatt maintains 80 km of designated **mountain biking** trails but – after much contention between bikers and hikers – now prohibits biking on walking trails not specifically marked "MTB." Four popular trails cross the Gornergrat and Rothorn areas – check with the tourist office for the latest map. For mountain biking rental and instruction, check in with the **Swiss Ski School**; see *Sports Services* below.

In the Air

 Air Zermatt offers **helicopter rides** around the Matterhorn, **heli-taxi transfers** from several airports, and **heli-skiing drops** to the Theodul Glacier. For more information and reservations, contact ☎ 027 966 86 86. Visitors can also take to the sky with the **Air Born Flight School**. **Tandem paragliding** rides are offered, and the Rothorn is a favorite launch point. For more information, drop by the **Haus Montana**, or contact ☎ 027 967 67 44.

On Snow & Ice

Summer Skiing

 Zermatt's Klein Matterhorn boasts the highest summer skiing area in the Alps. Skiers and boarders slide down the Theodulgletscher at Plateau Rosa, which – depending on snow conditions – offers anywhere between 6.2 and 21 km of marked pistes. One cable car and six drag lifts serve the 36-square-km area. When conditions cooperate, the glacier ice opens for skiing from early morning till midday between early July and late October. So then, a perfect summer day in Zermatt: Ski in the morning until the ice gets slushy, enjoy lunch at a mountain restaurant, and hike dry trails in the afternoon.

In the winter, **skiers** take to 394 km of pistes across Zermatt and connecting Cervinia. Zermatt's 194 km are graded 22% easy, 50% intermediate, and 28% difficult. Beginners are hard-pressed to find novice runs, heading for the blues on Gornergrat and Riffelberg. Intermediates enjoy the run of most area slopes, and advanced and expert skiers head off-piste with a guide – or take to the air for some of Europe's best heli-skiing. **Snowboarders** enjoy a growing selection of facilities, including three fun parks, a halfpipe, and a prepared mogul steep. A boarder-cross run and quarter-pipe are at Blauherd, and a new snow park at Rotenboden on the Gornergrat includes a number of obstacles, a kids' corner, an igloo, and a teepee bar. In summer, the Theodul glacier hosts the **Gravity Park**, the biggest snow park in Europe, with a 200-m super-pipe, a halfpipe, and several other obstacles.

> **TIP:** Skiers and boarders enjoy the relatively rare opportunity to slide across international borders. Although Cervinia, Italy, is an eyesore of a resort, it is

nice to ski over for a lunch of fresh pasta. (I liked the food and the views at **l'Etoile**, mid-mountain.) Beware, however; not all lift passes access both the Swiss and Italian lifts – check before you follow the Italian flags downhill into Italy. If you get stuck without the right pass, it's an expensive one-way ticket back to the peak.

Cross-country skiers are limited to just nine km of runs, but **winter walkers** enjoy 30 km of groomed hiking paths. Fans of ice sports take to two **ice-skating rinks** and 10 **curling rinks**. For **tobogganing**, head to the Gornergrat and the Rotenboden-Riffelberg 20-minute run; for a one-hour **dog-sledding** excursion along the foot of the Matterhorn, dial ☎ 027 967 77 09. In addition, the Alpin Center (see *Sports Services* below) offers a wide range of winter activities, including **snow shoeing**, **ice climbing**, and **ski touring**.

Sports Services, Outfitters & Guides

- The **Alpin Center Zermatt** consolidates the efforts of some 80 mountain guides who together offer a wide range of mountaineering options for visitors at all levels of ability. Climbing, high-mountain treks, and glacier excursions are on the menu here. Stop by the office at Bahnhofstrasse in the town center from 8:30 am-noon and from 4-7 pm daily. From more info, contact ☎ 027 966 24 60.

- The **Swiss Ski and Snowboard School** offers on-slope instruction in summer as well as winter. The school also runs mountain biking excursions in summer. For info and reservations, drop by the office on Bahnhofstrasse or contact ☎ 027 966 24 66, www.skischulezermatt.ch.

- **Stoked** is the town's alternative ski and snowboard school – and I've heard good things. They have a small, energetic team of instructors specializing in off-piste glacier adventures. Stoked runs the Snowflakes Kids Club and organizes some summer activities, too. For more info, stop by Hofmattstrasse 7 or contact ☎ 027 967 70 22, www.stoked.ch.

Where to Sleep

The **Grand Hotel Zermatterhof** ($$$$) teams up with Swiss Deluxe Hotel sibling **Mont Cervin** ($$$$) to offer the plushest accommodation in town. Both are in the center, both boast excellent cuisine, and both share the same rate structure. Book the Zermatterhof at ☎ 027 966 66 00, www.zermatt.ch/zermatterhof; the Mont Cervin at ☎ 027 966 88 88, www.zermatt.ch/montcervin.

HOTEL PRICE CHART	
Double room without tax; $$$-$$$$ always with bath.	
$	Under 120 CHF
$$	121-225 CHF
$$$	226-375 CHF
$$$$	Over 375 CHF

The **Hotel Monte Rosa** ($$$$) was once the Mont Cervie, the village's first hotel, a three-room establishment opened in 1838 by Josef Lauber. Since that day, it's witnessed many historical events, including the backside of guest Edward Whymper as he headed off for the Matterhorn summit. Today, the traditional rooms show individual décor, and all bask in the warmest of Swiss hospitality. Inquire at ☎ 027 966 03 33, www.zermatt.ch/monterosa.

The **Romantik Hotel Julen** ($$$-$$$$) is a family-run affair, an old chalet within sight of the Matterhorn peak. There's a kid-pleasing indoor pool, a garden, and a sauna. Most of the traditional, pine-paneled rooms have balconies. Book at ☎ 027 966 76 00, www.romantikhotels.com/Zermatt.

For clean-cut rooms with a commercial feel, head for the **Hotel Ambiance** ($$$). Excellent dining and big Matterhorn views make the short walk from the center worthwhile; ☎ 027 967 23 38, www.hotel-ambiance.ch.

The **Hotel Post** ($$-$$$) is the town's social center, offering three restaurants, three bars, and a disco all under one roof. The décor is cozy and eccentric, with cartoon characters lining the entry and knickknacks strewn about like something from an Old West tavern. It's comfy enough and very central, but it can also be loud – a mix to suit those looking for a party. Book at ☎ 027 967 19 31, www.hotelpost.ch.

For a remote night on the mountain, book the **Kulm Hotel** ($$) at Gornergrat. The fortress-like structure tops the 3,100-m peak at the terminus of the Gornergratbahn Railway. The rooms are Spartan, the views spectacular, and the mood convivial. Rooms share baths, and west-facing rooms are worth the bump in price for their Matterhorn views; ☎ 027 966 64 00.

Back in town, **Le Mazot** ($$) has freshly renovated rooms in the center above a restaurant of the same name. Its nine rooms are booked straight through the winter; ☎ 027 966 06 06, www.lemazotzermatt.ch.

The **Hotel Cima** ($-$$) occupies an old, narrow chalet, offering simple rooms and family-style hospitality. The appeal is all about location here; the house is just behind the sports fields, next to a playground, and a short walk from the train station and center; ☎ 027 967 23 37.

The cheapest cheerful place in town is the **Matterhorn Hostel** ($), a bunk-bedded establishment as simple as they come. It's in a chalet just south of the church; ☎ 027 968 19 19, www.matternhornhostel.com.

Where to Eat

 With over 100 restaurants in town and some 38 dining outlets on the mountain, Zermatt guests don't go hungry. Many of the best restaurants are in local hotels; most are pricey. For gourmet grub, try the dining rooms at the **Grand Hotel Zermatterhof** ($$$) and the **Monte Cervin** ($$$).

DINING PRICE CHART	
Average entrée, with tax.	
$	Under 15 CHF
$$	16-37 CHF
$$$	Over 37 CHF

The historical **Whymperstube** ($$$) at the Monte Rosa sets an elegant table with the highest quality regional dishes; ☎ 027 967 22 96.

The **Schonegg Gourmet-Stubli** ($$$) serves up creative cuisine in an intimate Baroque dining room; ☎ 027 966 34 34.

The small restaurant **Le Mazot** ($$$) grills excellent lamb specialties and offers fondue during the summer months. It has a handful of guest rooms upstairs, too; ☎ 027 966 06 06.

For traditional cuisine, the rustic **Stockhorn** ($$-$$$) does good grills and fondues across the river on the east bank; ☎ 027 967 17 47, www.grill-stockhorn.ch. Nearby, the tiny **Grill Restaurant Spycher** ($$-$$$) offers traditional dishes and a specialty flambée. Reserve at ☎ 027 967 2041. In the center, on the square just behind the church, **Chez Gaby** ($$) does grills and Swiss specialities; ☎ 027 967 31 34. The **Restaurant Stadel** ($$), also on the main drag, does the same; ☎ 027 967 35 36.

For less expensive fare, head for the Hotel Post, where the **Pizzeria Broken** ($-$$) spins a good pie, the **Old Spaghetti Factory** ($-$$) does decent pasta, and the **Brown Cow** ($-$$) dishes out sandwiches and snacks.

The **Papparela** ($) is popular for both après-ski and its pizzas. Finally, avoid the **Walliserkanne** – we've heard bad rumors, read bad reviews, and had a bad experience there ourselves.

Where to Party

Après-ski starts early on the mountain, with skiers dropping down to town via Furi and the **Hennu Stall**, a hut with a big deck, loud music, and a crowd. It's along the trail to town, just under the Matterhorn Express.

In the center, on the east bank of the river, après-ski revelers head for **Papperla** for drinks and pizza. Later, **Murphy's Bar** proves popular, too; it's an Irish Pub with nightly live music. For other options, simply wander down Bahnhofstrasse and shop for an appealing crowd.

At the Hotel Post, **Pink** offers live music, **Le Broken** does disco into the wee hours, and **Le Village** pumps a club mix. The **Brown Cow** draws a casual crowd, and the new **Papa Caesar's** chills out in lounge-like surrounds – both of these are also at the Hotel Post. Also on Bahnhofstrasse, **Grampi's** plays multiple roles as a pub, a pizzeria, and a late-night disco.

Behind the Hotel Monte Rosa, the **Pink Elephant** piano bar is a classier affair. The tiny old **Elsie's Place**, on the square across from the church, draws an elegant crowd for snails and cocktails, and the Hotel **Beau-Site** has a mellow piano bar and smoking lounge.

Zermatt's new **casino** opened during 2003 winter season near the Grand Hotel Zermatterhof. In order to avoid marring the quaint old street, the building is subterranean – only its entrance is visible from the street. The casino offers blackjack, roulette, and slots and, although there's no dress code, the mood is a touch upscale. Visit daily from 6-11 pm.

Where to Play

In summer, children head for the **Dwarves' Paradise**, a **playground** near the Blauherd cable station with swings, slides, ropeways, and climbing rocks. The **Kinderparadies** offers daycare programs between mid-June and mid-August for kids three months and older; ☎ 027 967 72 52, www.kinderparadies-zermatt.ch.

In 2003, Zermatt premiered the **Snowflakes Kids' Club**, a winter facility offering a play park and a novice snowboarding arena. Parents appreciate Zermatt's **kids-ski-free** program for kids through nine years of age – those nine-15 years old pay just half of the adult fare. Finally, the tourist office can help arrange **babysitting** services.

Festivals & Events

Zermatt offers so many activities that it's as if there's a festival on year-round. In winter, official events run to winter sports competitions, including the men's **FIS World Cup** races in December and several **freestyle skiing and boarding** events throughout the season – of which the **Triftji Bump Bash** in mid-April is most popular.

In summer, Zermatt welcomes a number of sporting events, including the **Zermatt Open**, an international tennis tournament; the **Zermatt Marathon**; and the **Matterhornlauf**, an uphill foot race from Zermatt to Schwarzsee. The **Folklore Festival** sees the return of traditional customs in mid-August, and fans of classical music should come to town for the **Riffelalp Concerts** in early September.

Saas-Fee

Although Zermatt is certainly the glamour-girl of the Valais, I have a soft spot for its less conspicuous neighbor, tiny Saas-Fee. While the village lacks Zermatt's jaw-dropping Matterhorn views, Saas-Fee offers intimate looks at the Feegletscher, or "fairy glacier," and has what is in our opinion a much more romantic ambiance. First developed in the 17th century as a summer farming community, Saas-Fee retains its traditional architecture, including one of the region's finest collections of traditional *stadel*, the farmers' huts built on stone pillars to deter rummaging rodents. Its clientele is largely Swiss and German, with less than one percent of its winter guests arriving from North America.

Saas-Fee lies to the east of Zermatt, on the opposite side of the towering Dom. Like Zermatt, the resort is reached via a climb up the forked valley south of Visp – to reach Saas-Fee, drivers at Stalden take the left fork toward Saastal instead of the right fork toward Täsch. (Although only a few km apart as-the-crow-flies, the drive between Saas-Fee and Zermatt takes around an hour.) Also like

Zermatt, the village of Saas-Fee is technically car-free, served only by a swarm of electric taxi carts. The swarm here, however, is considerably smaller and less menacing. Drivers park in the nine-story cliff-side garage on the village edge and, from the garage loading bays, they telephone hotels for pickup. (Visitors arriving by train must bus in from Brig or Visp.)

Guests here split into two distinct camps – those who've come for the small-resort exclusivity, and those who've come for the big-mountain recreation. Both camps enjoy the views from the Allalin, where the world's highest revolving restaurant, the **Drehrestaurant Metro-Alpin**, does a full rotation each hour. Steps away, adventurers stroll through the largest ice pavilion in the world (the **Mittelallin Eispavillon**), a cave carved out of the glacier and embellished with sculptures and a chapel.

Active visitors enjoy **summer skiing** on top of the glacier each morning and **hiking** and **biking** throughout the region on some 350 km of trails. With 13 nearby peaks towering to 4,000 m and more, Saas-Fee remains an excellent **climbing** base, and even those new to the sport should try the cable-, rope-, and ladder-equipped route through the **Alpine Gorge**. In winter, 100 km of groomed runs offer **skiing** and **snowboarding** for all levels, and several easy slopes run along the glacial ice, giving even beginning skiers an intimate look at dramatic blue crevasses. In addition, and a particular hit with families, the whole of the Hannig area is reserved for **non-ski** winter activities – a gondola-served mountain where non-skiers enjoy **winter hiking**, **tobogganing**, and **dining** in mountain huts.

 Want to stay? There are several special places from which to choose. Those seeking luxury should plunk down their platinum cards at the **Ferienart Walliserhof** ($$$$), a modern chalet with four restaurants and a fireplace next to its indoor pool; ☎ 027 958 18 00, www.ferienart.ch. Less expensive lodging can be found at the trendy **Hotel Dom** ($$), where fun-loving, kitchy décor draws a young snowboarding crowd to the hotel's popular lounge and basement bar, Popcorn; ☎ 027 957 51 01, www.uniquedom.com.

Those more serious about their sports head for the homey old **Hotel Britannia** ($$), a family-run hostelry with simple rooms – some freshly renovated, others old and dark. All, however, share the same lovely dining room, delicious food, and big terrace views. An excellent base for climbers, the Britannia is run by Jacques and Lori Bigler, who guide walks and are themselves accomplished climbers. Book early at ☎ 027 957 16 16, www.saas-fee.ch/britannia.

The excellent tourist office is at the top of town near the parking garage. For more information, contact ☎ 027 958 18 58, www.saas-fee.ch.

Interlaken & the Jungfrau

Set in the larger area of the Bernese Oberland, the Jungfrau tourist region enjoys the distinction of being Europe's most visited Alpine playground – and its easy to see why. At its center lies Interlaken, a large town encircled by mountains and flanked by two long lakes, the **Thunersee** and the **Brienzersee**. In the town hub, an impressive network of mountain railways, passenger ferries, and cable cars make it easy to explore the surrounding Alpine grandeur. To the

The Jungfrau Region

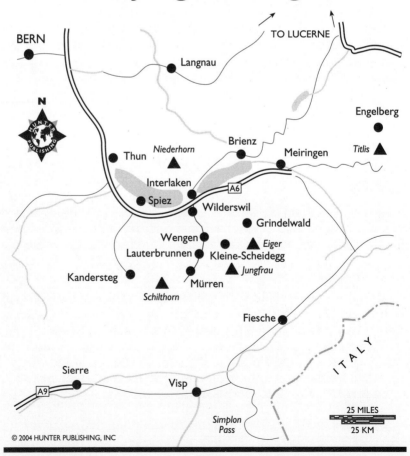

© 2004 HUNTER PUBLISHING, INC

south of the town stretches the dramatic **Lauterbrunnen Valley**; the car-free villages of **Mürren** and **Wengen** perch high above. The resort of **Grindelwald** hums with activity, and the majestic mountain trio – the **Eiger**, the **Mönch**, and the **Jungfrau** – soar in the south.

■ Interlaken

Population: 15,000

Base elevation: 567 m

Lake & mountain tourist town

At the heart of the Alps lies Switzerland; at the heart of Switzerland lies the Jungfrau region; and at the heart of the Jungfrau lies Interlaken.

Tucked away in what is arguably the most spectacular Alpine scenery in the world, Interlaken enjoys renown for its diversity of outdoor adventures and its role as the Jungfrau region's mountain transportation hub. It's an inviting town – a busy, bustling place with back alleys few tourists take time to explore.

History & Orientation

 Interlaken got its start during the 12th century, when a cloister took up residence on the land bar that now hoists up the town. Although a worthwhile destination in its own right, the town's tourist industry blossomed due to its convenient location, just north of the famous Jungfrau peaks: the Eiger, the Jungfrau, and the Mönch – names, by the way, that translate to the Ogre, the Virgin, and (in between, piously separating the two) the Monk. The valley village of Lauterbrunnen lies directly south of the Interlaken, and the resort villages of Grindelwald, Wengen, and Mürren perch in the mountains above. The region's resort villages grow smaller and quieter from east to west. Farthest east, Grindelwald buzzes with big-resort energy; over the hill to the west, Wengen slows down a bit, banning cars from its streets; and across the Lauterbrunnen Valley, the pedestrian-only village of Mürren hides out in splendid isolation.

Interlaken rests on a land bar between Lake Thun, or the Thunersee, and Lake Brienz, or the Brienzersee. However, this is not a lakefront town, per se. The town center clusters directly between the two shorelines, a fair distance from each. The Aare River runs through town between the lakes, and a ship canal forges in from the Thunersee in the west.

The Town

Interlaken has two train stations, pragmatically named the **Ostbahnhof** and the **Westbahnhof**, or the East and West stations. Ferry terminals lie just behind each; Thunersee boats dock behind the West Station; Brienzersee boats dock behind the East Station. The main boulevard, the **Höheweg**, runs from one station to the other paralleling the Aare River; midway, the **Höhematte Park** offers some semblance of a town center. The town's grandest hotel, the **Victoria Jungfrau**, fronts the park, and the **Metropole Tower** rises at its southwestern corner. A bit farther east, Höheweg briefly intersects the pedestrian zone, which centers on the streets of Jungfraustrasse, Marktgasse, Postgasse, and Neugasse.

Getting Here & Around

Visitors arriving by **air** should fly in to the international airports at Zürich, 129 km north, or Geneva, 214 km west. Allow 2½ hours driving time from Zürich, and 2½ hours driving time from Geneva. Those arriving by **car** enjoy easy access via the A8 Autobahn from Thun.

Once in town, **buses** run the city streets, and the Post Bus network well covers the surrounding region. **Boats** ply the waters of both the Thunersee and the Brienzersee, but the ferry loops make more sense as recreation than as transportation – see *Adventures in Water* below. Mountain trains depart the Interlaken Ost station for Mürren, Wengen, Grindelwald, and the Kleine Scheidegg. Mountain transport by railway is covered below under *Adventures by Rail*.

> **TIP:** Guests staying in the Jungfrau region should receive at check-in their **Eiger, Mönch, and Jungfrau Gästekarte**. The card brings a number of small price reductions that together can add up to significant savings.

Getting Connected

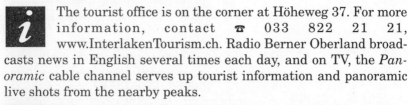

The tourist office is on the corner at Höheweg 37. For more information, contact ☎ 033 822 21 21, www.InterlakenTourism.ch. Radio Berner Oberland broadcasts news in English several times each day, and on TV, the *Panoramic* cable channel serves up tourist information and panoramic live shots from the nearby peaks.

The main post office is at Postplatz near the Interlaken West train station.

WWW For Internet access, head for the **Weltr@um Café** at Rosengarten 5. On Centralstrasse, **Yess** has terminals as well.

The Sights

 Although most tourists blow through town en route to the mountains just south, Interlaken itself offers several worthwhile sights – and several back alleys worth strolling. Walkers should wander down Höheweg, into the Kursaal gardens, around the Höhematte Park, and through the small but quaint pedestrian zone along Blumenstrasse, Neugasse, Marktgasse, and Jungfraustrasse. The **Museum of Tourism** offers an interesting look at the development of the region's tourism industry, with a focus on mountain transportation and winter sports facilities. It's open May to mid-October, Tuesday through Sunday from 2-5 pm, 5 CHF.

The **Model Railway Exhibition**, or Modelleisenbahn-Treff, offers a suitable follow-up to the Tourist Museum. Its model trains run up, into, and around an intricate tangle of tracks. It's on Rugenparkstrasse, near the Interlaken West train station, and is open mid-April through mid-October, 10 am-12 pm and 1:30-6 pm; ☎ 033 823 25 55, 7 CHF.

Just outside of town is Interlaken's newest attraction, the much-awaited **Mystery Park**. This museum and amusement park explores the world's oddest phenomena across seven themes, including ancient writings, the Giza pyramids, Mayan calendars, and outer space. It's open daily, 10 am-5:30 pm; 48 CHF. For more information, contact ☎ 033 827 57 57, www.mysterypark.ch.

The Adventures

In addition to the astounding array of outdoor recreation around the surrounding Jungfrau region – see *Grindelwald, Lauterbrunnen, Mürren,* and *Wengen*, listed separately below – Interlaken itself offers a wide range of lake, air, and mountain adventures.

On Foot

 A vast array of hikes wind throughout the Jungfrau region, with most **walkers** basing themselves in Grindelwald, Wengen, Mürren, or Lauterbrunnen – indeed, some of the Alps' most traveled trails are here. **Climbers**, too, like the region. Although most stay at higher altitudes, climbers staying in Interlaken can easily make arrangements with any of the town's adventure outfitters or the guiding specialist school, Swiss Mountain Guides (see *Sports Services* below, page 332).

Best among Interlaken's local hikes are those starting from the upper stations of the local mountain trains at Schynige Platte and Heimwehfluh. Experienced hikers should try the six-hour **Faulhorn Trail** from Schynige Platte to First Peak above Grindelwald. The trail passes through and above stunning mountain scenery, passing by the Bachalpsee and two mountain restaurants along the way. Take the Schynige Platte train to start, and return via the First cableway to Grindelwald and then railway back to Interlaken. (The reverse works just as well.)

In Water

 Interlaken loves water – even its name means "between lakes." And, indeed, the town sits between two long lakes on a land bar that was itself under water in ages past. A waterway runs through town center, connecting the two lakes, and snow-capped mountains drip clear water into several Alpine lakes. The Brienzersee sees relatively little recreational action – its banks are steep and its winds calm – but the breezy Thunersee offers a wide range of wet sports.

Swimmers head for **Neuhaus** at the northeastern edge of the Thunersee. Here, a grassy beach, lake-swimming facilities, and sand volleyball courts round out the summer facilities. A restaurant serves up food, and two outfitters offer **sailing**, **windsurfing**, and **pedal boat rentals** in addition to **wakeboarding**, **water-skiing**, and pulls on **tubes and banana-floats**. For more information, contact the sailing school's **Wake Point**, ☎ 033 822 83 30, www.swiss-sail.ch; or the **Hang Loose Surfshop** at ☎ 079 023 52 28, www.surfshop-hangloose.ch.

Whitewater sports excursions are offered by several outfitters, most notably **Alpin Raft** – see *Sports Services* below, page 332. In addition, the **Bödelibad** swimming complex offers a 25-m **indoor pool** year-round and a 50-m **outdoor pool** in summer. **Lake diving** is offered by a school in the Thunersee village of Gunten – contact the Interlaken tourist office for more information.

Summertime **fishing** is possible without permit from the shores of both the Thunersee and the Brienzersee. Permkljits for other bodies of water – or for fishing from a boat – are available at the tourist office. The tourist office also stocks info on limits, seasons, and bait regulations; stop by before you cast off. Favorite fishing holes include the Bortsee, the Bachalpsee, and the Lütschine River; all three requiring the extra permit. For **fly-fishing** guidance and instruction, contact **Pascal Zeller** at ☎ 033 823 60 88.

On the Lakes

Passenger boats make the rounds on the Thunersee year-round and on the Brienzersee from April to October. Regular service makes possible day-trips to a number of lakeshore destinations, and less frequent lake cruises feature a variety of themes. On the **Brienzersee**, boats run from behind the Interlaken East train station to docks at Brienz and Iseltwald. Round-trips to Brienz take approximately 2½ hours. The lake is the more attractive of the two and, a less subjective claim to fame, boasts the greatest average depth of all the lakes in Switzerland.

The **Thunersee** proves more popular for day excursions. Its fleet of 10 boats departs from the docks behind the Interlaken West train station, heading across the large lake to docks, including Beatenbucht and the lovely lakeside city of Thun. The round-trip takes approximately four hours. For more information, contact www.bls.ch.

AUTHOR'S PICK Children will want to meet the Thunersee's resident dragon, the fabled Ponzo. The large lizard figures prominently in the attractions around **Beatenberg**, a hillside town best reached by fanciful rides on the steam-breathing **Dragon Ship.** From the Beatenbucht boat dock, Ponzo's funicular roars up the mountain to Beatenberg; from there, a gondola rises to the peak of the **Niederhorn**, stopping midway at Vorass for those wishing to roll back down. (Trottibike scooters and mountain bikes are for rent at the valley station and can be carried up.) At the top of the Niederhorn, views, paragliders, trails, and a mountain restaurant delight adventurers of all ages. The Dragon Ship also calls at the Beatushöhlen-Sundlauenen dock and its **Dragon's Den**, a fascinating historical site also known as St. Beatus Caves.

BOAT EXCURSION ROUNDTRIP COSTS		
To	**From**	**Cost**
Thun	Interlaken West	40 CHF
Spiez	Interlaken West	28 CHF
Beatenbucht, Beatenberg & Niederhorn Loop	Interlaken West	56 CHF
Brienz	Interlaken East	32 CHF

On Wheels

Mountain bikers enjoy some 420 km of marked mountain biking routes in the Jungfrau region. In addition, 360 km of marked biking routes wind around the shores of the Thunersee. From Beatenberg, experienced riders set out on a difficult nine-km loop around the Niederhorn. **Trotti-bike scooters** are for rent at the Mittelstation Vorass above Beatenberg; ride down via either a six-km or a 12-km trail.

Back in Interlaken, **Daniel's Rentals** rents **motorcycles, jeeps, scooters**, and **bikes**. It's next door to Balmer's Hostel; ☎ 079 286 58 44. **Skaters** and **skateboarders** head for the Interlaken airfield, where a skate park is illuminated until 1 am in good weather. For inline skate rental, try **Eiger Sport** at Bahnhofstrasse 2.

■ Big-Mountain Excursions

AUTHOR'S PICK Chief among Interlaken's attractions are the famed peaks to its south – the Eiger, Mönch, and Jungfrau – and the opportunity to scale them via railway, funicular, and cable car. As the region's hub for mountain transportation, Interlaken offers a convenient base from which to set out exploring. Although expensive, these rail routes are some of the most memorable in Europe, and I hope you'll do at least one. Each can be completed in a half-day if you choose the quickest connections, but we'd recommend lingering awhile in the villages along the way. The following are just two of the region's big-mountain excursions.

The Jungfraujoch, nicknamed The Top of Europe, is the region's classic mountain excursion loop. In fact, when you return home from Switzerland, "Did you go up the Jungfrau?" is probably the first question you'll get. The outing departs from Interlaken's east train station, passes into the **Lauterbrunnen Valley**, then loops up to **Klein Scheidegg** via either **Wengen** or **Grindelwald**. (We think the clockwise, Grindelwlad-first route offers the more dramatic approach, but reasonable people disagree. To see it all, complete the loop on your way back down.) From Klein Scheidegg, the Jungfraujochbahn railway climbs up a tunnel just inside the Eiger's North Face, making two in-mountain stops at viewpoints along the way – viewpoints also used as rescue stations from which to aide stranded climbers. At the top, 3,454 m up, visitors enjoy panoramic views from the terrace, visits to the Sphinx research center, and wanders through the tunnels and the Ice Palace, a cave carved out of the Aletsch Glacier. In summer, huskies pull sleds, guides lead treks, and skiers, climbers, and sledders play on the glacial ice. It's a spectacular journey that may well produce your trip's most memorable moments. Transportation links operate year-round. Allow at least six hours. www.jungfraujoch.ch.

Above: St. Moritz with Muottas Muragl in background

Below: Hotel Waldhaus, St. Moritz

Above: Zürich Old Town and River Limmat

Below: Winterthür

...ch amd the lake, with St. Peters Church in front and Fraumünster Cathedral behind.

Grindelwald cable car with the Wetterhorn behind

The Schilthorn lies across the Lauterbrunnen Valley from the majestic trio, the Eiger, Mönch, and Jungfrau – offering an ideal vantage point from which to view the big-picture panorama. The Schilthorn loop starts with a train ride from Interlaken to **Lauterbrunnen**, continues with a climb via Mountain Railway to Grütschalp and along the cliff to **Mürren**. After visiting the lovely little car-free village, visitors ascend to Piz Gloria on the Schilthorn summit. Here, views stretch out in all directions, and a revolving restaurant serves meals. Much is made of the mountain station's role in the James Bond flick *On Her Majesty's Secret Service*. Piz Gloria provided the primary set for the film – clips screen today in the mountaintop theater. Adventurers return to the valley via cableway to **Stechelberg**, traveling back to Interlaken by bus. Although it's not as renowned as the Jungfraujoch loop, the Schilthorn is the favorite excursion of many visitors who've done both. They laud its 360° panoramic views, its *007* connections, and its proximity to charming, cliff-side Mürren. Transportation links operate year-round except during maintenance closures for a few days in late April, and for three weeks late November through early December; links as far as Mürren operate year-round. Allow at least five hours. www.schilthorn.ch.

> **TIP:** The Berner Oberland's Panorama cable channel broadcasts live shots from rotating cameras perched at mountain stations. Although weather conditions can change quickly on the mountain, it's worthwhile to check conditions before you hop the train or lift. These are expensive excursions, and bad weather or low visibility greatly diminishes their worth.

■ Local Mountain Excursions

Although less glamorous than the Jungfrau and Schilthorn loops, several worthwhile excursions ascend the foothills at Interlaken's doorstep. Perfect for family outings and area orientation rides, these trips are far less expensive than the state-of-the-art, peak-scaling outings above.

Schynige Platte should be your choice if you only have time for one local mountain excursion. The trip starts out with a short train ride from Interlaken East Station to Wilderswil and a transfer to the Schynige cogwheel railway. At the top, views reach out to the Eiger, Mönch, and Jungfrau, and trails head off in several directions. The Schynige Platte Hotel offers dining service on its terrace, and an Alpine garden boasts over 500 species of plants. Transportation links operate from the end of May through mid-October; allow at least three hours.

Those traveling with children should request the booklet Tammi & Tomi: The Last Screw, *from the valley station of the Schynige Platte train. The book tells the story behind the local Teddyland hoopla, and kids enjoy searching out the story's scenes.*

The **Harder Kulm** funicular departs from the northern edge of town, across the river from Interlaken East train station. In just eight minutes, visitors rise to sweeping views of the Thunersee, the Brienzersee, and the Jungfrau rising above in the south. At the top there's a short walking loop, the Goblin's Path, and at the bottom, a tree nursery and a small animal park with chamois and marmots – both the nursery and park are free. Transportation links operate May through October; allow at least one hour.

Visitors ascend **Heimwehfluh** in just five minutes via a nostalgic old funicular, departing a base at the southwestern edge of town just behind the Interlaken West train station. At the top, views stretch over the lakes and back to the Jungfrau. Although more a hill than a mountain, the Heimwehfluh proves popular with families, who enjoy a large playground, a show model railway, and two summer toboggan runs – one a slide, one on rails. The funicular operates from April through October; allow at least one hour.

MOUNTAIN RAIL EXCURSIONS ROUNDTRIP COSTS		
To	**From**	**Cost**
Jungfraujoch loop (rail)	Interlaken East	168 CHF*
	Lauterbrünnen	155 CHF*
	Kleine Scheidegg	102 CHF*
Kleine Scheidegg loop (rail)	Interlaken East	66 CHF
	Lauterbrünnen	53 CHF
Schilthorn loop (rail & cable car)	Interlaken East	106 CHF
Schilthorn roundtrip (cable car)	Stechelberg	95 CHF
Schilthorn roundtrip (cable car)	Mürren	63 CHF
Mürren loop (rail & cable car)	Interlaken East	41 CHF
	Lauterbrünnen	24 CHF
Schynige Platte rountrip (rail)	Interlaken East	57 CHF
Harder Külm roundtrip (funicular)	Interlaken East	22 CHF
Heimwehfluh roundtrip (funicular)	Interlaken West	10 CHF
*Save 20-30% by taking an early train and descending the Jungfraujoch before noon.		

In the Air

 During my last visit to Interlaken, I collected a dozen brochures from outfitters offering airborne sports – and I wasn't even looking that hard. The region's favorable wind conditions make flying extremely popular here, and activities range from paragliding jumps to glacier flights. **Bungee-jumpers** leap out of cable cars, off bridges, and into canyon gorges. **Hang-gliding** and **paragliding** excursions are offered by at least 100 outfitters; make arrangements through **Alpin Center** or **Alpin Raft**, both listed below under *Sports Services*. For **ballooning**, contact **Max Michel**, ☎ 031 911 13 08 or the tourist office.

Skydive Switzerland and **Scenic Air** pair up to offer a good range of outings, including **tandem skydiving** from planes and helicopters, **scenic flights**, and **glacier-landing flights**. In addition, they offer **fly-to-ride heli-sking** and an **airborne ski shuttle** to Zermatt and the Matterhorn. For more info, contact ☎ 033 826 77 17, www.skydiveswitzerland.com, www.scenicair.ch.

 For a memorable adventure – or perhaps a positive reply to a marriage proposal – Scenic Air will lift you high above the region's lakes and mountains, land on ancient glacial ice and, on request, provide a champagne picnic.

On Snow & Ice

 Interlaken's rail network makes it a reasonable location from which to explore the region's **skiing and snowboarding** slopes, a network of some 205 km of runs and 45 lifts jointly marketed under the moniker of the Jungfrau TopSki Region. Cooperating ski areas include Grindelwald, Wengen, and Mürren (see separate listings below). The old railways provide much of the transfer service between the areas; they're a quaint but painfully slow way to get around, however, and snow-sport enthusiasts shouldn't plan to visit more than one resort each day. For example, transfer from Mürren to Kleine Scheidegg above Grindelwald will take you approximately 1½ hours; the trip from Interlaken to above Kleine Scheidegg takes just slightly less. Nonetheless, if you're prepared for the haul, Interlaken makes a good-value base.

For local on-ice sports, head to the **Bödeli** recreation complex. Its artificial rink is open to the public for **ice-skating**, and equipment is for rent. For more information, contact ☎ 033 822 61 63.

Switzerland

Snowshoeing is on the menu at several local adventure outfitters. The local specialist, however, is **Base Camp**; ☎ 033 823 93 23, www.basecamp.ch.

Ice-climbing, glacier trekking, and **high-mountain tours** are offered by several outfitters, in particular the mountaineering specialists at **Swiss Alpine Guides** – see *Sports Services,* below.

In the Extreme

Interlaken caters to its youthful crowd with the Alps' widest selection of extreme sports outfitters – **Alpin Raft**, **Outdoor Interlaken**, and **Alpin Center** are three of the most reputable; contact info for each is listed below under *Sports Services*. With 14 years in the businesss, Alpin Raft offers a good selection of activities and an admirable safety record. The group specializes in **whitewater** activities, including **rafting** on four rivers and **canyoning** at six locales. Its **bungee-jumping** venues include a glacier and a canyon, and its air team offers **sky diving, paragliding**, and **hang gliding**.

Outdoor Interlaken offers a similar program. An affiliate of the Swiss Ski and Snowboard School, Alpin Center focuses on ski instruction and guiding in addition to its all-season offerings.

For a rip-roaring good time, call Alpin Center and book an appointment for **zorbing** (shown above) – a new adventure sport that involves rolling down a hill inside an inflatable transparent ball.

Sports Services, Outfitters & Guides

■ The **Swiss Ski and Snowboard School** offers a wide range of winter sports programs in addition to its **Alpin Center** adventure sports program. For more information, stop by their shop in Wilderswil or contact ☎ 033 838 55 23, www.alpincenter.ch.

■ **Swiss Alpine Guides** runs a selection of adventure sports, but really shines as an all-season mountaineering school. Private guiding, private instruction, and group courses are offered – options cover terrain from rock to ice. Check in at ☎ 33 822 60 00, www.swissAlpineguides.ch.

■ The **Intersport Rent Network** offers a good selection of new equipment from 11 shops in five villages around the Jungfrau region. Each offers rentals, service, and the kicker here – equipment exchange whenever and wherever you want it. Just take your rented equipment to any of the network's shops to swap. For more info, check in at Intersport Oberland at Postgasse 16 in Interlaken; ☎ 033 822 06 61.

■ **Alpin Raft** – see *In the Extreme* above; ☎ 033 823 41 00, www.alpinraft.com.

■ **Outdoor Interlaken** – see *In the Extreme* above; ☎ 033 826 77 19, www.outdoor-interlaken.com.

Where to Sleep

Hotel Victoria-Jungfrau ($$$$) is the queen bee in Interlaken, a grand old Belle Époque affair dominating the center and sprawling along the Höhematte Park. It's next to the casino, equidistant from either train station, and equipped with an in-house daycare program. Book at ☎ 033 828 28 28, www.Victoria-jungfrau.ch.

In a lovely location near the Interlaken East train station, fronting the Aarve River, the **Lindner Grand Beau Rivage** ($$$-$$$$) has much of Victoria's old-world grandeur but at substantially lower rates. Inquire at ☎ 033 826 70 07, www.lindnerhotels.ch.

The **Hotel Metropole** ($$$), in the center in the town's highest tower, has modern commercial rooms, an indoor pool, expense-account prices, and a businesslike manner; ☎ 033 828 66 66, www.metropole-interlaken.ch.

The **Hotel du Lac** ($$$) sits on the waterway between the boat dock and the Interlaken East train station, a good locale for early-morning rail departures into the mountains. Unless you're a huge fan of trains, book a water-view room; ☎ 033 822 29 22, www.bestwestern.ch/dulacinterlaken.

The **Hotel Neuhaus** ($$-$$$) has lakeside rooms and cheery décor on the grassy beach at Thunersee. Also available are family rooms, with two separate sleeping areas. Contact ☎ 033 822 82 82, www.hotel-neuhaus.ch.

For lodging along the center's Jungfraustrasse pedestrian street, try the homey **Hotel Toscana** ($$$); ☎ 033 823 30 33, www.ho-

HOTEL PRICE CHART	
Double room without tax; $$$-$$$$ always with bath.	
$	Under 120 CHF
$$	121-225 CHF
$$$	226-375 CHF
$$$$	Over 375 CHF

Switzerland

tel-toscana.ch. Or nearby, the inexpensive **Hotel Blume** ($-$$); ☎ 033 822 71 31, www.hotel-blume.ch.

There is no shortage of hostel accommodations. Best among the bunch for my buck is still **Balmer's Herberge** ($), Switzerland's classic youth hostel stay. The central, chalet-style complex is rowdy, energized perhaps by the extreme sports outfitter that books adventure outings – canyoning, rafting, bungee-jumping, ice climbing, ski tours and such – directly at the hostel. Nightly movies, a guest kitchen, a coin laundry, and e-mail access are offered. In summer, out near the autobahn, **Balmer's Tent** ($) bunks overflow guests. Contact Balmer's at ☎ 033 822 19 61, www.balmers.com. We've heard good things, too, about the **Backpacker's Villa** ($), an old chalet in the center near Höhematte Park, ☎ 033 826 71 71, www.villa.ch; and the basic **Happy Inn Lodge** ($) sits above the popular bar Brasserie 17, ☎ 033 822 32 25.

> **TIP:** Interlaken offers a good range of budget accommodations, making it an attractive base during the winter season, when rates in the mountain resorts soar.

The best of the summertime **camping** ($) is lakeside at Neuhaus at **Alpenblick**; ☎ 033 823 14 70, www.camping-alpenblick.ch. Or, beautifully set at the foot of a cliff and waterfall, the **Jungfrau** in Lauterbrunnen. The latter rents bungalows as well; ☎ 033 856 20 20, www.camping-jungfrau.ch; open winter, too.

Where to Eat

Great gourmet fare can be found at the **Jungfrau Brasserie** ($$$) in the Victoria Jungfrau Hotel. Its elegant Art Nouveau dining room dishes up creative Swiss specialties; reserve a table at ☎ 033 828 28 28.

DINING PRICE CHART	
Average entrée, with tax.	
$	Under 15 CHF
$$	16-37 CHF
$$$	Over 37 CHF

At the eastern end of town **La Bonne Fourchette** ($$$) offers elegant French cuisine served in a fireside dining room and accompanied by live music. It's in the Hotel Beau Rivage; contact ☎ 033 826 70 07 for reservations.

Near the Interlaken West train station, at Bahnhofstrasse 4, the inconspicuous **Le Caveau** ($$-$$$) has a small, simple dining room and delicious French and Swiss specialties, including local fish dishes and meat fondue; ☎ 033 823 24 65.

Out at the lake, the **Neuhaus Zum See** ($$-$$$) does good regional specialties and has an outdoor terrace directly on the Thunersee lakeshore; ☎ 033 822 82 82.

For reasonably priced Swiss specialties, head for my favorite restaurant in town, the **Loöwen** ($$), on the main pedestrian square at Marktgasse 10; ☎ 033 821 05 05. Across the square, try also the restaurant **Bären** ($$) in the hotel of the same name – I've heard its fondues are excellent; ☎ 033 822 76 76.

In the pedestrian area, along Jungfraustrasse, try the **Trattoria Toscana** ($$) for good Italian; ☎ 033 823 30 33. And **El Azteca** ($$) at the Hotel Blume offers Tex-Mex – they have a good veggie fajita; ☎ 033 822 71 31.

Fronting the casino and the Kursaal gardens, **Fujiyama** ($$) has the town's best Japanes cuisine. Next door, the Victoria-Jungfrau offers chic styling and good Italian fare in its **Pastateca** ($$); ☎ 033 828 28 28.

Budgeting visitors enjoy the cheerful **PizPaz** ($), where a long list of pizzas and a good corner locale draws a young crowd. It's at Centralplatz; ☎ 033 822 25 33. Try, too, the self-service restaurant in the **Coop** ($) at Interlaken East.

Where to Party

Much of Interlaken's nightlife is geared to the youthful crowd attracted by its good selection of hostels. First, the ever-popular **Brasserie 17** has live music each Thursday from September through June starting at 9 pm. It's in the Happy Inn at Rosenstrasse 17; ☎ 033 822 32 25. In the pedestrian zone, the **Löwen** on the Marktstrasse serves beer till late and, just around the corner at Postgasse 3, the **Hüsi Pub** is the town's favorite dive bar with DJs, darts, and video games. **Johnny's Club** in the Hotel Carlton draws a local crowd with frequent live music, and the **Black & White** disco gets rowdy late night on Höheweg.

For more elegant evenings, the **Restaurant Shuh** has tea on the menu, a mature crowd at the tables, and a pianist at the keyboard. Check in at Höheweg 56; ☎ 033 822 94 41. The **Interlaken Casino** is located amid the gardens of the Kursaal at Strandbadstrasse 44. It offers slots, roulette, and blackjack; ☎ 033 827 61 00, www.casino-kursaal.ch.

Evening entertainment can be had at Spycher Restaurant's **Folklore Show**, where a dinner, music, and dance production runs daily from May through October; ☎ 033 827 61 00. Also entertaining, the **William Tell Open Air Theatre** stages the classic Swiss tales on a grand scale with some 180 actors and dozens of farm animals. The play runs one or two times each week from mid-June through early September. For more info, contact ☎ 033 822 37 22, www.tellspiele.ch.

Where to Play

The Jungfrau region offers more to families and children than any other mountain destination I know. In and around Interlaken, kids enjoy family-oriented activities like lake cruises aboard the Dragon Boat, cable car and train rides, year-round snow play, wildlife parks, model railways, hiking, horse-drawn carriage rides, and the new **Mystery Park**. (And the list could go on.) A **children's train** runs through the center during summer, and the **Toy Library Jojo** allows checkout of games and toys; contact ☎ 033 822 87 86 for more information. **Playgrounds** are at Höhematte Park, near the east school, in the Kursaal garden, and on the mountain at Heimwehfluh.

> **TIP:** Although most families come to Interlaken to play together, the tourist office can provide current information regarding daytime childcare and babysitting.

Festivals & Events

Interlaken and the Jungfrau host many popular events, both in the town and in the mountains. As the mountains are easily reached via Interlaken, I include the events of both Interlaken and the mountain resorts here.

The year kicks off in mid-January, when the **FIS World Cup** races hit town for the **Lauberhornrennen** in Wengen. Mürren cuts loose a week later with the **Infernorennen**, a legendary race that is, together with the Kandahar race, one of the two oldest surviving ski events in the world. It was first held in 1928, and today, each year 1,800 amateurs to experts come to town to rip down the 12-km course, one after the other, all day long. Also in mid-January, Grindelwald hosts the **World Snow Festival**, an impressive ice festival during which snow-carvers whittle away at blocks that areeach the size of a small house.

In March, the **Horischlitten Race** sees the racing of traditional long-horned sleds down the Eiger Run. In early April, the region hosts the **Snowpen Air Rock Concert**, an outdoor party on the Kleine Scheidegg slopes. And thus, with an echo off the Eiger, the winter season clangs to a close.

May brings the **World Barbecue Gold Cup** to the Kursaal and Casino park, and June hauls in the **International Trucker and Country Festival**, drawing top names in country music and an appreciative crowd. In mid-August Interlaken celebrates its **Village Festival** with musical entertainment, games, and folklore, and for two weeks between mid- and late August, the **Interlaken Music Festival** offers a wealth of classical music. The summer ends in September with the **International Jungfrau Marathon**, a grueling race from Interlaken up to Wengen and Klein Scheidegg. The course has a vertical climb of 1,525 m and is aptly nicknamed the most beautiful marathon course in the world.

 For more information, contact the tourist office on the corner at Höheweg 37; ☎ 033 822 21 21, www.InterlakenTourism.ch.

Grindelwald

The busy resort of Grindelwald sprawls out in a wide valley 25 km southeast of Interlaken. The resort lies at the center of the Jungfraujoch rail loop (covered in detail in the Interlaken section) – an excursion so popular as to crowd the village and its main thoroughfare with day-trippers year-round. The 3,970-m North Face of the Eiger and the 3,701-m Wetterhorn dominate the valley from above. The Jungfrau and the Mönch tower just behind, glaciers lap at the valley floor, and mountain rail- and cableways chug in all directions.

LIFT PASS PRICE SAMPLES

Winter

1-day Grindelwald & Wengen	55 CHF
6-day Grindelwald & Wengen.	254 CHF
6-day Jungfrau region	282 CHF
Jungfrau supplement with 3-day or more pass. .	50 CHF

Pedestrian:

Round-trip to First.	48 CHF
Round-trip Jungfraujoch	150 CHF

For all this hustle and bustle, however, Grindelwald's mountain transportation network moves at a sluggish pace. Old mountain trains crawl up toward the Eiger and Kleine Scheidegg, and in winter the cableways to First and Männlichen often back up with crowds. That said, Grindelwald remains one of the best hiking bases in the Alps, with 300 km of hiking trails winding through the area in summer – and a whopping 80 km are groomed for winter walking as well. Mountain bikers ride on 160 km of marked routes, and all manner of extreme adventures can be arranged – check in with the tour-

Switzerland

ist office for more info. The year-round sports center offers an enormous indoor swimming pool, wellness facilities, curling rinks, and an indoor ice rink and stadium. In winter, skiers and snowboarders head for the First area above town or hop a train to the Kleine Scheidegg at the foot of the Eigerwand and Jungfrau. Non-skiers, too, enjoy winter activities – a wide range of fun including some 57 km of tobogganing runs.

Top Tobogganing

Grindelwald and its surroundings offer some of the most expansive sledding runs in the Alps. It also boasts the **world's longest sledding run**, a 15-km trail from First down to Grindelwald via Faulhorn and Bussalp. Other trails include the 4½-km **Speed Run** from Bussalp to Weidli and the groomed **Eiger Run** from near the Wengernalp Railway down to Grindelwald Grund. Just like ski runs, sledding runs here are graded with easy, intermediate, and advanced designations. Toboggan rentals are available; several runs are illuminated for nighttime sledding, and several mountain huts offer atmospheric fondue evenings – followed, of course, by a high-speed slide back to the village. Check with the tourist office to see what's on.

Want to stay? Grindelwald has all manner of accommodations; I recommend finding a hotel off the main road and a room with an Eiger view. For rustic luxury in the center, try the **Schweizerhof** ($$$$), a sprawling old chalet just above the train station. The rooms are simple and cozy; the food is gourmet. Reserve at ☎ 033 853 22 02, www.hotel-schweizerhof.com.

Above the village, 100 m above the First cableway valley station, the **Hotel Bodmi** ($$-$$$) is a modern chalet offering family-run accommodations and big views. The hotel sits near the ski school in winter and in a pasture in summer; apartments are available here, too. Contact ☎ 033 853 12 20, www.bodmi.ch.

> **TIP:** Those here solely to ski or hike may appreciate the isolation of Klein Scheidegg – a cluster of hotels dwarfed at the foot of the Eiger Wall. Consider the historical **Scheidegg Hotel**, a creaky old house at the base of the Jungfraujoch railway; ☎ 033 855 12 12, www.scheidegg-hotels.ch.

For more information, check with Grindelwald Tourismus. It's in the sports center; ☎ 033 854 12 12, www.grindelwald.com.

Lauterbrunnen

The Lauterbrunnen Valley stretches from Interlaken south toward Stechelberg. It's a narrow, steep-walled glacier gorge – cliffs rise on both sides, and waterfalls plunge all around. The village of Lauterbrunnen has just 1,000 residents, most of them employed in the tourist industry. They adeptly cater to the busy crowds that pass through or park cars here en route to auto-free Wengen, soaring above in the east, and Mürren, dangling cliff-side to the west. Although few tourists stop here for long, the valley makes a good-value accommodations base and is itself well worth exploring.

AUTHOR'S PICK Aside from the general attraction of its staggering natural beauty, the Lauterbrunnen Valley's main tourist draw is the spectacular **Trümmelbach Falls**, a collection of 10 glacier waterfalls roaring inside the mountain. An elevator and a network of walkway galleries climb alongside the chutes, where up to 21,000 gallons of water per second drain down from the Eiger, Mönch, and Jungfrau above. The glacial falls are the only accessible subterranean waterfalls in Europe. Trümmelbach is open from April through November from 9 am-5 pm; for more info, dial ☎ 033 855 32 32. Two other waterfalls in the valley are worth seeking out as well. The **Staubbachfall** drops some 300 m from a cliff near Mürren and, at the end of the valley, the **Sefinenfall** plunges straight to the valley floor.

Want to stay? Lauterbrunnen has a nice selection of good-value accommodations. I liked the **Hotel Schützen** ($$), a chalet property squeezed between the main road and the valley wall. Rooms are dark and simple, but most have balconies; there's a pleasant terrace restaurant and big views of the Jungfrau and waterfall; and in winter, the ski run from Mürren empties out right behind the hotel (although poor snow conditions frequently close the route). Book at ☎ 033 855 20 32, www.hotelschuetzen.com.

Lauterbrunnen's busy tourist information office is just across from the train station. Inquire at ☎ 033 856 85 68, www.wengen-muerren.ch.

Wengen

Perched across the Lauterbrunnen Valley from Mürren, over the Männlichen from Grindelwald, and around the corner from the Jungfrau, Mönch, and Eiger, the village of Wengen is the Jungfrau

Switzerland

region's high-altitude middle ground. The car-free village sits at 1,274 m, some 400 m above the Lauterbrunnen Valley floor. (Visitors should park cars in the garage at Lauterbrunnen and ride the train up to the village.) Particularly popular with British families, the resort offers an ambiance quieter than that of Grindelwald and an infrastructure somewhat more developed than that of tiny Mürren.

Wengen is above all a quiet place for a restful holiday. In summer, trails head off in all directions; in winter, ski runs wind down to town from just below the Eiger Wall. A new cable car plies to the Männlichen Peak directly from the center of town, and the Jungfraujoch train route comes through town, too; both operate year-round. Kids enjoy a big outdoor swimming pool in summer and village-center nursery slopes in winter. Parents appreciate the sport center's childcare center, which accepts children from 18 months of age. Several hotels offer public use of their indoor pools, and there's outdoor ice skating and curling in the winter.

LIFT PASS PRICE SAMPLES

Winter

1-day Grindelwald & Wengen	55 CHF
6-day Grindelwald & Wengen.	254 CHF
6-day Jungfrau region	282 CHF
Jungfrau supplement with 3-day or more pass . .	50 CHF

Pedestrian:

Loop via Männlichen & Kleine Scheidegg	99 CHF
Round-trip to Jungfraujoch	138 CHF

Want to stay? Wengen's accommodations tend toward aging Belle Epoque grandeur. Many require half- or full-board meal arrangements, which works out well since there are few non-hotel restaurants in town. Our pick for luxury is the **Regina** ($$$-$$$$), a lovely old villa with a hilltop locale, flower-strewn balconies, a wellness program, and the town's best restaurant. Book a room at ☎ 033 856 58 58, www.wengen.com/hotel/regina.

A five-minute walk south of the center, the **Hotel Hirschen** ($$-$$$) is a homey old chalet with basic rooms and a good location at the foot of the home run in winter and at the head of the hiking trails in summer. It's known more for its food than its rooms – the restaurant serves up grilled and meat fondue specialties and hosts a weekly barbeque in summer. Contact ☎ 033 855 15 44, www.hirschen-wengen.ch.

Wengen's information office is in the center along the main pedestrian drag. Head around the corner to your left as you exit the train station. For more info, contact ☎ 033 855 14 14, www.wengen-muerren.ch.

■ Mürren

Cable car ascending the south side of the Schilthorn above Mürren, with the Eiger in the distance.

Spectacular, magnificent, astounding, and extraordinary; one tends toward superlatives when describing the village of Mürren. Allow us just a few.

Set splendidly – *impossibly* – on the precipice of an 800-m cliff, the tiny village of Mürren glories in Alpine tradition, its car-free alleys winding among rustic old chalets, its balconies strewn with flowers or tucked under thick duvets of snow. It's the place I run to for a romantic weekend, a tranquil retreat amid the Alps' most majestic terrain. In short, I'm an unabashed fan.

Mürren owes its allure to three attributes. First, its location is unmatched for sheer beauty. The resort runs steeply up the hillside along the ledge of a granite wall, gazing east across the Lauterbrunnen Valley toward an in-your-face panorama of the Eiger, Mönch, and Jungfrau peaks. Second, the village bans cars from its narrow alleys, allowing access only via rail from Lauterbrunnen or cableway from Stechelberg – ditch your car in a lot at either base. Mürren's 500 residents and its visitors alike move about on foot and by train and cableway; in winter, toboggans prove the most efficient means of transport – rent yours on arrival from the local sporting goods store. Third, the village enforces strict architectural codes. While several of its hotels are grand old remnants of the Belle Epoque boom, its homes are rustic wooden chalets, with most façades stacked with firewood in winter and bursting with flowers in summer.

Switzerland

Much of the James Bond flick On Her Majesty's Secret Service *was filmed on location on Mürren's Schilthorn Mountain and inside Piz Gloria, its futuristic lift terminal. The resort milks the association for all it's worth, offering 007 deals on everything from breakfast to souvenir pins. As kitschy as it sounds, the rotating restaurant's 007 breakfast is a darn nice way to start the day. Inquire at your hotel for reservations.*

Mürren sits at the foot of the Schilthorn, a 2,970-m peak popular with day-tripping tourists year-round. In summer, hiking trails head up from the village toward the peak and down toward the hamlet of Gimmelwald and on to the Lauterbrunnen floor. In winter, skiers enjoy access to the Jungfrau's TopSki network – although in practice Mürren is a long haul by lift and rail to the other included resorts. The local pistes have a good variety of runs, and several mountain huts offer atmospheric dining and après-ski. In town, visitors swim in the sports center's indoor pool, stroll cleared walking trails, and ice-skate on a large outdoor rink. For dinner, don't miss the traditional Swiss specialties served up on the back porch of the ramshackle old Stägerstübli; ☎ 033 855 13 16.

Lift Pass Price Samples

Winter

1-day Mürren	55 CHF
6-day Mürren	239 CHF
6-day Jungfrau region	282 CHF
Jungfrau supplement with 3+ -day pass	50 CHF

Pedestrian:

Round-trip to Schilthorn	64 CHF
Round-trip to Jungfraujoch	170 CHF

Want to stay? Like many others, we're impressed with the hospitality of the **Hotel Alpenruh** ($$$), a chalet hotel with big balconies, big views, and a convenient location near the village station of the Stechelberg cable car, the lift by which visitors enter town. For more info, check ☎ 033 856 88 00, www.hotelschilthorn.ch.

At the opposite end of the village, across from the railway station, the **Eiger Guesthouse** ($-$$) offers a solid budget option, and the excellent bar downstairs draws a friendly and young British clientele. To reserve, contact ☎ 033 856 54 60, www.muerren.ch/eigerguesthouse.

> **TIP:** Overnight guests enjoy the atmospheric events at several mountain huts. The **Bergrestaurant Winteregg** offers an Alpine Breakfast with folk music each Sunday during summer; in the winter, the hut has fondue and grill evening every Saturday. For more info or reservations, dial ☎ 033 855 18 93. The **Allmendhübel** does weekly fondue nights as well – guests can tote toboggans up on the funicular and sled home after dinner. Contact ☎ 033 855 25 12 for reservations.

For more information, stop in at the tourist information office in the sports center or contact ☎ 033 856 86 86, www.wengen-muerren.ch.

Zürich & Central Switzerland

Although not normally fans of urban chaos, I was delighted with the city of Zürich. Long a bastion of conservative Swiss norms, the metropolis thumps today with an emerging artistic beat. Set on the northern edge of the Alps, the lakeside town has a large, well-preserved old town and an impressive wealth of art and architecture. Well-connected links head north to the museum town of Winterthür and the spectacular Rheinfalls. To the south, at one point of the spidery Vierwaldstättersee, the city of Lucerne draws tourists year-round for its lovely lakeside old town and its easy access to the nearby mountain recreation areas, including the famed Titlis Peak above Engelberg.

■ Zürich

Population: 363,000

Base elevation: 409 m

Gateway tourist city

Zürich's newest marketing slogan, "Live it, Love it," sums up the city's newfound lust for life. Once a stronghold of religious piety, then a bastion of world finance, the Zürich of today has let down its counter-cultural hair. Ready for the excitement of a city break? Join pleasure-seeking weekenders from all over Europe as they flock to Zürich for shopping, dining, art, theater, and a thumping underground nightlife.

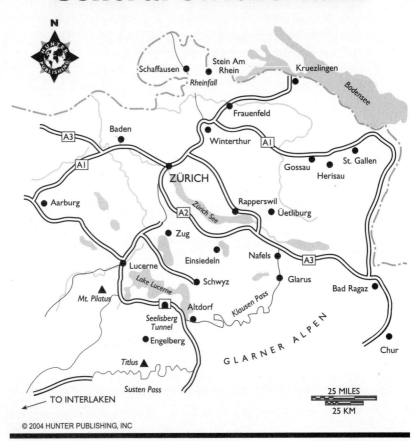

Central Switzerland

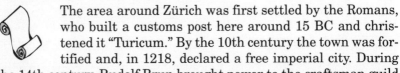

© 2004 HUNTER PUBLISHING, INC

History & Orientation

The area around Zürich was first settled by the Romans, who built a customs post here around 15 BC and christened it "Turicum." By the 10th century the town was fortified and, in 1218, declared a free imperial city. During the 14th century, Rudolf Brun brought power to the craftsman guild houses – many of which are still in operation – and the city signed on to the Swiss Confederation. A new wave of cultural change came in 1523, when local preacher Huldrych Zwingli shepherded the Reformation into Switzerland, and the city's Grossmünster Church became a haven for students and dissident Catholics from all over Europe. Based largely on the discipline, individualism, and work ethic instilled by Zwingli and his "pray and work" motto, Zürich built its wealth and, in the 19th and 20th centuries, emerged as an economic leader in industry, insurance, and banking. It is only recently that the city has indulged its much more hedonistic bent.

The city of Zürich nestles among the wooded, rolling hills of central Switzerland and sprawls along the banks of the Limmat River and the northern shore of Lake Zürich – in German, the *Zürichsee*. Although it's Switzerland's largest city, although it's sometimes raucous, and although it's always expensive, vibrant Zürich enjoys what independent researchers have deemed "the highest quality of life in the world."

The Town

Most of Zürich's sights lie south of the Hauptbahnhof train station on a triangular peninsula bordered by the Sihl and Limmat rivers and the lakeshore. **Bahnhofstrasse**, the wide boulevard running from the station down to the Bürkliplatz docks, is the home of Zürich's famed banks and boutique shops, while the quaint **old town** and **Schipfe** district tuck away along cobblestone alleys between Bahnhofstrasse and the western bank of the Limmat River. Just across the river, the trendy **Niederdorf**, or "**Dörfli**," district stretches south toward the lake in a delightful web of hip shops, seedy bars, and popular streetside cafés. Farther south, lakeside parks and promenades line both the east and west shores of **Lake Zürich**. Heading south on the western shore, visitors will find **Mythenquai**; down the eastern shore, the **Utoquai** and the parks at **Zürichhorn**.

Getting Here & Around

 International **air** travelers will arrive at the international airport, just 10 minutes by rail from the city center. The airport offers the services of 152 airlines, making it Switzerland's largest. Zürich is a major **rail** hub, as well – 95% of Swiss rail destinations are reachable with no more than one transfer. Drivers will find the city a challenge, as both navigation and parking are difficult, and once a parking spot is secured, most will be happier moving about on foot.

First and foremost, Zürich is a city of pedestrians. The compact center is easily accessed on foot, and walking, biking, and riding trams prove the most efficient and enjoyable means of travel. Better still, the extensive public transportation network proves surprisingly economical. **Bikes** are rented here for *free* – just show an ID and place a deposit at the train station – and inexpensive **tram** passes are offered by the trip, day, or week.

> **TIP:** For active visitors, the new **Zürich Card** can be a bargain. Cardholders enjoy free, unlimited use of all public transport in the greater Zürich area – including trains, buses, trams, boats, and funiculars. Also included is admission to 43 of the city's museums, welcome drinks at selected restaurants, and substantial discounts on several city tours and attractions. Cards can be purchased for either 24 or 72 hours (15 CHF and 30 CHF respectively) at the Hauptbahnhof tourist office, at your hotel, or at the Bürkliplatz boat docks.

Although ferries do ply up and down the Limmat and between several lakeside villages, most tourists in Zürich board boats for purely recreational reasons. Check out the wide array of boat tours available at the Bürkliplatz docks, or hop aboard a riverboat at any Limmat landing.

Getting Connected

The tourist information office is in the main train station at the northern end of Bahnhofstrasse. The often-crowded office doles out loads of brochures, makes hotel reservations, and sells the already popular Zürich Card. The office is open in the winter from 8:30 am-7 pm Monday through Saturday, 9 am-6:30 pm Sunday; and in the summer from 8 am-8:30 pm Monday through Saturday, 8:30 am-6:30 pm Sunday. For more information, dial ☎ 01 215 40 00, www.zuerich.ch.

The main post office, *Sihlpost*, is at Käsernenstrasse 95/97, just around the corner at the southwest end of the train station. It's open Monday through Friday from 6:30 am-10:30 pm and on Saturday from 6:30 am-10 pm. A second branch is in the Hauptbahnhof near the southern entrance of the station.

WWW Several cafés offer Internet access and other business services, the best of which is the aptly dubbed **Internet Café** at Uraniastrasse 3, a five-minute walk southeast of the main train station. Other options include **Cybergate Stars**, on Bahnhofplatz, and **Quanta**, at Limmatquai 94.

The Sights

A pedestrian's paradise, Zürich is best toured on foot. That said, and although it has its share of attractions, the city is loved more for its pulsing ambience than its circuit of "sights." So relax and wander. Instead of setting out to look *at* something, set out to simply look *around*.

Zürich gurgles with the sound of water. Its cobbled squares have more than 1,100 ornamental fountains, all of which – according to locals – bubble with pure, potable H_2O. Take a drink, not a dip, as bathing in fountain waters is generally frowned upon.

The city's central districts are well worth a wander, and visitors should note a few of the old city's most recognizable landmarks. Built in the 12th century, the **Grossmünster Cathedral** dominates the eastern bank of the Limmat River. The church is historically significant as the base of the Swiss Reformation movement as instigated by Huldrych Zwingli. Visitors can climb the church tower for magnificent city views from mid-March through October, 9:15 am-5 pm. Facing off from across the river is the **Fraumünster**, a 13th-century church built on the sight of a much older convent. One of Zürich's artistic highlights, the lovely structure is graced within by five enormous stained-glass windows, created in 1967 by then 80-year-old Mark Chagall. View the interior Monday through Saturday from 10 am-4 pm. Nearby, at the end of the oh-so-quaint Augustinergasse, the tower of **St. Peters Kirche** claims the largest clock face in Europe – the monster timepiece spans 8.7 m. Just north up the alley, **Lindenhof Park** offers a pleasant place to relax with Zürich locals amid shaded city views.

Zürich's Museums

With over 50 museums to choose from, Zürich offers collections ranging from art and design to history and industry. Two of the best are the Zürich Art Museum and the Swiss National Museum:

■ The **Zürich Art Musuem**, or Kunsthaus Zürich, has an outstanding collection of Italian and Dutch paintings from the 17th and 18th centuries and a good schedule of rotating and temporary exhibits. It's high on the east bank at Am Heimplatz 1 and open Tuesday through

Thursday, 10 am-9 pm, and Friday through Sunday, 10 am-5 pm; ☎ 01 253 84 84.

■ **Swiss National Museum**, or Schweizerisches Landesmuseum, occupies a modern replica of a Höhenzollen castle. Inside, the enormous collection includes displays of ancient and religious art, historical Swiss costumes, traditional interior design, and military history. The imposing grounds include a large, water-bounded park between the Limmat and Sihl rivers. The museum is just north of the Hauptbahnhof and is open Tuesday through Sunday from 11 am-7 pm; ☎ 01 218 65 11.

Zürich's **shopping** districts stretch north to south, from the train station toward the lake, in three distinct swathes. So, take your pick: chic, hip, or charm? **Bahnhofstrasse** is Switzerland's most famous upscale shopping street. Lined with banks, boutiques, and exquisite chocolate shops, lime-tree- and Lamborghini-lined Bahnhofstrasse should please even the most discriminating couture-hound.

East of Bahnhofstrasse, on the western bank of the Limmat River, is Zürich's quaint old town and riverside **Schipfe** district. Here, a maze of steep cobbled alleyways winds through historical houses occupied by antique shops, book dealers, and specialty art, liquor, and tobacco outlets. Those shoppers with trendier tastes should head for the east bank of the Limmat and the gritty **Dörfli** district. A dining, drinking, and (table-) dancing hotspot after dark, Dörfli draws a young, artsy crowd during the day. Shops here peddle inexpensive clothing, costume jewelry, lingerie, and tattoos.

Also worth shoppers' notice is the Swiss Handicrafts Store, or **Schweizer Heimatwerk**. With a branch in each of the shopping districts, it offers high-quality crafts from all over Switzerland. Stop in at the Hauptbahnhof, on the river at Rudolf Brun-Brücke, in old town at Rennweg, or at Bahnhofstrasse 2.

Want to see more? The tourist office offers **guided city tours** by foot, bus, boat, and trolley. Two-hour walking tours depart daily at 3 pm from the Hauptbahnhof tourist office (adults 20 CHF, children 10 CHF).

The Adventures

 Zürich plays more to city pleasures than to outdoor adventures, but locals do enjoy boating, swimming, and hiking. **Boat tours**, many including meal service, depart from Bürkliplatz at the southern end of Bahnhofstrasse.

Ferries, too, depart here and make round-trip runs around the lake. **Boat rentals** are offered just to the west of Bürkliplatz and down either lakeshore at Mythenquai, ☎ 01 201 65 10, or Utoquai, ☎ 01 251 32 23. Lake **swimming** is popular at several locales. Try the grassy beaches along the lakeshore or the pools at both Mythenquai, ☎ 01 201 38 89, and Utoquai, ☎ 01 251 61 51. Great days out can include a combination of these activities. Hop a ferry from Bürkliplatz to either Mythenquai or Utoquai – both have ferry docks – and spend a sunny day boating, swimming, and people-watching.

 Hiking trails wind through the forested hills south and west of Zürich. Trains depart the main station every half-hour for the 20-minute ride to Uetliberg, just west of the city. A viewing platform offers the area's best views, and hiking trails fan out into the forest. One scenic route, the *Planetenweg* (approximately 1½ hours), leads from Uetliberg across the Albisgrat ridge to Felsenegg – watch for the to-scale planet markers along the way – and returns to Zürich via cableway to Adliswil and then by railway to Zürich. Ask at the tourist office for maps and more information.

Where to Sleep

 Steps away from the lake, the opera, and Bahnhofstrasse shopping, the 150-year-old **Hotel Baur au Lac** ($$$$) counts the world's most royal and rich among its clientele. Inquire at ☎ 01 220 50 20, www.bauraulac.ch.

The **Hotel Widder** ($$$$), Rennweg 7, is our favorite high-end choice in Zürich. The property includes eight historic townhouses in the heart of old town, each decorated in crisp, modern style. The restaurant is popular for its elegant Swiss cuisine; the bar for its live jazz. Book at ☎ 01 224 25 26, www.widderhotel.ch.

HOTEL PRICE CHART	
Double room without tax; $$$-$$$$ always with bath.	
$	Under 120 CHF
$$	121-225 CHF
$$$	226-375 CHF
$$$$	Over 375 CHF

The cheery, charming **Zum Kindli** ($$$) brings suitable Laura Ashley florals to an ideal townhouse location in Zürich's old town; ☎ 01 211 59 17.

On the eastern hillside near the art museum and university, the **Romantik Hotel Florhof** ($$$) has newly refurbished rooms, home décor, and a pleasant dining terrace; ☎ 01 261 44 70, www.florhof.ch.

Hotel Limmatblick ($$), on the east bank of the river near Dörfli, offers 16 small, artsy rooms with an eye on the Dadaist art movement. The tram hub is steps away, river views are available, and the Dada Bar downstairs often books live music. Dial ☎ 01 254 6000, www.limmatblick.ch.

For something a bit closer to home, try the **Royal Comfort Inn** ($$), on the hill just outside the Dörfli district. Bright décor, complimentary beverages, and friendly service spice up the small, simple rooms. Book at ☎ 01 226 59 59, ww.comfortinn.ch.

Hotel Otter ($$) draws a young funky crowd to its fanciful theme-decorated rooms. Choose from angel, flame, or island décor – the latter complete with hammock. The Wüste Bar serves drinks downstairs. Oberdorfstrasse 7, ☎ 01 251 22 07, www.wueste.ch.

The best of the budget accommodations here is the **Biber Hotel** ($), also known as the City Backpacker, with a community kitchen, Internet service, and super-cheap dorms. It's in the heart of the party-hearty Dörfli district, and no curfew is imposed. Reserve at ☎ 01 251 9015, www.city-backpacker.ch. Party-minded accommodations are also offered in Zürich West at **Hotel Limmat**, where simple rooms round out the services and the city's largest dance club, Club X-TRA. The hotel-disco is in Zürich West at Limmatstrasse 118. Reserve rooms with bath ($$) or without ($) at ☎ 01 448 15 95, www.x-tra.ch.

Where to Eat

 Dining out is one of Zürich's chief pleasures, and visitors will find all manner of cuisine at all price levels. Over 1,700 restaurants serve central Zürich, and a whopping 400 of these offer terrace or garden dining. For traditional Swiss cuisine, try **Adlers Swiss Churchi** ($$) in old town, ☎ 01 266

DINING PRICE CHART	
Average entrée, with tax.	
$	Under 15 CHF
$$	16-37 CHF
$$$	Over 37 CHF

96 66; the cozy **Pinte Vaudoise** ($$), ☎ 01 251 23 35; or the more elegant **Haus zum Rüden** ($$$), ☎ 01 261 95 66, where river views complement regional dishes. **Churrasco** ($$) is popular for its Argentinean grill and garden-style dining; ☎ 01 221 11 44. On Bahnhofstrasse at Paradplatz, **Bierhalle Kropf** ($$) is worth a stop for its restaurant's oh-so-elegant setting – and the beer's good, too. Just up the road at Bahnhofstrasse 21, **Sprüngli** offers the city's finest chocolates and, in the café, a tempting selection of snacks.

The least expensive dining options are found in the Dörfli district and in the extensive shopping area at the train station. Shop the **Bürkliplatz Street Market** on Tuesdays and Fridays for inexpensive produce and, along Bahnhofstrasse, try the department store cafeterias for good deals on fixed-price menus.

*For a Swiss-flavored night out, hop a train and make the 20-minute trip to **Uetliberg**. Sweeping city views and a feast of Neuchâtel fondue await. Tuesday through Saturday, adults 49 CHF, children 25 CHF. Book your train and dinner package at the tourist office.*

Where to Party

Leisure travelers come from around Europe to take part in Zürich's emerging nightlife and performing arts scene. The **Tonalle** hosts world-class philharmonic concerts, the **Opera House** ranks among Europe's best, and the **Maag Music Hall** features first-run musical events. The legendary **Schauspielhaus Theater** is now supplemented by the Schiffsbau entertainment complex in burgeoning Zürich West, where one-time industrial plants have been transformed into some of the trendiest hotspots on the continent. Movie theaters thrive throughout the city and, in summer, films play on giant outdoor screens along the lakeshore.

Over 300 of the city's nightclubs now stay open past midnight – by far the largest number in any Swiss city. Dance clubs and bars run the gamut from haughty to hip-hop, from ritzy to rave, and with every imaginable thing in between. So, what's your pleasure? Check the *ZüriTipp Events Guide* and the tourist office's *City Guide Zürich* to see what's on.

Where to Play

Families should head for the tourist office and request the *Kids Agenda,* a compilation of fun and games including playgrounds, museums, theaters, and other kid-friendly activities. Our favorite playground? Try the park just below Lindenhof and just behind Schipfe.

The **Zürich Zoo**, on the Zürichberg just east of town, draws families for its forested paths and natural animal habitats. The park is easily reached via Tram #6 and is open daily from 8 am-6 pm, March through October ,and from 8 am-5 pm, November through February; ☎ 01 254 25 00, www.zoo.ch. Adults 18 CHF, children 9 CHF. Other out-of-town jaunts popular with young travelers include the **Sihlwald Nature Center**, south of Zürich near the Silwald train station, and the **Wildpark Langenberg**, a wild animal park that's a 20-minute hike from the Wildpark-Höfli train station.

Festivals & Events

Zürich hosts an ever-growing number of festivals, events, and sporting competitions throughout the year. The year kicks off with **CSI Showjumping** in February, and April brings the **Sechselauten Spring Festival**, during which costumed guild members ride through town, ushering out winter and ringing in summer with the burning of a stuffed snowman.

Summer brings the **Swiss Inline Cup**, the largest inline marathon in the world; the Zürich Festival, a celebration of opera, music, and theater; and the **August Street Parade**, for which over a million costumed partiers take to Zürich's streets. The **Summer Theater Spectacle** hosts international performers on the Landiwiese stage and, in November, the always popular **Expovina** showcases wine-tasting on board Lake Zürich boats. During the Christmas season, Zürich hosts Europe's largest indoor **Christmas Market** in the lobby of its main train station and, on December 31, rings in the New Year with an enormous fireworks display.

Winterthür

The small city of Winterthür lies just 25 km north of Zürich, midway between the city and Rheinfall. First founded in the 12th century, Winterthür prospered in textile and machinery manufacture and became one of Switzerland's premier patrons of cultural pursuits such as music, art, and architecture. This legacy remains today in the city's well-kept Old Town and, most remarkably, in its exquisite museums.

Museum City

Winterthür is home to no fewer than 15 permanent collections, housed in everything from ancient castles to glassy modern structures. Most museums also host temporary exhibitions – check the tourist office's guide to find out what's in town. A few of the best permanent collections follow.

■ Two separate estates, at **Römerholz** and **Stadtgarten,** house the formidable collection of Oscar Reinhart, a local banking heir who bequeathed his cache to the city upon his death. Paintings span a range of artists, including Degas, Monet, Rembrandt, Rubens, and El Greco. The collections are open for viewing Tuesday through Sunday from 10 am to 5 pm (8 CHF each or 12 CHF for a combined ticket).

- The **Kunstmuseum** displays rotating collections of modern international art. Monet, Van Gogh, and Picasso are all represented here. The museum is open Tuesday through Sunday from 10 am to 5 pm (8 CHF); www.kmw.ch.

- The **Fotomuseum** shows off a wide range of photography in a brightly renovated warehouse. It's open Tuesday-Friday, noon-6 pm, and weekends, 11 am-5 pm (8 CHF); www.fotomuseum.ch.

- The **Villa Flora**, Tosstalstrasse 44, houses works by Cézanne, Van Gogh, Matisse, and Renoir. The villa is open Tuesday through Saturday, 2-5 pm, and Sunday from 11 am to 3 pm (6 CHF).

- **Technorama** shows off Switzerland's technological prowess with a host of kid-friendly interactive exhibits. It's open Tuesday-Sunday from 10 am to 5 pm (15 CHF).

TIP: If you're planning on making a full day's worth of museum rounds, museum passes covering one day or more are available. Check at the tourist office for the latest deal. If you need a ride, the Museums-Bus makes rounds between the main train station, the Stadtgarten, the Kunstmuseum, and the Römerholz during museum hours. The 5 CHF ticket is good all day, and includes stops at Villa Flora and the Fotomuseum on Sundays.

 Want to stay? Winterthür's summer-only **youth hostel** ($) occupies Schloss Hegi, a 15th-century castle. Dial ☎ 052 242 38 40. The **Hotel Krone** ($$) offers homey accommodations directly in the heart of Old Town. Check in at ☎ 052 208 18 18, www.kronewinterthur.ch.

 The tourist office is at the main train station. Check ☎ 052 267 67 00 or www.winterthur-tourismus.ch for more information.

Rheinfall

Europe's largest waterfall lies 50 km north of Zürich, on the border of Germany near Schaffhausen. At 150 m wide and 23 m high, the falls pump an average of 21,000 cubic feet of water per second – a sight certainly worth the short drive. Although they can be viewed from either side, the falls are most spectacular from Schloss Laufen, a hillside medieval castle. Short paths lead to the Känzeli and Fishnetz

Switzerland

platforms, both misty vantage points from which to view the raging waves. Boat rides, cliff climbs, and restaurant dining are available, and souvenir stands abound. Access to the falls is open daily.

 If you happen to be in Schaffhausen on August 1, don't miss the Swiss National Day celebration: historical city tours, hillside bonfires, and evening fireworks over the falls.

 Want to stay? The lovingly renovated **Rheinhotel Fischerzunft** ($$$) sits on a riverside lot near Shaffhausen's center. A good restaurant, riverside walks, and fresh décor make for a memorable evening. Check in at Rheinquai 8, ☎ 052 632 0505.

 The Rheinfall tourist office is in town at Industriestrasse 39. For more information, check ☎ 052 672 74 55, www.rheinfall.ch.

■ Lucerne

(Luzern)

Population: 61,000

Base elevation: 436 m

Lake & mountain tourist city

Nicknamed "The City of Lights" and regarded as the cultural capital of Switzerland, Lucerne draws tourist crowds year-round for its lovely lakeside location, its wealth of recreational activities, and its treasure-trove of historical buildings, towers, and bridges.

History & Orientation

 First founded as a Roman settlement and eventually home to an eighth-century monastery, Lucerne – or in German, *Luzern* – grew into a market center and was officially founded in 1178. During a brief annexation under Austrian Hapsburg rule, the fledging city pledged adherance to the Oath of Eternal Alliance – a pact that would prove the cornerstone of the modern Swiss Confederation. Lucerne's Catholic patrician class enjoyed expansive rule through the 19th century, and the material perks of that dominance are evident even today in the cultural wealth of the old city center. Thus, although the national capital was eventually set in Bern, and although financial control of the nation most definitely rests in Zürich, Lucerne remains without question Switzerland's premier tourist city.

The Tale of William Tell

Long lodged in the memories of Swiss nationals and foreign tourists alike is the fetching tale of William Tell. Under the rule of the Austrian Hapsburgs, local villagers were forced to bow to the governor's pole-mounted hat. As the story goes, the heroically rebellious Tell refused and was thus, as punishment, forced to shoot an apple off of his own son's head. An expert marksman – with two arrows in his quiver – Tell succeeded in his task. However, upon being queried regarding his intent for the second arrow, he admitted that, had the first gone astray and injured the boy, the second arrow was meant for revenge.

His now doubly offended oppressor packed Tell off to the dungeon, a trip entailing a boat ride across a stormy lake. However, as Tell was also an expert oarsman, he thrillingly lept ashore near Rütli, darted around the lake to meet the misguided boat, and sent that second arrow flying through the governor's heart. Thus, whether myth or memory, William Tell remains an icon of the Swiss ideal: a cooperative but fiercely independent individual forced to bow to no other man's hat.

The city of Lucerne clusters at the mouth of the Ruess River along the northwestern edge of Lake Lucerne, known in German as the *Vierwaldstättersee*. Pastoral villages and jutting mountain cliffs surround the sprawling body of water, and glorious peaks rise all around: Mt. Pilatus, the Stanserhorn, and Mt. Titlis to the south, and the Klewenalp, Mt. Rigi, and Bürgenstock to the north and east. Picturesque throughout the year, the region draws a steady stream of tourism for its architectural treasures, its cultural events, and its natural surroundings.

The Town

Many visitors will first become familiar with the newly built area around the train station and boat docks, on the southern riverbank next to the lake. Adjacent at Europaplatz, the Culture and Congress Center's jutting roof reflects the lights, crowds, and water below, creating a surreal scene that has quickly become a landmark as recognizable as the city's famed Kappelbrücke.

Such ultra-modern architecture stands in stark contrast to the charms of the old city center just north across the bridge, where cobblestone streets wind around medieval houses below the eight remaining towers of the 15th-century City Wall, or *Museggmauer*. Moving east along the lakeshore, follow the promenade to the quay's old hotel row and, eventually, to the Lido Park and the Swiss Transportation Museum. Alternatively, climb north along Löwenstrasse up from the promenade to the Gletschergarten and the Dying Lion Monument.

Getting Here & Around

 International travelers arriving by **air** should fly into the airport at Zürich, which lies 55 km northeast of Lucerne, or approximately one hour by car or rail. **Trains** depart hourly between Lucerne and Interlaken and the transportation hubs of Zürich, Bern, and Geneva. Lucerne is the departure point for Swiss Federal Railway's popular William Tell Express, a picturesque route by boat across the lake, then by train across the mountains south toward the southern lakes and Italy. Regional **buses** depart from in front of the train station.

Ferries serve the local lakeshores year-round, but service is minimal during the winter months. Boats leave from the docks conveniently located just in front of the train station and bus depot. Guests using multiple modes of transportation for day-trips or excursions should note the many money-saving combination passes.

For **drivers**, parking is tight and expensive in this pedestrian-oriented town. However, most hotels offer parking, and several multi-story garages are on hand. The Bahnhof garage is the most convenient large garage near the old city center's sights.

> **TIP:** The free Lucerne **Visitor's Card**, or Gästekarte, brings all manner of discounts on sightseeing, activities, and transportation. Your hotel can issue and validate a card upon your arrival.

Getting Connected

 The tourist information office is in the main train station at 3 Bahnhofstrasse; ☎ 0227 17 17, www.luzern.org. The well-stocked tourist center offers stacks of brochure information and the services of a friendly and knowledgeable staff. Guided tours and some transportation passes are sold here. The tourist office is open in winter from 8:30 am to 6 pm weekdays, 9 am-6 pm weekends, and in summer from 8:30 am to 8:30 pm weekdays, 9 am-8:30 pm weekends.

The post office sits just across the street from the train station at the corner of Bahnhofstrasse and Bahnhofplatz. It's open Monday through Friday, 7:30 am-6:30 pm, and Saturday, 8 am-noon.

 Internet access is offered at the tourist office and in many hotel lobbies.

The Sights

 Most tourists come to Lucerne for its medieval **Old Town**, a centuries-old center of shops, restaurants, and romantic architecture. The most instantly recognizable landmark here is the **Kappelbrücke**, a kinked bridge over the Ruess River well known for its Wasserturm tower, cycle of paintings, and the 1993 fire that destroyed much of it. The bridge structure has since been rebuilt as an exact replica of the original, the paintings painstakingly recreated and recently mounted along the bridge. Look for the visible line between the old and new wood. Follow the swans downstream to the 17th-century **Speuerbrücke** for a look at what is now the city's oldest covered bridge. Note, too, the morbid cycle of paintings here, including Megliger's disturbing *Dance of Death*. On the north side of the river, wander the old city streets and squares, now a pedestrianized haven of shops, restaurants, and hotels, and climb the Schirmer, Zyt, and Mannli Towers of the old **City Wall**.

Strolling out of the old town and along the lake's northern shore, walkers enjoy a long gravel path scattered with snack carts and park benches and fronting Lucerne's most elegant old hotels. A detour up Löwenstrasse leads to second cluster of city sights. Most notable here are the imposing twin towers of the **Hofkirche** and the poignant **Löwendenkmal**, or "The Dying Lion of Lucerne," a carved stone memorial to the Swiss soldiers who died in Paris in 1792 while defending the French King. Just beyond, the **Gletschergarten** provides an interesting look at the city's ancient geology, as well as a much more frivolous maze of mirrors. It's open daily from 9 am to 6 pm; ☎ 041 410 43 40, www.gletschergarten.ch.

Lucerne boasts an impressive collection of museums. Most noticeable is the ultra-modern Culture and Congress Center, alternatively known as the KKL, and its top-floor **Museum of Art**, which specializes in exhibitions of international contemporary art. It's next door to the train station at Europaplatz 1; ☎ 041 226 78 78, www.kunstmuseumluzern.ch.

The **Rosengart Donation,** Pilatusstrasse 10, opened in 2002 to display a rich collection of works by Klee, Picasso, Monet, Matisse, Miro, and Cezanne. For more info, dial ☎ 041 220 16 60 or see www.rosengart.ch. Also donated by the Rosengart family are the works displayed at the **Picasso Museum**, an intimate collection of drawings and photos featuring the work, life, and loves of the legendary artist during the final 20 years of his life. The collection is housed in the Am-Rhyn-Haus at 21 Furngasse; ☎ 041 410 17 73.

For music buffs, the **Richard Wagner Museum** pays homage to that famed composer at the site of his local residence, Villa Tribschen, the house in which he wrote *Siegfried-Idyll* for his long-time love, Cosima. It's located on the southern shore of the lake at Wagnerweg 27; ☎ 041 360 23 70.

AUTHOR'S PICK The **Swiss Transportation Museum**, or Verkehrshaus der Schweiz, sees more annual visitors than any other museum in Switzerland, and new arrivals will quickly understand why. The largely interactive museum is a huge hit with kids – and therefore a huge hit with parents, too. Major attractions include a full-sized planetarium, helium balloon rides, laser shows, and an IMAX theater. Multimedia displays on boat, rail, and aviation travel educate and entertain, and a 240-square-yard aerial photograph of Switzerland allows even the least adventuresome *Adventure Guide* reader to go home bragging, "I walked across Switzerland!" The museum is located at Lidostrasse 5, on the northern lakeshore approximately 1½ km from the town center. Ferries dock nearby. The museum is open daily from 10 am to 6 pm, except Christmas day; ☎ 0848 85 20 20, www.verkehrshaus.org.

The tourist office arranges **guided factory tours** to several local sites. Favorites include a brewery, an alphorn factory, a dairy, a glass factory, and a refuse incineration plant. (Okay, so this last one might not belong on our list of "favorites," but it is worth a mention.) The tourist office also gives **guided walking tours** through the city center daily from May through October and on Wednesdays and Saturdays from November through April. Walking tours depart at 9:45 am, take two hours, and cost 16 CHF per person.

The Adventures

Adventures around Lucerne come in three categories: lake outings, mountain outings, and combinations of the two. Visitors in search of **lake outings** can enjoy any number of boat tours – more than 20 ferries and tour boats ply the local waters. At the northwest shore near the old city center, **SNG** rents paddleboats, arranges watersports, and offers lake tours and boat taxi service. Dial ☎ 041 210 36 37, www.sng.ch. The city's main ferry service, however, is the **Lake Lucerne Navigation Company**, or Schiffahrtsgesellschaft Vierwaldstättersee, Switzerland's largest ferry operation. The company operates year-round service to all corners of Lake Lucerne, but boats run less frequently during the winter months. Tourists particularly enjoy the themed lake cruises here, which typically include some kind of sustenance such as fondue, cake, or a buffet meal. For more information, dial ☎ 041 367 67 67, www.lakelucerne.ch, or check with the information kiosk just across from the train station.

Mountain outings around Lucerne take day-trippers to several surrounding peaks for hiking, biking, skiing, and view-laden relaxing. Combination boat, train, and cable car passes make transportation a breeze. (The tourist office can help with routing and ticket arrangements.) Popular mountain outings include **Mt. Pilatus**, or "Dragon Mountain," where a cogwheel railway, gondola, and cable car will tug you up to several nice trails, a mid-mountain summer toboggan run, and soaring views from the silvery mountaintop lodge. Another is **Stanserhorn**, with its old funicular, marmots, and rotating restaurant. And there is also **Klewenalp**, where playgrounds, mountain-bike rentals, a petting zoo, and a rock-climbing garden please families of all ages. Specialist mountain-bikers enjoy a difficult circular run here from Buochs up to Stafel, a 3½-hour trek covering almost 19 miles.

At **Mt. Rigi**, home to Europe's first mountain railway, adventurers enjoy wintertime sledding and skiing and, in summer, some of the region's best mountain hiking – try the two-hour Seeweg route from Kaltbad along the cliffs to Unterstetten and Hinterbergen. Jutting into the lake is the **Bürgenstock**, a peaceful mountain peninsula overlooking five lakes.

Finally, if you only get one mountain day-trip outside of Lucerne, don't miss the resort of Engelberg and its **Mt. Titlis**, where the world's first revolving cable car, the Titlis-Rotair, totes visitors up to year-round glacier fun, including skiing, boarding, snow-biking, tubing, and sledding. For more info, see this guide's *Engelberg* chapter; call ☎ 041 639 50 60, or see www.titlis.ch.

Hiking, biking, and **skating** trails circle Lake Lucerne and web around the region's peaks – several of the best are mentioned above. Maps and route information are available at the tourist office. The train station offers bike and skate rental at service windows 23 and 24; ☎ 0512 27 32 63. The local ferry operator provides specialized sporting tours that include round-trip transportation between Lucerne and recommended hiking, biking, and skiing destinations. Bikes can accompany riders on any train, most boats, and some buses, normally for small extra fees.

Walking the Swiss Path

Seven hundred years after signing the 1291 pact that unified the first three Swiss cantons, Switzerland celebrated the anniversary by – what else – developing a new trail: The *Weg der Schweiz*, or Swiss Path. True to meticulous Swiss ways, the trail is divided into 26 sections, each representative of a Swiss canton, and each length proportionate to the population of the represented canton. The trail begins at Rütli Meadow, the site on which the Oath of Eternal Alliance was signed, and circles 35 km around the Urnersee to Brunnen. Plan two days to walk the entire trail, or walk shorter sections between village boat stops. Any area tourist office will have more information and maps.

Swimming options include the floating pools at Spitteler Quay and the grassy beaches at both Lido and Seepark. The **Dietschiberg golf** course offers public play on 18 holes from April through November. The course is the oldest in central Switzerland, with big, mature trees and big, sweeping views of the city, lake, and mountains. Call ☎ 041 420 97 86 or see www.golfclubluzern.ch.

*Travelers seeking more outlandish adventures should check with **Outventure**, an extreme sports operator that arranges guided outings around Lucerne and Engelberg. Adventurers can climb waterfalls, bungee-jump out of cable cars, and overnight in a self-built igloo. Find your Alpine adventure at www.outventure.ch or call ☎ 041 611 14 42.*

Where to Sleep

The city's three most elegant old hotels line up shoulder to shoulder along the promenade on the northern lakeshore of Lake Lucerne. Exuding old-world splendor from its aging pores, the sprawling **Hotel Schweizerhof** ($$$$) opened in 1845 and is now a national architectural landmark. Reserve at ☎ 041 410 04 10, www.schweizerhof-luzern.ch.

The **Palace Hotel** ($$$$) boasts lovely Jungendstil décor and a calendar brimming with cultural events; ☎ 041 416 16 16, www.palace-luzern.ch.

The **Grand Hotel National** ($$$$) trades on superb wellness facilities and an excellent, if pricey, Thai restaurant. Book the National at ☎ 041 419 09 09, www.national-luzern.ch.

At the opposite extreme of five-star ambiance gleams **The Hotel** ($$$$), a wonderfully modern, minimalist operation sporting scenes from great movies on its guestroom ceilings; ☎ 041 226 86 86, www.the-hotel.ch.

The **Romantik Hotel Wilden Mann** ($$$) rests just across the river from Lucerne's charming old town. Lovingly decorated, mix-and-matched guestrooms complement antique-laden public areas and a cozy Swiss *stübe* restaurant with outdoor service in summer; ☎ 041 210 16 66.

HOTEL PRICE CHART	
Double room without tax; $$$-$$$$ always with bath.	
$	Under 120 CHF
$$	121-225 CHF
$$$	226-375 CHF
$$$$	Over 375 CHF

The half-timbered **Rebstock** ($$$) sits below the steps of the Hofkirche, and its popular outdoor café takes full advantage of the adjacent sunny square.

Just across from the train station, the **Waldstätterhof** ($$$), ☎ 041 2 271 271, www.waldstaetterhof.ch, offers courtyard parking and recently refurbished rooms with bright, modern décor.

For a lakeside option, try the **Seeburg** ($$$), with its view-blessed terrace and aging **Seeburg Chalet** ($$), ☎ 041 375 55 55, www.hotelseeburg.ch.

The **Schiff** ($$) and **Des Alpes** ($$) share similar positions in the heart of old town on the northern bank of the Ruess River. Both have simple décor and some rooms with lake-and-mountain views. Book the Schiff at ☎ 041 418 52 52, www.hotel-schiff-luzern.ch; the Des Alpes at ☎ 041 410 58 25, www.desalpes-luzern.ch.

Jailhotel Löwengraben ($$), once a prison, now incarcerates a novelty-seeking, youthful clientele. The cells have been converted into reasonably comfortable bunk dorms and private rooms, and public areas include a popular disco. Get booked at ☎ 041 417 12 12, hotel@loewengraben.ch.

For lofty mountain lodging on Pilatus Peak, take the train up to the simple **Pilatus-Kulm** ($$); ☎ 041 670 12 55, www.pilatus.com. Our pick for camping out is the **Camping Lido** ($). The well-equipped grounds are nicely situated near the lakeshore, the Transportation Museum, and a ferry dock. Head for Lidostrasse 19 or contact ☎ 041 370 2146, www.camping-international.ch.

Switzerland

Where to Eat

Lucerne boasts a nice collection of restaurants, many of which are geared toward the city's ever-present tourist crowds. The **Stadtkeller** ($$$ with show), in the old town, has long been popular for its traditional Swiss cuisine and a folklore performance featuring alphorn blowing, flag twirling,

DINING PRICE CHART	
For an average entrée, with tax.	
$	Under 15 CHF
$$	16-37 CHF
$$$	Over 37 CHF

and yodeling. Dial ☎ 041 410 47 33 for lunch and dinner reservations.

Novelty dining floats lakeside at the **Schiffsrestaurant** ($$), a converted old paddle steamer with expensive food and extensive views – the ambiance of the deck-top bar is certainly worth the price of a drink.

Those headed for the Stanserhorn can lunch at the tourist oriented **Rondorama** ($$) a revolving restaurant at 6,300 feet.

For less conspicuous dining, try **Opus**, a delightful wine bar and terrace restaurant on the southern bank of the Ruess River near the Spreuerbrücke. Nearby, cheery **Sebastian's** ($$$) serves excellent seafood at the corner of Rütligasse and Pfistergasse.

Mr. Pickwick's Pub ($$), just in front of the Kappelbrücke, features English-style pub food and a great selection of beer.

Deep in the maze of old town at Eingasse 15, **Spycher** ($$) offers an interesting selection of Swiss and Oriental specialties – but don't let the odd mix scare you away; this friendly house serves up some of the city's best fondue. Dial ☎ 041 412 37 37 for reservations.

Lucerne is in general a rather pricey place to eat. For inexpensive and to-go meals ($), head for the downstairs deli at the train station or any of the small markets in the old town – the **Migros** grocery is at Hertensteinstrasse 44.

Where to Party

Yet another prison-themed attraction is **Sedel,** a graffiti-festooned concert venue and disco near Emmenbrücke and the youth hostel, home base for much of this club's rowdy clientele. Dial ☎ 041 420 63 10 to see what's on.

At Seidenhofstrasse 5, ☎ 041 227 66 66, the medieval **Adagio** draws more mature crowds with a mix of music and a more expensive selection of drinks, while **The Loft**, at Haldenstrasse 21, ☎ 041 410 92 44, thumps to a disco beat amid slick modern décor.

Freshly refurbished in 2002, the **Casino Lucerne** occupies an enviable lakeside lot on the northern edge of town at Haldenstrasse 6, ☎ 041 418 56 56. Live entertainment – in both Vegas and Swiss styles – and an elegant dining room supplement a fanciful gaming room with roulette, poker, blackjack, craps and slot machines. The casino is open daily from noon to 4 am for those at least 20 years of age.

Where to Play

 Families enjoy the playground, petting zoo, and activities atop **Klewenalp**, and several lakeside paths offer family-friendly strolls – particularly enjoyable when combined with a round-trip boat ride. Childcare services are available in the old town at **Kinderparadies**, Hertensteinstrasse 40, ☎ 041 410 44 15. On the sixth floor of the Hotel Waldstätterhof, the **Kinderstube** offers play time for kids 2½ years and older, Tuesday through Friday from 2-5 pm; ☎ 041 210 35 04. The tourist office can provide additional information regarding babysitting.

Festivals & Events

 Numerous music festivals highlight calendar, including the well-regarded **Luzern Festival**, a seasonal series of performances by eminent musicians. Check the tourist office to see who's in town.

From the end of February through early March bizarrely costumed revelers and musicians take to the streets in celebration of **Carnival,** a party renowned throughout Europe.

In late June, the colorful **Old Town Festival** is a traditional tourist favorite and, in early August, a spectacular fireworks show lights up the lake during **Seenachtsfest.**

■ Engelberg

Population: 3,500

Base elevation: 1,050 m

Mountain resort town

While most tourists base themselves in Lucerne and make quick trips up to see Engelberg's famed Titlis peak before running back to the city, I think Engelberg's outdoor attractions merit the opposite arrangement – an option particularly appealing during the cold winter months, when ski slopes are more inviting than lakeshores. All-season Engelberg is central Switzerland's most popular mountain resort.

Switzerland

History & Orientation

 Engelberg's founding dates to 1120 AD, when a group of monks built a monastery on a site in the upper valley. Through the Middle Ages, the group ruled the surrounding area with an iron religious hand – powers granted by the Pope and ungoverned by the Swiss Federation. But, a rotten run of luck struck in the 18th century, beginning with a fire in 1729 that destroyed the monastery in its entirety. The place was rebuilt in the Baroque grandeur you can still see today, but its glory days came to a quick end when Napolean's armies turned up on Switzerland's doorstep in 1798. Since then, the monastery has lived a quieter life, running a school, library, and dairy operation.

Today, bell-clad cows wander the slopes of the three mountain recreation areas that enclose the steep-walled Engelberg Valley. The Brunni rises to the north behind the village; the Fürenalp tucks in at the far western end of the valley; and, to the south, the Titlis dominates its less lofty neighbors. The winter season in Engelberg generally runs from Christmas through mid-April, and some glacier-based winter sports play from May through September. With the exception of a two-week maintenance period in November, cable cars run year-round. For summer-sport enthusiasts, the snow is melted and the mud is dry from mid-June through October.

The Town

The town of Engelberg clusters at the foot of the Brunni, on the northern bank of the Engleberger Aa River. Anchoring the town are the Eugenisee resevoir down-valley to the west, the monastery up-valley to the east, the sports center to the south, and the Brunni cable car to the north. Architecture includes an odd mix of old-world grandeur, traditional Swiss chalets, and modern apartment blocks. If the architecture offends the eye, however, the setting certainly will not – lofty peaks rise all around. The main street, Dorfstrasse, runs east to west through the center, crossed by both Bahnhofstrasse and Klosterstrasse, Engelberg's other main drags. Most of the town's restaurants and shops lie along these three streets.

Getting Here & Around

 Engelberg sits approximately 34 km south of Lucerne, 19 km down the Engelbergertal from the Stans Süd exit of the A2 autobahn. The trip takes just over an hour by **train** or about an hour by car. The Titlis cable car station and parking lot is on the right side of the main road on entry to Engelberg. The LSE (Lucerne-Stans-Engelberg) Railway runs hourly trains from Lucerne that arrive directly into Engelberg's town center. A **boat-train** combination route is also possible via boat over the Vierwaldstättersee and then by train to Engelberg.

Getting around Engelberg in winter is simple, given the free ski buses operating on five lines from mid-December through mid-April. Similarly routed shuttle **buses** that run from July through mid-October are free to Engelberg Guest Card holders and inexpensive for all others. For **taxi** service, try **Hans Fluckiger** at ☎ 041 637 21 21 or 079 422 61 61.

Mountain transportation options – available year-round – vary from a single ride on a single lift to all-day access on all area lifts. Rail pass holders should inquire for discounts.

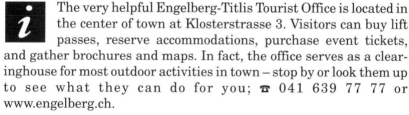

TITLIS LIFT PASS PRICE SAMPLES	
Winter	
1-day adult	52 CHF
6-day adult	250 CHF
Sledding day pass for Gerschnialp	32 CHF
Summer	
Pedestrian Round-trip to Titlis	76 CHF

Getting Connected

The very helpful Engelberg-Titlis Tourist Office is located in the center of town at Klosterstrasse 3. Visitors can buy lift passes, reserve accommodations, purchase event tickets, and gather brochures and maps. In fact, the office serves as a clearinghouse for most outdoor activities in town – stop by or look them up to see what they can do for you; ☎ 041 639 77 77 or www.engelberg.ch.

✉ The post office is located at Bahnhofplatz, right next to the train tracks.

WWW Internet access is offered in hotel lobbies throughout the village. Try also the **Salomon Station** at the Titlis cable car valley station and the **Von Holzen Camera Shop** at Dorfstrasse 31, next to the Ramada Treff Hotel.

The Sights

The **Engelberg Monastery**, or Benediktinerkloster, is home to a legacy of Benedictine monks that has been in residence since 1120 and today operates a religious school. Visitors can tour the imposing grounds Tuesday

Switzerland

through Saturday at 10 am and 4 pm. Inquire regarding English-language tours at the tourist office. The tour includes access to the fabulously Baroque Klosterkirche, home to an organ that, with its 7,000 whistles, is the largest in Switzerland. If you can catch a concert, by all means do.

Attached to the Engelberg Monastery is the Odermatt family's **Schaukäserei Cheese Factory**, producer of the creamy Engelberger Klosterglocke, a cheese made from milk gathered at 25 local mountain farms. The factory has a café and shop stocking locally produced cheeses, breads, and gift items. Highly sterile cheese-making demonstrations take place from behind a wall of glass. The showroom is open daily from 9 am to 5 pm; www.schaukaeserei-engelberg.ch, ☎ 041 638 08 88.

In the town center at the historic Wappenhaus, the small **Tal Museum Engelberg** stores some interesting artifacts related to the development of the Engelberger Valley. The museum's collection tracks the village's history from its founding in 1120 with the establishment of the Benedictine monastery to its present role as a health and winter sports resort. It's a small collection, but interesting enough. Check it out at Dorfstrasse 6; ☎ 041 637 04 14. It's open Wednesday through Sunday from 2 to 6 pm.

AUTHOR'S PICK

Rising from 1,020 to 3,020 m, the **Mt. Titlis** cable-car route whisks visitors up to the Titlis peak in three stages: a gondola, a cable car, and, finally, the world's first revolving cablecar, the Titlis-Rotair. The entire trip takes about 45 minutes one-way. At the top, visitors can wander through an ice cave bored 150 m through the glacier and, from the viewing platform, can ogle Alps as far as the eye can see. Here, snow fun is on hand year-round at the Glacier and Freestyle Park, with skiing, boarding, biking, tubing, and sledding on the glacier ice. (The Titlis peak protrudes into Swiss Air Force airspace, so fighter-jet fans should keep watch for F/A-18s dogfighting in the clouds above and thundering through the valleys below.) For more info on the Titlis-Rotair and Mt. Titlis activities, call ☎ 041 639 50 60 or see www.titlis.ch.

The Adventures

The sunny **Brunni** area is a multi-use mountain geared toward family fun. Hiking, biking, and skiing trails are well-maintained, and winter and summer tobogganing runs are available. The Ristis lift station caters to kids, who enjoy a petting zoo, playland, and both summer and winter toboggan runs. At 3,238 m, the **Titlis** is Engelberg's highest lift-equipped peak, and its Titlis-Rotair rotating cable car is the prime destination of most valley visitors. The bulk of the area's winter and summer activities are here, along with a nice collection of mountain restaurants. Several small lakes hide behind the nearby Jochpass. **Fürenalp** remains the smallest and least known of the local mountains, a boon to those looking to lose high-season crowds. Good trails, big views, and a handful of rustic huts make this small peak a place worth lingering.

For more info on mountain recreation activities, contact the **Brunni** at ☎ 041 639 60 60, www.brunni.ch; **Fürenalp** at ☎ 041 637 20 94, www.fuerenalp.ch; and **Titlis** at ☎ 041 639 50 50, www.titlis.ch. Also of note, the Information Engelberg Aktuell TV channel operates all day, every day, and provides weather reports, local event information, and outing suggestions. Tune in at hotels with cable service.

On Foot

Excellent **hiking** trails span 360 km throughout the Engelberg region, so there's plenty of room here to roam. Lifts serve trails around the Brunni, Titlis, and Fürenalp peaks, and free trail maps and route suggestions are available at the tourist office. For short hikes, I like the 3½-km **Rock and Water geology trail**, where signposted history lessons mark 345 million years of history, and the **Tickle Trail** at Härzli-See at the top of the Brunni chairlift, where barefoot walkers can tantilize their toes on a Kneipp therapy course. A more strenuous day-trek begins at the end of the valley road at End der Welt and hikes up along the treeline past Ober Zieblen to Fürenalp and its attractions. Hikers can descend by trail (via Stäfeli and Alpenrosli) or direct lift to Wasserfall, out near the golf course.

Mountain climbing, equipped *via ferrata*, trekking, and glacier rappelling – it's all here in Engelberg. Individuals head to Titlis or Wissberg at Fürenalp for **rock-climbing** and, for equipped climbing, to the via ferrata at Fürenflue on Fürenalp and Rigidalstock on Brunni.

Vie ferrate are high mountain routes with fixed climbing aids (wire ropes, rungs, pegs, ladders, and bridges).

Both **Outventure** and **Adventure Engelberg** arrange guided trips and, for practice, the **Sporting Park Engelberg** offers an indoor **climbing wall**. Weekly passes, one-time climbs, and instruction are available.

TIP: The **Engelberg Summer Pass** offers a week's worth of free participation in daily activities organized by local guides for guests of all ages and energy levels. Activities include wildlife observation hikes, trampoline courses, and – ladies, here's one worth looking into – snow-scooting on Mt. Titlis with a former Mr. Switzerland. Several scheduled activities are not included on the pass, although pass holders are offered substantial discounts. It's expensive (110 CHF adults, 90 CHF kids six-16, free for kids under six), but worth it if you're staying a week. Get more info, purchase a pass, and book activities at the tourist office.

In Water

 Kayakers head for the calm, clear Trübsee waters, **rafters** ride down the Engelberger Aa, and **canyoneers** slide down waterfalls and brave rapids between narrow cliff walls. Both Outventure and Adventure Engelberg arrange trips. Lake **fishing** at Eugenisee and at several of the lakes behind Jochpass opens to foreigners from mid-April to late October. Fishermen should pick up a day license at the tourist office.

The **Schwimmbad Sonnenberg swimming complex** maintains indoor and outdoor pools. The 25-m indoor pool is open daily from 10 am to at least 6 pm, while the giant, 50-m outdoor pool and children's play area are open only from May through August. The pools are managed by the **Sporting Park Engelberg** at ☎ 041 637 34 94. A handful of small pools and the most elaborate **sauna** facilities in town are open to non-guests at the **Felsenbad Sporthotel Eienwaldli** daily from 8:30 am to 8 pm for 2½-hour sessions. The hotel is on the southwestern outskirts of town near the campground and golf course and can be reached at ☎ 041 637 19 49 or www.eienwaeldli.ch.

On Wheels

 Daredevils enjoy thrill rides on the aptly named **devil's bike run** at **Jochpass**, where adrenaline-hounds mount fat-wheeled rollers and rip down a designated path. Younger kids and less adventuresome adults hire **trotti bike scooters** on the pleasant road from Gerschnialp down to Engelberg or glide down the 600-m **summer rodelbahn** at Ristis on Brunni.

Mountain bikers take to the lifts – with a nominal 3-5 CHF surcharge for bike transport – to access trails on all three of the area's mountains. I like the extensive network of lake-to-lake trails on the back side of the Jochpass and the sunny half-day ride from Engelberg up past Ristis to the Brunnihütte and its Härzli-See lake. Pick up the tourist office's summer brochure with suggested biking routes for all levels of fitness and skill, and rent a bike at **Bike'n Roll** at

Dorfstrasse 31; ☎ 041 638 02 55, www.bikenroll.ch. The shop also offers mountain biking lessons and guided tours.

In the Air

Paragliders head to several launch sites scattered across the Brunni, Fürenalp, and Titlis peaks. For paragliding courses, contact the **Euro-Flugschule** at ☎ 041 637 07 07, www.euroflugschule.ch. Tandem flights for beginners are offered by both **Outventure** and **Adventure Engelberg**. These same outfitters arrange both **"flying fox" ropes courses** through the trees and **bungee-jumping**, whereby airborne daredevils leap out of the Titlis cable car for a 130-m plunge above Gershnialp.

On Snow & Ice

Skiers flock from the city each weekend to enjoy the 82 km of groomed ski runs that wind through the Engelberger valley. The runs are served by a total of 24 lifts and are graded 30% beginner, 60% intermediate, and 10% advanced and expert. The main ski areas are the famed Titlis, the lift-linked Jochpass to the south, and the family-oriented Brunni to the north. Beginners head for the easy runs at Gerschnialp and Trübsee at Titlis, while intermediates have run of most of the Titlis area. Advanced and expert skiers leap off the sheer Laub Wall or maneuver a narrow run from Rotegg down to Stand. **Snowboarders** gather at Jochpass for play on the halfpipe, quarterpipe, and terrain park or year-round at the Titlis Glacier Park. **Families** enjoy the sunny (and less expensive) Brunni area on the north side of town for a range of snowplay activities. Kids head for the Yeti ski playground at Ristis and the beginner's tow at Klostermatte. **Night skiing** is held each Wednesday in January and February on the Brunni's lighted 1½-km trail and also, at each full moon, on the Titlis near Stand.

The Engelberg Valley offers 36 km of **cross-country ski** trails. The most extensive collection is at Gerschnialp, the plateau stretching out from the first stage of the Titlis cablecar route. When snow cover allows, the Sporting Park Engelberg maintains a long loop and lights it at night. Trail passes for this loop are free to holders of the Engelberg Guest Card – those without can pick up an inexpensive pass inside (6 CHF). In addition to downhill runs, sledding paths, and hiking trails, the free local trail map marks cross-country routes throughout the valley.

Switzerland

A Fun Run

When the snow is good, intermediate-level skiers can take advantage of the Titlis area's huge vertical drop – a total of 1970 m – by making the peak-to-valley run from the top of the new Jockstock-Express chairlift down to Engelberg. From the lift station, head for Jochpass, where freestylers can veer into the halfpipe or terrain park and diners can veer into the Jochstubli terrace restaurant (try the delicious *kurbis*, a pumpkin cream soup) or the Surfers Paradise Joch-Bar, an umbrella bar with loud music and a snowboarding crowd. On a sun-drenched day, the detour from here down to the old Engstlenalp lift shack is worth it for the smell of the wood alone. A hilly run leads down to Alpstubli and Kanonenrohr, where the trail drops under the treeline on its way to Untertrübsee. Passing hiking, cross-country, and sledding trails along the way, the route returns to the base of the Titlis cable car in Engelberg.

There are 38 km of groomed winter walking trails to keep cold-weather **hikers** and **snowshoers** happy. Sunny trails crisscross the Brunni area, and a short, snowy trail off the Titlis summit leads to the glacier lookout at Stotziegg. Pedestrians can purchase limited lift passes to access those trails at altitude, and the ski map offered free around town indicates winter walking trails in addition to skiing and sledding runs. In addition, several outfitters offer instruction and guided outings, including snow-shoeing, glacier trekking, and glacier rappelling. Contact the tourist office for more info.

Sledding fans rent toboggans at both the Brunnihütte, for the 2½-km slide down to Ristis, and the Gerschnialp, for the 3½-km run open there from Christmas until mid-March. On the Titlis, a **snow tubing** run operates year-round and, during the summer months, the new Titlis Glacier Park and Ice Flyer chairlift offer sliding via an inventive array of paraphernalia including standing and seated **scooters**, **boogie boards**, and **balance bikes**. Equipment use is free at the park, but guests must buy lift passes to the glacier and can, if necessary, rent boots and jackets at the Titlis photo studio. See what's on at the glacier at ☎ 041 639 50 50 or www.titlis.ch.

Sporting Park Engelberg offers introductory **curling** lessons with shoe and rink rental by arrangement. Public **ice-skating** takes place when more official events aren't on the ice – guests should check the sport center's Internet site or the local information channel for free-skate times, or check in at ☎ 041 637 34 94, www.sportingpark.ch.

In the Extreme

Outventure, one of my favorite European adventure outfitters, operates out of nearby Stansstad and serves both the Lucerne and Engelberg areas. Bungee-jumping from cable cars, abseiling waterfalls, and all-night igloo outings.... Those seeking outlandish adventures will find themselves in safe – if not necessarily *sane* – hands. Check out Outventure at www.outventure.ch or call ☎ 041 611 14 42.

Abseiling is sliding down a rope under control (from the German "ab," meaning down, and "seil," or rope).

Adventure Engelberg organizes kayaking, river rafting, trekking, bungee-jumping, canyoning, caving, and paragliding – often in conjunction with Outventure. Get more information and book activities at the Engelberg Tourist Information Center, or contact them direct at ☎ 041 639 54 59, www.adventure-engelberg.ch.

Sports Services, Outfitters & Guides

You pick the mountain, and the **Engelberg Bergführer** mountain guides will take you there. Make arrangements at their office in the tourist center; ☎ 041 639 54 57, www.bergfuehrer-engelberg.ch.

Adrenaline junkies should check out the wide range of guided all-season outings available at **Outventure** and **Adventure Engelberg**. (See *In the Extreme* above.)

Ski and Snowboard School Engelberg Titlis offers a full range of snowsport classes for children and adults. Several course lengths are available, as are special and private courses in ski racing, snowshoe trekking, and freeriding. The main office is in the Tourist Center and can be reached at ☎ 041 639 54 55, www.skischule-engelberg.ch.

Board Local at Dorfstrasse 43, ☎ 041 637 00 00, www.boardlocal.ch, specializes in snowboard rental and boarding instruction, and the **OKAY** snowboard shop offers rentals from a convenient location at the Hotel Bellevue, just across from the train station.

For general equipment rental, **Titlis-Sport** at Klosterstrasse 9, ☎ 041 639 60 70, www.titlis-sport.ch, is an Intersport outlet with a good inventory. Equipment can be booked online via the reservation network at www.intersportrent.ch. Also of note is the **Salomon Experience** rental station at the valley station of the Titlis-Rotair. They specializes in Salomon skis, of course, but they also rent snow-wear, snowshoes, and snow toys. Call ☎ 041 638 00 02 or search at www.t-r-s.ch.

Switzerland

Where to Sleep

Directly at town center, the **Ramada Treff Regina Titlis Hotel** ($$$-$$$$), a modern, sprawling four-star operation, dominates the hotel scene here with business-like rooms and apartments, view-blessed balconies, a pool and sauna, and an excellent staff. Reserve at ☎ 041 639 58 58, www.ramada-treff.ch.

HOTEL PRICE CHART	
Double room without tax; $$$-$$$$ always with bath.	
$	Under 120 CHF
$$	121-225 CHF
$$$	226-375 CHF
$$$$	Over 375 CHF

Also in the center, the quaint **Hotel Engelberg** ($$-$$$), ☎ 041 639 79 79, fronts a cobbled, pedestrian section of Dorfstrasse. Its balconies spew flowers in the summer, and the center's sights and shopping are all nearby.

The once-grand **Hotel Europe** ($$-$$$) just down the street offers an interesting choice of tower rooms, guest rooms, and apartments. This friendly hotel is, like the Bellevue, associated with the local hotel school. It houses a sauna and steam room and can be reached at ☎ 041 639 75 75, www.hoteleurope.ch.

Just across from the train station, the monstrous **Hotel Bellevue** houses both dorms ($) and rooms ($$) in a lovely, if decrepit, old mansion. Its grand lobby and large lounge belie the simple accommodations above. The Bellevue welcomes a young partying crowd and, as the hotel is a base of the Schiller Hotel Management School, guests can expect fairly hospitable housemates. The rowdy Yucatan bar and the OKAY snowboard shop occupy opposite corners of the hotel. Call ☎ 041 639 68 68 or see www.bellevue-engelberg.ch.

On the southeastern outskirts of town, the **Sporthotel Eienwaldli Hotel** ($$) has the valley's best spa facilities and a quiet, location near the golf course and campground. In addition to cozy traditional rooms, the hotel offers indoor pools with a waterfall and slide and a sauna facility with solarium and steam cave.

Campers enjoy the Bünter Family's **Campingplatz Eienwaldli** ($), a modern, well-equipped facility on the banks of the Aa River, near the golf course, and with access to the adjacent hotel's pool and sauna. Open year-round, but during high season reservations are recommended. Reach both the hotel and campground at ☎ 041 637 19 49, www.eienwaeldli.ch.

Staying up-mountain is an option year-round. Cozy accommodations are available at 1,300 m in the **Ritz-Gerschnialp** ($), ☎ 041 637 2212, a convenient location for cross-country skiers.

Farther up the Titlis slopes at 2222 m, next to the halfpipe and terrain park, is the **Berghaus Jochpass** ($$), ☎ 041 637 1187, www.jochpass.ch, where rooms and dorms come with half-board.

On the other side of the valley, the **Fürenalp** ($) offers dorm beds at 1,850 m from May to October. Inquire at ☎ 041 637 39 49.

Where to Eat

Engelberg has a good selection of restaurants – many of them hotel-based, and few of them cheap. Your best bet for an inexpensive meal is the **Coop** ($) grocery on Klosterstrasse just across from the tourist center. The **Zur Alten Post** ($) on Dorfstrasse offers

DINING PRICE CHART	
Average entrée, with tax.	
$	Under 15 CHF
$$	16-37 CHF
$$$	Over 37 CHF

standard café snacks and several more filling dishes, and the **Bierlialp Trattoria and Pizzeria** ($$) next to the tourist center does the best authentic Italian food in town.

Alpenclub, at Dorfstrasse 5, ☎ 041 637 12 43, is the food court of Engelberg, with a collection of cozy, casual restaurants, including a pizzeria ($$), a fondue corner ($$$), and a regional specialty grillroom ($$$).

For excellent local fare, try the regional specialties at the Hotel Engelberg's **Dorfstubli** ($$) across the street, or head for the Hotel **Schweizerhaus** at Dorfstrasse 42 for delicious grilled meats, including the house specialty, *Tararenhut-Erlebnis*, a table-top cone-shaped grill on which diners prepare their own meals. Reservations recommended at ☎ 041 637 11 05.

Where to Party

Across from the train station, the ever-popular **Yucatan** bar and restaurant claims the largest beer consumption in central Switzerland – a claim you'll not dispute after witnessing its après-ski crowd any sunny weekend winter afternoon. In addition to beer, the bar serves up simple Tex-Mex grub amid simple surroundings and the sounds of DJ'd or live music.

The Eden Hotel's **Unique Pub**, just across the street from the Yucatan, boasts "creative lounging" and a sunny terrace out back. In the center of town on Dorfstrasse, securely located next to the police station, the small **Casino** offers late-night slot-machine gambling, a bar, and occasional live music. Next door and down the alley, in the basement of the Alpenclub, the **Spindle Disco** rocks an 18-and-over crowd into the wee hours with a techno-house beat. The **Bierlialp**, at Dorfstrasse 21, has pizza and beer and a disco beat as well.

Where to Play

Hotels **Ramada Treff** and **Edelweiss** offer guests day-time **childcare** during high season, and the **Engelberg Titlis Ski School** accepts kids aged two and up for their daily, December-through-Easter kindergarten. The tourist office can provide a list of private babysitters, and Mini-Max, at Dorfstrasse 34, rents baby gear such as strollers and cribs. Favorite **playgrounds** include **Fürenalp**, the pond at **Grötzenwaldli**, and the petting zoo at **Ristis** on Brunni.

Festivals & Events

As in most Alpine villages, festivals and events enliven every month of the year. FIS World Cup **ski jumping** comes to town in December, and **snowboarding and freestyle competitions** run from October through May.

In May and June, farmers take their cattle to higher pastures and then, in September and October, bring them back to the valley with all the pomp and color such homecomings merit. The **24-hour Mountainbike Race** attracts downhillers from all over Europe and, in late October, the **Native Costume Festival** drums up revelers in historical regional dress.

The Graubünden

In the easternmost corner of Switzerland, the Graubünden region intersperses two world-class cosmopolitan resorts and many other tiny, traditional villages. The area first hit the tourism map in the early 1900s as a climatic health resort, and tuberculosis patients came from all around Europe to breathe its clean, dry air. A century later, the region has successfully morphed into a thriving Alpine center. Busy Davos is renowned for its research centers, athletic facilities, and international summit meetings; glitzy St. Moritz draws fur-clad crowds to its elegant boutiques and hotels; and Arosa attracts sports-minded families to its secluded slopes. As a whole, the Graubünden harbors an excellent network of hiking, biking, and skiing trails, and much of its historical Romansch culture remains intact.

The Graubünden Region

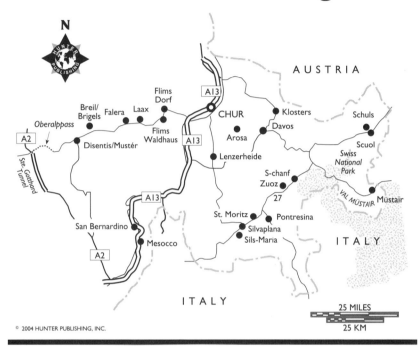

N

AUSTRIA

Flims Dorf
A13
Breil/ Brigels
Falera
Laax
CHUR
Klosters
Schuls
Oberalppass
Davos
A2
Flims Waldhaus
A13
Arosa
Scuol
Disentis/Mustér
Lenzerheide
Swiss National Park
Ste. Gotthard Tunnel
S-chanf
Zuoz
A13
27
VAL MÜSTAIR
Müstair
St. Moritz
Pontresina
San Bernardino
Silvaplana
Sils-Maria
ITALY
Mesocco
A2
ITALY

25 MILES
25 KM

© 2004 HUNTER PUBLISHING, INC.

■ St. Moritz

Population: 5,084

Base elevation: 1,768 m

Lake & mountain resort town

We choose St. Moritz as our main Graubünden base for its international fame and comprehensive array of outdoor activities. This is not a quaint Alpine village, nor is it the place for those seeking a wilderness retreat. It is, however, an ideal destination for celebrity hounds and fashion fanatics – and all those who believe a morning hike merits an afternoon massage and seven-course evening meal.

History & Orientation

First discovered by the Celts some 3,000 years ago, St. Moritz and its mineral springs have long drawn summer visitors from across Europe. With an illustrious guest list, including Paracelsus, Hermann Hesse, Friedrich Nietzsche, and Thomas Mann, this old spa town remains a

Switzerland

much-ballyhooed summer destination for the world's rich and famous.

It wasn't until 1834 that out-of-towners first stayed the winter, but the idea caught on quickly, and in 1864 the village's first wintertime hotel welcomed a group of trend-setting British vacationers. Since then, St. Moritz has become one of the globe's premier winter destinations and a pioneer in resort marketing – its latest ploys include pricey St. Moritz brands of coffee, mineral water, and music compilation CDs.

St. Moritz sits near the border of Italy in the southeastern corner of the Graubünden region. The town nestles in the famed Engadine Valley, a high-altitude expanse stretching 94 km along the Inn River. St. Moritz rests at an altitude of 1,800 m, and the relatively small difference in height between the valley floor and the surrounding peaks deceives the eye: although these mountains don't look so imposing, their heights hover around 4,000 m and justify the area's nickname, "The Rooftop of Europe."

Blessed with a stable, high-Alpine climate, St. Moritz boasts an average of 322 sunny days each year. Five major mountain peaks and 25 lakes scatter throughout the area, making this one of the Alps' most attractive natural playgrounds. The snow and ice here have hosted two Olympic Winter Games – in 1928 and 1948 – and over three dozen World Championship competitions. In February of 2003, St. Moritz once again made history as host of the Alpine Skiing World Championships.

The Town

So, its natural surroundings are exquisite; its history, distinguished; and its patrons, oh-so-refined. Even so, the town of St. Moritz remains a visually unappealing place. Its block-style architecture huddles around the western side of St. Moritz Lake (or in Romansch, "Lej da Murezzan"), an oblong body of water fed by the Inn River. St. Moritz-Dorf climbs up the hillside to the north, while St. Moritz-Bad – Dorf's poorer urban sister – sprawls out to the southwest.

St. Moritz Bad does appeal to budgeting travelers – although few frugal travelers dare set foot in St. Moritz at all. Hotel rates in Bad are generally less lofty than in Dorf, iron-rich spring waters bubble up in a public spa, and a large network of trails draws equestrians and cross-country skiers.

However, it is St. Moritz-Dorf that steals the show in the Engadine Valley, and so it is St. Moritz-Dorf I spotlight here. From the lakeshore and train station on the valley floor, multi-story hotel blocks step up the hillside toward the Corviglia ski slopes above. The town centers on Piazza da Scuola, a bustling square framed by the

Wengen and the Lauterbrunnen valley

Engelberg with the Benedictine abbey founded in the 12th century and Mt. Hahne

Above: Davos in the Landwasser Valley, seen from the Erbalp

Below: Arosa at sunset with the Schlesshorn in background

Gsteigwiler-Wildersil, in the Jungfrau, Switzerland

main shopping, dining, and promenading streets of Via Maestra and Via Viglia. Development scatters from this congested center out toward the Olympic Center to the east, St. Moritz-Bad to the southeast, and down to the lake below.

Dorf's terraced streets house a diverse but uniformly upscale collection of designer boutiques, gourmet restaurants, and posh hotels. The village's atmosphere smacks of exclusivity, its elegance attracts an illustrious clientele, and its social calendar includes some of Europe's most lavish affairs. This high-altitude attitude does, however, come at stratospheric cost: Prices here are the highest in the Alps. Like most mountain resorts, St. Moritz more or less shuts down between seasons – from late April through May and in November.

Getting Here & Around

 St. Moritz lies approximately 200 km, or a three-hour drive, from either Milan or Zürich. International arrivals can **fly** into either Zürich or Geneva and make connections either by plane or helicopter to the Samedan Airport just outside St. Moritz. Trains connect St. Moritz to the rest of Europe via Chur to the north and Tirano, Italy, to the south. The St. Moritz train station sits between the lakeshore and St. Moritz-Dorf.

The train station serves as hub for the Post **bus**, which services the Graubünden region, as well as the local Engadin bus, which makes rounds through St. Moritz. The regional train company is the **Rhaetian Railway** (☎ 081 833 59 12). For taxi service, try **Taxi Zentrale** at ☎ 081 833 11 12.

 AUTHOR'S PICK — Year-round lift service offers access to the area's outstanding mountain restaurants and far-reaching views. Highly recommended is a trip by foot or lift up to the Corviglia area behind St. Moritz. After transferring at Corviglia from the funicular to a cable car, guests climb to Piz Nair, the black mountain. On the way, look for the 2003 World Cup ski racing start platform – and just below, the world's steepest downhill start, a free-fall drop on which skiers reach speeds of up to 130 km an hour in the first seven seconds of the race.

LIFT PASS PRICE SAMPLES	
Winter	
1-day adult for St. Moritz area	56 CHF
6-day adult all-area pass	294 CHF
Summer	
Pedestrian round-trip to Piz Nair	30 CHF
6-day adult all-area pass	96 CHF

Getting Connected

 The St. Moritz Tourist Board is in the heart of the pedestrian old town at Via Maestra 12. Contact ☎ 081 837 33 33 for more information.

 The post office is on Via Serias just below the Badrutt's Palace Hotel.

 For public Internet access, try the **American Bar** or **Bobby's Pub** in the Galeria shopping center. The **Bibliothek** has computers as well.

The Sights

St. Moritz activities focus less on sightseeing than on shopping, spectacle, and sport. Visitors enjoy **shopping** on the Via Serlas and Via Maestra for goodies from Armani, Bvlgari, and Prada, and gift shops sell local crafts, woodcarvings, and chocolates. A few overpriced sporting goods outfitters are on hand to remind visitors that they are, after all, in the mountains.

View of St. Moritz from Suvretta onto Lake Champfer and Silvaplana, backdropped by Piz da la Margna.

St. Moritz is a favorite venue for refined spectator sports such as polo, sailing, equestrian competitions, classic car rallies, and greyhound racing. Such events take place throughout the year – check with the tourist office to see what's on. Also popular are the many concerts staged year-round in local gardens, hotels, spas, forests, churches, and squares. Many feature world-renowned musicians, and many are free of charge.

Worth an uphill stroll is a visit to the village's own version of the **Leaning Tower**. The 12th-century structure, once the bell tower of the now-demolished St. Mauritius Church, stands 33 m and leans 5½ degrees. A handful of small museums rounds out the sightseeing options here. The **Engadine Museum** houses a worthwhile collection of cultural and historical displays in one of the valley's few remaining traditional buildings (Via dal Bagn 39; ☎ 081 833 43 33). Just up the hill, the **Segantini Museum** honors Giovanni Segantini, an artist famed for his poignant depictions of Alpine life. Segantini spent his last years in the Engadine Valley, and this museum boasts the world's largest collection of his work (Via Somplaz 30; ☎ 081 833 44 54).

The Adventures

Recreation opportunities are immense. Major lift systems congregate in the Corviglia area directly above St. Moritz and sprawl out across Diavolezza, Corvatsch, Pontresina, and Muottas Muragl. The lift system operates year-round, serving skiers in winter and hikers in summer. The lake offers a playground for both summer water sports and winter ice recreation, and walking trails are maintained throughout the year.

On Foot

 Some 500 km of well-marked trails wind throughout the Engadin region, and various outfitters offer a total of 600 guided mountain excursions – many of them with themes such as minerals, game, botany, glaciers, or flora and fauna. Trams and cable cars run year-round to the peaks of Piz Nair, Corvatsch, and Lagalb, and all are excellent bases from which to begin hikes among mountain restaurants. The hiking and walking terrain varies from easy to extreme, so everyone will find suitable trails.

Piz Nair soars above St. Moritz, making it a tempting destination for all. Athletic visitors set out for the 3½-hour hike, but less ambitious walkers can take the funicular and cable car to reach the same viewpoint. The Pass Suvretta route takes walkers off the back side of the Piz Nair peak – reached by either lift or the hike above – over to the Pass Suvretta, and down into the Engadine Valley. The four-hour

Switzerland

route transverses bleak, high-Alpine pastures, passes Lac Suvretta, follows a meandering stream, and finally arrives back in St. Moritz Dorf.

Shirley Temple's movie classic Heidi *was filmed in this region, and a 1790s-era hut from the original set has been moved here. A flat, kid-friendly flower trail leads from the Chantarella funicular station to the hut and, from there, down to St. Moritz via a forested path signposted with the fairy-tale of Schellen-Ursli. The whole loop takes less than two hours.*

Canyoning, climbing, and mountaineering activities are all available, too. See the *Sports Outfitters* box below for contact information.

On Horseback

For those interested in traveling by hoof, **St. Moritz Stables** offers year-round equestrian services. Established almost 100 years ago, the lakeside center offers equestrian training, maintains bridle paths, and guides trail rides. Full-day rides into the Roseg Valley include a picnic and magnificent mountain scenery; ☎ 081 833 57 33.

In Water

St. Moritz is best known for its healing waters. The **St. Moritz Spa Centre** trades on its historical reputation and a long list of spa treatments. Visitors can relax with beauty treatments, mud baths, massages, peat packs, and various baths spiked with additives such as carbonic acid. Make reservations at ☎ 081 833 30 62.

Kite- and wind-surfers love the Engadine during the month of August, when Maloja winds bring clear skies and cool breezes to the lakes of Silvaplana and St. Moritz. World-class events and regattas – including the colorful Windsurfing Marathon in July – dot the summer social calendar. A sailing club, ☎ 081 833 40 56, and a rowing club, ☎ 081 837 33 88, offer instruction and boat rentals. **Whitewater rafting** excursions are operated by **St. Moritz Experience** (see *Sports Outfitters* below). Half- and full-day trips make runs down The Inn river along the Scuol-Giarsun and the Pontresina-Samedan stretches.

The **Cantonal Fisch-Farming Institution** (☎ 081 833 67 52) licenses visitors for **fishing** during the May-September season. The

Engadine mountain lakes are home to perch and various trout species, but be forewarned: The privilege of fishing here does not come cheap. Licenses cost 46 CHF for a day; 132 CHF for a week and 220 CHF for 15 days.

On Wheels

No fewer than six outfitters rent **mountain bikes** and equipment. The most convenient may be the rental service located in the train station, but our fave remains the specialist shop **Bike Side** at ☎ 081 833 05 55. A good route? The **Poschiavo Trail** offers a mild downhill grade suitable for all mountain bikers. The 22-km trail starts atop Lagalb – take the cable car up from Diavolezza – and descends 2,893 m into Poschiavo. The train and tourist offices offer a package deal including round-trip train transport, bike transfer, cable car ticket, and lunch at the Punschlaver Teller.

A popular destination for **inline skating**, St. Moritz caters to skaters with a five-km circuit at Samedan Airfield and an 8.6-km route from La Punt to S-chanf. Additional trails wind through the relatively flat St. Moritz-Bad. The Engadin Inline Marathon clogs the main road from Maloja to S-chanf each June. Thousands of skaters turn out for the 42-km race, the world's original inline distance event. For rental information, contact **Samedan Tourismus** at ☎ 081 851 11 60, www.samedan.ch.

In the Air

Paragliders and **hang-gliders** take off from the mountain station at Corviglia. Regularly scheduled flights launch each hour from 10 am to 4 pm, and flights from other locations can be arranged.

AUTHOR'S PICK

Want to try it? Put yourself in the hands of a pro. ***Heinz Zwyssig*** *has been flying since 1976 as a paragliding instructor and guide, and was captain of the Swiss national team for eight years. In 2003, he celebrated his 4,000th flight over St. Moritz. For more info, contact Mr. Zwyssig at ☎ 079 353 21 59, www.luftarena.ch; 230 CHF per flight.*

On Snow & Ice

The **ski slopes** around St. Moritz are some of the most extensive in Switzerland, with 60 lifts servicing 350 km of flatteringly rated runs. Officially rated 16% easy, 71% intermediate, and 13% difficult, the runs cater to intermediate-level skiers (many of whom will feel comfortable on the area's "difficult" runs, too). This is St. Moritz, after all, and *looking* good on the slopes is much more important than *being* good on the slopes. Advanced skiers in search of greater challenge should hire a guide and/or a helicopter and head off-piste. Several local guiding services offer heli-skiing and backcountry treks.

Although certainly not the most obvious **snowboarding** destination, snobby St. Moritz has bent its rigid ways a bit to include some good facilities for boarders. There's a halfpipe and fun-park in Corviglia and two more fun-parks at Corvatsch. The runs are wide, and the off-piste snow is deep. The Wave Division, ☎ 081 830 01 01, of the **Swiss Ski School** offers specialized instruction and guiding.

St. Moritz is one of the world's premier destinations for **cross-country skiing**. Over 150 km of prepared trails wind through the valley bottom around St. Moritz Dorf and at Pontresina. The **Swiss Cross-Country Ski School,** ☎ 081 833 62 33, offers instruction in skating and classic techniques from December through April. The Cross-Country Ski Marathon takes place each March, with 12,000 participants mob trails to make the 42-km trek over and around the Upper Engadine lakes.

Many St. Moritz trails are groomed for **winter walking**, and the tourist office offers walking maps. **Philosophers' Way** stretches out along the Muottas Muragl plateau. Placards with quotes from renowned philosophers punctuate the two-km trail. The mountain views are mesmerizing, and the thoughts are worth pondering. **Segantini Path** memorializes local artists. The peaceful, wooded trail winds two km from Hotel Soldanella to Suvretta.

Horse-drawn sleighs slide through the Staz forest and over the valley's frozen lakes. Sleighs can be hired next to the Catholic church in St. Moritz Bad. A new **toboggan run** winds from Muottas to Punt Muragl, dropping 700 m over four km. Sliders can rent sleds at the bottom of the Muottas funicular.

To pick up the pace a bit, try the **Olympic Bob Run**, the world's only natural bobsled run. Since its opening in 1890, the track has hosted more than 30 World Championships. The track is open to novices from late December through early March – two riders pair up in each four-man sled with a driver and a brakeman. Rides are not cheap but do include a photo, pin, and certificate; ☎ 081 833 31 17. Need something more? Check out the Cresta Run (see *In the Extreme* below).

The new **St. Moritz Ice Arena** offers open-air skating and organized hockey games from July through April; ☎ 081 833 50 30. The **Al Parc Curling Center** tops a natural ice arena near the Kulm Hotel. Private and group instruction for new and experienced curling fans is available from late December through early March; ☎ 081 833 45 88.

In the Extreme

The **Cresta Run** clings tight to its reputation as the most testosterone-charged activity in the Alps. Male club members – for those are the only kind – belly down onto skeleton toboggans and rip headfirst through a tube of natural ice. The British-founded tradition is over 100 years old. Steep club initiation fees entitle member males to five runs during the season, from late December to March. If you have the head to try it, wear a helmet. Inquire at ☎ 081 833 31 17.

 **Rap jumping** combines the adrenalin-pumping thrill of bungee, with the control of abseiling, and for anyone who finds normal abseiling a bit tame, rap jumping is the adrenalin roping sport (not for the faint-hearted). Rap jumping has been described as ultra low level skydiving, or beginner's base jumping. There is, however, a complete safety presence, with a belay (brake control) at the top of the wall, able to stop you at any stage.

Sports Services, Outfitters & Guides

■ **St. Moritz Experience** guides lead touring over the Morteratsch Glacier, canyoning in a nearby gorge, high-mountain trekking, and multi-sport days, including climbing, abseiling, rap jumping, hydrospeeding, tubing, sailing, mountain biking and more. Teens can meet like-minded friends while on teen-only treks. With activities geared toward adrenaline-craving youth, these trips are hipper than a video arcade and a pocket full of quarters. Contact ☎ 081 833 77 14.

■ The **Schweizer Bergsteigerschule,** or Swiss Mountaineering School, just down the road in Pontresina, is the largest such school in Switzerland. The guides here take a more technical approach to year-round tours and instruction. The group runs multi- and single-day guided adventures on foot, rope, ski, and snowshoe. Check in at ☎ 081 838 83 33, www.bergsteiger-pontresina.ch.

■ **Engadin Adventure** in nearby Scuol is associated with the Swiss Outdoor Association, offering rafting, biking, and various day tours. Contact ☎ 081 861 14 16, www.engadin-adventure.ch.

■ Two ski schools together offer one of largest instructor forces in the Alps, and many hotels staff in-house teams. (With all the money that passes through St. Moritz, there's a huge demand for private instruction.) The **Swiss Ski School** is the time-honored leader here, ☎ 081 830 01 01, but we've heard better things about **Suvretta Snowsports**, ☎ 081 836 36 00.

Where to Sleep

Over half the hotels here rate four or five stars, so there's a lot to choose from in the splurge category. Rates across all categories skyrocket in winter. Forerunners in the center of town include the elegant old **Hotel Kulm** ($$$$; see *The House that Badrutt Built* below); ☎ 081 836 80 00, www.kulmhotel-stmoritz.ch, and a monstrous 1896 reproduction

HOTEL PRICE CHART	
Double room without tax; $$$-$$$$ always with bath.	
$	Under 120 CHF
$$	121-225 CHF
$$$	226-375 CHF
$$$$	Over 375 CHF

of a Gothic fortress, **Badrutt's Palace Hotel** ($$$$); ☎ 081 837 10 00, http://www.badruttspalace.com. Several fabulous new suites were added in 2003 but, as we go to press, ongoing garage construction below the hotel mars the atmosphere some. Ask before you book.

The House that Badrutt Built

In 1856, hospitality pioneer Johannes Badrutt upgraded a local pension into St. Moritz's first hotel, the Hotel Külm. Later, he became the first to suspect that this spa-town's summer guests might like the resort in winter, too. He invited a privileged few Englishmen to be his guests at the Külm for the winter of 1864, and winter tourism was born.

The Badrutt family went on to expand the Hotel Kulm, adding recreation facilities such as curling and ice-skating rinks, and to open the huge Badrutt's Palace Hotel (above) in 1896. Today, thousands of travelers visit St. Moritz each winter – and some of them pay upwards of $2,000 a night to sleep here, in the house that Badrutt built.

For slightly less grand surroundings, try the elegant old **Hotel Schweizerhof** ($$$). Its friendly staff, central location, historical interior, and upper, lake-view rooms make this a memorable stay; ☎ 081 837 07 07, www.schweizerhofstmoritz.ch.

The **Hotel Crystal** ($$$) has modern rooms just below the Corviglia funicular station; ☎ 081 836 26 26, www.crystalhotel.ch. Also in the center, the small **Languard** ($$$) tucks away next door to the Kulm, mixing antique and modern furnishings. There is no restaurant on the premises, but the breakfast room offers one of the best lake views in town; ☎ 081 833 31 37, www.languard-stmoritz.ch.

Not pretty, but near the center, the **Hotel Soldanella** ($$) has decent accommodations on the western edge of Dorf, near the museums and the Segantini Weg path; ☎ 081 830 85 00, www.hotel-soldanella.ch.

For a quiet, rural location across the lake, try the **Landhotel Meierei** ($$-$$$). It's a lovely walk of reasonable distance into town, and the restaurant and terrace are favorite stops for lakeside strollers; ☎ 081 833 20 60, www.hotel-meierei.ch.

In Bad, the freshly renovated **Kempinski Grand** ($$$$) reigns supreme with a location near the baths and the city's glitzy casino; ☎ 081 836 21 11, www.kempinski-stmoritz.com. Around the block, the **youth hostel** ($) sports modern comfort in both dorm and room accommodations; ☎ 081 833 69 48, www.youthhostel.ch. The similarly spartan **Hotel Stille** ($) next door draws crowds of kids to its bar and sometime-disco; ☎ 081 833 69 48, www.hotelstille.ch. The Olympiaschantz **campground** ($) offers sites just southwest of Bad between June through September; ☎ 081 833 40 90.

Where to Eat

St. Moritz has no shortage of gourmet dining rooms – 20 restaurants in the area rate a Gault Millau "gourmet" standard, in total earning a whopping 298 points. **Jöhri's Talvo** ($$$), in a 17th-century house in Champfer, tops the gourmet rankings here with its seafood specialties; ☎ 081 833 44 55. **Jorimann's Refugium** ($$$) runs a close second with creative takes on regional specialties; ☎ 081 833 30 00. Our favorite, however, is **Chesa Veglia** ($$-$$$), a rustic old house in the center with a lovely terrace, traditional fare, and wood-fired pizzas. It's well run by Badrutt's Palace Hotel; reserve at ☎ 081 837 28 00.

DINING PRICE CHART	
Average entrée, with tax.	
$	Under 15 CHF
$$	16-37 CHF
$$$	Over 37 CHF

Switzerland

The Hauser ($$), a restaurant in the hotel of the same name, breaks the local mould with Australian specialties, including kangaroo, ostrich, and alligator; ☎ 081 837 50 50.

On the mountain, the cozy **El Paradiso** ($$) perches on the slopes of the Corviglia area. Its food is traditional, the views from its pillow-padded terrace chairs are astounding, and its atmosphere is as convivial as mountain restaurants come.

For wood-fired pizzas, try the Schweizerhof's mountain hut, **Acla Clavadatsch** ($$); ☎ 081 833 55 30. In Bad, try **Caruso** ($) for pizza; ☎ 081 836 00 00. Or **La Fontana** ($$) for traditional cuisine; ☎ 081 833 12 66.

Hanselmann's pastry shop hides mounds of delectable goodies behind its glossy window displays. The shop is just below the tourist office, and its wares are well worth the splurge of cash and calories. Cheaper options, such as a **Coop** grocery and take-away pizza, cluster along the road between Dorf and Bad.

Where to Party

As with local restaurants, most of the town's 20+ bars and discos are hotel-run. All nightclubs are expensive. At Badrutt's Palace, stylishly clad guests lounge at the **Renaissance** and at the **Mexican Bar**, and the **Hotel Schweizerhof** offers three separate bars, including rooms for country-western music, sing-along piano tunes, and dancing. The glamorous new **St. Moritz Casino** opened in December 2002 at the Kempinski Grand Hotel des Bains in Bad. It's open 8 pm-4 am daily, with slots, roulette, black jack, and stud poker.

For a younger crowd, the **American Bar** and **Bobby's Pub** at the Galeria center both chill with a hip casual beat from après-ski on. The cozy, informal bars offer Internet access, too. For an outdoor in-town après-ski party, try the **Roo Bar** at the Hotel Hauser. Later, dance your way to the **Prince** on Via Maistra or, in the Hotel Steffani, the **Vivai Dance Club**.

Where to Play

The **Kids' Club** at the Hotel Schweizerhof offers hotel-based **childcare** and children's activities. Non-guest families are accommodated on a space-available basis daily from 9:30 am to 5:30 pm. (Badrutt's Palace and the Kempinski Grand both offer in-house childcare for guests.) The best **playgrounds** are at the school just above the Segelhaus sailing center in Dorf and at the end of Via Tegliatscha in Bad.

Festivals & Events

St. Moritz schedules almost 300 special events each year. Sporting events range from serious competitions, such as World Cup ski races, to mass spectacles, such as inline skating, windsurfing, and cross-country ski marathons. Cultural events, too, crowd the Engadine calendar, and each year the town offers over 200 free indoor and outdoor concerts.

During the winter season, the lake provides a frozen stage for a number of time-honored events – events as patrician as they are unusual. The **on-snow** and **on-ice competitions** include horse jumping, polo, and golf played with red balls. The February **horse races** include betting opportunities, a **skijoring race**, and the most elegant **parties** of the social season.

March brings the **Gourmet Festival**, a **Music Festival**, and **Chalandamarz**, a celebration of youth and spring. Summertime features include a well-regarded **Opera Festival** and, in July and August, the **Engadiner Concert Weeks**.

The Glacier Express

Several scenic train routes pass through St. Moritz, and the Engadine Swiss make much of this skillfully engineered network. However, the Glacier Express is the most famed of all Swiss rail routes. The train links the western Alps to the eastern Alps, running from St. Moritz to Zermatt via Chur. Travelers view glaciers, peaks, and waterfalls through panoramic windows as the train passes through 91 tunnels and viaducts and over 291 bridges during the 7½-hour trip (one per day in winter; two-three per day in summer). The cost from St. Moritz to Zermatt is 218 CHF first class, 131 CHF second class. Reserve through travel agents, at any Swiss train station or check www.glacierexpress.ch. If you go, be sure to book a table in the old-fashioned dining car, where good food is topped off with wine served in glassware angled to offset the train's steep climb.

Silvaplana

Just six km upstream from St. Moritz, the village of Silvaplana guards the Julier pass from the western shore of Lake Silvaplana. The small village huddles across a busy road from its namesake lake. (Lake Silvaplana is just one of four lakes in the Upper Engadine chain derived from a single ancient lake.) A land bar connects the village center to Surlej, the small hamlet at the base of the Corvatsch cable car and slopes.

Although often discounted as an insignificant suburb of St. Moritz, I see Silvaplana as the ideal location from which to explore the natural wonders the village shares with its more glorified neighbor. It's quieter here, and less expensive, and the traditional village center is much more in tune with what most visitors to the Swiss Alps might expect. Silvaplana is also much more sports-minded than well-manicured Moritz. So, for adventurers looking to get their hands dirty, this is the better base.

In summer, Silvaplana is first and foremost a place of pilgrimage for lovers of windy watersports. Kitesurfing, sailing, windsurfing, and paragliding thrive here on afternoon thermals whipped up by the Maloja Winds. In addition, hiking, biking, climbing, and fishing supplement summertime snowsports at Corvatsch.

CORVATSCH

Atop the cable car route up Corvatsch at 3,303 m sits the region's newest summertime attraction, **GletscherWorld**. The glacier here was opened in 2003 for warm-weather play (although extremely warm weather that particular summer put a slight crimp in plans). Now, atop Corvatsch, snow-play is available year-round. Visitors can snowshoe or air-board on the icy slopes, check out the inside of a glacier, and dine in the Engadine's highest restaurant. If you go, don't miss the dizzying panorama from the upper viewing terrace. For more information check ☎ 081 838 73 73, www.corvatsch.ch.

In winter, guests enjoy access to the same ski runs and uplift system that have made St. Moritz famous – 60 lifts and 350 km of runs in all. The local runs, at Corvatsch and Furtschellas, are mostly easy intermediate trails, and other winter sports beckon as well: cross-country skiing, dog-sledding, ice-skating, snowshoeing, and kite-skiing are all available here. Each Friday, floodlights brighten the Corvatsch slopes for a nighttime ski and snowboard party.

Want to stay? I like the simple, central, fun-loving **Ferienhotel Julier Palace** ($$); ☎ 081 828 96 44, www.julierpalace.com. The Camping Silvaplana **campground** boasts an enviable lakeshore locale next door to the sport center. It's not luxurious, but it's ideal for budgeting guests here to play on the lake; ☎ 081 828 84 92.

 The tourist office is on the main village road next to the post office. Its helpful staff offers schedules, maps, postcards, brochures, and lift tickets and can make suggestions regarding the wide choice of sports outfitters and schools. Contact ☎ 081 838 60 00, www.silvaplana.ch.

The Swiss National Park

(Parc Naziunal Svizzer)

 The Swiss National Park is, as you might guess from its name, Switzerland's only national park and the nation's largest nature reserve. Established in 1914, the park sits along the border of Italy and on the eastern doorstep of Zernez, 35 km northeast of St. Moritz and just over the Flüela Pass from Davos. Entry is free, and the gates remain open from June through October.

The park dedicates its efforts and its substantial wealth of territory to the preservation of nature and its processes. Human interaction is minimized: Fires are left to burn unopposed, only one road crosses the grounds, and strict stay-on-the-path, don't-pick, don't-feed regulations are meticulously enforced. The results of this management are extraordinary, and visitors hiking the pristine, rugged terrain enjoy frequent sightings of red deer, chamois, ibex, bearded vultures, and, of course, those ever-amusing marmots.

The best way to explore the park is, of course, on foot. A great introductory hike is the popular nature trail from Il Fuorn. Enriching the circular path are signposts describing ecology and wildlife of the area – in English and for kids, too.

 The four-hour loop is painstakingly documented in the *Along the Nature Trail* guidebook. However, for those with kids – or for those adults who'd like a lighter look at the park's flora and fauna – I recommend instead the children's version of the guide. Both books are available at the Park House.

 Want to stay? In the middle of the park on the main road, the **Hotel il Fuorn** ($$) offers simple accommodations and a restaurant with regional and trout specialties. Inquire at ☎ 081 856 12 26, www.ilfuorn.ch. In Zernez, the **Hotel**

Bar-Post ($$) has been housing travelers since 1905. It's smack in the center of the small village, just 500 m from the National Park information house. Dial ☎ 081 851 55 00, www.baer-post.ch.

 For more information, check in at the Nationalparkhaus (National Park House), along the main road on the eastern outskirts of Zernez. The center houses an information desk, a gift shop, a small museum, and a theater with an interesting 15-minute video. (The staff will screen the English version on request.) The park house is open daily from June through October, 8:30 am to 6 pm. (A new information center is in the works and should open sometime in 2005.) Inquire at ☎ 081 856 13 78, www.nationalpark.ch.

■ Davos

Population: 12,700

Base elevation: 1,560 m

Mountain resort town

Davos, the highest resort town in Europe, imbues a beautiful Graubünden valley with a flurry of relentless commotion. Its tourist marketing folks pitch the resort as a center for health, research, congress, sport, relaxation, and culture. The first four attributes are inarguable, and Davos' health-focused legacy now ranks it among the world's finest sports training centers. It's those last two claims – holiday and culture – that give us pause, for Davos is neither a restful nor a traditional place. No, Davos is a cosmopolitan town, all science and sport, bustling with activity, and rarely any lederhosen in sight.

History & Orientation

 The history of Davos begins with the valley's settlement by migrating farmers, who arrived here from the Valais in the 13th century. Several centuries later, in 1848, the German doctor Alexander Spengler moved in and soon determined that the region's dry, dust-free Alpine climate eased the symptoms of tuberculosis. Sanatoria sprung up all around, and the town soon boomed with clinical trade. However, as more effective treatments for tuberculosis became available during the early 1900s, the influx of sanatorium patients dwindled, and the town needed a new gig. Enter skiing. Davos' deserted sanatoria morphed niftily into hotels, uplift networks were installed on the mountain, and *voila* – an Alpine ski resort was born.

As one of Europe's most important climatic resorts, Davos saw the arrival of many illustrious artists and writers, who came here to "take the cure" or to visit friends and family. One noted visitor had a lasting influence on the resort's reputation. In 1912, writer Thomas Mann came to Davos to be at the side of his ailing wife. He left four weeks later with a less-than-complimentary impression of sanatorium life that was to become the impetus behind his famed novel *The Magic Mountain*. The novel's fictional sanatorium setting was largely based on what is today's luxurious Steigenberger Belvedere.

Modern Davos still relies heavily on its clinical, research, and sports-science trades. Local clinics specialize in the treatment of allergies and respiratory illnesses, and local research institutes explore the natural sciences, focusing on biomedicine, air quality, radiation, and physio-meteorological observation.

It's also a competitive international convention venue; the World Trade Organization meets here each January, and numerous medical

View of Davos Square, with the cable car to Ischalp and Jakobshorn and the Schatzalp and Parsenn in the background.

Switzerland

conferences convene throughout the year. All of this attention on science and medicine makes Davos a highly suitable sports training ground. World-class athletes train here at the Sports and High Altitude Center, reaping both the stamina-building benefits of the Davos' 1,560-m altitude and the scientific developments of its research institutes.

Davos lies in the Graubünden region, the easternmost province of Switzerland. The town crawls along the Landwassertal Valley at the northern edge of the Engadine, 11 km south of Klosters and 14 km west of the Flüelapass. Arosa lies just west, but a now navigatable road connects the two resorts.

The Davosersee, the local lake, shimmers at the northern edge of town, several side valleys lie perpendicular to the Landwassertal, and lifts rise in all directions from the valley floor to six recreational mountain areas. The Pischa, Jakobshorn, and Rinerhorn rise along the Landwassertal valley to the east; opposite, the Schatzalp and the Parsenn rise to the west; and the Gotschna and Madrisa areas flank Klosters to the north.

The Town

Davos stretches along the Landwassertal from the **Davoser See** in the north to **Davos Platz** in the south. Quieter **Davos Dorf** lies in between, the Schiabach and Dischmabach streams separating the two neighborhoods. Train stations anchor either end of the stretch, and two streets run the length of the town, both roughly paralleling the Landwasser River. The busy upper road, **Promenade**, funnels one-way traffic south; closer to the river, the lower **Talstrasse** funnels traffic north. Clustered between the two roads, about halfway down the stretch, are the **Kongresszentrum Convention Center**, the **Kurpark**, and the **Sportzentrum** sports center. Most of Davos' action lies between the sports center and the train station at Platz.

Getting Here & Around

Visitors arriving by **air** should fly into the international airport at either Zürich or Innsbruck, both about 150 km from Davos. Hourly **trains** connect Davos and Zürich. Two train stations serve Davos; one at Platz, and one at Dorf. Local **buses** run between the two. All local buses are free to holders of the Davos Guest Card.

> **TIP:** Guests at local hotels receive the free **Davos Guest Card**, good for unlimited travel on local bus lines (although your dog must pay a surcharge) and for discounts at mountain lifts, the sport center, ice-skating, and paragliding among many others.

The town's mountain attractions are scattered in seven areas: **Pischa**, **Jakobshorn**, **Rinerhorn**, **Schatzalp/Strela**, **Parsenn**, **Gotschna**, and **Madrisa**. For more information on mountain transport in Davos and Klosters check www.bbdk.ch.

Lift Pass Price Samples

Winter

1-day adult all-area pass	61 CHF
6-day adult all-area pass	279 CHF
Pedestrian round-trip to the Jakobshorn	32 CHF

Summer

Pedestrian round-trip to the Jakobshorn	80 CHF

Getting Connected

 The main tourist information office is at Promenade 67 in Davos Platz. Its seasonal hours are rather fickle, but generally run from 8:30 am to 6 pm, with shortened days on Saturdays and (sometimes) Sundays. Contact the main tourist office at ☎ 081 415 21 21, www.davos.ch. A second tourist office is in Davos at Bahnhofstrasse, directly across from the train station.

Post offices are in Davos Platz at Bahnhofstrasse 3 and in Davos Dorf at Gahnhofstrasse 9.

WWW For 24-hour Internet access, head for **After Hours** at Promenade 64 in Platz. Other outlets include the **Esso-Bar** at Talstrasse 22 and **Expert RoRo** at Promenade 123 in Dorf.

The Sights

 The "sights" of Davos are exclusively museums. The town's most famous collection, the **Kirchner Museum**, honors the expressionist artist Ernst Ludwig Kirchner with the world's largest display of his work. The artist lived here from 1917 to 1938, the date of his suicide. The architecturally intriguing museum stands at Ernst Ludwig Kirchner-Platz in Davos Platz and is open year-round, Tuesday through Sunday, 2-6 pm, from 10 am at Christmas, Easter, and mid-July through September; ☎ 081 413 22 02, www.kirchnermuseum.ch; 8 CHF.

The Davos Museum, or **Heimatmuseum**, offers a look at regional folk history and art at Museumstrasse 1 in Davos Dorf. It's open

Wednesday, Friday, and Sunday from 4 to 6 pm; ☎ 081 413 61 17; 5 CHF.

Also interesting, the **Winter Sports Museum**, at Promenade 43 in Davos Platz, documents the history of the sports for which the town is famous. The collection is open Tuesday and Thursday from 4:30 to 6:30 pm and, additionally in winter, on Saturday during the same hours; ☎ 081 413 24 84; 5 CHF. Finally, several **show factories** demonstrate the processes behind the production of milk, cheese, and beer. The tourist office has more information and can arrange tours.

The Adventures

On Foot

 Hikers enjoy 450 km of marked and maintained walking and hiking trails. The trails escape the city's bustle, climbing through Alpine meadows and along sparkling brooks. Mountain lifts assist. **Walkers** take to several easy routes, including the geology trail through the Zügen Gorge and, at Schatzalp, the stroll through the Alpine botanical garden. **Climbers** head for the climbing garden near Seehorn, accessed from Davos Dorf via the Fluelastrasse.

On Horseback

 For on-hoof adventures, carriage and sleigh rides trot up the area's quieter side valleys. Contact the **Führhalterverband** for more info, ☎ 081 413 41 41.

State-of-the-Art Sports

Developed in 1996, the **Davos Training and High-Altitude Center** grooms the world's finest athletes across all sporting disciplines. It's one of Europe's finest sports training venues, and it welcomes amateur athletes as well. The center encompasses a restaurant, lecture rooms, and a sports medicine department in addition to a track stadium, multiple ice arenas, a ball sports area, and a soccer pitch. World-class competitions are staged here, too, including ice hockey's Spengler Cup, the Davos Nordic Skiing Word Cup, and the Swiss Alpine Marathon. Want to play too? See what's on and what's open at ☎ 0814 415 36 00, www.davos.ch.

In Water

 The town's watersports revolve around the small **Davosersee**, or Davos Lake, where the watersports center houses both a sailing and windsurfing school. Contact the sailing school at ☎ 081 416 59 18; and the windsurfing school at ☎ 081 413 19 40. Summertime fishing is an option after obtaining the proper permits – head for town hall and the police station for more information. Swimmers enjoy the free lakeside bathing area at the Davosersee and, in town, an indoor swimming pool. The swimming complex is at Promenade 90 in Platz, near the convention center. The pool is open daily, but hours vary by season. From more information, dial ☎ 081 413 64 63.

On Wheels

 Bikers in Davos hit 115 km of maintained trails. Experienced bikers rave about the 20-km downhill route from Weissfluhjoch to Küblis. For guided tours and instruction, contact **Bike Experience** at ☎ 079 312 79 11, www.bike-experience-davos.ch.

> **TIP:** Hikers and bikers wishing to trek cross-country should inquire at the tourist office regarding **Hike-Easy/Bike-Easy** packages. The self-guided itinerary includes accommodations, lunchpacks, maps, and – most delightfully – luggage transfer between evening stops. Programs run from Davos to Lenzerheide to Arosa or vice-versa, lasting four to seven days.

In the Air

 Davosers first took to the air in 1912, when a local resident built the region's first hang-glider. By the 1930s, a local airfield was one of Europe's favorite gliding venues. Today, a variety of operators offer airborne sports, but the best by our estimation is the Delta- und Gleitschirmflugschule Davos – Anglophones simply call it **Davos Sport**. Their five tandem pilots offer a variety of flight packages. For more information contact Hans Guler at ☎ 081 413 60 43, www.davos-sport.ch. **Swissraft** can arrange balloon tours. Contact ☎ 081 911 52 50 for more information.

On Snow & Ice

 In the Davos **skiing** region, 53 lifts serve 320 km of marked runs graded 30% easy, 49% intermediate, and 21% expert – although few runs here really merit the black rating. The runs are scattered over six mountains, which can prove an inconvenience if you plan to move around a lot. **Snowboarding** got an early start in Davos – at least by European standards. By 1990, Davos had gained a reputation among boarders as the place to practice their new sport. Development of the Jakobshorn continues, and the funpark, boarder-cross, and pipes at "Fun Mountain" continue to draw Europe's best.

The town grooms 75 km of **cross-country skiing** trails, of which 35 km are designated for skating technique. The trails wind through the Landwassertal and its satellite valleys; one trail near the center has floodlights. All trails are free of charge. In winter, the **Langlaufzentrum**, or cross-country ski center, at Hertistrasse offers locker rooms, beverages, and a wax room; ☎ 081 416 44 55. The **Swiss Snowsportschool** offers instruction (see *Sports Services* below). **Winter walkers** and **snow-showers** take to 84 km of cleared walks and mountain trails, and sledders dive down three **toboggan runs** – a two-km trail at Gotschna, a 2½-km run at Schatzalp, and a steeper, 3½-km plunge at Rinerhorn.

Davos on Ice

 Davos ranks among the Alps' premier training grounds for **on-ice sports**. In addition to the stamina-building benefits of training at altitude, skaters and curlers enjoy superb facilities – the largest rink, a whopping 22,000 square m.

The sport center has a covered outdoor rink of artificial ice, a stadium, and an enormous natural rink as well; the first is open year-round as training and event schedules allow. Skate rental is available, and entry is 5 CHF. One other small rink ices over from December to mid-February. It's in the center of Davos Dorf near the Parsenn funicular station and is open daily from 10 am to 4 pm; if weather allows, also on Thursday evening from 8 to 10 pm.

The **Sportzentrum Davos** runs a wide range of on-ice activities, including curling, speed skating, and ice-stick shooting. The center's well-regarded ice-skating lessons are offered in three languages, booking at a rate of 25 CHF per 20-minute session. Call ☎ 081 415 36 00 or see www.davos.ch for more information.

If you decide to slide on one of the tobogganing trails, rent a high-quality sled – one with the Davoser trademark. Local toboggan-makers gained an early reputation as excellent craftsmen, and Davos-made sleds still rank among the world's finest .

Sports Services, Outfitters & Guides

The **Swiss Snowsportschool** and the **New Trend** ski school together employ a total of 150 ski instructors each year. Of the two, I like New Trend, both for its small classes – ski classes are limited to six participants, snowboarding classes to eight – and for its Top Secret specialist snowboarding division. Contact the Swiss School at ☎ 081 416 24 54, www.ssd.ch. Book classes with the New Trend ski school at ☎ 081 413 20 40, www.newtrenddavos.ch; with their Top Secret snowboarding division at ☎ 081 413 73 74, www.topsecretdavos.ch.

Intersport Ettinger is our choice for sports equipment rental. The shop has three outlets conveniently located in town near the bases of the Parsennbahn, the Jakobshornbahn, and the Rinerhornbahn lifts. The shops both sell and rent all-season sporting equipment. For more information, contact ☎ 081 410 12 12, www.ettinger.ch.

Where to Sleep

Unlike most ski resorts, Davos does a booming business in the summer season as well — 40% of its annual profit is made during the summer months. Prices are high throughout the year. One of the two five-star places in the valley is the **Steigenberger Belvedere** ($$$$), a sanatorium-hotel that made history as the inspiration for Thomas Mann's *The Magic Mountain*. To-

HOTEL PRICE CHART	
Double room without tax; $$$-$$$$ always with bath.	
$	Under 120 CHF
$$	121-225 CHF
$$$	226-375 CHF
$$$$	Over 375 CHF

day, the magic here comes in the form of luxurious surroundings, gourmet cuisine, and excellent service. The hotel stretches along the main road at Promenade 89; ☎ 081 415 60 00, www.davos.steigenberger.ch. Also lovely, the **Arabella Sheraton Seehof** ($$$$) presides over a busy square and Dorf's central pond, which in winter becomes the neighborhood ice rink. The elegant hotel boasts a nice wellness center, a traditional restaurant and bar, and an inviting beer garden. Reserve at ☎ 081 416 12 12, www.arabellasheraton.com.

For gamblers, the **Hotel Europa** offers commercial accommodations next door to the casino; ☎ 081 415 41 41. We've also heard good things about the homey hospitality of the **Crystal Hotel** ($$$) at Eisbahnstrasse 2; ☎ 081 414 01 00, www.crystal-davos.ch.

High on a hill above town, accessed via the Schatzalp funicular, the venerable old **Berghotel Schatzalp** ($$$) has a wonderful away-from-it-all ambiance and lovely views from its galleried balconies. Reserve at ☎ 081 415 51 51, www.schatzalp.ch.

We liked the **Hotel Pischa** ($$) for its simple rooms, big balconies, and view-blessed breakfast terrace. The hotel fronts the woods at Strelastrasse 2, a steep climb up from Platz; ☎ 081 413 55 13.

At the far southern edge of town, a good walk up the hill, the **Larix** ($$-$$$) is the closest one will come to an Alpine chalet. The small, cozy hotel has an outstanding restaurant; it's at Obere Albertistrasse 9; ☎ 081 413 11 88, www.hotel-larix.ch.

The **Seehorn Garni** ($$) has rooms near the lake; ☎ 081 416 62 51, www.davos-seehorn.ch. The **Alpina** ($$) has rooms with balconies and views on a quiet side street above town center; ☎ 081 416 47 67, www.alpina-davos.ch.

Even the **HI youth hostel** ($-$$) here is pretentiously pricey, marketing itself as "Switzerland's most exclusive." (It's a sad day, in this traveler's opinion, when *hostels* become exclusive.) The old **Beau Site** sanatorium still has its grand balconies, big valley views, and good location near the Parsennbahn funicular. Reserve a room in this "youth palace" at ☎ 081 420 11 20, www.youthhostel.ch/davos. The tourist office can assist in booking less expensive private rooms.

Where to Eat

 For culinary excellence, head for **Hubli's Landhaus** ($$$) out in Davos Laret, north of town. With 16 Gault-Millau points and a Michelin star to boot, this little dining room is a gourmet's choice; ☎ 081 417 10 11.

DINING PRICE CHART	
Average entrée, with tax.	
$	Under 15 CHF
$$	16-37 CHF
$$$	Over 37 CHF

The traditional restaurant **Pot-au-Feu** ($$), at Mattastrasse 4 in Platz, does good Swiss specialties like fondue, pot-au-feu, and grills at reasonable rates; ☎ 081

413 50 68. Budgeting diners can try the **Coop Grischuna** ($) at Bahnhofstrasse 1 in Platz.

For a romantic evening above town, try the **Wintergartenrestaurant Larix** ($$$) at the chalet-style Larix Hotel. The cuisine is classic French-Swiss. Reserve at ☎ 081 413 11 88, www.hotel-larix.ch.

At the **Restaurant Schatzalp**, high above Davos, traditional fondues and other regional specialties are served within view of the stars and the city lights; ☎ 081 415 51 60. Finally, and perhaps most appealing, the **Restaurant Teufi** ($$) invites Davos guests on a one-hour horse-drawn sleigh or carriage ride en route to their forest-ensconced restaurant. Meat fondues and a rustic ambiance await. Make arrangements in advance at ☎ 081 416 35 82, www.teufi.ch.

AUTHOR'S PICK A particular hit with kids, the **Au Hof**'s Thursday morning farmer's breakfast invites guests to start their day right. It's still a European breakfast – there are no waffles in sight – but the hearty homemade offerings here come with an invigorating dose of fresh Alpine air. Reservations must be made with the tourist office a day in advance; open early July through mid-October.

For late-night grub, the **Crazy Cow** ($$) serves food till 11:30 pm. It's open seven days each week at Talstrasse 31; ☎ 081 410 03 50, www.crazycow.ch. If you get the munchies even later, **After Hours** serves 24-hour take-away at Promenade 64. Alternatively, head for the **Bar-Café Esso** ($); granted, it's odd to hang out at a gas station, but this little convenience store has pool tables, darts, and food shopping until 2 am. It's at Talstrasse 22.

Where to Party

Davos offers a wide range of bars, pubs, and clubs – but the crowds seem to congregate in a very specific few. From après-ski on, **Paulaner's** at the Arabella Sheraton Seehof Hotel draws a crowd with a rustic ambiance and a summer-only beer garden. Sunny afternoons make popular, too, the terrace at the **Choccolino Café**, in Platz at Promenade 45.

For nighttime action, head for the small **Chämi Bar** at Promenade 83 and, to dance till dawn, party your way to the **ExBar** down the street. It's lively all night and doesn't go dark till 6 am. The Hotel Europe provides one-stop nightlife; here, the **Cabanna** disco and a separate **Tonic piano bar** play late into the night, and next door, the **Davos Casino** spins blackjack, roulette, and slot machines daily from 1 to 3 pm.

Where to Play

 Children's programs run throughout the year, organized by the tourist office and local businesses in the summer and, additionally, by the ski schools in the winter. Popular activities include fairytale afternoons, inline-skating, pony riding, ice-skating, and family films. **Childcare** is offered by some hotels, and the tourist office can assist with other arrangements. **Playgrounds** entertain at the Kurpark in Davos Platz and at Seehof Lake in Davos Dorf.

Festivals & Events

 As you might expect, Davos' festivals revolve around sport. Literally hundreds of events, competitions, and congresses take place here each year; we'll cover only a few. Early in winter, in mid-December, the **Davos Nordic Skiing World Cup** races run along the Flüelatal Valley. During the week between Christmas and New Year, ice hockey comes to town in a big way. The **Spengler Cup** rocks Davos Ice Stadium with competitions between top international teams.

Then, in late January, the annual meeting of the **World Economic Forum** draws the world's attention. Summer events include the popular **Davos Night Race** in mid-July, the **Swiss Alpine Marathon** in late July, and the **International Music Festival**, a celebration of young classical musicians. Concerts run for two weeks in July and August. Finally, for five evenings in July, Davos' main street grinds to a halt for the **Verkehrsfrei Promenade**, for a few hours becoming a pedestrian-only area with food, drinks, and outdoor entertainment.

■ Arosa

Population: 2,500

Base elevation: 1,800 m

Mountain resort town

It's not a quaint mountain village, but rather a bustling resort town in a splendid setting and in which there's always something to do. Arosa ranks among the biggest resort villages in Switzerland, remaining popular with summertime walkers, wintertime skiers, and families all the year through. Travelers be forewarned. What they say is true: Arosa grows on you.

History & Orientation

 Although the middle section of the Schanfigg Valley has been populated since 800 AD, the village of Arosa grew up around two remote convent farms, Merans and Pradaz, both first mentioned in documents in the early 13th century. Walser populations from Davos moved in during the 14th century, bringing with them new governance, dialects, and farming methods. After successive rule under the Counts of Vaz, Toggenburg, Montfort, and Austria, the farmers finally ended up selling their land to the town of Chur, today the capital city of the Graubünden. Tourism took flight in the mid-19th century and, with the development of a tuberculosis sanatorium, in a span of only 60 years the population rose from 71 residents to 3,724 – more than the town claims today.

The Town

After the long drive here through remote hamlets and lush forests, visitors arriving by car are greeted with a jolt – the abrupt transition from pristine wilderness to the blocky sanatorium-style architecture of Ausserarosa. (Train arrivals are greeted a bit more gently, with a circular approach around the pleasant Untersee.) Arosa, at first glance, is not a pretty town.

The main road into town becomes Poststrasse. With few exceptions, most of Arosa's sights, restaurants, and shops lie along this road. The resort has two distinct neighborhoods: bawdy, overbuilt Ausserarosa and traditional, peaceful Innerarosa farther up-valley. The town's main action occurs in Ausserarosa, home to the train station, the valley station of the Weisshornbahn cable car, and the village's two small lakes, the Obersee and the Untersee. Traveling up Poststrasse, visitors pass the tourist office, casino, and movie theater before arriving in quiet Innerarosa. Here, in the upper valley's original settlement, old chalets, grazing cows, and a mountainside chapel create a scene more in tune with most visitors' expectations. Just below, the Hornli-Express gondola departs for the surrounding peaks.

Getting Here & Around

 For travelers entering Switzerland by **air**, the nearest international airport is at Zürich, 163 km northwest. Those arriving by **car** will come to Arosa via Chur, the Graubünden canton's capital city. From Chur, the road to Arosa climbs 30 km, up 1,150 m, and around 365 curves – one for each day of the year, which is precisely how long you'll swear it took to drive. Alternatively, the Rhaetische Bahn railway offers frequent train service to Arosa from the doorstep of Chur's main station.

So, then, you have two options for travel between Chur and Arosa: (1) park your car at the station in Chur and take the train for the one-hour scenic train ride up the dramatic Schandigg Valley, or (2) endure one or two white-knuckled hours driving the cliff-side of that dramatic valley, possibly stuck in traffic, probably slowed by considerable construction – all the while *wishing* you had taken the train. Those who do the latter on their first visit do the former on their second.

*For a fresh take on rail travel, hop aboard one of the Rhaetische Bahn's **aussichtswagen**, open-air view cars attached to the regular trains between Chur and Arosa. Trains run only in good weather from July to September, from Chur to Arosa at 9:02 am and from Arosa to Chur at 12:04 pm. Inquire at either station, or find more info at www.rhb.ch.*

Once in town, visitors enjoy the frequent-and-free bus service. (Drivers should note the enforced midnight-6 pm ban on private traffic.)

Mountain transportation includes a gondola and a cable car in summer and a total of 13 lifts in winter, with valley-level hubs behind the train station and at Innerarosa. Check the tourist office or www.arosabergbahnen.ch for current schedules.

Lift Pass Price Samples

Winter

1-day adult . . . . 54 CHF

6-day adult . . . . 251 CHF

Pedestrian round-trip to Weisshorn . . . . 16 CHF

3-day pedestrian lift pass. . . . . 70 CHF

Summer

Cable car transport free with Arosa Card

Getting Connected

The Arosa Tourist Information Office is located on Poststrasse at the Alt Post. The office is open in summer Monday-Friday, 8 am-12 pm and 2-6 pm, and on Saturday, 9 am-1 pm; in winter, Monday-Friday, 9 am-6 pm, Saturday,

9 am-5:30 pm, and Sunday 4-6 pm. Contact ☎ 081 378 70 20 or check www.arosa.ch for more information.

 The post office is at Oberseeplatz in the center of Ausserarosa.

 Access the Internet at the **LOS Café Bar** in the center on Poststrasse.

All-Inclusive Arosa

Arosa is pioneering a new concept in resort management – a concept I hope will catch on elsewhere, too. During the summer months, *all* visitors staying in *all* types of accommodations receive an **Arosa Card** at check-in. (Day visitors can purchase a card for just 8 CHF at the train station, cable car valley stations, or tourist office – for more info check www.all-inclusive.ch.) The card entitles holders to unlimited use of many once-costly Arosa attractions, including the Hornli and Weisshorn cable cars, the beach facilities at Untersee, boat rental at both lakes, an indoor ice rink, the local bus service, and a parking garage. In effect, visiting families are freed from vacation budgeting concerns – no matter how many times the kids want to ride a cable car, skate on ice, or float a boat. *Bravo*, Arosa!

The Sights

 The **Bergkirchli**, a 500-year-old mountain chapel above Innerarosa, offers summertime concerts by candlelight each Wednesday evening. Instrumental and vocal performances are highlighted by the church's 1760-era organ. The **Schanfigg Heimatmuseum**, also in Innerarosa, presents a small display of local history. Opening hours for both the Bergkirchli and the Schanfigg Heimatmuseum are changeable – check with the tourist office for a current schedule.

Two nighttime attractions merit attention. First, each Wednesday evening in winter, the Mountains of Fantasy produces an impressive open-air **laser and effects show** on the snowy slopes above town. Also, each Tuesday, Saturday, and Sunday evening in summer, the new Obersee Wasserspiele **fountain show** pumps water through 1,000 spouts, electricity through 200 bulbs, and sound through 30 speakers to spectacular effect. Both shows are free to Arosa visitors.

The Adventures

Arosa's adventures focus on its fabulous ring of mountains and, less significantly, on its two small lakes. (Both of these, however, are more akin to swimming holes than "lakes" – one for people, and one for waterfowl.) The forested terrain surrounding the village offers a splendid Alpine setting, and a concentrated uplift system makes trail walking an easy option for all.

On Foot

 Mountain walking, hiking, and **wandering** are Arosa's summertime *raison d'etre*, and 200 km of footpaths surround the town. Pedestrians should stroll around the Obersee for a glance back at the village and its Alpine backdrop, down through the forests around Untersee, and up to peaceful Innerarosa for a look at its traditional chalets and mountain church. Well-maintained gravel paths criss-cross the mountains above, and mountain huts provide refreshments. Popular routes include hikes up to (or down from) the Weisshorn cable car's two stations, trips to Maran's Alpine garden and cheese-making dairy, and meanders along the Planetweg, a 2.2-km stroll through our solar system that's laid out on a 1-to-2,800,000,000 scale.

The trail map from the tourist office marks trails for all abilities. In addition, the tourist office and other outfitters arrange all manner of **guided outings**, including a farmer's breakfast at a mountain hut, rock-climbing, Alpine tours, and animal-spotting safaris.

In Water

 Arosa boasts no fewer than 10 nearby lakes. All are small, and only the Obersee and the Untersee (the two village lakes) have seen considerable development. **Rowboats** are available at Obersee and Untersee, and the dock at Obersee also offers **pedal boats** and **aquabikes**. The use of boats is free to holders of the Arosa Guest Card. From June through mid-September **trout fishing** is an option at both Obersee and Untersee, although on Sundays fishing is prohibited. Permits are available at the tourist office.

Arosa's time-honored **swimming hole** is the Untersee, a small forest lake decked out with a beach (complete with imported sand), swimming platforms, volleyball courts, a nice playground, a heated wading pool, rowboats, grilling pits, and a restaurant. Untersee activities are free with the Arosa Guest Card. Swimmers will find **pool** and **spa facilities** at many of the area's hotels, several of which open their doors to non-guests. Offerings vary by season and occupancy rates. Check the tourist office for current options.

On Wheels

 Mountain biking is less popular than walking in Arosa, but bikers do enjoy access to 60 km of designated trails. Rent bikes at the **Parkhel Arosa**; ☎ 081 377 01 65. **Trotti-bikes** – something between a bike and a scooter – can be rented at the train station. Pre-reservation is strongly urged; ☎ 081 377 14 90. Advanced trotti-riders can take the Weisshorn cable car to Mittelstation and then ride down via Maran to Arosa. **Skateboarders** head for the summer-only fun-park in the lakeside lot behind the train station.

EASY BIKE/EASY HIKE

For adventurers hoping to cover a lot of ground by bike or foot, Graubünden-area tourist offices have paired up to offer luggage forwarding between resort villages. The program highlights several unguided itineraries ranging from four to seven days, most traveling between Davos, Arosa, and the town of Lenzerheide. Packages include accommodations in hotels or mountain huts, some meals, trail maps, cable car rides, and point-to-point luggage transportation. Contact the Arosa or Davos tourist office to make arrangements for late-June to mid-October trips.

In the Air

 Rides up Arosa's summertime **cable car** and **gondola** provide spectacular views of the surrounding Alps. The Weisshornbahn climbs from the Obersee to 2,653 m, while the Hornli-Express climbs from Innerarosa to 2,513 m. Keep watch for marmots on the way up. Both mountain stations have restaurants.

For a tour of the area by **balloon** (three-four hours), contact Mr. Vollenweider at ☎ 01 391 37 14; for **paragliding**, contact Jogi at ☎ 079 449 88 13. The tourist office can make arrangements as well.

On Snow & Ice

 Arosa's downhill attractions include 60 km of groomed runs and 40 km of marked off-piste routes. The uplift system networks three cable cars and gondolas, six chairlifts, and four drag lifts. Known by most as a resort for beginning and intermediate skiers, Arosa now appeals to more ad-

Switzerland

vanced skiers with the promotion of **FreeRide Mountain**, a collection of lift-served off-piste routes descending from the Sattelhütte on Brüggerhorn and the Stoffelhütte atop the Weisshorn. (Check current off-piste conditions at the checkpoints marked with a red target on the ski map.)

Snowboarders head for the halfpipe at the Brüggerhorn Mittelstation, and 25 km of trails of loipe keep **cross-country ski-ers** doing loops. Some 10 km of **sledding runs** weave down the mountain, and walkers enjoy 60 km of groomed **winter walking trails**. Many paths cut through the ski slopes and climb up to the mountain huts, making lunch meetings between skiers and non-skiers perfectly feasible. (Arosa is unique in that all of its mountain restaurants can be reached on foot.)

Adventurers can enjoy several odd-hour mountain excursions during the winter high season. Watch the sun rise from the **Weisshorn** peak (at left) on Thursday mornings, enjoy a sunset fondue at the **Weisshorngipfel** each Tuesday, and combine nighttime skiing with a **Tschuggenhütte** fondue dinner each Friday evening. Check in with the tourist office for reservations.

Arosa celebrates ice sports with three separate **ice rinks**. The indoor **Eissporthalle** at Obersee is open throughout the year, although it is frequently used for hockey games and such, so the open-skate schedule varies. Check the posting on the front door to see when the ice is free. Two outdoor rinks open in winter – the artificial rink near Obersee and the natural rink at Innerarosa. The Eissporthalle also offers weekly beginners' courses in **curling** and **eisstockshiessen**, or ice stick shooting, a similar game played outdoors and without the broom. The ice sports center has more information; ☎ 081 377 17 45.

Sports Services, Outfitters & Guides

The **Swiss Ski and Snowboard School Arosa** offers a range of snowsport classes for children and adults, including skiing, telemarking, and snowboarding. (**Banana's Snowboarding School** is an SSSA affiliate.) Private instruction is also available. Contact ☎ 081 377 11 50, www.sssa.ch.

The **ABC Ski and Snowboard School**, the lesser known of the ski schools here, tops out its competitor with just one bonus: the school guarantees classes with no more than eight students. ABC offers snow-biking each Tuesday and

Thursday afternoon from 2 to 4 pm. Reserve ahead at ☎ 081 356 56 60, www.abcarosa.ch.

Specher Sport is Arosa's favorite all-season outfitter. Its two outlets, one in Innerarosa and one in Ausserarosa, both lie along Poststrasse; ☎ 081/377 12 07.

Carmenna Sport also offers equipment service and is with Swissrent-a-Sport, so it's possible to reserve rental equipment ahead of your visit at ☎ 081 377 12 05, http://www.carmennasport.ch.

Where to Sleep

For luxury, the five-star **Arosa Kulm Hotel and Alpine Spa** ($$$$), ☎ 081 378 88 88, www.arosakulm.ch, rules the roost. Perched on a knoll alongside the main road in Innerarosa, the hotel was the valley's original guesthouse (although constant renovation has done away with much of its visible history). For my money, however, I forego a star and recommend instead the fresh-faced **Hotel Belarosa** ($$$$); ☎ 081 378 89 99, www.belarosa.ch. The hotel shows bright rustic décor, superb wellness facilities, and a room count made up mostly of suites.

HOTEL PRICE CHART	
Double room without tax; $$$-$$$$ always with bath.	
$	Under 120 CHF
$$	121-225 CHF
$$$	226-375 CHF
$$$$	Over 375 CHF

For mid-range accommodations in the center of Ausserarosa, try the simple **Hotel Obersee** ($$-$$$); ☎ 081 377 12 16, www.hotelobersee.ch. It's just across from the Eishalle and has the town's rowdiest disco in the basement.

For something a bit above the nightlife noise, try the hillside **Hotel Alpina** ($$-$$$); ☎ 081 377 16 58, www.arosa.ch/hotels/alpina, just off of Poststrasse. With lovely lake and mountain views from some of its balconies, several apartments to let, and a brightly painted plastic cow out front – who could pass that up?

Several affordable hotels line Poststrasse as it climbs toward Innerarosa. It's a busy road and a steep walk (although bus service eases the burden), but the south sides of these hotels offer peaceful mountain, forest, and valley views. I like the **Hotel Alpensonne** ($$-$$$); ☎ 081 377 15 47, www.hotelalpensonne.ch. Here, 200 m below Innerarosa, the Bareit family offers homey rooms, a friendly staff, and bonuses like shelves of used books, a small sauna, and buckets of toys for the kids. Some rooms share baths, but rooms with south-facing balconies are decked out with big views and old wicker patio furniture – each chair with a pad and blanket. Try also the clean **Quellenhof** ($$-$$$), just down the road; ☎ 081 377 17 18, www.quellenhof-arosa.ch.

Finally, for budget accommodations, nothing here beats the three **Backpacker's** ($) properties scattered around the valley. Each caters to a young clientele with double, multi-bed, and dorm rooms. There's a downtown property in the center, ☎ 081 377 13 87; the nearby chalet property, ☎ 081 378 52 52; and the mountain lodge above town, just off a ski run, ☎ 081 378 84 23. Information on all three can be found at www.backpackers-arosa.ch.

Where to Eat

Arosa's restaurants are almost exclusively hotel-based.

Below the Kulm along Poststrasse, the restaurant **Alpensonne** ($$), ☎ 081 377 15 47, highlights seasonal game, fondue, and a long wine list – all at reasonable prices. Request a table by the

DINING PRICE CHART	
Average entrée, with tax.	
$	Under 15 CHF
$$	16-37 CHF
$$$	Over 37 CHF

window for a lovely mountain-and-forest view. Under the Hotel Obersee and across from the Eishalle, the popular **Poltera Stube Gästhaus** ($$) offers traditional fare alongside its claim to fame, the *Flamme Spiess*, a spit of skewered meat cooked tabletop over an open flame. Make reservations at ☎ 081 377 18 12.

For chicken specialties, head down toward Untersee to the Hotel Beau Rivage and its restaurant, **The Chicken Farm** ($$). The **Grottino Pizzeria** ($) on in the center on Poststrasse serves up two menu pages worth of pizzas and 65 different grappas.

For one-stop variety, try the **Hotel Post** on the lakefront at Obersee, where varied fare is offered in a pizzeria ($$), café ($), and traditional fondue *stüberl* ($$$). Pick up picnic fare at the **Coop** ($) grocery on Poststrasse just below the tourist office, or try **Heidi's** ($) deli up in Innerarosa.

Where to Party

Arosa is essentially a family resort, but a good collection of small haunts offers a respectable array of après-ski and late-night action. The **Halli Galli** disco under the Hotel Obsersee, the **Crazy** nightclub at Hotel Post, and **The Kitchen** at the Hotel Eden all get lively in the evening. The piano bar, **Im Gada,** at the Hotel Carmina draws happy crowds as well.

The town **casino** deals up blackjack, roulette, 85 slot machines, a restaurant and bar, and superb views over the Untersee. Place your bets from 5 pm nightly at Poststrasse just below the tourist office. Next door, a **movie theater** screens first-run films in German, French, and English.

Where to Play

Arosa remains a family-oriented resort, and children's activities abound. Nice **playgrounds** corral kids near the Obersee soccer field (or winter ice rink) and at Innerarosa next to the tennis courts (or winter ice rink). The tourist office can provide a list of **babysitters** and assist with equipment rental.

Festivals & Events

In summer, Arosa's event calendar is crowded with music festivals, golf tournaments, and mountain-biking competitions. From June through October, the town hosts a varied program of **music courses**, and associated recitals abound. **Jazz Days** come to town in mid-July, and Arosa's **Summerfest** takes place the first weekend in August.

In winter, Arosa's ice highlights **hockey, ice-skating**, and **curling events** – and several competitions each year bring the world's finest athletes to town. Comics take the stage at **Humor Festival** in December – although much is lost if you don't speak German. Mid-January highlights the **Pferderennen**, or on-snow horse races, and early April brings a slew of on-mountain concerts during the **Caliente Fiesta Tropical**. To see what's on, check www.arosa.ch/events.

Chur

With 5,000 years of history, Chur is Switzerland's oldest city. The settlement has been continuously inhabited from Neolithic ages, and the modern city is the Graubünden region's cantonal capital, its educational center, and its department-store shopping hub. Huddled between the mountains and the A13 Autobahn, Chur offends the eye with sky-rise apartment blocks that rise all around. But, better things lie within, and it's worth a brief stop on your way by.

Chur's claim to fame is its **medieval old town**. An 800-year-old cathedral rises above a maze of cobbled alleys and squares, where pedestrians enjoy quaint shops, cozy pubs, and old-world architecture, much of which dates from the mid-15th-century, when a fire destroyed the center. Worth a look are the Rathaus, or town hall, the Altes Gebäu at Poststrasse 14, and the lovely old Bärenloch area. Pick up a map at the tourist office, or join a guided walking tour. The 90-minute tours depart the Rathaus on Poststrasse at 2:30 pm each Wednesday from April through October.

Aside from its church and the attractions of its medieval center, Chur focuses its marketing efforts on the tourist excursions that can be easily made from its doorstep, including Arosa, Klosters, Davos, Heidiland, vineyards, and a total of 26 health resorts. The city is also the intersection of several tourist train routes; the Bernina Express, the Arosa Express, and the Glacier Express all stop here.

If you need to stay, Chur's only four-star hotel shines just across from the train station. Contact **Hotel ABC** ($$$); ☎ 081 252 60 33, www.hotelabc.ch. Near the center, the three-star **Hotel Chur** ($$) specializes in arranging active daytrips; ☎ 081 254 34 00, www.hotelchur.ch.

 The city's small tourist office is at Grabenstrasse 5, just around the corner from Poststrasse and the old quarter. They don't publish much in English but do distribute a small, almost-legible map of the city center. Contact the office at ☎ 081 252 18 18, www.churtourismus.ch.

 The Graubünden region is home to the story of *Heidi*, the children's book by Johanna Spyri. The story is set in Maienfeld, just north of here, and the surrounding region milks its claim to fame for every ounce of potential tourist gold.

Lenzerheide

For a rural, family retreat where few foreign tourists tread, head for Lenzerheide. The valley of Lenzerheide-Valbella rests below the Rothorn peak, a 20-minute drive southeast from Chur. Hiking, biking, and low-key relaxing are the attractions here. Summertime guests swim in the **Heidsee**, walk its grassy shores, and hike up and along the surrounding foothills. Boat rentals, playgrounds, and a small rappelling wall please youngsters, and trout-fishing licenses are available at the tourist office. Lifts climb to the top of the **Rothorn**, where panoramic views of some 1,000 peaks await. Nearby, in Churwalden, the Alp Pradaschier offers a 3.1-km rail-rider toboggan run, a year-round track that's the largest of its kind in the world and is a superb hit with kids.

Hike-Easy/Bike-Easy: The Lenzerheide-Valbella Valley lies amid an excellent network of mountain-biking and hiking trails. A stop here is part of the Hike-Easy/Bike-Easy itinerary, a self-guided tour on foot or bike between Davos and Arosa. The package deal entails a four- or seven-day ride or walk and includes accommodations, maps, bike rental, and – most impressively – luggage transfer between overnight destinations. Contact the Arosa or Davos tourist offices for more information.

Want to stay? In the village center, try the homey **Hotel Spescha** ($$); ☎ 081 384 62 63. For a tasty treat, stay in the **Guarda Val** ($$$-$$$$), a rustic farmhouse on the outskirts of Lenzerheide at Sporz. The comfortable hotel boasts a well-regarded gourmet restaurant; ☎ 081385 85 85, www.guardaval.ch.

 Find the tourist office in the center along the main road, Voa Principala; ☎ 081 385 11 20, www.lenzerheide.ch.

Language Primer

English	German	French	Italian
Basics			
Hello	Guten Tag/Gruss Gott	Bonjour/Salut	Buongiorno/Ciao
Good evening	Guten abend	Bonsoir	Buona sera
Goodbye	Auf Wieder-sehen/Tschuss	Au revoir/Salut	Arrivederci/Ciao
Yes	Ja	Oui	Si
No	Nein	Non	No
It's OK	Alles gut	Ca marche/Tres bien	Va bene
Please	Bitte	S'il vous plait	Per favore
Thank you	Danke	Merci	Grazie
You're welcome	Bitte	Je vous en prie	Prego
Excuse me	Entschuldigung	Excusez-moi	Mi scusi
I don't understand	Ich verstehe nicht	Je ne comprends pas	Non capisco
Help	Hilfe	Au secours	Aiuto
I'm lost	Ich habe mich verlaufen	Je suis perdu(e)	Mi sono perso (persa)
Left	Links	Gauche	Sinestra
Right	Recht	Droite	Destra
Straight	Geradeaus	Tout droit	Sempre diritto
North	Nord	Nord	Nord
South	Sud	Sud	Sud
East	Ost	Est	Este
West	West	Ouest	Ovest
Signs			
Open	Offen	Ouvert	Aperto
Closed	Geschlossen	Fermé	Chiuso
Entrance	Eingang	Entrée	Ingresso/Entrata
Exit	Ausgang	Sortie	Uscita
Forbidden	Vorboten	Interdit	Vietato
Toilets	Toiletten	Toilettes	Bagni
Women	Damen	Femmes	Donne/Signore
Men	Herren	Hommes	Uomini/Signori

English	German	French	Italian
Questions			
Do you speak English?	Sprechen Sie Englisch?	Parlez-vous anglais?	Parle inglese?
How much is. . .	Wieviel kostet. . .	Combien coute?	Quanto costa.
Where is. . .	Wo ist. . .	Ou est. . .	Dove. . .
When. . .	Wann. . .	A quelle heure. . .	Quando. . .
I'd like. . .	Ich mochte. . .	Je voudrais. . .	Vorrei. . .
Meetings			
My name is. . .	Ich heisse. . .	Je m'appelle. . .	Mi chiamo. . .
What is your name?	Wie heissen Sie?	Comment appelez-vous?	Como si chiama?
I come from. . .	Ich komme aus. . .	Je viens de. . .	Vengo da. . .
Where are you from?	Woher kommen Sie?	Vous venez d'ou?	Da dove viene?
Sleeping			
Hotel/guesthouse	Hotel/Pension/Gastehaus	Hotel	Albergo/Pensione
Youth hostel	Jungendheberge	Auberge de jeunesse	Ostello
Camping place	Campingplatz	Camping	Campeggio
Night	Nacht	Nuit	Notte
Single room	Einzelzimmer	Chambre simple	Camera singola
Double room	Doppelzimeer	Chambre double	Camera doppia
Dorm room	Schlafsaal	Dortoir	Dormitorio
Eating			
Breakfast	Fruhstuck	Petit-déjeuner	Prima colazione
Lunch	Mittagessen	Déjeuner	Pranzo/Colazione
Dinner	Abendessen	Diner	Cena
Menu	Spiesekarte	Menu	Menu/Liste
Restaurant	Restaurant/Gaststatte	Restaurant	Ristorante
Supermarket	Supermarkt	Supermarché	Supermercato
Market	Markt	Marché	Mercato
Bakery	Backerei	Boulangerie	Panetteria
Traveling			
Ticket	Karte	Billet	Biglietto
One-way	Eizelkarte	Aller simple	Sola andata
Round-trip	Ruckfahrkarte	Aller retour	Andata e ritorno
Bus	Bus	Bus	Autobus
Stop	Haltestelle	Arrêt	Fermata
Train	Bahn	Train	Treno
Train station	Bahnhof	Gare	Stazione
Boat	Boot	Bâteau	Barca
Cable car	Luftseilbahn	Télépherique	Funicolare
Chair lift	Sesselbahn	Telesiege	Seggiovia

English	German	French	Italian
Days			
Monday	Montag	Lundi	Lunedi
Tuesday	Dienstag	Mardi	Martedi
Wednesday	Mittwoch	Mercredi	Mercoledi
Thursday	Donnerstag	Jeudi	Giovedi
Friday	Freitag	Vendredi	Venerdi
Saturday	Samstag	Samedi	Sabato
Sunday	Sonntag	Dimanche	Domenica
Times			
Today	Heute	Aujourd'hui	Oggi
Tomorrow	Morgen	Demain	Domani
Morning	Morgen	Matin	Mattina
Noon	Mittag	Midi	Mezzogiorno
Afternoon	Nachmittag	Après-midi	Pomeriggio
Evening	Abend	Soir	Sera
Numbers			
0	Null	Zero	Zero
1	Ein	Un	Uno
2	Zwei	Deux	Due
3	Drei	Trois	Tre
4	Vier	Quatre	Quattro
5	Funf	Cinq	Cinque
6	Sechs	Six	Sei
7	Sieben	Sept	Sette
8	Acht	Huit	Otto
9	Neun	Neuf	Nove
10	Zehn	Dix	Dieci
11	Elf	Onze	Undici
12	Zwolf	Douze	Dodici
13	Dreizehn	Treize	Tredici
14	Vierzehn	Quatorze	Quattordici
15	Funfzehn	Quinze	Quindici
16	Sechzehn	Seize	Sedici
17	Siebzehn	Dix-sept	Diciassette
18	Achtzehn	Dix-huit	Diciotto
19	Neunzehn	Dix-neuf	Diciannove
20	Zwanzig	Vingt	Venti
21	Einundzwanzig	Vingt et un	Ventuno
30	Dreizig	Trente	Trenta
40	Vierzig	Quarante	Quaranta
50	Funfzig	Cinquante	Cinquanta
60	Sechszig	Soixante	Sessanta
70	Siebzig	Septante (Soixante-dix)	Settanta

English	German	French	Italian
80	Aachtzig	Huitante (Quatre-vingt)	Ottanta
90	Neunzig	Nonante (Quatre-vingt-dix)	Novanta
100	Hundert	Cent	Cento
1,000	Tausand	Mille	Mille
1,000.000	Eine Million	Un million	Un milione

prochain arret
Pardon
viandes
sans

Index

Index